Biblical women in early modern literary culture

MANCHESTER
1824

Manchester University Press

Biblical women in early modern literary culture
1550–1700

edited by
VICTORIA BROWNLEE
and LAURA GALLAGHER

Manchester University Press

Published by Manchester University Press.

Published by Manchester University Press
Altrincham Street, Manchester M1 7JA, UK
www.manchesteruniversitypress.co.uk

British Library Cataloguing-in-Publication Data
A catalogue record for this book is available from the British Library

Library of Congress Cataloging-in-Publication Data applied for

ISBN 978 07190 9155 1 *hardback*

First published 2015

Typeset in Dante by
Koinonia, Manchester
Printed and bound in Great Britain by
TJ International Ltd, Padstow

For our parents – Roberta and David Brownlee and Christine and Gabriel Gallagher – with love

Contents

List of contributors

Victoria Brownlee is an Irish Research Council post-doctoral fellow at University College Dublin. She has written on early modern women's writing and the Bible and has recently completed a monograph entitled *Biblical Readings and Literary Writings: 1550–1640*.

Dympna Callaghan is William L. Safire Professor in Modern Letters at Syracuse University. Her most recent book is *Who Was William Shakespeare? An Introduction to the Life and Works* (2013). Her previous books include *Woman and Gender in Renaissance Tragedy* (1989), *Shakespeare Without Women* (2000), *Romeo and Juliet: Texts and Contexts* (2003), *Shakespeare's Sonnets: An Introduction* (2006), and the Norton Critical Edition of *The Taming of the Shrew* (2009). She is co-author of *The Weyward Sisters: Shakespeare and Feminist Politics* (1994) and editor of, among others, *A Feminist Companion to Shakespeare* (2001) and *The Impact of Feminism in English Renaissance Studies* (2007). She is General Editor of the series Arden Shakespeare: Language and Writing, and co-editor with Michael Dobson of the Palgrave Shakespeare Studies series.

Danielle Clarke is Associate Professor of English Renaissance Language and Literature at University College Dublin. She is the author of *The Politics of Early Modern Women's Writing* (2001), editor of *Three Renaissance Women Poets: Isabella Whitney, Mary Sidney and Aemilia Lanyer* (2000) and co-editor of *'This Double Voice': Gendered Writing in Early Modern England* (2000) and *Teaching the Early Modern Period* (2011). She has also written numerous articles and essays on women's writing and is now working on a book-length project on the negotiation of form, genre and language in Renaissance women's poetry.

Laura Gallagher is a postdoctoral teaching assistant in the School of English at Queen's University, Belfast, and a Learning Development Assistant at the University's Learning Development Service. She completed her doctoral thesis, 'The Virgin Mary in the Early Modern Literary Imagination', in 2012 and is currently working on related articles.

Beatrice Groves is the Research Lecturer in Renaissance Literature at Trinity College, University of Oxford. She has published widely on early modern literature including the monograph *Texts and Traditions: Religion in Shakespeare 1592–1604* (2007). She has recently completed a book entitled *Jerusalem Destroyed: the Fall of a City in Early Modern English Literature.*

Elizabeth Hodgson is Associate Professor in the Department of English at the University of British Columbia. In addition to articles and essays on John Milton, Katherine Philips and Aemilia Lanyer, she is the author of *Gender and the Sacred Self in John Donne* (1999). Her next book, *Grief and Women Writers in the English Renaissance*, is forthcoming from Cambridge University Press.

Lisa Hopkins is Professor of English at The Humanities Research Centre at Sheffield Hallam University. She has written on Shakespeare, Marlowe and Ford as well as Jane Austen and Bram Stoker. Her publications include *Shakespeare on the Edge: Border-Crossing in the Tragedies and the Henriad* (2005), *Christopher Marlowe, Renaissance Dramatist* (2008), *The Cultural Uses of the Caesars on the English Renaissance Stage* (2008), *Relocating Shakespeare and Austen on Screen* (2009), and *Drama and the Succession to the Crown, 1561–1633* (2011). She is the co-editor of *Marian Moments in Early Modern British Drama* (2007), *Shakespeare* – the journal of the British Shakespeare Association, and the Arden Early Modern Drama Guides.

Michele Osherow is Associate Professor of English and Director of the Judaic Studies Program at the University of Maryland, Baltimore County. She is author of *Biblical Women's Voices in Early Modern England* (2009) and has written several essays on early modern appropriations of Old Testament narratives. She is currently researching a book on contemporary American productions of Shakespeare and is resident dramaturg for the Folger Theatre (Folger Shakespeare Library, Washington, DC).

Thomas Rist is Senior Lecturer in the Department of English at the University of Aberdeen. He is author of *Shakespeare's Romances and the Politics of Counter-Reformation* (1999) and *Revenge Tragedy and the Drama of Commemoration in Reforming England* (2008). He is co-editor of *The Arts of Remembrance in Early Modern England: Memorial Cultures of the Post Reformation* (2013) and has published a number of articles and essays on early modern literature and religious interaction. He is currently editing the Arden Early Modern Guide to *The Spanish Tragedy*.

Adrian Streete is Senior Lecturer in Renaissance Literature in the School of English at Queen's University, Belfast. He is the author of *Protestantism and Drama in Early Modern England* (2009), editor of *Early Modern Drama and the Bible: Contexts and Readings, 1570–1625* (2011), and co-editor of *Refiguring Mimesis: Representation in Early Modern Literature* (2005), *Filming and Performing Renaissance History* (2011), and *The Edinburgh Companion to Shakespeare and the Arts* (2011). He has published a variety of essays and articles on early modern literature and has recently completed a book funded by the Leverhulme Trust examining anti-Catholicism and apocalypticism in seventeenth-century drama.

Alison Thorne is Senior Lecturer in the Department of English at the University of Strathclyde. She is the author of *Vision and Rhetoric in Shakespeare: Looking through Language* (2000) and co-editor of *Rhetoric, Women and Politics in Early Modern England* (2007). She is the author of a number of articles and chapters on Shakespeare and feminine speech genres and is currently writing a book on the politics of female supplication in the literature and culture of early modern England.

Acknowledgements

The idea for this volume emerged in September 2010 during our first effort at organising an international conference as doctoral candidates at Queen's University, Belfast. For that reason, we are grateful to the energetic bunch of scholars and postgraduates who participated in 'Biblical Women: Reading and Writing Women in the Sixteenth and Seventeenth Centuries', and also to the Arts and Humanities Research Council for generously sponsoring the event. Since our first correspondence, the contributors to this volume have offered support and encouragement, and we are grateful for their hard work, enthusiasm and patience at every stage. Our thanks also to all those at Manchester University Press for their diligent assistance and expert guidance throughout the process, to Ann-Maria Walsh for pointing us in the direction of Erhard Schön's 'Twelve famous women of the Old Testament', and to the Irish Research Council for supporting the use of the image.

In the School of English at Queen's we were fortunate to encounter a great number of stimulating and encouraging scholars and we had the privilege of being part of the Renaissance research cluster. We benefited enormously from the wisdom and insights of Mark Burnett, Emma Rhatigan, Adrian Streete and Ramona Wray. To Adrian we owe a particular debt. His belief and interest in the project has been unwavering, and without his encouragement we might never have begun. We are grateful to him for generously gifting us so much of his time.

We lastly want to thank our families for their constant love and support, and for repeatedly asking after the progress of the 'biblical women book'. Our 'biblical women' ran parallel with graduations, relocations, new jobs and a marriage and we thank our wonderful husbands, Danny O'Neill and Andy Carroll, for their sacrifices, good humour and reassurance through it all. Your love meant everything, and always will.

Introduction: Discovering biblical women in early modern literary culture, 1550–1700

Victoria Brownlee and Laura Gallagher

The essays collected in this volume consider how biblical women were read, appropriated and debated in a wide range of early modern texts. By 'biblical women' we mean those women whose stories appear in the Old and New Testaments, as well as archetypes of femininity, such as those described in Book of Proverbs or Book of Revelation.[1] The literature within which these biblical women are considered includes plays, poems, works of political theory, devotional prose, biblical commentaries and sermons, as well as conduct and life writings, and, as a result, a variety of writers are examined. Essays considering Edmund Spenser, William Shakespeare and Aemilia Lanyer sit alongside those that explore the work of more unfamiliar names, such as Robert Cleaver, Thomas Nashe and Henry Constable, testifying to the multiplicity of biblical appropriation in England from 1550–1700. For as *Biblical Women in Early Modern Literary Culture* demonstrates, mothers and poets, dramatists and politicians, as well as sermonisers and biblical commentators, read, applied and re-imagined the narratives of the Bible's women, and often in markedly different ways.

Although many of us might struggle to place Puah, Peninnah or Priscilla within biblical history, an early modern reader was much less likely to do so. Instead, flitting between Old Testament and New, and shuffling across several biblical narratives within a handful of lines, early modern writers display nuanced familiarity with the scriptural figures they address, and anticipate a similarly sophisticated biblical knowledge among their readers. Aemilia Lanyer's *Salve Deus Rex Judaeorum* (1611) is a case in point. This sequence of lyric poems exhibits a striking awareness of the Bible's women, evident in the clever re-reading, and reframing, of the narratives of Eve and Mary in particular.[2] Yet, before the main Passion poem begins, Lanyer showcases her biblical knowledge in the dedicatory letter 'To the Vertuous Reader', and issues an emotive call to her audience to remember the Bible's 'wise and virtuous' women who are used by God to 'bring downe' the 'pride and arrogancie' of men:

As was cruell *Cesarus* by the discreet counsell of noble *Deborah*, Iudge and Prophetesse of Israel: and resolution of *Iael* wife of *Heber* the Kenite: wicked *Haman*, by the di[v]ine prayers and prudent proceedings of beautifull *Hester*: blasphemous

Holofernes, by the inuincible courage, rare wisdome, and confident carriage of
Iudeth: & the vniust Indges, by the innocency of chast *Susanna:* with infinite
others, which for breuitie sake I will omit. As also in respect it pleased our Lord
and Sauiour Iesus Christ, without the assistance of man ... to be begotten of a
woman, borne of a woman, nourished of a woman, obedient to a woman; and
that he healed woman, pardoned women, comforted women: yea, euen when he
was in his greatest agonie and bloodie sweat, going to be crucified, and also in the
last houre of his death, tooke care to dispose of a woman: after his resurrection,
appeared first to a woman, sent a woman to declare his most glorious resurrection
to the rest of his Disciples. Many other examples I could alleadge of diuers faithfull
and virtuous women ... All which is sufficient to inforce all good Christians and
honourable minded men to speake reuerently of our sexe, and especially of all
virtuous and good women (1611: F3v).

In providing a truncated survey of women's importance across biblical history,
the dedicatory letter anticipates the interpretative project of the central poem
which similarly traces a virtuous band of New Testament women who, unlike
their male counterparts, are constant in their support of Jesus.

The Old Testament women that Lanyer cites in this portion of the dedication
exert political, social and spiritual influence as they counter the evil of men:
Deborah who worked to orchestrate Israel's attack on the Canaanite army led
by Sisera (Judges 4:4–17); Jael who, having offered the fleeing Sisera shelter in
her tent, killed him by hammering a tent peg so deeply into his skull as he slept
that she 'fastened it to the ground' (Judges 4:21); Queen Esther who petitioned
the King to have the enemy of the Jews, Haman, hanged (Esther 5–7); Judith
who saved her town from Nebuchadnezzar's army by decapitating his general,
Holofernes (Judith 8–13); and Susanna whose steadfastness in the face of accusations of promiscuity lead those who had given false witness against her to be
sentenced to death (Daniel 13). The violence within these biblical narratives does
not detract from Lanyer's praise of the women mentioned as variously noble,
discreet, resolute, prayerful, beautiful, courageous, wise, confident, innocent
and chaste. Rather, details of the unsavoury actions that secure these women's
achievements are, unsurprisingly, excluded from Lanyer's defence of women.

Such omissions are suggestive of the way in which biblical women's narratives could be trimmed, reframed and appropriated in line with the agenda and
purpose of individual writers. In Lanyer's case, this series of abridged Old Testament narratives functions to assert the historic significance of women more
generally; an objective that becomes clearer as she turns her attention to the
women of the New Testament. Instead of focusing on their personal qualities, the women of the Gospels are honoured by cataloguing the privileged and
affectionate encounters they shared with Jesus: Mary was his mother, Mary
Magdalene was the chosen witness of his resurrection (Mark 16: 9–20), and the
various women healed, pardoned and comforted by Jesus were the recipients
of Messianic notice and time.[3] In these lines, Lanyer emphasises the deliberate

selection of women for important, spiritually significant tasks. The concise list of Jesus' debts to his mother in particular, and her centrality in the subsequent Passion poem, becomes indicative of women's spiritual relevance across sacred and secular history. The biblical women cited in this passage are understood to be participants in a larger sequence of female virtue (as opposed to male immorality) as they sit among 'infinite others' in the Bible, as well as the 'faith-full and virtuous women ... in all ages', who are similarly constant in their devotion to Christ.

As it establishes a constellation of godly women across Christian history, this dedicatory passage alerts us to an exegetical methodology that was funda-mental to the interpretation of the Bible's contents in this period. Lanyer's deft movement between both Testaments of Scripture and into the early modern present relies on biblical typology; a reading practice that, as many of the essays in this volume attest, regularly underpins the secular application of the Bible's female figures. Understood typologically, Lanyer's Old Testament women find their antitypes in New Testament female figures that, in turn, prefigure her patronesses and general audience of women. This passage importantly reminds us, then, that the Bible's women were not wedged in a remote biblical past. Instead, their narratives, understood to be part of an 'omnipresent history' (Killeen, 2010: 493), had enduring relevance for the immediate circumstances of early modern readers.

While the Bible's women had, as Lanyer's work suggests, assumed resonance within the early modern present, this volume unravels how the process of reading their lives produced multiple, rather than uniform, interpretations. Subsumed within a range of social, political and cultural debates, the varied applications of biblical women illuminates how the Bible, as Christopher Hill explains, 'could mean different things to different people at different times, in different circum-stances' (1993: 5). For writers like Lanyer, the Bible's cast of virtuous women could be turned to extol feminine virtues and advocate equality; yet, in the hands of other early modern readers, its women, both faithful and disobedient, were deployed as markers to guide and circumscribe female behaviour. While some of the essays that follow consider the complex ways in which biblical women were positioned as both positive and negative exemplars, others trace the wider application of these narratives. For the invocation of the Bible's women in discussions of female behaviour sits alongside their deployment in discourses on monarchy and doctrine, discussions of travel and grief and debates on England's enemies and foreign policies. During a period when individuals and authori-ties were biblically motivated and informed, the Bible's women were entangled with, and central to, an impressive array of (competing) ideologies.

The Bible in early modern English society and culture

It is difficult to overestimate the reach and importance of the Bible within early modern society. Biblical images, narratives and text were visible and audible in daily life and the Bible's pages were widely available, in a variety of formats and languages, across Europe. More than 140 editions of the Geneva Bible were printed in England alone between 1575 and the 1640s which, along-side other translations, resulted in as many as one million copies of the verna-cular scriptures in circulation by the mid-seventeenth century (Wright, 1943: 53; Molekamp, 2013: 14). From the earliest days of the Reformation, a healthy publishing industry grew up in support of biblical reading in the form of inter-pretative aids such as paraphrases, commentaries and religious pamphlets (Watt, 1991; Green, 2000). But access to biblical content was not restricted to those who could read. Weekly church services included Psalm singing, Bible readings and expository preaching, and many of the laity were compelled to attend catechising classes.[4] Biblical knowledge was also developed in less regimented ways, through the popularity of public sermons, such as those delivered at St Paul's Cross (see Morrissey, 2011; McCullough et al., 2011), and the circulation of didactic woodcuts and ballads in the period's cheap print (Watt, 1991: 140–67). The narrative of Daniel 13, for example, forms the basis of a ballad entitled 'The constancy of Susanna', which, by re-telling Susanna's story, anticipates that its readership will 'learne thus to liue godly' (*An excellent ballad*, 1640). Many such biblically derived ballads achieved long-lasting popularity and some, including 'Sampson judge of Israell' and 'David and Berseba', were circulated in broadside form for several decades.[5] As the existence of these ballads suggests, traditional literary genres participated in the dissemination of biblical content, and the popularity of biblical poetry and drama in the sixteenth century is suggestive of the way in which the period's literature was implicated in the legacy of the religious Reformation.

Poetic paraphrases of biblical texts were widely available from London's booksellers and, for writers such as William Baldwin, this poetry offered readers a wholesome alternative to 'baudy balades of lecherous love' (1549: 4). While Baldwin bills his verse paraphrase of the Song of Songs as an alternative to the period's love poetry, his work also seeks, like the majority of biblical paraphrases on this text, to guide the reader towards an appropriate interpretation of the Song's meaning. Because the Song of Songs was, at face value, an erotic dialogue between two lovers, poetic translations offered a means of dissemi-nating an alternative, spiritual reading of the book's contents in a popular and accessible format.[6] Among Protestant and Catholic commentators, Scripture's most sustained expression of female desire was rendered into an account of divine devotion; as Francis Quarles explains in his poetic retelling of the Song, the lovers are 'CHRIST, the *Bridegroome*; the CHVRCH, the Bride' (1680: 3).[7]

While biblical poetry addressing the Song of Songs was commonly mobilised to reinforce dominant readings of the Bride's body as the figurative body of the Church, in the case of other biblical women, the genre was used to advance divergent readings of their narratives. Edward Gosynhyll's poetic retelling of the opening chapters of Genesis finds Eve's creation from Adam's rib evidence of her inferiority as well as her 'euyull ... styffe, and sturdye' nature (1541: B4r); whereas, in Lanyer's *Salve Deus*, Eve's creation from Adam's body logically makes him the source of her error (1611: D3v). Used to reinforce and debate exegetical positions, poetry addressing the Bible's women could also have an important devotional function. The anonymous ballad 'The Wracks of Walsingham', for example, provides an outlet for lamenting the loss of England's Catholic past by remembering the destruction of the country's most famous Marian shrine during the reign of Henry VIII (Jones, 2002), and Robert Southwell's *Moeoniae* (1595), written at a time when Marian devotion was prohibited, demonstrates that poetry continued to provide a space to reflect on the Virgin's importance and intercessory powers. Such poems suggest that poetic reflections on the Bible's women could be used to express religious sorrow, venerate the saints and bemoan the visible losses of the Reformation.

In the biblically infused culture of early modern England, drama was also, as Paul Whitfield White has shown, 'an effective disseminator of religious ideas and cultural practices' (2008: 211). Of course, this usage was not new. Throughout the medieval period religious plays and pageants were popularly used by the Church to commemorate events in the Christian calendar. Biblical narratives, such as the accounts of Creation and the Passion, were central to these performances, and recent scholarship has demonstrated that traces of this tradition remain visible in the work of rural touring companies and commercial theatres in Elizabethan England (see O'Connell, 2000; White, 2008; Streete, 2011).[8] Certainly, biblically orientated drama continued to be written and performed throughout the reign of Queen Elizabeth I, as the large number of dramas claiming biblical sources in their titles suggests. Many of these plays are devoted to the lives of biblical men, such as Theodore de Bèze's *A tragedie of Abrahams sacrifice* (1577) and Robert Greene's lost play *Job* (c.1586), but evidence suggests that the narratives of the Bible's women were also regularly translated into drama throughout the Tudor period. The life of Mary Magdalene, who held a central role in medieval cycles addressing the Passion (see Coletti, 2004), was the subject of John Burgess' *St Mary Magdalene* (1507; see Harbage, 1988) and Lewis Wager's play *A new enterlude ... entreating of the life and repentance of Marie Magdalene* (1566), while the story of the Old Testament's Queen Esther was retold in *A new enterlude of Godly Queene Hester* (c.1527–30, published 1561; Greg, 1904). Records also testify to a number of plays addressing, or affording considerable space to, Eve, Susanna, Bathsheba, Salome and the Whore of Babylon.[9] Many of these biblical plays, much like medieval mystery cycles, sought to familiarise audiences with scriptural narratives and were used for didactic purposes. Yet, Scripture's female figures could also be excavated from the broader biblical narratives they inhabit and redeployed to tell alternative stories. The Whore of Babylon is a case in point. She appears in Thomas Dekker's 1607 play, *The Whore of Babylon*, in a tale warning of the religious and political threat England faced from Catholicism and its southern-European allies, a relocation that, as Victoria Brownlee's essay (Chapter 13) suggests, proliferated in reformed exegesis and poetry as well as plays.

While the Bible's women appeared in dramatic re-readings as well as re-tellings of their scriptural narratives, they were also reimagined more abstractly on the early modern stage. In a biblically saturated culture, as Beatrice Groves reminds, even a fleeting scriptural reference or allusion 'could open up a fund of associations, ambiguities and analogies' (2007: 25).[10] Scripture's ideological currency means, then, that a lack of visibility does not assume a lack of presence when it comes to biblical women in drama. The Bible's women may be discerned at the level of topical reference and linguistic implication. For example, the Virgin Mary is evoked in Cassio's praise of Desdemona's beauty and virtue in *Othello* (Maillet, 2007); Shakespeare's famous description of Cleopatra's barge recalls the description of the Whore of Babylon in Rev. 17:1–10 (Barroll, 1958; see too: Davidson, 2002; Hamlin, 2013: 219–20); and, as Lisa Hopkins' essay in this volume (Chapter 12) suggests, it is possible to read Helena's pilgrimage to Compostela in *All's Well That Ends Well* in light of Mary Magdalene's common association with narratives of exploration.

The oblique influence of biblical women's narratives on early modern drama testifies to the broader force of these stories in early modern literary culture. Much more than a source of literary inspiration, their narratives operated as filters through which personal and political circumstances were conceived, and provided imagery and discourse that could be mobilised to comment on any issue. The ideological resonance of the Bible's women in this period is suggested by the fact that they appear as glancing references, as well as literary subjects, across a broad spectrum of the period's writing. Their names are regularly invoked, often without explanation, in political discourse. For example, in a treatise on female monarchy, the Scottish reformer John Knox refers to Queen Mary I as that 'cursed Iesabel of England' (1558: 55). Replacing Mary's name with Jezebel's, Knox's biblical reference advances a political comment by connecting the legacy of a notoriously idolatrous Old Testament queen with that of a current monarch. Such shorthand use of the Bible's women proliferates in early modern political writings including, as Adrian Streete's essay (Chapter 4) explores, in the radical political theories of the 1550s; in these tracts, figures such as Deborah, Jezebel, Athalia, Judith and Jael are frequently drawn into discussions of Christian liberty.[11] The pointed citation of biblical women's names by Knox and his contemporaries illuminates how even the briefest scriptural reference could elicit a wealth of associated meanings and significances.

Yet, the reverse is also true. While writers undoubtedly harness the symbolic attachments of the Bible's female figures, in doing so, they also participate in the ideological inscription of biblical women's narratives by redeploying them within particular debates and contexts.

Moving a biblical woman from the pages of Scripture into a new polemical context or genre is, then, an act of translation rather than a transferal. It necessitates some form of interpretation on the part of author and reader. Whether biblical women are used at length or in brief, recalled directly or indirectly, their relocation will always involve an element of revision. This revision may range from a subtle shift in emphasis to an imaginative embellishment, or involve the exclusion or magnification of particular aspects of the biblical narrative. Whatever the case, ideological forces exert influence on the interpretative process ensuring that biblical readings can neither be neutral nor, as the reformers claimed, merely literal.

Reading and applying the Bible in early modern England

The very process of reading and interpreting the Bible was loaded with significance and, as such, an appreciation of biblical reading practices is essential for assessing the shared and varied applications of the Bible's women in the period. From the second half of the fourteenth century, the Bible held a fundamental position for those seeking to reform the Church and, for magisterial reformers such as Martin Luther and John Calvin, only Scripture's pages could prescribe the principles of faith.[12] Across Europe, the doctrine of *sola scriptura* was widely accepted by individuals and authorities that embraced religious reform and, in England, the newly established Church likewise preserved the authority of the Bible alone. Article six of the Thirty-nine Articles clearly states that 'Holye Scripture conteyneth all thinges necessarie to saluation: so that whatsoeuer is not read therein, nor may be proued therby, is not to be required of anye man ... or be thought requisite necessarie to saluation' (Church of England, 1571: 5). Disavowing the edicts of Popes, councils and centuries of tradition, the doctrine of *sola scriptura* was conceived as a response to the hermeneutic principles of the late medieval Church.[13]

During the medieval period, the Vulgate Bible, written in Latin, was the preserve of scholars rather than individuals. This scholarly engagement with Scripture was, however, extremely complex due to a tendency to approach the biblical text via the *Glossa Ordinaria*.[14] Within the *Glossa*, the words of the Old and New Testaments were surrounded by an expansive compilation of exegesis written by several authors over a number of centuries. The result of this tradition of biblical reading was, according to Alister McGrath, that the 'direct' influence of the Bible 'diminished considerably' between the twelfth and fourteenth centuries (1987: 123). His point here is not that the Bible ceased to be important but rather that its influence was felt in a more indirect way. Certainly, as the developed pattern of reading Scripture according to a number of higher (that is non-literal) senses suggests, biblical exegesis remained an important part of theological discussion throughout the medieval period.

Medieval exegetes, and Catholic commentators who followed in this tradition, commonly understood Scripture according to a four-fold methodology referred to as the *Quadriga*. According to this system, once the literal sense of a passage had been established, three further senses could be discerned: that is, the allegorical, moral (sometimes termed tropological) and anagogical.[15] From the earliest days of the Reformation, reformers ridiculed this highly theorised methodology on the basis that it distorted Scripture's meaning (see Luther, 1830: 402). Instead of four senses, they asserted that 'Scripture hath but one sense, which is the literall sence. And that literall sence is the rote and ground of all' (Tyndale, 1528: R2v). The reformers' claims for the literal were bound up with the accusation that Catholicism had abandoned this manner of reading Scripture; William Tyndale argued that, within the Roman Catholic Church, 'the literall sence is become nothi[n]ge at all. For the pope hath take[n] it cleane awaye' (1528: R1r–2v). Self-proclaimed champions of literalism, the reformers exuded particular venom for allegory, a reading practice that, in keeping with its association with Catholicism, Luther terms a 'beautiful harlot who fondles men' (1968: 347).[16]

Despite the verbal claims of the reformers, the Reformation did not rescue the literal, or the Bible for that matter, from a medieval Church that had simply forgotten it.[17] In accordance with the schema of the *Quadriga*, the literal sense remained important to medieval as well as Catholic commentators and, as the publication of an English translation of the Latin Vulgate suggests, biblical reading was not the preserve of Protestants alone.[18] One must be cautious too about taking at face value the reformers' renunciation of figurative readings. The reformers' brand of 'literalism' accommodated the use of allegory in interpretation of certain biblical texts, such as the Song of Songs and the Book of Revelation, and permitted the use of typology. Indeed, in spite of the reformers' vocal attempt to distinguish their exegetical practices from the institutionalised readings of the late medieval Church, a distinctive pre- and post-Reformation hermeneutic is, ultimately, difficult to identify.[19] Instead, the reformers' continued use of interpretative methodologies such as typology illuminates the contested nature of reformed literalism and suggests that figurative modes of reading continued to hold considerable sway within their exegesis. This mixed exegetical mode, so to speak, is reflected in the essays that follow.

Biblical typology was among the most influential, and common, reading practices of the early modern period and, as suggested earlier, was fundamental to the application of Scripture to the secular present.[20] At its heart, typology was as a means of establishing the hermeneutic unity of the Old and New Testaments and was predominately Christological in focus. Understood typologically, Old Testament figures and events had resonance beyond their historic moment and foreshadowed Christ's birth, life and death. For example, the High Priest in Exodus, acting as an intercessor for the people with God, might be seen, as William Perkins explains, as 'a type of Christ' (1609: 67). During the sixteenth and seventeenth centuries, however, this exegetical methodology was expanded outwards to include secular history within a continuing process of typological fulfilment; a shift that was no doubt motivated by the reformed insistence on the application of Scripture to the self.[21] Within this enlarged application, a biblical type could, as Lanyer's work suggested, find its antitype, or fulfilment, in the early modern present as well as within the pages of Scripture. A typological reading of the Bible marked Scripture's contents with living relevance and, although this reading practice is not always visible, its applicatory principles underpin the flexible readings of the Bible's women considered in many of this volume's essays.

Commenting on the fluidity of biblical readings in this period, Debora Kuller Shuger reminds that biblical narratives have 'a sort of extradogmatic surplus of undetermined meaning – or rather meaning capable of being determined in various ways' (1994: 5). Thus, Mary's virginity might be reminiscent of England's Virgin Queen Elizabeth; praise of her might, as Thomas Rist's essay (Chapter 10) discusses, slide into admiration of Henrietta Maria, and consideration of her could, as Laura Gallagher's essay (Chapter 11) suggests, provide a tool for meditation and affective piety. These alternative determinations of Mary's relevance are bound up with questions of female power and authority and demonstrate that biblical readings 'cannot and should not be reduced to theological positioning (although they have theological implications)' as they 'take shape at the intersection between the biblical text and other cultural materials' (Shuger, 1994: 5).

The essays that follow seek to investigate this 'intersection' by unravelling the rhetorical potential of the Bible's women across political, cultural, gendered and theological discourses. In doing so, the volume as a whole addresses a series of pertinent questions. It begins with a central question: which biblical women are appropriated in the period and to what ends? The volume then diverges into a series of interlinking queries: how do reading practices embellish, alter and shape contemporary applications of the Bible's women? In what ways does a typological understanding of Scripture enrich the perceived significances of the Bible's women? Does genre influence the ways in which these women were understood? Or, what responses do particular genres invite? To what extent is the reception of biblical women influenced by confessional identity? How is female rule or, more broadly, female power understood when refracted through biblical women? To what extent do biblical women provide a model for female speech and self-expression? To what degree do archetypes of biblical femininity operate as both positive and negative exemplars for early modern women? Are the Bible's women sexualised in contemporary exegesis and, if so, what effect does this have on their appropriation and appreciation? The essays collected here by no means provide exhaustive answers to these questions but, in attending to these broader issues, they hope to illuminate the pervasive impact of biblical women on early modern culture and stimulate their further discussion within scholarship.

Biblical women in early modern literary culture: the essays

Over the last decade, early modern scholarship has familiarised us with the significance of male biblical leaders, such as Moses and David, within contemporary debates on kingship and authority.[22] More recently, important discussions of how the Old Testament judge Deborah operated as an antecedent for Queen Elizabeth, and considerations of the Virgin Mary's presence in post-Reformation England have reminded that the Bible's women, as well as men, had significant, and diverse, ideological resonance.[23] The essays within this volume seek to build on this developing corpus of work by locating the Bible's more familiar women, such as Eve, Mary and Mary Magdalene, alongside their less familiar (by modern standards), but nonetheless significant, counterparts such as Zipporah, Michal and Esther.[24] In doing so, the essays, each of which addresses a particular biblical woman or archetype of femininity, offer a purview of the diverse ways in which the women of the Old and New Testaments were read and represented in early modern England.[25]

The essays that follow traverse a range of genres and examine literature written by a variety of confessionally diverse writers. By considering literature intended for assorted audiences, *Biblical Women in Early Modern Literary Culture* showcases the diverse contexts in which the Bible's women were deployed, and illuminates the transferability of biblical appreciation across apparent religious divisions. The volume has been split into two sections: Part One considers women and feminine archetypes of the Old Testament and the essays gathered in Part Two address the New Testament. This structure reflects the division of Scripture in early modern Bibles and speaks to the contemporary method of reading the Bible from the Old Testament to the New. Nevertheless, in spite of this division, the essays regularly make cross references between the two Testaments highlighting how, in line with the conventions of early modern exegesis, they were understood to exist in a reciprocal relationship. Within each section, the essays are broadly organised according to the sequential appearance of the women/feminine archetypes in the Bible. The biblical women studied extend from Eve in Genesis to the Whore of Babylon in Revelation, and the essays vary between those that examine dominant trends in appropriation to those that consider appropriations of a particular interest group or individual. Mindful that the Bible contains many women beyond those that are addressed in the essays, each section opens with an overview surveying how the women of the Old and New Testaments were understood in the period. These overviews work to situate the discussions that follow within a broader context of biblical reading.

Unsurprisingly, the volume's opening essay considers the Bible's first woman, Eve, and traces changes in her representation across the seventeenth century. Although Eve's temptation was routinely appropriated as part of the formal *querelle des femmes* controversies in the early part of the century, Elizabeth Hodgson explores how Eve is rendered a more sympathetic figure through her elision with Eden in the work of Aemelia Lanyer and Ester Sowernam. The mid-century writings of Royal Society horticulturalists, such as Abraham Cowley and John Evelyn, similarly appropriate Eve, but particularly her beautiful garden, as nostalgic propaganda for a particular pre-lapsarian mode of living. However, in these writings, the subtleties of Eve's guilt are subsumed and glossed over through emphasising the delights of the garden landscape. This shifting understanding of Eve across the period re-emerges and is re-appropriated inconsistently in John Milton's *Paradise Lost* (1674): his Eve, as in the early century, is the paradigmatic first woman and is also, like later writings addressing the Fall, defined according to perceptions of Eden. Eve's shifting significances across the century pinpoint how this biblical woman was ideologically permeable and readily 'redeployable even within her own habitat' of the garden.

The ideological flexibility of the Bible's women is further revealed in Adrian Streete's examination of radical political theories written during the 1550s by Protestant political theologians such as John Knox, Christopher Goodman and John Ponet. The subject of Christian liberty and the rights of subjects in these tracts is infused with a profound misogyny, and a deprecation of female rule, but Streete draws attention to how this outlook contradicts dominant readings of Old Testament female leaders including Deborah, Jezebel, Athalia, Judith and Jael. The appropriation of these female figures in resistance theory reveals a crucial tension. While on the one hand, 'wicked' biblical women are invoked to condemn female rule; on the other hand, 'good' biblical women are marked out as exemplars of godly resistance to tyranny. Moreover, the very fact that God allows female monarchs to rule at all obliges such writers, if not exactly to rethink, then certainly to confront a number of biblically endorsed patriarchal dicta concerning women's political and social subordination to men. As such, the essay demonstrates how the fraught ideological landscape of the 1550s encouraged, almost inadvertently, a reconsideration of the political uses of biblical women as a way of reconceptualising the lived reality of female monarchical rule.

Consideration of the way in which female power was perceived and understood through biblical women is extended in Michele Osherow's essay. Drawing attention to the popularity and esteem of Moses and King David in the early modern period, Osherow identifies how their wives, Zipporah and Michal respectively, suffered intense criticism at the hands of early modern exegetes.

Although the Bible recounts how each woman single-handedly saved the life of her husband, their decisive behaviour was understood by some readers, particularly male sermon writers, as highly unorthodox and, although unpunished on earth, worthy of divine retribution. The disapproval in early modern readings of both women centres on their fearless engagement with the locus of maleness. Both wives' stories are steeped in images of castration: Zipporah circumcises her son and casts the foreskin at Moses' feet, and, at the start of her narrative, Michal's value is set at 200 Philistine foreskins and once married, she will disobey her father and later mock her spouse. The essay thus reveals how early modern commentary grappled with, and censored, the wives' critique and emasculation of their husbands.

Echoing Osherow's attentiveness to political context and powerful femininity, Alison Thorne examines how the story of persecution, supplication and redemption in the Book of Esther was understood and applied by early modern readers. Opening with a study of the multiple reversals of fortune in the Esther narrative, and considering how this reflects Esther's supplication, Thorne then indicates how interpretation of this biblical text was conditioned by the socio-political, religious and aesthetic values prescribed by genre, focusing on biblical exposition in conduct literature. The specific context of the political instability of the 1640s and 1650s reveals Esther's relevance as a model to women petitioners of the civil war. Esther's image was, as Thorne explains, 'firmly associated with the interlocking themes of piety, self-sacrifice and concern for welfare of the body politic' and, as such, provided an inspirational model for women to vocalise their opinions on the contemporary upheavals.

Danielle Clarke's contribution also focuses on the relevancy of biblical women to issues surrounding female speech by considering the reception, use and circulation of the Book of Proverbs in conduct literature. For female readers, this biblical book expounded various negative assessments of the effect and status of the speaking woman; yet, in Proverbs 31, the ideal is articulated. Through examining the interpretation and application of feminine precursors found in the Book of Proverbs, Clarke considers how these biblical women became standards by which contemporary women might be judged. The essay explores how Proverbs 31 in particular was frequently adopted as a means to praise exemplary women, particularly in printed funeral sermons and life writings such as maternal advice manuals and diaries. Addressing these diverse genres, this essay is highly attuned to how the circulation, delivery and tone of genre inflected understanding of female biblical models.

Appropriately, the first essay in the New Testament section is attentive to the relationship between Scripture's two Testaments. Beatrice Groves illuminates how readings of the 70 AD fall of Jerusalem in early modern literature, particularly in Thomas Nashe's *Christ's Tears over Jerusalem* and Thomas Dekker's plague pamphlets, were influenced by the stress on femininity, and especially maternity, found in the biblical prophecies of that event. Groves argues that these early modern writers synthesize the weeping mothers found in Lamentations and Luke with Miriam, the violent mother of Josephus's *Jewish War*, to create a maternal figure who wept lovingly over her child before killing him. Miriam's story embodies the scriptural tropes of failed maternity which congregate at the site of the fall of Jerusalem: the weeping, widowed city and cannibalistic mothers of Lamentations; the daughters of Jerusalem in Luke who will desire not to have borne children or given suck; and the Lucan Christ, who is figured as a mother-hen whose wings cannot gather in her offspring. Groves suggests that this description of Christ figures him in both 'a feminine, and a disturbingly predatory position', a construction that in many senses resonates with contemporary understandings of the vengeance of a loving God.

The focus shifts again with Thomas Rist's essay on the appropriation of the Virgin Mary in Catholic poetry of the early seventeenth century, but the discussion continues to press the impact of religious-politics, genre and typology on perceptions of this emotive biblical woman. Opening with Ben Jonson's poetic comparison of the Virgin Mary and Henrietta Maria, the essay finds evidence of Mary's survival in the recusant poetry of Henry Constable and Richard Verstegen. Within the work of these writers, Rist considers Mary's feminised role as mediatrix, including its political dimension and erotic potential, before moving to consider reoccurring descriptions of Marian violation. Images of Marian defloration are, he contends, tragic rather than salvific and, as such, embody the perceived tragedy of Mary's removal from the English Church.

Laura Gallagher's essay also explores the particular significance of the Virgin Mary to recusants and remains attentive to the influence of genre. She argues that devotional prose texts intended for an English Catholic audience construct the Virgin Mary's grief at the cross in terms that recall medieval mourning rites and the conventions of the evocative *Stabat Mater Dolorosa*. However, in doing so, such texts are found to actively participate in, and negotiate, the early modern controversies surrounding the performance of grief. Mary's mourning does not simply operate as a static image of medieval Catholicism. Instead, the traditional conventions and motifs associated with the Virgin's mourning provide a means of ruminating on the nature, gender and significance of grief generally, and Marian grief specifically, in the early modern period. The appropriation of the voice, tears, visual experience, and bodily pains of the mother was intended to enable the reader to fully appreciate, and share in, Jesus' sacrifice. Through a process of accommodation and negotiation, then, the essay contends that the mournful Virgin of the Catholic past could be utilised in emerging Christocentric devotion to highlight the significance of Jesus' death, assert Mary's role as intercessor, and provide a tool for meditation and affective piety.

The focus on place in Groves' essay, and the political specificity of biblical women highlighted in several preceding essays, is powerfully evoked in Lisa

Hopkins' study of Helena in *All's Well that Ends Well*. Hopkins asserts that the pilgrimage-minded Helena should be read in the light of two holy women, Mary Magdalene and St Helena of Britain, both of whom went on long journeys in search of truth and salvation. Considering how the Magdalene paradigm is directly evoked within the play, the discussion is particularly interested in the ways in which Mary Magdalene became associated with New World exploration, an examination that opens into a discussion of St. Helena of Britain. Outlining how St Helena is similarly connected to exploration and linked specifically to encoded ideas about British nationhood, patriotism and Protestantism, Hopkins' dual consideration of St Helena and Mary Magdalene offers a new reading of Shakespeare's Helena.

Victoria Brownlee's essay fittingly draws the volume to a close with a discussion of the politically charged Whore of Babylon from the Book of Revelation. Acknowledging how this biblical book was popularly mapped onto the on-going struggle between Protestantism and Catholicism, Brownlee examines the exegetical practices that facilitated the translation of the Whore from biblical to secular history. Mindful of the reformers' commitment to a literal reading of Scripture, Brownlee traces how John's description of this biblical woman's body, as well as her seductive and deceiving nature, became tell-tale signifiers of her Catholic identity. The Whore's bedecked appearance, seductive capabilities and position as a spiritual mother were, for many reformed readers, understood to plainly detail the threat posed to believers, and the English state, by Catholicism. Within this tradition of reading, which stretches from sermons and commentaries to literary works including Edmund Spenser's *The Faerie Queene* and Thomas Dekker's *The Whore of Babylon*, the Whore's narrative becomes central to how Protestants understood themselves and their enemies. This final essay reinforces, then, the complex ways in which the Bible's women were deployed in response to national and international issues, as well as personal circumstances.

As each of the volume's essays demonstrates, early modern readings of the Bible implicated the female figures of the Old and New Testaments within an assortment of, often disparate, cultural debates. And what we discover when we look at these readings, is that the scriptural accounts of the Bible's women are not neatly reproduced. Indeed, this volume uncovers a series of biblical women who are re-read, reimagined and refigured anew within specific contexts, and for a variety of rhetorical and religious purposes. The hope is that, in doing so, the essays gathered here will foster greater awareness of, and stimulate interest in, biblical women's nuanced specificity and applicability in the early modern period.

Notes

1 The Book of Proverbs, which is addressed to Solomon's 'sonne' (1:10), offers paternal advice by describing several female types which include the harlot (Prov. 7), wisdom as a woman (Prov. 8) and the virtuous wife (Prov. 31). The Woman Clothed with the Sun (Rev. 12) and the Whore of Babylon (Rev. 17) are also used symbolically in the Book of Revelation. For more on these various women see Clarke and Brownlee's essays in this volume (Chapters 7, 13). It should be said that Susanna and Judith, whose stories appeared in a separate section between the Old and New Testaments called the Apocrypha in many Protestant Bibles, have also been included in the Old Testament Overview (Chapter 2) as their narratives remained popular with early modern writers.

2 For more on Lanyer's representation of Eve and Mary, as well as further discussion of how *Salve Deus* responds to particular theological and devotional debates, see Lewalski (1985); Beilin (1987: 177–207); Schoenfeldt (1997); Grossman (1998); Phillippy (2001); Hodgson (2003); White (2003); Bennett (2004); Coles (2008); DiPasquale (2008); Mascetti (2011) and Molekamp (2012).

3 The women who supported Jesus include Joanna (Luke 8:3); Susanna (Luke 8:3); Martha and her sister Mary (Luke 10:38–42 and John 11:1–6; 19–40) and the daughters of Jerusalem (Luke 23:28–31).

4 Religious conformity was enforced by law, and church attendance was compulsory. Those who failed to attend services faced hefty fines which, by 1581, could be as much as twenty pounds per month (Groves, 2007: 11–12). Servants as well as the children within households attended catechism sessions run by the master of the house or within the local church. For more on catechising see Green (1996).

5 See Watt (1991: 336–41) for a full list of ballads with their circulation and publication dates.

6 According to Lewalski the Song of Songs was 'second only to the book of Psalms in the frequency with which it was rendered into verse' in the seventeenth century (1979: 53).

7 Although Catholic and Protestant exegetes agreed on a spiritual interpretation of the Song of Songs as an account of divine, rather than human, devotion, some Catholic readers associated the Bride with Mary rather than the Church. For a discussion of the Song of Songs in medieval and Catholic literature see Astell (1990) and Matter (1990), and for more on how this biblical text was read in the seventeenth century see Clarke (2011).

8 For more on the religious drama of the medieval period, as well as a discussion of the dramatic usage of biblical narratives to mark religious festivals, see Muir (1995) and Coletti (2004).

9 The women listed appear in the following plays: Thomas Garter's *The commody of the moste vertuous and godlye Susanna* (1578); George Peele's *The loue of King Dauid and fair Bethsabe* (c.1594, published 1599); Thomas Dekker's *The Whore of Babylon* (1607). For a full listing of plays performed during this period see Harbage (1964).

10 A number of scholars have sought to examine biblical allusions in Shakespeare's dramatic works; see for example Shaheen (1999); Marx (2000); Freinkel (2002); and Groves (2007). For the influence of the Bible on drama beyond Shakespeare see Streete (2011).

11 Killeen (2010: 491) has shown how the wicked biblical Kings Rehoboam and Jeroboam were similarly used as shorthand in the political writings of the seventeenth century.

12 Prior to the Reformation, steps had been taken to produce a vernacular Bible in English by John Wycliffe, and in Czech by Jan Hus. For more on this see Spinka (1966) and Dove (2007). For an overview of development of the Bible in English see Daniell (2003).

13 For discussion of how medieval reading practices shaped the doctrine of *sola scriptura* see Gerrish (1982: 51–68) and McGrath (1987: 119–44).

14 For an overview of the Bible's influence in the medieval period, and consideration of the interpretative impact of the *Glossa Ordinaria*, see Smalley (1983).

15 For more on the distinctions between these senses see McGrath (1988: 157). It should be said that while the term '*Quadriga*' typically refers to the four senses cited, this was not a fixed interpretative system and '*Quadriga*' could be used to refer to some or all of these approaches: see Evans (1984: 114–22).

16 As Dolan explains, the reformers persistently associated 'the Roman church with fallen women' which allowed them to 'acknowledge its seductive appeal while simultaneously repudiating it' (1999: 52). The accusation of harlotry made against the Roman Catholic Church was rooted in, and bolstered by, associating Catholicism with the Whore of Babylon who appears in Revelation 17. See Brownlee's essay in this volume (Chapter 13).

17 McGrath (1987: 148–53) outlines the importance of the literal within the *Quadriga* as well as the influence of humanism on the hermeneutics of various reformers. See also Muller's discussion of literal interpretation (1996).

18 This translated version of the Latin Vulgate is often referred to as the Douay-Rheims Bible (New Testament, 1582; Old Testament, 1609–10). It was translated into the vernacular by English Catholics living in exile in France during the reign of Elizabeth I. For more on this Bible and the Catholic Reformation more generally see Mullett (2002).

19 Recent work on the hermeneutic practices of medieval and reformed exegetes has pointed to the continuing influence of intellectual movements, including scholasticism and humanism, as well as medieval schools, such as *via moderna*, on reformed thought and techniques of interpretation. See McGrath (1987: 52–9, 69–92) and Cummings (2002: 78).

20 The reformers attempted to reconcile their use of typology to their commitment to literalism by differentiating between this reading practice and allegory. For a discussion of the difficulties of this distinction, and a consideration of the reformers' continued reliance on figural readings, see Luxon (1995); Freinkel (2002) and Brownlee (2012). It should be said that typology was not a new reading practice developed after the Reformation, nor was it uniquely practiced by Protestant readers. This reading practice can be traced back to early Church writers (see Daniélou, 1960) and remained important throughout the medieval period during which the terms 'typology' and 'allegory' were used, almost interchangeably, to describe non-literal interpretations (see Miner, 1977; Keenan, 1992).

21 Lewalski (1977: 81) attributes the expansion of typology in the sixteenth and seventeenth centuries to the reformed directive for individuals to scrutinise Scripture for personal relevance. See also Galdon (1975: 5) and Keenan (1992: 262) for the development of typological applications.

22 Marx's (2000) consideration of Moses, David and Job, Streete's (2009) work on Christ, and Killeen's (2010) study of Old Testament kings attest to a growing interest in examining the diverse, and contested, ways in which male figures from Scripture were conceptualised in the period's writings. Before this, Campbell (1959) also considered how the Bible's male heroes were used in poetry.

23 McLaren (2003), Walsham (2003) and Osherow (2009), have considered Deborah, and discussions of Mary include Hackett (1994); Ellington (2001); Buccola and Hopkins (2007); Espinosa (2011); and Waller (2011).

24 Beilin (1987) and Almond's (1999) studies of Eve importantly demonstrate how she informed conceptions of gender in the early modern period. Badir (2009) considers the vast writing dedicated to Mary Magdalene.

25 In focusing on the women from both the Old and New Testaments, this volume builds on Ephraim (2008) and Osherow's (2009) important studies dedicated to the women of the Hebrew Bible.

References

An excellent ballad intituled, the constancy of Susanna. (c.1640) London: John Wright.

Almond, P.C. (1999) *Adam and Eve in Seventeenth-Century Thought.* Cambridge: Cambridge University Press.

Astell, A.W. (1990) *The Song of Songs in the Middle Ages.* Ithaca, NY: Cornell University Press.

Badir, P. (2009) *The Maudlin Impression: English Literary Images of Mary Magdalene, 1550–1700.* Notre Dame, IN: University of Notre Dame Press.

Baldwin, W. (1549) *The canticles or balades of Salomon, phraselyke declared in Englysh metres.* London: William Baldwin.

Barroll, L. (1958) 'Enobarbus' Description of Cleopatra.' *Texas Studies in English,* 37: 61–78.

Beilin, E.V. (1987) *Redeeming Eve: Women Writers of the English Renaissance.* Princeton, NJ: Princeton University Press.

Bennett, L. (2004) *Women Writing of Divinest Things: Rhetoric and the Poetry of Pembroke, Wroth and Lanyer.* Pittsburgh, PA: Duquesne University Press.

Bèze, T. de (1577) *A tragedie of Abrahams sacrifice.* London: Thomas Vautroullier.

Brownlee, V. (2012) 'Reforming Figures: Biblical Interpretation and Literature in Early Modern England.' PhD thesis, Queen's University Belfast.

Buccola, R. and Hopkins, L. (eds) (2007) *Marian Moments in Early Modern British Drama.* Aldershot: Ashgate.

Campbell, L.B. (1959) *Divine Poetry and Drama in Sixteenth-Century England.* Cambridge: Cambridge University Press.

Church of England (1571) *Articles, whereupon it was agreed by the archbishoppes and bishoppes of both prouinces, and the whole cleargie.* London: Richarde Jugge and John Cawood.

Clarke, E. (2011) *Politics, Religion and the Song of Songs in Seventeenth-Century England.* Basingstoke: Palgrave Macmillan.

Coles, K.A. (2008) *Religion, Reform, and Women's Writing in Early Modern England.* Cambridge: Cambridge University Press.

Coletti, T. (2004) *Mary Magdalene and the Drama of Saints: Theater, Gender, and Religion in Late Medieval England.* Philadelphia, PA: University of Pennsylvania Press.

Cummings, B. (2002) *The Literary Culture of the Reformation: Grammar and Grace*. Oxford: Oxford University Press.

Daniell, D. (2003) *The Bible in English: its History and Influence*. New Haven, CT: Yale University Press.

Daniélou, J. (1960) *From Shadows to Reality: Studies in the Biblical Typology of the Fathers*. Westminster: Newman Press.

Davidson, C. (2002). 'Antony and Cleopatra: Circe, Venus and the Whore of Babylon'. *History, Religion and Violence: Cultural Contexts for Medieval and Renaissance English Drama*. Ed. C. Davidson. Aldershot: Ashgate. 64–94.

Dekker, T. (1607) *The Whore of Babylon*. London: Eliot's Court Press.

DiPasquale, T. (2008) *Refiguring the Sacred Feminine: The Poems of John Donne, Aemilia Lanyer and John Milton*. Pittsburgh, PA: Duquesne University Press.

Dolan, F.E. (1999) *Whores of Babylon: Catholicism, Gender, and Seventeenth-Century Print Culture*. Ithaca, NY: Cornell University Press.

Dove, M. (2007) *The First English Bible: The Text and Context of the Wycliffite Versions*. Cambridge: Cambridge University Press.

Ellington, D.S. (2001) *From Sacred Body to Angelic Soul: Understanding Mary in Late Medieval and Early Modern Europe*. Washington, DC: Catholic University of America Press.

Ephraim, M. (2008) *Reading the Jewish Women on the Elizabethan Stage*. Aldershot: Ashgate.

Espinosa, R. (2011) *Masculinity and Marian Efficacy in Shakespeare's England*. Farnham: Ashgate.

Evans, G.R. (1984) *The Language of the Bible: The Earlier Middle Ages*. Cambridge: Cambridge University Press.

Freinkel, L. (2002) *Reading Shakespeare's Will: The Theology of Figure from Augustine to the Sonnets*. New York: Columbia University Press.

Galdon, J.A. (1975) *Typology and Seventeenth-Century Literature*. Paris: Mouton.

Garter, T. (1578) *The commody of the moste vertuous and godlye Susanna*. London: Hugh Jackson.

Gerrish, B.A. (1982) *The Old Protestantism and the New: Essays on the Reformation Heritage*. Chicago: University of Chicago Press.

Gosynhyll, E. (1541) *Here begynneth a lytle boke named the Schole house of women wherin euery man may rede a goodly prayse of the condicyons of women*. London: Thomas Petyt.

Green, I.M. (1996) *The Christian's ABC: Catechisms and Catechizing in England c.1530–1740*. Oxford: Clarendon Press.

——. (2000) *Print and Protestantism in Early Modern England*. Oxford: Oxford University Press.

Greg, W.W. (1904) *A new enterlude of Godly Queene Hester*. Louvain: A. Uystpruyst.

Grossman, M. (ed.) (1998) *Aemilia Lanyer: Gender, Genre and the Canon*. Lexington, KY: University Press of Kentucky.

Groves, B. (2007) *Texts and Traditions: Religion in Shakespeare, 1592–1604*. Oxford: Oxford University Press.

Hackett, H. (1994) *Virgin Mother, Maiden Queen: Elizabeth I and the Cult of the Virgin Mary*. Basingstoke: Palgrave Macmillan.

Hamlin, H. (2013) *The Bible in Shakespeare*. Oxford: Oxford University Press.

Harbage, A.B. (1964) *Annals of English Drama, 975–1700*. London: Methuen & Co.

Harbage, A. (1988) *Annals of English Drama, 975–1700*. 3rd edn. Ed. S. Schoenbaum. London: Routledge.

Hill, C. (1993) *The English Bible and the Seventeenth-Century Revolution*. London: Allen Lane.

Hodgson, E.M.A. (2003) 'Prophecy and gendered mourning in Lanyer's *Salve Deus Rex Judaeorum*.' *Studies in English Literature*, 43.1: 101–15.

Jones, E. (ed.) (2002) *The New Oxford Book of Sixteenth-Century Verse*. Oxford: Oxford University Press.

Keenan, H.T. (1992) *Typology and English Medieval Literature*. New York: AMS Press.

Killeen, K. (2010) 'Chastising with Scorpions: Reading the Old Testament in Early Modern England'. *Huntington Library Quarterly*, 75:3: 491–506.

Knox, J. (1558) *The first blast of the trumpet against the monstruous regiment of women*. Geneva: J. Poullain and A. Rebul.

Lanyer, A. (1611) *Salue Deus Rex Judaeorum*. London: Valentine Simmes.

Lewalski, B.K. (1977) 'Typological Symbolism and the "Progress of the Soul" in Seventeenth Century Literature.' *Literary Uses of Typology from the Late Middle Ages to the Present*. Ed. E. Miner. Princeton, NJ: Princeton University Press. 79–114.

——. (1979) *Protestant Poetics and the Seventeenth-Century Religious Lyric*. Princeton, NJ: Princeton University Press.

——. (1985) 'Of God and Good Women: The Poems of Aemilia Lanyer'. *Silent but for the Word: Tudor Women as Patrons, Translators and Writers of Religious Works*. Ed. M. Hannay. Kent, OH: Kent State University Press. 204–24.

Luther, M. (1830) *Commentary on Galatians*. London: James Duncan.

——. (1968) *Luther's Works: Volume 5 (Lectures on Genesis, Chapter 26–30)*. Ed. J.J. Pelikan, W.A. Hansen, G.V. Schick and P.D. Pahl. St Louis: Concordia Publishing House.

Luxon, T.H. (1995) *Literal Figures: Puritan Allegory and the Reformation Crisis in Representation*. Chicago: University of Chicago Press.

Maillet, G. (2007) 'Desdemona and the Mariological Theology of the Will in *Othello*'. *Marian Moments in Early Modern British Drama*. Ed. R. Buccola and L. Hopkins. Aldershot: Ashgate. 87–110.

Mascetti, Y. (2011) '"Here I have prepar'd my Paschal Lambe": Reading and Seeing the Eucharistic Presence in Aemilia Lanyer's *Salve Deus Rex Judaeorum*.' *Partial Answers*, 9.1: 1–14.

Marx, S. (2000). *Shakespeare and the Bible*. Oxford: Oxford University Press.

Matter, E.A. (1990) *The Voice of My Beloved: The Song of Songs in Western Medieval Christianity*. Philadelphia, PA: University of Pennsylvania Press.

McCullough. P.E., Adlington, H., and Rhatigan, E. (eds) (2011) *The Oxford Handbook of the Early Modern Sermon*. Oxford: Oxford University Press.

McGrath, A.E. (1987) *The Intellectual Origins of the European Reformation*. Oxford: Blackwell.

——. (1988) *Reformation Thought: An Introduction*. Oxford: Blackwell.

McLaren, A. (2003) 'Elizabeth I as Deborah: Biblical Typology, Prophecy and Political Power.' *Gender Power and Privilege in Early Modern Europe*. Ed. P. Richards and J. Munn. London: Longmans. 90–107.

Miner, E.R. (1977) *Literary Uses of Typology: From the Late Middle Ages to the Present*. Princeton, NJ: Princeton University Press.

Molekamp, F. (2012) 'Reading Christ the Book in Aemilia Lanyer's *Salve Deus Rex Judaeorum* (1611): Iconography and the Cultures of Reading.' *Studies in Philology*, 109.3: 311–32.

——. (2013) *Women and the Bible in Early Modern England: Religious Reading and Writing.* Oxford: Oxford University Press.

Morrissey, M. (2011) *Politics and the Paul's Cross Sermons, 1558–1642.* Oxford: Oxford University Press.

Muir, L.R. (1995) *The Biblical Drama of Medieval Europe.* Cambridge: Cambridge University Press.

Muller, R.A. (1996) 'Biblical Interpretation in the Era of the Reformation: The View from the Middle Ages.' *Biblical Interpretation in the Era of the Reformation: Essays Presented to David C. Steinmetz in Honor of his Sixtieth Birthday.* Ed. D.C. Teinmetz, R.A. Muller and J.L. Thompson. Grand Rapids, MI: W.B. Eerdmans. 3–22.

Mullett, M.A. (2002) *The Catholic Reformation.* London: Routledge.

O'Connell, M. (2000) *The Idolatrous Eye: Iconoclasm and Theater in Early-Modern England.* Oxford: Oxford University Press.

Osherow, M. (2009) *Biblical Women's Voices in Early Modern England.* Aldershot: Ashgate.

Peele, G. (1599) *The loue of King Dauid and fair Bethsabe.* London: Adam Islip.

Perkins, W. (1609) *Christian oeconomie: or, A short survey of the right manner of erecting and ordering a familie according to the scriptures.* London: Felix Kyngston.

Phillippy, P. (2001) 'Sisters of Magdalen: Women's Mourning in Aemilia Lanyer's *Salve Deus Rex Judaeorum.*' *English Literary Renaissance,* 31.1: 78–105.

Quarles, F. (1680) *Divine poems containing the history of Jonah, Esther, Job, Sampson: together with Sions sonnets, elegies.* London: Tho. Sawbridge.

Schoenfeldt, M. (1997) 'The Gender of Religious Devotion: Aemelia Lanyer and John Donne.' *Religion and Culture in Renaissance England.* Ed. C. McEachern and D. Shuger. Cambridge: Cambridge University Press. 209–33.

Shaheen, N. (1999) *Biblical References in Shakespeare's Plays.* Newark, DE: University of Delaware Press.

Shuger, D.K. (1994) *The Renaissance Bible: Scholarship, Sacrifice, and Subjectivity.* Berkeley: University of California Press.

Smalley, B.M. (1983) *The Study of the Bible in the Middle Ages.* Oxford: Blackwell.

Southwell, R. (1595) *Moeoniae. Or, Certaine excellent poems and spirituall hymnes: omitted in the last impression of Peters complaint being needefull thereunto to be annexed, as being both diuine and wittie.* London: Valentine Sims.

Spinka, M. (1966) *John Hus and the Czech Reform.* Hamden: Archon Books.

Streete, A. (2009) *Protestantism and Drama in Early Modern England.* Cambridge: Cambridge University Press.

——. (2011) *Early Modern Drama and the Bible: Contexts and Readings, 1570–1625.* Basingstoke: Palgrave Macmillan.

Tyndale, W. (1528) *The obedie[n]ce of a Christen man and how Christe[n] rulers ought to governe.* Antwerp: J. Hoochstraten.

Wager, L. (1566) *A new enterlude, neuer before this tyme imprinted, entreating of the life and repentaunce of Marie Magdalene.* London: John Charlewood.

Waller, G. (2011) *The Virgin Mary in late Medieval and Early Modern English Literature and Popular Culture.* Cambridge: Cambridge University Press.

Walsham, A. (2003) 'A Very Deborah?" The Myth of Elizabeth I as a Providential Monarch.' *The Myth of Elizabeth.* Ed. S. Doran and T. Freeman. Basingstoke: Palgrave Macmillan. 143–68.

Watt, T. (1991) *Cheap Print and Popular Piety, 1550–1640*. Cambridge: Cambridge University Press.

White, M. (2003) 'A woman with Saint Peter's keys?: Aemilia Lanyer's *Salve Deus Rex Judaeorum* (1611) and the priestly gifts of women.' *Criticism*, 45.3: 323–40.

White, P.W. (2008) *Drama and Religion in English Provincial Society, 1485–1660*. Cambridge: Cambridge University Press.

Wright, L.B. (1943) *Religion and Empire: The Alliance between Piety and Commerce in English Expansion, 1558–1625*. Chapel Hill, NC: University of North Carolina Press.

PART I

Women and feminine archetypes of the Old Testament

2

Overview: Reading Old Testament women in early modern England, 1550–1700

Victoria Brownlee and Laura Gallagher

The Old Testament reveals a female cast that is as significant as it is varied: its pages weave together the stories of mothers, daughters, wives and queens, as well as female prophets, judges and military leaders, who shape biblical history. The biblical books of Ruth, Esther and Judith are each devoted to the lives of their female title figures, and in the Song of Songs, a female voice is heard more clearly than in any other biblical text.[1] Even those Old Testament books preoccupied with the histories of Israel's patriarchs pause to note women's contribution to sacred history. In Genesis, the bodies and decisions of women, such as Sarah, Rebecca and Rachel, enable the establishment of the Israelite nation; and Exodus 1–4 reveals a catalogue of women, including Shiphrah, Puah, Moses' mother, Miriam, pharaoh's daughter, and Zipporah, who successively protect Moses. In many cases, very little is known about the various women who occupy the narratives of Israel's leaders: the decisions of the Widow of Zarephath (1 Kings 17:8–24); Potiphar's wife (Gen. 39), and the two harlot mothers of 1 Kings 3 affect the lives of Elijah, Joseph and Solomon, yet each remains nameless. The fleeting presence of the countless Old Testament women identified only by husbands and fathers is, then, not a marker of insignificance by biblical standards, nor, for that matter, by early modern ones. In fact, the amount of biblical text occupied by an Old Testament woman is rarely a useful gauge of her importance to early modern readers. Jephthah's daughter, whose story is told in Judges 11:29–40, attracted considerable attention as writers debated the theological implications of her sacrifice, while Queen Athaliah, whose wickedness is referenced in a handful of verses scattered across 2 Kings 8 and 11, and 1 Chronicles 8 and 22, became an important reference point for sixteenth-century political theorists.[2] The woman first mentioned in Scripture, Eve, is perhaps a more familiar case in point, for, although only mentioned in Genesis 2:22–5, Genesis 3 and briefly at the beginning of the book's fourth chapter, she incited more comment than any other biblical woman (and most men) in the period.[3]

Early modern readings of Eve were as paradoxical as they were numerous. Even a cursory glance at the arguments that rage within Ester Sowernam (1617) and Rachel Speght's (1617) responses to Joseph Swetnam's *The araignment of lewd, idle, froward, and unconstant women* (1615) will provide a flavour of the ferocity, and complexity, of the debates Eve stimulated.[4] Eve's story was implicated in discussions about original sin, democracy, nakedness, sexual libertinism and polygamy, but it was most consistently invoked in debates on the nature of women and the relationship between the sexes.[5] Eve's creation from Adam's 'rybbe' (Gen. 2:22) precipitated divergent assessments of women's status, and these ranged from claims that the female body was the '*epitome* ... and full perfection' of creation, to declarations that woman was 'second to man' (Austin, 1637: 180; Charron, 1608: 13).[6] Of course, disagreements over how to read Eve's creation in Genesis 2 were further complicated by the additional account of humankind's creation in Genesis 1:27. Writers seeking to re-evaluate established gender hierarchies regularly looked to this earlier version and were quick to point out that it 'makes no such distinctions and differences as men do' between the order and origin of male and female creation (Fell, 1667: 3).

Eve's engagement with the serpent in Genesis 3 also provoked interpretative disagreement. Although the burden of responsibility for the Fall was typically attributed to Eve, writers such as Lanyer, who unearths Adam's complicity (see 1993: 84–92), as well as John Evelyn and Abraham Cowley, offer, as Hodgson's essay (Chapter 3) suggests, a more positive reimagining of Eve's narrative. While the identification of male, as well as female, writers with Eve and her garden recovered her as a more sympathetic figure in some intellectual circles, other voices acknowledge Eve's continuing tenacity in debates over female behaviour into the later decades of the seventeenth century (see Tattle-well and Hit-him-home, 1640 and Fell, 1667). By this point, Eve's actions in Genesis 3 evoked a set of established assumptions about female weakness, disobedience and pride that, although increasingly challenged, continued to inform restrictions on women's behaviour. In line with the early modern concern with female speech, misogynist readings of the Fall often express particular discomfort with Eve's words. John Abbot's reading of Genesis 3 suggests that Eve erred specifically because of her open mouth and, addressing her, he charges: 'No sooner weare you made, but you must walke, / To recreat yourself, and enter talke' (1623: 22). As is so often the case in early modern readings of female speech, Eve's willingness to 'talke' is connected to her chastity.[7] It is because Eve converses 'with Satan' that Abbot imagines her pregnant with sinful conservation – her 'bellies full of chat' (1623: 23) – and suggests that she bequeaths a propensity to damnable chatter to her descendants.

Abbot is not alone in expressing distain for Eve's speech, nor is she the only target for those seeking to biblically denigrate the female voice. The Bible's first female prophet, Miriam, who was punished with leprosy for speaking out against her brother Moses (Numbers 12:1–10), was regularly vilified for intemperate speech.[8] Giacomo Affinati, in a treatise praising female silence, claims Miriam's 'murmuring' to be 'an infectious disease' and, in doing so, suggests that her leprous state is the manifestation of a deeper, inner corruption (1605: 147). Yet, just as Miriam's outburst could be used to denigrate women's speaking, other aspects of her narrative could be turned to authorise the female voice. Rachel Speght makes this clear when, detailing the causes for which women were made, she claims that a woman must use 'her voice to sound foorth [God's] prayses, like *Meriam*, and the rest of her company; ... to giue good councell vnto her husband, the which hee must not despise. For *Abraham* was bidden to giue eare to *Sarah* his wife. ... *Leah* and *Rachel* councelled *Iaacob* to do according to the word of the Lord: and the Shunamite put her husband in mind of harbouring the Prophet *Elisha*' (1617: 11). In reading Miriam's song of praise to God in Exodus 15:20–1, as well as the words of Sarah, Rachel and the Shunamite wife, Speght recovers women's words that praise, counsel and secure the protection of God's people. For Speght, these Old Testament narratives reveal that the Bible does not straightforwardly demand female silence but affords women powerful, effective voices.[9]

The voices of these Old Testament women could be used to counter cultural restrictions on female speech but they could also be used to sanction women's written words. Identification with the speaking women of the Bible was an important authorising tactic of early modern women writers, and the prayer of Hannah (1 Sam. 1), as well as the songs of Miriam (Exo. 15) and Deborah (Judg. 5), acquired particular resonance.[10] Speght looks to Hannah and Deborah who 'sang hymnes of thankesgiuing vnto the Lord' (29); Fell celebrates the voices of '*Hulda, Miriam*, and *Hanna*'; and the female petitioners of the 1640s and 1650s, as Thorne's essay (Chapter 6) suggests, invoked Esther as a radical model. Lanyer's opening praise of a series of Old Testament women used to bring down the 'pride and arrogancie of men' also reads as a catalogue of biblical women's discourse: Deborah is praised for 'discreet counsel', Esther for 'divine prayers' and Judith for 'rare wisdom' (1993: 49). Even the Book of Proverbs, which as Clarke's essay explores shaped various negative assessments of the speaking woman, endorses the voice of the exemplary wife who 'openeth her mouth with wisdome' (Prov. 31:26) and could be turned to authorise women's literary endeavours. Dorothy Leigh, for example, draws on the model of maternal instruction prescribed in the Book of Proverbs by including a citation from Proverbs 1:8 on the frontispiece of *The Mothers Blessing* (1616).

Other women writers deployed the female voices of the Old Testament in support of more audacious claims. In addition to relieving women from the social expectations of silence, their examples were understood to make female preaching and teaching permissible. In *Womens speaking justified* (1667), Fell cites the words of the prophetess Hulda (2 Kings 22:14–22; 2 Chron. 34:22–8), Hannah's prayer (1 Sam. 1:11), the Queen of Sheba's 'preaching' (1 Kings 10:6–9), as well as the wise counsel of Judith and Esther (detailed in the biblical books devoted to them), to show that '[priests] make a Trade of Womens words to get money by, and take Texts, and Preach Sermons upon Womens words; and still cry out, Women must not speak, Women must be silent' (16).[11] Tracing 'Womens words' across the Old Testament, Fell lays claim to a biblical tradition of female preaching that has been appropriated by men. For Fell, those men who deny women the right to speak express an attitude clearly at sea from biblical standards; they are 'far from the minds of the Elders of *Israel*, who praised God for a Womans speaking' (16).

By foregrounding priests' reliance on the words of the Bible's women, Fell's work reminds us that the female figures of the Old Testament were important to early modern men as well as to women. Hannah, the first person other than a prophet to talk to God in the sanctuary, and the only woman whose prayer is recorded in Scripture, became, as Michele Osherow explains, 'a paradigm for Protestant expression and belief' (2009: 45–6). Hannah's silent, direct prayer to God prompts Henoch Clapham to commend her example, alongside Moses', to all readers of *A Tract of Prayer* (1602): 'Prayer, is nothing else but a powring foorth of the soules-sense according to the instinct and motion of GOD his holy Spirit. And herevpon it is, that *Moses* is sayd to *cry* (Exod. 14. 15.) though he vttered no worde: and *Hannah to pray* (1 Sam. 1. 12.) though she spake onely in her hart. And this is called Prayer *Mentall*' (A3r). Marked as a model of prayer for men and women, Hannah demonstrates that Old Testament women could function as exemplary figures that transcend gender boundaries.

Biblical women also exceed gendered readings when they are invoked in theological debates on church worship. John Case, for example, looks to the Old Testament to support the use of appropriate music citing the Psalms as well as the songs of 'Miriam ... Debora & Baruck' (1586: 131). Alternatively, Rahab, the harlot who sheltered Joshua's spies in Jericho (Josh. 2), frequently appeared in discussions over the relationship between faith and works. Her actions were commended in the Book of James and, as a result, she was said to possess a 'living faith' that all believers should exhibit (Bullinger, 1624: A4v; see James 2:28). But just as James's commendation of Rahab's works prompted some commentators to disagree over the extent to which her actions contributed to her justifica-tion, others puzzled over how to reconcile her lies to the King about the spies' whereabouts with her praiseworthy faith (see Coverdale, 1537: D8r; Coignet, 1586: 262; Jackson, 1615: 15–26; Goodwin, 1659: 49–50). The Queen of Sheba was more symbolically drawn into the period's theological debates. Because she was, as John N. King explains, 'a traditional type for the Church', her image was deployed to visualise King Henry VIII's newly established authority over the Church in England (1989: 92). She appears kneeling to Henry, figured as the Old Testament King Solomon, in Hans Holbein's officially commissioned miniature, 'Solomon Receiving the Homage of the Queen of Sheba' (c.1534), and also in a stained-glass window commemorating Henry's reign in King's College Chapel.[12] As these images attest, the Bible's female figures can be found in a variety of genres and in works that, although biblically inspired, might be political in emphasis.

Biblical women were also mobilised in the period's domestic writings. Susanna's unswerving protection of her chastity, as recounted in Daniel 13, was regularly cited in conduct and marriage manuals for women. Robert Greene's *The myrrour of modestie* offers a prose retelling of her narrative in the 'hope most will treade' in her example (1584: n.p.) and, concerned that women be chaste, Leigh calls her readers to emulate Susanna who became 'famed through the world for chastity' (1616: 29). Susanna's beauty and heroic protection of her body from wicked voyeurs also drew the attention of dramatists and poets. She appears in Thomas Garter's play *The commody of the moste vertuous and godlye Susanna* (1578), in Robert Roche's 1599 poem, *Eustathia, or the constancie of Susanna*, and in countless lyrics and paintings across the sixteenth century.[13] Indeed, according to Theresa DiPasquale, Susanna's story was 'one of the most popular subjects of medieval and Renaissance art and literature' (2000: 365). Of course, not only were Old Testament women important to domestic writings on chastity, they also powerfully informed early modern conceptions of maternity. Thomas Bentley's *The monument of matrons* commends Hannah, Bathsheba and Christ's mother Mary as exemplars of 'motherlie and carefull affection' (1582b: B2r) and Elizabeth Clinton's *The Countesse of Lincolnes nurserie* (1622) looks to Eve, Sarah and Hannah to encourage women to breastfeed. On the basis of these women's narratives, Clinton boldly implores her readers to fulfil their maternal duty: 'Now who shall deny the own mothers suckling of their owne children: to bee their duty, since euery godly matrone hath walked in these steps before them: Eue the mother of al the liuing; Sarah the mother of al the faithfull; Hannah so gratiously heard of God' (5). What is interesting about Clinton's use of these particular Old Testament women is that the narratives of Eve (Gen. 4:1), Sarah (Gen. 18:13–4), and Hannah (1 Sam. 1:19) each attribute their pregnancies to God, rather than their respective husbands Adam, Abraham and Elkanah (Osherow: 2009: 71). In selecting these examples, then, Clinton both erases the contribution of fathers and foregrounds how motherhood has been a divinely valued, and historically significant, task across the pages of Scripture.

For those women who penned maternal advice books offering religious instruction to their children, Hannah, whose husband permitted her to 'Do what semeth … best' in her labour to return their son, Samuel, 'unto the Lord' (1 Sam. 1:23, 28), was a compelling predecessor. The work of Elizabeth Grymeston (1604), Dorothy Leigh (1616) and Elizabeth Jocelin (1624) invoke, in varying ways, Hannah's example, attesting to the way in which this Old Testament matriarch accrued special resonance among early modern mothers.[14] Although a more complex figure than Hannah, Bathsheba's attendance to the godly instruction of her son Solomon, as detailed in Proverbs 31:1–9, attracted similar praise. *The monument of matrons* draws a clear connection between the knowledge of

the 'wise and learned king' and that of his 'godly, wise, and learned' mother
(Bentley, 1582b: 134). Here, Bathsheba's example proves that a proper demonstration of motherly love will involve godly instruction: 'she, to shewe her duetie
& motherly affection towards him her childe, taught him the doctrine and
preceptes of good life, and howe he shoulde rule and gouerne to the glorye of
God' (134). While, as this reading suggests, Bathsheba like Hannah was understood to model a form of maternity that is rich in spiritual consequence, writers
praising her maternal wisdom often skirted around the circumstances leading
up to Solomon's birth.

Bathsheba enters the biblical narrative in 2 Samuel 11 as the object of King
David's lust. This lust leads David into adultery and deceit, but also causes him
to orchestrate the death of Bathsheba's husband Uriah on the frontlines of battle
(1 Sam. 11:1–17). Although the biblical text suggests that Bathsheba is passively
subject to the whims of her King, some early modern readers were clearly
uncomfortable with accepting David's role as the narrative's sole conspirator.[15]
Henry Cornelius Agrippa makes Bathsheba complicit along with David when
he identifies her as '*Bathsheba* the Adulteress' (1676: 265), John Lightfoot infers
a similar meaning when he describes her as 'an Adulteresse' (1644: 55) and John
Oliver terms her 'guilty of adultery' (1663: 107). Such straightforward denounce-
ments of Bathsheba's innocence are reasonably uncommon in early modern
readings of this narrative; yet, other writers apportion blame to Bathsheba in
more subtle ways. Francis Sabie's poem 'Dauid and Bathsheba' (1596) suggests
that Bathsheba willingly submits to David's advances when, reminiscent of
a courtship scene, he describes how 'she came, he wooes, she gaue consent'
(F2r). There is also an indirect suggestion that Bathsheba might be partially
culpable in the opening scene of George Peele's *The Love of King David and Fair
Bethsabe* (c.1594, published 1599). In devoting almost fifty lines to a description of
Bathsheba bathing, which in the biblical narrative is recounted in a solitary verse
(2 Sam. 11:2), the play seems to assign at least part of the burden of responsibility
to her irresistible body. As the audience consider the contours of Bathsheba's
body along with the watching David, his singular responsibility is diffused; his
actions are, to some extent, mitigated by the magnetism of her beauty.[16]

Samuel Cobb's late seventeenth-century poem *Bersaba*, which also begins
with a lengthy reflection on Bathsheba's naked body, more obviously lessens
David's blame with the claim that 'Ev'n Love himself admir'd her won'drous
shape' (1695: 4). Yet, in distinction to Peele's Bathsheba who, on meeting David,
attempts to dissuade his advances, Cobb's Bathsheba is represented as the stereo-
typical lusty female:

> Her Heart straight blushes with a secret Fire,
> Her wanton Breast glows with a new Desire.
> She tries all Arts that Woman's Wit can find,
> And only Love fills now her lab'ring mind. (4)

Here, it is Bathsheba's desire, as well as David's, that motivates the adultery. The poem's ending reveals, however, that both parties do not share equal blame. The final lines, which recall David the Psalmist rather than the adulterer, reveal that he suffers from 'No unchast Desire ... / nor could *Bersaba* now Beguile' (15). Evidently, it is the bewitching Bathsheba who, reminiscent of the Genesis serpent who 'begules' Eve (Gen. 3:13), leads David astray.

What is explicit in Cobb, and implicit in Peele, is the disarming potential of female beauty. Because Bathsheba's appearance caused the downfall of the period's most favoured biblical king, her name occasionally crops up alongside those of Jezebel, Delilah and Potiphar's wife who each use their bodies to seduce Israel's leaders.[17] These women are, however, much more frequently invoked than Bathsheba to warn of the dangers of the female body.[18] In *Samson Agonistes* (1671), John Milton presents Delilah's appearance as powerfully alluring but false, and Samson realises much too late that he has been beguiled by 'fair fallacious looks, venereal trains, / Softn'd with pleasure and voluptuous life' (37). Although the biblical text makes no reference to Delilah's use of adornment, Milton's Dalila, 'bedeckt, ornate, and gay' and moving in a cloud of 'odorous perfume' (46–7), embodies the familiar connection between jewellery and corruption, particularly corrupted female sexuality.[19] Her imagined 'ruffes and cloathes' cause her to be counted, alongside Jezebel, among the Bible's proud, 'hurtfull wives' who 'joy' in 'their husbands harmes' in the marriage guidebook *Matrimoniall honovr* (D.R., 1642: 298). Although Jezebel, who in 2 Kings 9:30 'peinted her face, and tired her head', is similarly vilified for a love of outward embellishment, readings of her ornamentation frequently have a more politicised edge. For many writers, her painted face connected her to the infamously painted Whore of Babylon and, consequently, to Rome.[20] Henry Ainsworth makes these connections clear when, drawing on the words of Revelation 17:2, he describes the Roman Catholic Church as 'this *Iezebel*' who has 'enamoured the Nations with her beauty ... and made them drunken with the wine of her fornications (1624: 90; see also Abbot, 1604: Ff2v). Jezebel was, then, not simply used to dissuade women from cosmetics and embellishment. In many Protestant writings she also can be found operating as a potent symbol of Catholicism and its perceived corruption.

Unsurprisingly, in marriage and domestic writings Jezebel is regularly cast as the quintessential wicked wife. She is attacked for imprudence and idolatry as well as 'chiding and bawling' speech (Gouge, 1622: 285), and, because she 'provok[es] *Ahab* to be farre worse then himselfe', is even credited with responsibility for her husband's sin (D.R., 1642: 34). But, by early modern standards, Jezebel was by no means the only wayward wife in the Old Testament. Zipporah (wife of Moses), Michal (first wife of David), Job's wife, Delilah and Eve, were all used to describe the undesirable wife, while Sarah, Hannah, Ruth, Susanna, Abigail and Esther were hailed as virtuous wifely exemplars.[21] Although Old Testament women were frequently categorised as godly or wicked, the biblical narratives within which these women reside often reveal more complex figures than marriage and conduct writings suggest. Take Abigail, for example. 1 Samuel 25 details how she makes reparations to David and his army for Nabal's churlishness by executing a plan without her husband's consent. The biblical text clearly states that, as she boldly rides out to meet David, 'she tolde not her husband Nabal' (1 Sam. 25:19). The consignment of food Abigail provides, and the persuasive speech she makes before David, alter the army's course of action and save her household from death. But the narrative does not end here. Abigail's unauthorised resourcefulness is cited a direct cause of her Nabal's death: 'In the morning when his wife tolde him … his heart died within him' (1 Sam. 25:37).

The Abigail who is praised by early modern writers as 'a true Idea of a virtuous wife' at times bears little resemblance to the one in the biblical account (Ferrers, 1622: A8r). Conduct writings commonly overlook Abigail's wifely disobedience and focus instead on her prudence, wisdom and beauty.[22] In fact, she even appears in Robert Cleaver's treatise on household order as an example wifely obedience:

> A good wife therefore is knowne, when her words, and deeds, and countenance, are such as her husband loueth. She must not examine whether he be wise or simple, but that she is his wife, and therefore being bound she must obey: as *Abigail* loued her husband, though he were a foole, churlish, and euill conditioned. (1621: O6v)

While it is ironic that Abigail, who not only questions her husband's judgement but devises a plan to override his decision, is extolled as an archetype of wifely love and obedience, such selective reading of her narrative is by no means unusual within the tradition of biblical exemplarity. As writers excised portions of biblical narrative, and accentuated some characteristics and not others, the reputations of certain female figures fared rather better than others. Thomas Grantham's 1641 sermon on marriage illuminates this inconsistency in how Old Testament women were read when, commenting on the compatibility of spouses, he cites the following examples: '*Nabal* and *Abigail*, *Nabal* a foole and churle, and of so base a disposition … and she a kinde complementall woman she fell at *Davids* feet, and offered to wash the feet of his servants. *David* and *Michal*, *Michal* a scoffing woman, deriding *David* for dancing before the *Arke*, and he a man after Gods own heart' (1–2). Just as Grantham chooses to foreground Abigail's submission to David, if not to her husband, rather than her wifely disobedience, his derision of Michal reflects only part of her story. Earlier in their marriage, Michal rescued David from the clutches of Saul, a moment which, as Osherow's essay (Chapter 5) explains, is rarely celebrated in early modern readings of her narrative.

While the errors of some Old Testament women like Michal are amplified, those of others are diminished. Rebecca, whose beauty and 'comly behaviour'

(Hilder, 1653: 39, 54) in covering her face before meeting Isaac is much admired by early modern writers, cunningly deceives her husband into conferring the blessing due to Esau, as the first-born son, onto her favoured son Jacob. But unlike Michal who is condemned for the lies she tells to protect David, Rebecca is guilty of the rather lesser crime of rashness.[23] A number of commentators downplay her deception on the basis that it expedites, rather than alters, God's providential plan. Calvin's commentary on Genesis elucidates this rationale. Because Jacob's election was ordained by 'immutable decree', he claims that Rebecca's actions 'sprang from no other thing, then from fayth' which manifested itself as 'rash and undiscrete zeale' (1578: 569–70). Abraham Wright similarly finds her guilty of 'presuming upon the Oracle of God' but points out that 'her desire was good' (1662: 41–2). Evidently, viewing Rebecca's lies from the vantage of God's plan for Jacob, commentators on Genesis found her actions understandable if not excusable.

The 1568 play *A newe ... comedie ...vpon the historie of Iacob and Esau*, however, mobilises Rebecca's audacious disregard for patriarchal authority to interrogate political and gendered hierarchies. Michelle Ephraim's discussion of the play suggests that Rebecca operates as a figure of Queen Elizabeth and contends that the drama's embellishment of her matriarchal role in many senses 'naturalizes the usurpation of men by women' (2008: 59).[24] While Rebecca may indeed be understood to figure Elizabeth in *Jacob and Esau*, it was the Old Testament judge Deborah who was more commonly used to celebrate, and authorise, the authority of England's Queen. Deborah's wisdom and position as a respected judge in Israel marked her as a suitable predecessor of Elizabeth, but it was her deliverance of the Israelites from the idolatry of the Canaanites (Judges 4) that sealed her identification with Elizabeth who freed England from the Catholicism imposed under Mary (Doran, 1996: 11; Ephraim, 2008: 49).[25] Elizabeth was commemorated as an English Deborah in her coronation pageant on Fleet Street and Andrew Willet remembers 'our worthy Deborah our late Soueraigne Q. Elizabeth' as he marks the coronation of James I in *Ecclesia triumphans* (1603: 103).[26] While these examples demonstrate that Deborah functioned as a model for Elizabeth throughout her reign, the Queen's image was not exclusively fashioned through this biblical figure.[27] Over the course of her reign, Elizabeth was likened, often concurrently, to the biblical Queens Esther and Sheba, the warriors Jael and Judith, as well as male leaders including Moses, David and Solomon.[28]

Esther's victory over Haman and protection of the Jews marked her, like Deborah, as an antecedent of the rescuing Queen Elizabeth.[29] Yet, as a biblical queen of doubtful parentage, Esther perhaps acquired special resonance with the newly crowned daughter of Anne Boleyn (Ephraim, 2008: 29). It has been suggested that the need to biblically legitimate Elizabeth might, for example, have motivated the publication of *The Godly Queene Hester* early in the Queen's reign, particularly as the wisdom and decisive authority of the play's Hester powerfully attests to the effectiveness of female leadership.[30] More specifically, the narratives of biblical women such as Esther, Deborah and Sheba were important to conceptions of female rule because they represented women's involvement in executions, battle and command. John Bridges looks to the deliverance of Israel at the hands of Deborah and Jael, as well as the Queen of Sheba's command over her train, to demonstrate that 'women princes' may not only wield sovereign power but 'gouern ouer all their armies ... *without* shame' (1587: 769–70).[31] A document attributed to Queen Elizabeth also seeks to understand her military role through a biblical lens when, before her troops at Tilbury, it describes her to be in possession of a 'Masculine Spirit, like another *Deborah*' (1688: 1). This comment is revealing because it demonstrates that early modern readers often found it difficult to reconcile Deborah's (and Elizabeth's) actions with her gender.[32] For this reason, it is not uncommon to find the impressive feats of Deborah, Jael and Judith couched in masculine terms. Thomas Heywood praises Deborah as a 'Heroicke and masculine spirited Championesse' and describes Judith as having 'Put on a masculine spirit' to behead Holofernes (1640: 15, 20). Although Heywood suggests here that Deborah and Judith confound gendered expectations, particularly the convention of female weakness, his descriptions do so by tying the bravery, leadership and strength that these women exhibit to maleness.

Readings of Old Testament women are, it seems, often bound up with early modern assumptions about femininity. And these assumptions regularly inflect the lessons male writers extrapolate from the narratives of the Bible's women: the Bible's 'good' wives could be used to teach early modern women about obedience and chastity, while its assumed wicked women might be used to warn of the dangers of female speech, ornamentation and seduction. But the powerful voices and effective actions of Old Testament women are difficult to occlude, and early modern women writers, and some men, found in their examples a means to authorise their own words, challenge established notions about female preaching, and re-establish motherhood as a vocation rich in spiritual significance. Moreover, consideration of Old Testament women reveals that they transcend, as well as prescribe, gender boundaries. The Bible's female figures were important to men, as well as to women; their images were mobilised by monarchs, and their stories appear in a spectrum of theological and political debates. Irrespective of subject matter or genre, Old Testament women are, as the following essays attest, hard to evade.

Notes

1 In the Geneva Bible, as well as in early editions of the Authorised Version, the Book of Judith, along with the story of Susanna (Daniel 13), is included among the Apocrypha. Although texts gathered in the Apocrypha were not, according to the instructions offered in the Geneva Bible (1560), to be 'expounded publikely in the church' or

used to 'proue any point of Christian religion', they were nonetheless deemed useful for the 'advancement and furtherance of the knowledge of the historie, & for the instruction of godlie maner' (Apocrypha: The Argument). As a result, the Apocrypha retained familiarity among Protestants throughout the sixteenth and seventeenth centuries, with portions of its texts even included in the Church's lectionary.

2 For an overview of how Jephthah's daughter was read in relation to sacrifice see Shugar (1994: 128–66) and Thompson (2001: 100–78). In addition to sermons and commentaries, Jephthah's daughter appears in two plays: John Christopherson's *Jephthah* (1544) and George Buchanan's *Jephthah* (1554). Ephraim (2008: 89–154) has also argued that the narrative of Jephthah's daughter informs the representation of Jewish daughters in Christopher Marlowe's *The Jew of Malta* (c.1590), and William Shakespeare's *The Merchant of Venice* (1596–97). For discussion of Queen Athaliah's use by political theorists see Streete's essay in this volume (Chapter 4).

3 For an assessment of Eve's popularity in the early modern period see Beilin (1987: 247–85); Almond (1999); McManus (2000: 193–206); and Peters (2003: 130–54).

4 For consideration of the pamphlet debate stimulated by Swetnam's text, and the importance of Genesis to debates on women more generally, see McManus (2000: 193–206).

5 See Almond (1999: 2) for a full list of debates in which Eve's narrative became embroiled, as well as Crowther (2010).

6 Biblical references have been taken from *The Geneva Bible* (1560, rpt 2007).

7 Scholars who have studied the connection between female chastity and silence include Callaghan (1989); Trill (1997); and Luckyj (2002). It is worth mentioning that although the voice of the Bride in the Song of Songs offers a powerful expression of female desire, medieval and early modern readers favoured, as the volume's Introduction (Chapter 1) explains, a spiritual reading of this text and commonly understood the Bride to be a figure of the Church. See the studies of Matter (1990); Astell (1990); and Clarke (2011).

8 For more on how Miriam's speech is read in the period, and a sustained discussion of the female voices of the Old Testament more generally, see Osherow's excellent study (2009: 11–43).

9 In 1 Corinthians 14:34–5 Paul advised women to be silent in church and his words were commonly invoked to constrain female speech.

10 For a detailed overview of early modern readings of these women see Osherow's (1999) various chapters on Miriam (11–44), Hannah (45–76) and Deborah (77–110).

11 Leigh (1609: 27–8) also cites Anna, Miriam and Hulda as examples of women who teach.

12 For a discussion of the biblical iconography used throughout these windows and Henry's use of Solomonic imagery more generally, see King (1989: 86–9).

13 For an overview of poetry devoted to Susanna's story see Campbell (1959: 124–7). For connections between Garter's Susanna and Queen Elizabeth see Ephraim (2008: 71).

14 See Osherow (2009: 66–9) for the influence of Hannah's story on Grymeston and Jocelin. Leigh (1616: 41) cites Hannah.

15 Those who wished to relieve David of some blame were perhaps influenced by the fact that he was, as King (1982: 81) terms, 'the most enduring biblical type for Tudor kingship'. It should be said that David's redemption, as recounted in the Psalms, was the focus of many writings in the period. Between 1530 and 1600 there were more

than seventy translations of the Psalms printed (Zim, 1987: 2–3).

16 See Ephraim (2008: 69–88) for a more extended discussion of how Bathsheba's body
    is represented in Peele's play.

17 See for example Bentley's list and comments (1582c: 94). Jezebel adorns herself in the
    hope of impressing Jehu in 2 Kings 9:30 and her marriage to Ahab lead him, and Israel,
    into idolatry; Delilah seduces Samson into revealing the secret of his strength which
    leads to his capture by the Philistines and later death (Judges 16); Potiphar's wife
    attempted to seduce Joseph and his refusal of her advances resulted in his imprison-
    ment (Gen. 39:7–20).

18 See for example the descriptions of Delilah in Bentley (1582c: 139–40) and *The deceyte
    of women* (1557: f1v–2v); of Jezebel in Ainsworth (1624: 90), Tuke (1616: B2r) and Brath-
    waite (1631: 194); and of Potiphar's wife in Batt (1581: 52v), Pricke (1609: M1r) and
    Greenham (1612: 637).

19 For a discussion of the early modern connection between jewellery and corruption
    see Shell (1999: 29) and Streete (2009). It is worth noting that although the empha-
    sis on Dalila's ornamented appearance prompts us to sympathise with the duped
    Samson and even excuse his poor judgement, Milton (1671) also complicates Dalilia's
    character by, for example, making her Samson's wife and adding a scene in which she
    visits him in prison. Martin (2004) suggests that in making these additions, Milton
    asks readers to rethink their assumptions of Delilah.

20 For more on the Whore of Babylon's connection with ornamentation and Rome see
    Brownlee's essay in this volume (Chapter 13).

21 See Gouge's list (1622: 285) as well as Bentley's (1582a: 72). Ruth is remembered in
    Milton's 'Sonnet Nine' as a dutiful homemaker and an ideal wife (Jeffery, 1992: 669).
    She was also commonly praised in the period for constancy of faith and love (Agrippa,
    1542: 21; Hill, 1660: 20–1).

22 See for example Hayward (1614: 574) and A.L. (1653: 3–4).

23 See Ephraim (2008: 49–56) for more on how Rebecca's actions were read as haste or
    rashness in the period.

24 Ephraim has also connected Rebecca's nurse Deborra with the Deborah of Judges
    4, and read her as a figure of Elizabeth (2008: 49–68). Pasachoff (1975) too has read
    Rebecca as Elizabeth Tudor.

25 Protestants understood themselves to fulfil the role of God's chosen people (see King,
    1982: 410).

26 See Osherow (2009: 81–6) for more on Elizabeth as Deborah in the Fleet Street
    pageant.

27 For a discussion of Elizabeth's image see Marcus (1990) as well as Levin (1994).

28 For an example of Elizabeth's concurrent identification with a range of biblical
    figures see Bentley (1582b: 262). For discussion of Elizabeth's identification with male
    biblical figures including David see Marcus (1990: 135–53) and Osherow (2009: 82–91,
    115–21). Elizabeth's association with Solomon was celebrated in a Latin play, *Sapientia
    Solomonis*, which was performed on 17 January 1565 before Elizabeth I and Princess
    Cecilia of Sweden who, having travelled to visit England's Queen, is addressed as the
    Queen of Sheba (see Payne, 1975: 27–9).

29 Norden (1596: 8) praises Elizabeth as 'a Hester in this land' because of her role in
    religious reform. See also Brenz's comparisons (1584: A1v–4r).

30 The play was written perhaps as early as 1525 but remained unpublished until 1561. Ephraim (2008: 29) argues for a connection between the play's reprinting and Elizabeth's reign, while other scholars read the play's Hester as Catherine of Aragon: see for example Bevington (1968: 87–93) and Blackburn (1971: 70–6).

31 Although not a regular feature in writings on Esther, Quarles's poetic retelling of Esther's narrative in *Hadassa* (1621) devotes considerable space to her involvement in the execution of Haman and his sons.

32 See Osherow's (2009: 82–3) discussion of how female weakness influences readings of Deborah, as well as Levin's (1994) consideration of Elizabeth's use of androgynous imagery.

References

Abbot, G. (1604) *The reasons which Doctour Hill hath brought, for the vpholding of papistry.* Oxford: Joseph Barnes.

Abbot, J. (1623) *Jesus Praefigured.* Antwerp: s.n.

Affinati, G. (1605) *The dumbe diuine speaker, or: Dumbe speaker of Diuinity.* London: R. Bradock.

Agrippa, H.C. (von Nettesheim) (1542) *A treatise of the nobilitie and excellencye of woman kynde.* London: Thomae Bertheleti.

——. (1676) *The vanity of arts and sciences.* London: J.C.

Ainsworth, H. (1624) *An arrow against idolatrie Taken out of the quiver of the Lord of hosts.* Amsterdam: G. Thorp.

Almond, P.C. (1999) *Adam and Eve in Seventeenth-Century Thought.* Cambridge: Cambridge University Press.

A newe mery and wittie comedie or enterlude, newely imprinted, treating vpon the historie of Iacob and Esau (1568) London: Henrie Bynneman.

Astell, A.W. (1990) *The Song of Songs in the Middle Ages.* Ithaca, NY: Cornell University Press.

Austin, W. (1637) *Haec homo wherein the excellency of the creation of woman is described, by way of an essay.* London: Richard Olton.

Batt, B. (1581) *The Christian mans closet.* London: Thomas Dawson.

Beilin, E.V. (1987) *Redeeming Eve: Women Writers of the English Renaissance.* Princeton, NJ: Princeton University Press.

Bentley, T (1582a) *The fift lampe of virginitie conteining sundrie forms of christian praiers and meditations.* London: H. Denham.

——. (1582b) *The monument of matrones conteining seuen seuerall lamps of virginitie, or distinct treatises.* London: H. Denham.

——. (1582c) *The sixt lampe of virginitie conteining a mirrour for maidens and matrons.* London: Thomas Dawson and Henry Denham.

Bevington, D.M. (1968) *Tudor Drama and Politics: A Critical Approach to Topical Meaning.* Cambridge, MA: Harvard University Press.

Blackburn, R.H. (1971) *Biblical Drama under the Tudors.* Paris: Mouton.

Brathwaite, R. (1631) *The English gentlewoman.* London: B. Alsop and T. Fawcet.

Brenz, J. (1584) *A right godly and learned discourse vpon the book of Ester.* Trans. J. Stockwood. London: John Wolfe.

Bridges, J. (1587) *A defence of the gouernment established in the Church of Englande*. London: John Windet and T. Orwin.

Bullinger, H. (1624) *Looke from Adam, and behold the Protestants faith and religion evidently proued out of the holy Scriptures*. London: John Haviland.

Callaghan, D. (1989) *Woman and Gender in Renaissance Tragedy: A Study of King Lear, Othello, The Duchess of Malfi and The White Devil*. New York: Harvester Wheatsheaf.

Calvin. J. (1578) *A commentarie of Iohn Caluine, vpon the first booke of Moses called Genesis*. London: Henry Middleton.

Campbell, L.B. (1959) *Divine Poetry and Drama in Sixteenth-Century England*. Cambridge: Cambridge University Press.

Case, J. (1586) *The praise of musicke*. Oxenford: Joseph Barnes.

Charron, P. (1608) *Of Wisdome three bookes written in French by Peter Charro[n]*. London: Eliot's Court Press.

Clapham, H. (1602) *A tract of prayer*. London: W. White.

Clarke, E. (2011) *Politics, Religion and the Song of Songs in Seventeenth-Century England*. Basingstoke: Palgrave Macmillan.

Cleaver, R. (1621) *A godly forme of houshold government for the ordering of priuate families*. London: R. Field.

Clinton, E. (1622) *The Countesse of Lincolnes nurserie*. Oxford: John Lichfield.

Cobb, S. (1695) *Bersaba, or, The love of David a poem*. London: J. Whitlock.

Coignet, M. (1586) *Politique discourses upon trueth and lying*. London: John Windet.

Coverdale, M. (1537) *A goodly treatise of faith, hope, and charite*. Southwarke: James Nicolson.

Crowther, K.M. (2010) *Adam and Eve in the Protestant Reformation*. Cambridge: Cambridge University Press.

DiPasquale, T.M. (2000) 'Woman's Desire for Man in Lanyer's *Salve Deus Rex Judaeorum*.' *Journal of English and Germanic Philology*, 99: 356–78.

Doran, S. (1996) *Monarchy and Matrimony the Courtships of Elizabeth I*. London: Routledge.

Elizabeth I (1688) *Queen Elizabeth's opinion concerning transubstantiation*. London: F.E.

Ephraim, M. (2008) *Reading the Jewish Woman on the Elizabethan Stage*. Aldershot: Ashgate.

Fell, M.A. (1667) *Womens speaking Justified, proved and allowed of by the Scriptures*. London: s.n.

Ferrers, R. (1622) *The worth of women*. London: William Jones.

Garter, T. (1578) *The commody of the moste vertuous and godlye Susanna*. London: Hugh Jackson.

Giacomo, A. (1605) *The dumbe diuine speaker ... A learned and excellent treatise, in praise of silence*. London: R. Bradock.

Goodwin, J. (1659) *The banner of justification displayed*. London: E.C.

Gouge, W. (1622) *Of domesticall duties eight treaties*. London: John Haviland.

Grantham, T. (1641) *A marriage sermon: A sermon called a wife mistaken*. London: s.n.

Greene, R. (1584) *The myrrour of modestie*. London: Roger Warde.

Greenham, R. (1612) *The workes of the reuerend and faithfull seruant af Iesus Christ M. Richard Greenham*. London: Thomas Snodham and Thomas Creede.

Grymeston, E. (1604) *Miscelanea. Meditations. Memoratiues*. London: Melch. Bradwood.

Hayward, J. (1614) *The strong helper, offering to beare euery mans burthen*. London: John Beale.

Heywood, T. (1640) *The exemplary lives and memorable acts of nine the most worthy women in the world three Iewes. Three gentiles. Three Christians*. London: Tho. Cotes.

Hilder, T. (1653) *Conjugall counsell, or, Seasonable advice, both to unmarried, and married persons.* London: John Stafford.

Hill, W. (1660) *A New-Years-gift for women.* London: T.N.

Jackson, T. (1615) *Iustifying faith, or The faith by which the just do liue.* London: John Beale.

Jeffery. D.L. (1992) *A Dictionary of Biblical Tradition in English Literature.* Grand Rapids, MI: W.B. Eerdmans.

Jocelin, E. (1624) *The mothers legacie, to her vnborne childe.* London: John Hauiland.

King, J.N. (1982) *English Reformation Literature: The Tudor Origins of the Protestant Tradition.* Princeton, NJ: Princeton University Press.

———. (1989) *Tudor Royal Iconography: Literature and Art in an Age of Religious Crisis.* Princeton, NJ: Princeton University Press.

L., A. (1653) *A question deeply concerning married persons and such as intend to marry propounded and resolved according to the scriptures.* London: Tho. Underhill.

Lanyer, A. (1993) *The Poems of Aemilia Lanyer: Salve Deus Rex Judaeorum.* Ed. S. Woods. Oxford: Oxford University Press.

Leigh, D. (1616) *The Mothers Blessing.* London: John Budge.

Leigh, W. (1609) *The first step, towards heaven.* London: Nicholas Okes.

Levin, C. (1994) *The Heart and Stomach of a King: Elizabeth I and the Politics of Sex and Power.* Philadelphia, PA: University of Pennsylvania Press.

Lightfoot, J. (1644) *The harmony of the foure evangelists among themselves, and with the Old Testament.* London: R. Cotes.

Luckyj, C. (2002) *'A moving rhetoricke': Gender and Silence in Early Modern England.* Manchester: Manchester University Press.

Marcus, L.S. (1990) 'Shakespeare's Comic Heroines, Elizabeth I, and the Political uses of Androgyny.' *Women in the Middle Ages and the Renaissance: Literary and Historical Perspectives.* Ed. M.B. Rose. Syracuse, NY: Syracuse University Press. 135–53.

Martin, C.G. (2004) 'Dalila, Misogyny, and Milton's Christian Liberty of Divorce.' *Milton and Gender.* Ed. C.G. Martin. Cambridge: Cambridge University Press. 53–76.

Matter, E.A. (1990) *The Voice of my Beloved: The Song of Songs in Western Medieval Christianity.* Philadelphia: University of Pennsylvania Press.

McManus, B. (2000) 'Eve's Dowry.' *Women, Writing, and the Reproduction of Culture in Tudor and Stuart Britain.* Ed. M. Burke. Syracuse, NY: Syracuse University Press. 193–206.

Milton, J. (1671) *Paradise regain'd a poem in IV books: to which is added Samson Agonistes.* London: J.M.

Norden, J. (1596) *A progresse of pietie.* London: I. Windet.

Oliver, J. (1663) *A present for teeming women.* London: Sarah Griffin.

Osherow, M. (2009) *Biblical Women's Voices in Early Modern England.* Aldershot: Ashgate.

Pasachoff, N.E. (1975) *Playwrights, Preachers and Politicians: A Study of Four Tudor Old Testament Dramas.* Salzburg: Inst. f. Engl. Sprache u. Literatur.

Payne, E.R. (ed.) (1975) *Sapientia Solomonis.* New Haven, CT: Yale University Press.

Peele, G. (1599) *The loue of King Dauid and fair Bethsabe.* London: Adam Islip.

Peters, C. (2003) *Patterns of Piety: Women, Gender, and Religion in Late Medieval and Reformation England.* Cambridge: Cambridge University Press.

Pricke, R. (1609) *The doctrine of superioritie, and of subiection.* London: T. Creede.

Quarles, F. (1621) *Hadassa: or The history of Queene Ester.* London: Felix Kingston.

R., D. (1642) *Matrimoniall honovr, or, The mutuall crowne and comfort of godly, loyall, and chaste marriage*. London: Th. Harper.

Roche, R. (1599) *Eustathia, or the constancie of Susanna*. Oxford: Joseph Barnes.

Sabie, F. (1596) *Adams complaint. The olde worldes tragedie. Dauid and Bathsheba*. London: Richard Johnes.

Shell, A. (1999) *Catholicism, Controversy, and the English Literary Imagination, 1558–1660*. Cambridge: Cambridge University Press.

Shuger, D.K. (1994). *The Renaissance Bible Scholarship, Sacrifice, and Subjectivity*. Berkeley: University of California Press.

Sowernam, E. (1617) *Ester hath hang'd Haman: or An answere to a lewd pamphlet, entituled, The arraignment of women*. London: Thomas Snodham.

Speght, R. (1617) *A mouzell for Melastomus, the cynicall bayter of, and foule mouthed barker against Euahs sex*. London: Nicholas Okes.

Streete, A. (2009) '"An old quarrel between us that will never be at an end": Middleton's *Women Beware Women* and Late Jacobean Religious Politics.' *Review of English Studies*, 60.244: 230–54.

Swetnam, J. (1615) *The araignment of lewd, idle, froward, and vnconstant women or the vanitie of them, choose you whether*. London: George Purslowe.

Tattle-well, M. and Hit-him-home, I. (1640) *The womens sharpe revenge*. London: I. Okes.

The deceyte of women, to the instruction and ensample of all men yonge and olde (1557) London: W. Copland.

The Geneva Bible: A facsimile of the 1560 edition (2007) Ed. L.E. Berry and W. Whittingham. Peabody, MA: Henderson Publishers.

Thompson, J.L. (2001) *Writing the Wrongs: Women of the Old Testament among Biblical Commentators from Philo through the Reformation*. Oxford: Oxford University Press.

Trill, S. (1997) 'Introduction.' *Lay by your needles ladies, take the pen: Writing Women in England, 1500–1700*. Ed. K. Chedgzoy, M. Osborne and S. Trill. London: Edward Arnold.

Tuke, T. (1616) *A discourse against painting and tincturing of women*. London: Thomas Creede and Bernard Alsop.

Willet, A. (1603) *Ecclesia triumphans: that is, The ioy of the English Church*. Cambridge: John Legat.

Wright, A. (1662) *A practical commentary or exposition upon the Pentateuch*. London: G. Dawson.

Zim, R. (1987) *English Metrical Psalms: Poetry as Praise and Prayer, 1535–1601*. Cambridge: Cambridge University Press.

3

A 'Paraditian Creature':
Eve and her unsuspecting garden
in seventeenth-century literature

Elizabeth Hodgson

In the early seventeenth century in England a flurry of texts emerged formally debating the moral and ethical value of womankind. In these debates both misogynist and anti-misogynist arguments claim that the Bible's first woman, Eve, exemplifies the status and value of all women after her.[1] Eve, the first human to fall, was regularly used to define and malign woman, and her eating of the forbidden fruit was, for some, biblical evidence of womankind's inherent fallibility. As Joseph Swetnam famously argued, Eve 'by her aspiring minde and wanton will ... procured mans fall, and therefore euer since [women] are & haue been a woe unto man' (1615: sig. B1r). In the succeeding decades of the seventeenth century, however, Eve is surprisingly imagined by English writers as the world's first and noblest gardener. The seeds of this alternative reading of Eve's role are apparent even in the pro-woman debaters of the early century, while the polemical arguments about her originary sin are still dominant. This pattern is certainly clear in Aemelia Lanyer, who creates an Eve worthy of sympathy, one whose tangential connections to her lost garden are a recurring, and defining trope, in *Salve Deus Rex Judaeorum* (1611). Ester Sowernam's 1617 prose tract likewise explicitly foregrounds Eve's position as a 'Paraditian Creature' (A4r). Then, as the century progresses, Eve is increasingly reinvented as a particular subject and citizen of Eden, the patroness, labourer and goddess of an English georgic paradise, with a distinctive ethical function not immediately connected to her original sin.[2] In these later texts, Eve is more likely to look after sacred fruit than mistakenly to eat it. Writers such as the horticulturalist mystics Abraham Cowley and John Evelyn increasingly reveal an Eve who is conflated both with Adam and with the garden itself. Over this century, then, Eve gradually becomes assimilated with her garden, revealing the complex ways in which the Bible's first woman is ideologically permeable, redeployable even in her own habitat.

Even before the formal debates on womankind of 1615–20, Aemelia Lanyer's 1611 Passion poem *Salve Deus Rex Judaeorum* launched an explicit defence of womankind by both defending Eve and juxtaposing her devout daughters with a series of Edenic gardens (Lanyer, 1993). Lanyer's poem nests 'Eves apologie' within a series of sacred and unobtainable gardens – the biblical gardens of Eden and Gethsemane and the abandoned grounds at Cookham. These beautiful, yet mournful, spaces bear the marks of the old and the new Paradise. They embody worlds lost but also regained through the specific alliance between God and womankind which, for Lanyer, begins with Eve in Genesis. *Salve Deus'* first Edenic garden is designed to show how virtuous women wait tenderly upon their Lord in these sacred precincts. The poem's dedication, entitled 'To all virtuous ladies in generall',[3] invites its devout women to a place which is part Eden, part Solomon's garden and part the happy fields of Revelation: 'those pleasant groves ... by the well of life' (15). This biblical paradise is adorned with 'sweet odours, mirrhe, gum, aloes' from the Song of Solomon; 'the beauteous lilly of the field' from Matthew 6:28; and 'fields of rest' and 'cristal springs' from Psalm 23 (15). The invited women are dressed as the virtuous maidens ready for the divine 'Bridegroome' (12) of Revelation 19. They are to 'annoynt [their] haire with *Aarons* pretious oyle,'[4] 'to be transfigur'd with our Loving Lord' (14) in the 'fields of rest' to which 'Gods holy Angels' will lead them (15). This new Paradise is born of Eden's own 'earth / Whereof at first your bodies formed were' (15). It leads into Heaven itself by Christ's redeeming 'torments' (15), so that these women are made like Eve in her paradisal garden. Lanyer keeps hinting here at Eve's Edenic home: by picturing not only its divine beauty but also the serpents entering the garden; by describing the earthly stuff of which the women are made; and by implying that the garden can make them 'immortall, subject to no death' (15). This new Eden is the natural home of the devout women who serve and care for their saviour. As the female denizens of Eden, they are reminders and figures of Eve herself.

Having set a biblical Eden as both origin and goal for virtuous womankind, Lanyer turns to Eve directly. Lanyer's defence of Eve implies not only that a virtuous Eve redeems all the women who follow her (including Lanyer's patronesses) but even more that Eve's sympathy, her tender-heartedness, is what connects her and her daughters to the Son of God.[5] In the poem's 'Apologie' for Eve, Eve's innocence and 'harmelesse Heart' (85) leads her to sin, but this fault is revealed in terms that generate sympathy for her plight: 'Our Mother Eve, who tasted of the Tree, / Giving to *Adam* what shee held most deare, / Was simply good, and had no powre to see, / The after-comming harme did not appeare' (84). Eve is described as naively ignorant, 'simply good' in every sense because she did not understand the serpent's cunning and because her only motive was 'too much love' for Adam.[6] Eve is thus not only harmless and innocent but to be pitied: she is a 'poore soule', 'poor *Eve*' and the first of 'poore women' (85). She is to be sympathised with, rather than condemned, just as Jesus himself should be as he stands before Pilate, a typological connection directly drawn in the following line: 'Her weakenesse did the Serpents words obay; / But you in malice Gods deare Sonne betray' (86). There is, Lanyer suggests, a clear distinction between the sin of the kind-heartedly mistaken Eve and the malicious evil of those who condemn Jesus.[7] 'Eves apologie' thus follows on from Pilate's wife's pleas for Jesus to be spared because the poem sees Eve's error as a mistake motivated by love, and it is love which drives the women of *Salve Deus* to have pity on Jesus as well. Eve's fault becomes no fault, because it is an error of sympathy, and sympathy is, as Lanyer explains, the virtue which the male characters in the crucifixion narrative conspicuously lack: 'Whom, if unjustly you condemne to die, / Her sin was small, to what you do commit; / All mortall sinnes that doe for vengeance crie, / Are not to be compared unto it' (86). The unjust condemnation of Jesus resonates with the unjust condemnation of Eve as both are abused victims of male malice. In this reading, male cruelty becomes the most significant and historically sustained sin, rendering Eve a type of Jesus himself.[8]

This fascinating implied allegiance between Eve and Jesus is obliquely represented in Lanyer's narration of another garden – this time, the garden of Gethsemane. In a lengthy discussion of Jesus praying in the garden while his disciples sleep, Lanyer's text emphasises not only the relative indifference and cold-heartedness of the disciples but also the ways in which Jesus' temptations position him as a new Eve:

> Now went our lord unto that holy place,
> Sweet *Gethsemaine* hallowed by his presence,
> That blessed Garden, which did now embrace
> His holy corps, yet could make no defence
> Against those Vipers, objects of disgrace,
> Which sought that pure eternall Love to quench:
> …
> Sweet Lord, how couldst thou thus to flesh and blood
> Communicate thy griefe? tell of thy woes?
> Thou knew'st they had no powre to doe thee good,
> But were the cause thou must endure these blowes,
> Beeing the Scorpions bred in *Adams* mud,
> Whose poys'ned sinnes did worke among thy foes. (67)

In these lines, Gethsemane is a 'blessed Garden', but one that contains 'Vipers' seeking to destroy 'pure eternall Love', just like the serpent/Satan in Eden. Gethsemane's venomous snakes and scorpions are 'bred in *Adams* mud', an evocative phrase which juxtaposes the Edenic temptation and Calvary's tortures.[9] Like Eve, then, Jesus is tempted and betrayed in the garden by the viper Judas and, by extension, his sinful forerunner Adam (see Mark 14). The garden in which Lanyer's virtuous dedicatees meet their 'bridegroom' and the figure of Eve who is 'simply good' coincide in this new temptation in the new garden. In this way, the biblical paradise found and lost is connected through Eve and her descendants.

The lineage which Lanyer claims, the 'golden chain' (21) connecting Eve's
virtues to those of womankind, are manifest in another contemporary paradisal
garden marked by absence and loss.[10] This is a contemporary English one, the
garden at Cookham, and it too is a Paradise without an Eve. Cookham's garden
begins Lanyer's narrative of the crucifixion:

> And pardon (Madame) though I do not write
> Those praisefull lines of that delightful place,
> As you commaunded me in that faire night,
> when shining *Phoebe* gave so great a grace,
> Presenting *Paradice* to your sweet sight,
> Unfolding all the beauty of her face
> > With pleasant groves, hills, walks and stately trees,
> > Which pleasures with retired minds agrees. (51–2)

In these lines Lanyer imagines a paradisal garden, 'that delightful place', which
functions as the original Edenic garden in symbolising 'th'all-creating Providence
… all by him begunne' (52). Though Lanyer does not specify the garden to which
she is referring, whether it be Cookham or Eden itself, these lines suggest that
there is a beautiful garden which Cumberland knows and to which the poem
can only allude in passing. That garden clearly reminds Lanyer of Cumberland's
own 'sad Soule, plunged in waves of woe' (52) and also of Jesus, who 'through
Afflictions' of his own will 'enroule … all thy glorious Trialls' (53).[11] The binding
agents here include both the garden itself, which 'to retired minds agrees' (52)
and the constancy of loss, absence, regret, sorrow and tribulation. This juxtaposition of the absent garden, the sorrowing owner, and the grieving Lord are
another instance of Lanyer's strategic evocations of a paradise lost.

The extended elegy entitled 'The Description of Cooke-ham' at the end
of *Salve Deus* supplies the lost garden to which Lanyer is referring. Here the
Edenic garden (Cookham's grounds) and its godly patroness (Anne Clifford) are
both remembered through their mutual partings. As Shannon Miller explains:
'elegiac in tone as well as invoking a prelapsarian Edenic space, the account of
this garden resonates intriguingly with the re-written Fall narratives' of the later
formal debates on Eve and womankind (2008: 57). Eve and Eden are certainly
the implicit correlatives to Cookham's elegiac beauty and its devout womanly
inhabitants because the garden and the poem's women overflow in the same
mournful sympathy which Lanyer has made Eve's chief virtue, or virtuous
fault.[12]

The gardens of Cookham are clearly intended to resonate with God's
creativity as set out in Genesis: the speaker explains that the trees and flowers
all reveal how 'their Creators powre, which there you saw, / In all his Creatures
held a perfit Law' (133). The Cookham garden is the 'perfit' book of Nature,
revealing in unaltered, undiminished form the will of the Creator. Its central
value, though, is that it echoes Eve's sympathy for Jesus in mourning for the

women who leave it. In this sense, Cookham's garden brings Lanyer's argument full circle by showing how paradise lost sympathises with its women just as 'poor Eve' is forgiven by her own sympathetic heart. When the Cookham garden loses its women, then 'the trees ... Forsooke both flowres and fruit, when once they knew / Of your depart, their very leaves did wither' (135). The poem describes the grasses turning grey, the brooks freezing over, their 'dying bodies half alive, halfe dead' with the loss of their chief heroine.[13] In this image of an abandoned, postlapsarian garden, from which the central women are exiled, the notion of blame or guilt is carefully excised. Eve's forbidden tree becomes a royal oak in whose shade Clifford meditates upon the scriptures. As Miller argues, the 'departure from Eden is not a consequence of their actions' (2008: 59). Lanyer's Clifford women, like Eve, are blameless and devout. Their garden is sacred and particularly sympathetic. In these ways, it is Eve's garden as Lanyer imagines it throughout *Salve Deus*: a sacred paradise for virtuous women who in every sense are Christ-like in their losses and bound together with Eden because they share a mutual tenderness of heart. As Eve loves Adam and Christ, so the garden loves its devout mistress. This is a feminised affective landscape of particular ethical force because the story of redeemed womankind for Lanyer begins with Eve.

Lanyer's *Salve Deus* in its composite form thus keeps generating a similar set of congruencies between a sympathetic Eve and the divine godhead in the context of the sacred garden. As other devout women are placed in Edenic gardens to show their devotion, or removed from those gardens to show how the garden is likewise sympathetic to them and to Christ, Eve's poor kindness is the leitmotif in the landscape of *Salve Deus*. While Lanyer never makes the argument that Sowernam will use, of Eve's direct descent from the garden, she most certainly suggests that the tender-heartedness linking Eve to Jesus and Jesus to women makes possible, and is symbolised by, that abandoned but beautiful Edenic landscape. Lanyer's ethical, apologetic reading of the first woman keeps imagining that her defence can be suggested by a sympathetic Eve and a sympathetic landscape.

Lanyer's brief defence of Eve is expanded upon over the next ten years in Jacobean England. In the formal controversies debating women's virtues and ills in the later 1610s and 1620s, Eve is explicitly attacked and defended in hierarchical and ethical terms precisely because she is seen as the model for all women to follow. In the pro-women works of this period, Eve is directly defended by her associations with Eden. This is especially evident in Ester Sowernam's work. Sowernam notes in *Ester hath hang'd Haman: Or An Answer to a ... The Arraignment of Women* (1617) that Eve (as a representative of all women) is 'a Paraditian Creature. Who as shee commeth out of the Garden, so shall you finde her a flower of delight, answerable to the Countrey from whence she commeth' (1617: A4r).[14] Eve, in some sense, becomes the garden, 'a flower ... answerable to [her] Countrey'. Sowernam suggests that Eve emerges from Eden not in exile but like

a child being born, bearing the genetic stamp of her parental Paradise. The way
to read Eve is to read the Garden itself:

> That delight, solace, and pleasure, which shall come to man by woman, is prognos-
> ticated by that place wherein woman was created: for she was framed in Paradice,
> a place of all delight and pleasure, euery element hath his creatures, euery creature
> doth corresponde the temper and the inclination of that element wherein it hath
> and tooke his first and principall *esse*, or being. So that woman neither can or may
> degenerate in her disposition from that naturall inclination of the place, in which
> she was first framed, she is a Paradician, that is, a delightfull creature, borne in so
> delightfull a country. (6)

As Miller suggests, this passage implies and assumes that 'Eden is located in
Eve, and thus within all women' (2008: 28). Sowernam claims that there is a
kind of permanent genetic imprint of the paradisal garden on the soul of Eve
and every woman after her, as if the garden has made her, and that therefore
she and every woman after her continue that perfection of Paradise. Eve's exile
from the garden, in Sowernam's paradigm, can have no discernible effect, for she
in many ways *is* the garden forever. Sowernam argues that 'The Countrey doth
also the woman more grace, / For Paradice is farre the more excellent place'
(50), implying that Eden 'graces' Eve with its own virtues.

   The difficulty with reading Sowernam as an early eco-feminist defender of
Eve is that Sowernam also persists in implying that Eve is superior *to* the garden
by virtue of being made after it. Sowernam repeatedly claims that Eve is more
perfect than everything made before her because 'euery succeeding worke was
euer more excellent then what was formerly Created: hee wrought by degrees,
prouiding in all for that which was and should be the end' (5). In what Linda
Woodbridge calls the 'exhausted ... mode of the formal controversy [that] Eve
was the last and therefore the highest creation' (1986: 97), Sowernam argues that
Eve is 'created out of a subiect refined, as out of a Quintessence' (6), by a process
of purification of not only the earlier Creation but of Adam himself.[15] In this
paradigm, Sowernam suggests that Eve is a more perfect version of Paradise, an
improvement upon her prior landscape.

   As conventional as her 'highest creation' argument is, however, when
Sowernam makes Eve a creature of Paradise she creates for herself a rather
startling problem. In Sowernam's arguments Eve both is and is not a flower – a
product – of Eden; she supersedes Adam because she comes from the garden,
but she also surpasses the garden as the next, improved Creation. Sowernam,
by attempting to defend Eve in these two different ways, makes the first woman
both a product of, and a mistress over, her own Edenic garden. Sowernam
summarises her readings of Genesis as if these arguments are consistent: 'First,
that woman was the last worke of Creation ... She was created out of the chosen
and best refined substance: She was created in a more worthy country' (1617:
15); but the philosophical tensions between original and subsequent creation

nonetheless underlie Sowernam's image of Eve in the Garden. What it means for Eve to come 'out of Paradise' remains not so much a solution (as Miller would claim), or a hackneyed cliché (as Woodbridge would read it), but for Sowernam, and for many Jacobean readings of Eve, an unanswered question.

In the decades that follow Lanyer's sympathetic Eve and empathetic gardens, and Sowernam's rather confused representation of an Eve redeemed by Eden, the Bible's first woman is further transformed and more radically reimagined. Eve becomes entirely synonymous with her redemptive garden during the civil wars and upheaval of the 1650s and 1660s, when England's legendary character as 'this other Eden, demi-paradise' (Shakespeare, 2002: 2.1.42) seems to be dissolving into wrack and ruin. In Miller's view, the Eve 'who defended herself in the terms of the Fall ... went underground at mid-century' (2008: 33). While this fallen Eve may disappear from view, Eve remains, transposed from sinner to gardener, signified by and ennobled through the dream of her perfect lost Eden. The ethical question of Eve becomes not 'did Eve sin?' but 'can her Eden save us?' In this context, Eve is no longer a sinner but a horticulturalist, even more closely identified with her garden; and therefore like the garden far more obviously blameless than in those apologetic texts of the early century. The trade-off for Eve's disappearing sin is, however, that she becomes almost indistinguishable from Adam as the first agricultural labourer in the best Edenic garden. Even more, Eve, Adam and the garden engage in a kind of mutual transubstantiation of natural spiritual innocence in these texts. Eve almost disappears, as Andrew Marvell would say, into 'a green thought in a green shade' (2005: 101).

The ethical and nationalist flavour of Eve's Eden becomes the mystical correlative to the 'debating regarding ... the forests and wastes of England' which reached 'an incendiary intensity' during the civil wars (Theis, 2008: 229). Royalists, Parliamentarians and other revolutionaries (like the Diggers) not only made competing land-use claims and launched economic disputes over natural resources, but they also strained after new millennialist or authoritarian models of a paradisal England.[16] This combination of devotional nostalgia for the prelapsarian world and a scientific attempt to reconstruct England as a garden colours the Royal Society writers (Samuel Hartlib, John Evelyn, John Beale, Abraham Cowley) as they produced a torrent of works on orchards, vegetable gardening, bee-keeping, landscape architecture, pruning, grafting, cultivation and forestry in this era.[17] John Beale's *Herefordshire orchards, a pattern* (1657) notes that 'we do commonly devise a shadowy walk from our Gardens through our Orchards ... into our Coppice-woods or timber-woods. Thus we approach the resemblance of Paradise, which God with his own perfect hand had appropriated for the delight of his innocent Masterpiece' (48). Beale's description of how to plan a garden so that it is most like the divine original 'appropriated for ... his innocent Masterpiece' shows how this group of writers use the Edenic garden along with Adam and Eve ('his innocent Masterpiece') to validate their agricultural and landscaping advice. They see attention to agricultural matters as mechanisms for recreating Edenic innocence in England. This 'Eden of the improvers' is both a nostalgic past but also 'something in the future to be brought into being' (Lowe, 1992: 67). In these narratives, the human masterpiece of Eve becomes almost the same as that of Adam, and even more synonymous with Eden itself.

John Evelyn exemplifies this part-nostalgic, part-millennialist search in the 1650s and 1660s for 'the remains of Eden' (Parry, 1992: 144) in which Adam and Eve are innocent in an innocent garden. Evelyn's arguments depend upon a syllogism not unlike Sowernam's, but with a different conclusion: Eve and Adam are pure and unfallen; their garden is unfallen; therefore, gardens retain that same prelapsarian virtue that they had during Eve's and Adam's tenure. Evelyn's *Silva* (1670) makes this claim about the original sacerdotal groves of Eden and Adam and Eve's priestlike roles therein. His *Acetaria. A discourse of sallets* goes back to Eve and Adam's life in Eden when they breathed 'the pure *Paradisian* Air, sucking in a more *aethereal*, nourishing, and baulmy *Pabulum*, so foully vitiated now' (1699: 125). The air of Paradise is a kind of food for virtue, a 'nourishing, and baulmy *Pabulum*' free of 'intemperance ... and effeminacy' (125). Evelyn implies a kind of oddly exculpatory status for Adam and Eve's eating and drinking when he argues that they 'at first knew what Plants and Fruits were good, before the Fall' (128), as if Eve and Adam had a kind of intuitive relationship to vegetables against which that one error in eating is irrelevant.

Evelyn argues that Adam and Eve must have dwelt in Paradise for some time before the Fall, and he rhapsodises about 'the Paradisian Fare, their innocent and healthful Lives in that delightful Garden ... *Adam*, and his yet innocent Spouse, fed on Vegetables and other Hortulan Productions before the fatal Lapse' (1699: 147). The pure wisdom of Eve ('his yet innocent Spouse') is signified by, and likewise signifies, the purity of the vegetarian menu on which they dined. Even when Evelyn does discuss the Fall itself, Eve is not treated as an ethical subject, though her diet is. While Evelyn describes the environment as 'more innocent' than Eve or Adam, he also explicitly argues that Eve could not have 'so quickly forg[o]t the Injunction ... and all other their Obligations in so few Moments' (147–8). Evelyn proposes that only extended time, and multiple efforts of Satan, could have led to such a 'forgetting'. His primary interest in crediting Eve with more resistance than Genesis seems to describe, however, is to make her a testimonial for the nutritious diet of herbs and vegetables on which the first couple so long subsisted. The fantasy of Paradise, to which Evelyn clearly hopes that the English can return, is one in which Adam and Eve are what they eat, and what they eat is a heavenly pablum of the garden itself. In this scenario, Eve may have eaten wrongly once, but Evelyn wants to argue that she ate well for much longer. Evelyn proclaims her relative strength of will, her innocence, her innate wisdom, but only because he wants to represent both Eve and Adam as symbols of the salad days which he hopes to reinvent.

Abraham Cowley employs the same nostalgia for Eden and its curative properties for current English woes, but Cowley is also prepared to suggest that Eve interrupts his homosocial fantasy of a new English Eden. Cowley's ode 'Of Solitude', his treatise 'Of Agriculture', and particularly his essay and ode 'The Garden' all frame the same complex, escapist, ethical praise for the woodland or garden spaces of Eden. He repeatedly describes an agricultural life as inherently prelapsarian, noting 'the Innocence of this Life' (1721: 653) for the farmer who can 'see, like God, that all his Works are Good' (655). 'The first ... in the World, were a Gard'ner'; 'we were all born to this art, and taught by Nature to nourish our Bodies by the same Earth out of which they were made' (655). Cowley makes it clear that this prelapsarian craft is all the nobler because of its origins in Eden. Like Sowernam, Cowley interprets Eden as a purifying force for all of its subjects, Eve and Adam included.

More thoroughly than Evelyn does, though, Cowley reveres the paradisal garden to the exclusion of Eve. Cowley, in fact, replaces Eve with the garden itself as man's first helper. In 'Of Solitude,' Eve interrupts Adam's perfect rural solitude:

> Oh Solitude, first State of Humankind!
> Which bless'd remain'd, 'till Man did find
> Ev'n his own Helper's Company,
> As soon as two (alas!) together join'd,
> The Serpent made up three. (645–6)

Cowley, unlike Evelyn, is willing to treat Eve as the interrupter of the joys of Adam. The puns in 'Ev'n his own Helper's Company' and 'alas' gender the loss of original solitude but also the Fall itself, as if Eve brings the Serpent with her. The privacy of Eden and the privacy of his own woodland retreats are both marred by the daughters of Eve.

Cowley's poem, 'The Garden' circles around again to the problem and blessing of Eve in the garden:

> When God did man to his own Likeness make, ...
> He thought it fit to place him, where
> A kind of Heav'n too did appear,
> As far as Earth could such a Likeness bear:
> That Man no Happiness might want,
> Which Earth to her first Mother could afford:
> He did a garden for him plant,
> By the quick Hand of his Omnipotent Word.
> As the chief Help and Joy of human Life,
> He gave him the first Gift; first, ev'n before a Wife. (677–8)

Cowley sees Paradise replacing the celestial realms, 'a Kind of Heav'n ... / As far as Earth could such a Likeness bear'. Earth, which Cowley elsewhere calls 'our Mother' (653), now provides hortulan happiness to *her* 'first Mother', Eve. God apparently 'plants' the garden as Eve's superior predecessor – it is 'the chief Help and Joy of human Life ... / first, ev'n before a Wife'. Thus, the garden of Eden functions first as Adam's 'chief Help', as well as a gift to Eve. Here again, the garden and Eve operate in a curious synthesis, one which ultimately leaves Eve as the surplus helper whom Adam does not quite need. In this sense, Eden both predates and continues to surpass Eve as the source of goodness to Adam.

What both Cowley and Evelyn are working toward, then, is a view of Paradise in which Adam and Eve, when present, reflect the perfections of their vegeta- tive environment. Eve is not so much a denizen of Eden as Eden is a feature of Eve. This paradigm shift is inconsistent about Eve's guilt – in some instances she is the first mother of Mother Earth, in others the one who brings the serpent into the garden – because it is the perfect, innocent, noble first garden which is really what Cowley and Evelyn are seeking to honour, define and recreate. Their praise of its solitude, its vegetarian bounty, its purer air, its sacramental trees, may become praise (or blame) of Eve or Adam, but that is only a necessary correlate to the garden itself. Far more explicitly and urgently than Lanyer, and with very different motives, Evelyn and Cowley desire this lost garden. They are sometimes willing to allow Eve to inhabit it.

After Eden's appropriation of Eve in the middle of the century, she re-emerges as a central ethical figure in John Milton's *Paradise Lost* (1674).[18] Milton's Eve has been the subject of much critical debate, not least because Milton clearly reverts to an earlier paradigm and invites assumptions that his Eve 'is the representation of the first or perfect female human subject' (Edwards, 1997: 239).[19] In this sense, the epic relies on the Jacobean rhetoric which judges Eve as the paradigmatic first woman.[20] Milton also, however, borrows from Evelyn and Cowley a less representative Eve who is, and who is defined by, her garden.[21] As for Milton's peers, *Paradise Lost*'s gardener Eve does not necessarily redeem all womankind by caring for her flowers. Nor is Milton's Eden itself 'a place where equality of gender exists in surprising ways' (Hiltner, 2008: 7).[22] What Milton does add to the century's view of Eve is a very curious mix: *Paradise Lost* both insists upon Eve's subordinate, secondary and originary role and also grants her a particularly affective identification with the garden. Milton's Eve is thus a complex revisiting of this shifting ideology of Eve, one which does not and cannot resolve itself (despite critics' efforts) into a single ethical reading.

The terms by which Eve represents womankind are in many respects far more explicitly evaluative, frequently punitive (even by seventeenth-century standards), and more constraining in *Paradise Lost* than in most of Milton's contemporaries (see also Sumers, 2004: 200–25). Miller argues that Milton 'enacts the anti-woman debates ... by dramatising disagreements ... between Adam and Eve' (2008: 22), but the Miltonic narrator also pronounces on Eve's illusory beauty, her subor- dinate role, and her vulnerability to temptation, all of which replay the formal controversies.[23] The first description of Eve in Book IV insists upon this hierarchy, declaring that Adam is 'for God only, shee for God in him', 'both / Not equal, as their sex not equal seem'd' (Milton, 1957: 4.299, 296–7). Eve describes Adam as 'my Guide / And Head' (4.442–3), 'Preeminent by so much odds' (4.447). Her charms are 'submissive,' (4.497), Adam's love is 'superior' (4.499). Adam makes explicit Eve's exemplary status when he proclaims in response to her comments that 'nothing lovelier can be found / In Woman, than to study household good' (9.232–3). All of these statements about Eve create a hierarchy which Milton clearly treats as both natural and predictive. Comparative and negative terms, hierarchical language and categorical labels ('my Guide and Head', 'Woman') abound in this text. Though many Milton apologists have sought to provide glosses on these descriptions (exculpatory of both Eve and of Milton), the poem keeps circling back to this classification of Eve as the first woman and the second in power to her husband (see McColley, 1999 and Schoenfeldt, 2001). Along-side the passages which make Milton sound like an early Jacobean misogynist debater, however, Milton also incorporates the rhetoric of his contemporaries, making Eve a reflection of her own garden, a garden herself. Here Milton's innovation is not only that his Eve floats between being Adam's help-meet and the garden's, but also that her role vis-à-vis the garden is particularly affective even while it is mutually constitutive. The poem proffers a series of efforts, ambivalent and opportunistic, to conflate a present Eve with a present garden through their mutual affections.

Milton's Eve in Book IV of *Paradise Lost* insists on an emotional connection to her garden which is reminiscent of her bond to Adam himself. Adam reminds her that:

> With first approach of light, we must be ris'n,
> And at our pleasant labor, to reform
> Yon flow'ry Arbors, yonder Alleys green,
> Our walk at noon, with branches overgrown,
> That mock our scant manuring, and require
> More hands than ours to lop th[e]ir wanton growth:
> Those Blossoms also, and those dropping Gums,
> That lie bestrown unsightly and unsmooth,
> As riddance, if we mean to tread with ease. (4.624–32)

Adam, with his task-oriented approach to the Garden, implies a correlation between horticultural 'reform' and self-discipline; as Lewalski suggests, 'this activity mirrors the gardening Adam and Eve have also continually to carry on within themselves' (2008: 18). Adam speaks a language of constraint and management, using terms like 'must', 'require' and 'riddance' to enforce his policing of the garden's acknowledged luxuriousness. In contrast, Eve, in her semi-sonnet, asserts a bond of affection, first to the garden and then to Adam:

> Sweet is the breath of morn, her rising sweet,
> With charm of earliest Birds; pleasant the Sun
> When first on this delightful Land he spreads
> his orient Beams, on herb, tree, fruit, and flow'r, ...
> But neither breath of Morn when she ascends
> With charm of earliest Birds, nor rising Sun
> On this delightful land, nor herb, fruit, flow'r ...
> Or glittering Star-light without thee is sweet. (4.641–56)[24]

Eve's chiasmic sonnet affirms the personalised affection with which she regards Eden as 'sweet', 'delightful', and full of 'charm'. Eve is thus framed by Milton as an associative figure who responds almost as much to the garden as to Adam.[25] She gives both Adam and the garden her affection here, and though she declares in the end that Adam makes Eden 'sweet', Milton suggests clearly that Eve loves and feels bound to her paradisal surroundings as well.

This associative, affective connection with Eden is made more explicitly part of Eve's role in the many places where Eve expresses fondness for the plants and flowers of Eden and vice versa, as if they are her children and her companions. When Raphael visits Adam, Eve 'Rose, and went forth among her Fruits and Flow'res, ... Her Nursery; they at her coming sprung / and toucht by her fair tendance gladlier grew' (8.44–7). Milton's pun ('Eve / Rose') makes the flowers both Eve herself and her offspring: they are affectively responsive to her, 'gladlier' in her presence. Eve may be seen as the 'genius loci',[26] but her role here is both to enliven the garden and be adored by it, in a process of interanimation and familial bonds which is more emotive than spiritual, less functional than constitutive.[27] Marshall Grossman argues that Eve is created for 'supplementing a gap in the Symbolic of Eden' (2003: 425) as Adam experiences it, but outside of Adam's perspective the symbolic of Eden continues to be Eve's function and place.

Milton makes these associations through many symbolic gestures mutually defining Eve herself as 'the fairest ... flower' (9.432) and the plants of the garden as versions of Adam and Eve:

> On to th[e]ir morning's rural work they haste
> Among sweet dews and flow'res; where any row
> Of Fruit-trees overwoody reach'd too far
> Th[e]ir pamper'd boughs, and needed hands to check
> Fruitless imbraces: or they led the Vine
> To wed her Elm; she spous'd about him twines
> Her marriageable arms, and with her brings
> Her dow'r th'adopted Clusters, to adorn
> His barren leaves. (5.211–19)

The garden here enacts human overreaching but even more human affection, as the vine and elm 'imbrace.' Milton reverses the classical epithalamic image in which the groom is the tree and the bride the twining vine.[28] The images of Eve as a flower as well as a gardener, and these tropes in which the garden is inter-animated by the affective bonds between humans and plants, create a kind of sympathetic synthesis of Eve with her environment. It is not just, as Flannagan notes, that 'both Eve and Eden are associated with fecundity as represented in gardens, grains, fruits, flowers' (1998: 475),[29] but that Eve and Eden generate each other. The plants and flowers become more human, more affective, as they 'embrace' and bring 'dowrs' to each other: this is both what Eve does herself and what she creates in them.

It is not surprising, then, that Eve's plea after the Fall is to continue living 'in these pleasant Walks' (11.179) and her most significant lament is for the loss of the garden:

> Must I thus leave thee Paradise? thus leave
> Thee Native Soil, these happy Walks and Shades,
> Fit haunt of Gods? ... O flow'rs,
> That never will in other Climate grow,
> My early visitation, and my last
> At Ev'n, which I bred up with tender hand
> From the first op'ning bud, and gave ye names,
> Who now shall rear ye to the Sun ...? (11.270–8)

Eve here speaks to the flowers as if they are indeed her children 'bred up with tender hand' and named by her. The garden is her 'native' soil, 'fit haunt of Gods', the place she sees as fittingly her own. Eve's relationship to Eden is made by Milton into an actual relationship, a mutually animating bond.

In this sense, then, Milton makes Eve, both in affective and in symbolic terms, a part of her garden and Eden: the structure of who Eve is. Milton, like Lanyer and the Stuart controversialists, constantly suggests that Eve is the first woman, symbolic of womankind. Milton insists (unlike Lanyer or Sowernam) that as the first woman Eve is inherently subordinate and inferior to Adam. Milton also just as consistently asserts Eve's affective bonds to the paradisal place. These two functions of *Paradise Lost* do not cancel each other out or explain each other, they cohabit within the poem. Milton, in his effort to capture and recapture paradise, uses Eve not only to reacquire Eden (as his Royal Society colleagues do) but also as the first of womankind in all her loves and losses. Borrowing the hierarchical paradigms of the Swetnam/Sowernam debates, Lanyer's sympathetic Eve, and the Eve who vanishes into an innocent Eden of his colleagues, Milton allows each version of Eve to coexist uneasily in *Paradise Lost*, to vanish and reappear like the garden itself in his culture's imagination.

Milton's indeterminate synthesis of the ethical Eve and the gardener Eve thus points back to Eve's cultural travels in seventeenth-century England. The first woman of Genesis in Jacobean culture is super-saturated with predictive force as she is used to explain all subsequent women's ethical behaviours. Eve is here the best specimen of female tendencies, habits, vices and virtues. This version of Eve as archetypal woman and first sinner, with its roots in both biblical Jewish and medieval Christian culture, is the primary way in which Eve has continued to be imagined. As the early Stuarts praise or blame Eve, however, they start even in their judgements to consider how her natural environment might contribute to her status. As the seventeenth century progresses, these readings shift ground, as Eve begins to become a prop in her Edenic garden for the Georgian fantasists and mystical horticulturalists of the 1650s. It is important to note here, though, that while Lanyer and Sowernam in varying ways both suggest that Eve's original garden can be used to explain her fallen virtues, Eve does not become a new ethical figure of eco-feminism in the later century. Rather, for the civil-war writers upon whom Milton also builds, paradise lost, paradise within and paradise rediscovered require Eve as their supplement or signifier. In this complex shift in the Eve paradigm, the Bible's first woman loses her predictive force for women as she grows roots in her Edenic landscape. This does not mean that Eve becomes unambiguously noble as the first gardener in paradise. Rather, she sits briefly and uneasily in this century as a version of the garden itself. The biblical Eve as first female, first created, first sinner, in this quite distinctive moment in her cultural history, becomes inconsistently defined by her unsuspecting garden.

Notes

1 On the *mulier* debates, see particularly Shepherd (1985); Woodbridge (1986); and Jordan (1990).

2 Lewalski rightly notes that 'the term 'paradise' carries multiple significances' (2008: 16).

3 Susan Wiseman suggests that this dedication 'makes the shift from classical to Christian' (2007: 138).

4 Psalm 133:2. All italics are as the original text, unless otherwise stated.

5 For detail on Lanyer's figuration of Eve see Beilin (1987); Lewalski (1993: 231); and McGrath (2002: 215–20).

6 As Miller notes, Milton's Satan describes Eve as 'stupidly good' (*Paradise Lost*, 9.465). She argues that Milton thus nullifies Lanyer's attempt to exculpate Eve via ignorance (2008: 63).

7 On the innocence which Lanyer attributes to Pilate's wife, see Campbell's excellent essay (1995).

8 Linda Woodbridge notes how Sowernam likewise repeats this suggestion that 'much misogyny ... results from men's attempt to shift guilt onto someone else', starting with Adam in the garden (1986: 98).

9 On Lanyer's use of the details of Christ's Passion, see James (2009: 58–72).

10 See on the question of a feminine biblical lineage, Lewalski (1991); Loughlin (2000); and Tinkham (2009).

11 Woods thinks Cookham is the most likely referent here (Lanyer, 1993: 51, note on lines 15–17).

12 Anne Clifford is made a semi-biblical character in her own right, associated in the

poem with Miriam, David, Moses and Joseph.

13 Hammons notes how derelict Lanyer makes Cookham seem in this poem (2005: 404).

14 Jones explains the 'quasi-scholastic' reasoning by which Sowernam argues for Eve's selective environmental genetics (1990: 54).

15 Shepherd notes as well how the formal controversy includes 'much witty play ... on the story of woman's creation from a finer substance ... and on woman as the last and most perfect of God's works' (1985: 18).

16 Edwards cites Winstanley on 'lopping off the tree of Tyrannie' (2008: 263).

17 Hartlib alone published and compiled several works on these topics in the 1650s, including *The English improver, or a new survey of husbandry* (1649), *Samuel Hartlib his legacy of husbandry* (1655), *The compleat husbandman* (1659), and *The reformed commonwealth of bees* (1655). John Beale, in addition to his work on orchards, was busy drafting works on 'A physique garden' and 'A garden of pleasure' (Parry, 1992: Appendix 3). Evelyn published not only *Silva* but also *Kalendarium hortense* (1666), *De acetaria* (1699), and *Elysium Britannicum* (2001). Parry in 'John Evelyn as Hortulan Saint' notes also Ralph Austen's *Treatise of fruit trees, with the spiritual use of an orchard* (1653) and Thomas Browne's (1658) *The garden of Cyrus* (Parry, 1992: 138). For more on the Royal Society, first proposed by this group as a research centre for natural philosophers and scientists, see especially Hunter (1989); Leslie (1992); and Harris and Hunter (2003).

18 *Paradise Lost* criticism is a vast field; in this context, I can only provide the briefest of samplings.

19 Key readings of gender in *Paradise Lost* include McColley (1983); Nyquist (1987); Edwards (1997); and Martin (2004).

20 Miller argues that *Paradise Lost* debates labour and household economy by re-engaging the empowerment/voice debates of the earlier tracts on Eve and women (2008: 67–74). I am arguing that the garden itself serves this function in the 1650s, and that Milton is responding to and building on that trope. Note Martin's (2004) discussions of the ambiguities in Milton's Eve as a prototypical woman.

21 Milton dedicated his 'On education' to Hartlib and corresponded with several founders of the Royal Society. Edwards notes that *Paradise Lost* responds to 'seventeenth-century natural history and ... the experimental philosophers' (1999: 9), but even more than their experiments, Milton appears to be driven to respond to their ideologies of Eve in Eden.

22 On eco-critical and naturalist readings of *Paradise Lost*, see McColley (1993); Evans (1996); Edwards (1999); and Hiltner (2008).

23 Miller's first chapter (2008: 31–46) outlines many traces of the controversies' terms and arguments in *Paradise Lost*.

24 McColley, among others, notes the poetic structure of this passage (1988: 107).

25 Revard elides Adam's and Eve's responses to paradise by discussing 'their commitment to the garden' (2008: 32), though she notes Eve's distinctively poetic praise.

26 Lewalski cites Hiltner (2008: 18).

27 Amy Tigner makes equally fascinating connections between Eve and the culinary productiveness of the garden (2010: 241).

28 Cf Catullus LXI: 'ac domum dominam voca/ conjugis cupidam novi,/ mentem amore revinciens/ ut tenax hedera huc et huc/ arborem implicat errans.' (Goold, 1989: 112).

29 See Kilgour (2004: 1–17) for more on Eve's iconographic links to the garden.

References

Beale, J. (1657) *Herefordshire orchards, a pattern for all England written in an epistolary address to Samuel Hartlib, Esq.* London: Roger Daniel.

Beilin, E.V. (1987) *Redeeming Eve: Women Writers of the English Renaissance.* Princeton, NJ: Princeton University Press.

Campbell, G. (1995) 'The Figure of Pilate's Wife in Aemilia Lanyer's *Salve Deus Rex Judae-orum.' Renaissance Papers.* Ed. G.W. Williams and B.J. Baines. Raleigh: Southeastern Renaissance Conference. 1–15.

Cowley, A. (1721) 'Several Discourses by way of Essays in Verse and Prose.' *The works of Mr. Abraham Cowley consisting of those which were formerly printed, and those which he design'd for the press, now published out of the author's original copies, with the Cutter of Coleman-Street.* Vol II. 12th edn. London: Gale Ecco. 622–727.

Edwards, K.L. (1997) 'Resisting Representation: All about Milton's "Eve."' *Exemplaria: A Journal of Theory in Medieval and Renaissance Studies,* 9: 231–53.

——. (1999) *Milton and the Natural World: Science and Poetry in Paradise Lost.* Cambridge: Cambridge University Press.

——. (2008) 'Eden Raised: Waste in Milton's Garden.' *Renaissance Ecology: Imagining Eden in Milton's England.* Ed. K. Hiltner. Pittsburgh, PA: Duquesne University Press. 259–71.

Evans, J.M. (1996) *Milton's Imperial Epic: Paradise Lost and the Discourse of Colonialism.* Ithaca, NY: Cornell University Press.

Evelyn, J. (1666) *Kalendarium hortense, or, The gard'ners almanac.* London: Jo. Martyn and Ja. Allestry.

—— (1670) *Silva, or, A discourse of forest-trees, and the propagation of timber in His Majesties dominions as it was deliver'd in the Royal Society.* London: Jo. Martyn and Ja. Allestry.

——. (1699) *Acetaria. A discourse of sallets.* London: s.n.

——. (2001) *Elysium Britannicum or The Royal Gardens.* Ed. J. Ingram. Philadelphia: University of Pennsylvania Press.

Flannagan, R. (ed.) (1998) *The Riverside Milton.* Boston: Houghton Mifflin.

Goold, G.P. (ed.) (1989) *Catullus.* London: Duckworth.

Grossman, M. (2003) 'The Rhetoric of Feminine Priority and the Ethics of Form in *Paradise Lost.' English Literary Renaissance,* 33: 424–43.

Hammons, P.S. (2005) 'The Gendered Imagination of Property in Sixteenth- and Seven-teenth-century English Women's Verse.' *CLIO: A Journal of Literature, History, and the Philosophy of History,* 34.4: 395–418.

Harris, F. and Hunter, M. (eds) (2003) *John Evelyn and His Milieu.* London: British Library.

Hiltner, K. (ed.) (2008) *Renaissance Ecology: Imagining Eden in Milton's England.* Pittsburgh, PA: Duquesne University Press.

Hunter, M. (1989) *Establishing the New Science: The Experience of the Early Royal Society.* Woodbridge: Boydell Press.

James, F. (2009) '"A christal glasse for Christian women": Meditations on Christ's Passion in the Devotional Literature of Renaissance Women.' *Journal of International Women's Studies,* 10.3: 58–72.

Jones, A.R. (1990) '"Counterattacks on "the bayter of women": Three Pamphleteers of the Early Seventeenth Century.' *The Renaissance Englishwoman in Print: Counter-balancing the Canon.* Ed. A.M. Haselkorn and B.S. Travitsky. Amherst, MA: University of Massachusetts Press. 45–62.

Jordan, C. (1990) *Renaissance Feminism: Literary Texts and Political Models*. Ithaca, NY: Cornell University Press.

Kilgour, M. (2004) 'Eve and Flora (*Paradise Lost* 5.15–16).' *Milton Quarterly*, 38: 1–17.

Lanyer, A. (1993) *The Poems of Aemilia Lanyer: Salve Deus Rex Judaeorum*. Ed. S. Woods. Oxford: Oxford University Press.

Leslie, M. (1992) 'The Spiritual Husbandry of John Beale.' *Culture and Cultivation in Early Modern England: Writing and the Land*. Ed. M. Leslie and T. Raylor. Leicester: Leicester University Press. 151–72.

Lewalski, B.K. (1991) 'Re-writing Patriarchy and Patronage: Margaret Clifford, Anne Clifford, and Aemelia Lanyer.' *Yearbook of English Studies*, 21: 7–25.

——. (1993) *Writing Women in Jacobean England*. Cambridge, MA: Harvard University Press.

——. (2008) 'Milton's Paradises.' *Renaissance Ecology: Imagining Eden in Milton's England*. Ed. K. Hiltner. Pittsburgh, PA: Duquesne University Press. 15–30.

Loughlin, M.H. (2000) '"Fast Ti'd Unto Them in a Golden Chaine": Typology, Apocalypse, and Woman's Genealogy in Aemilia Lanyer's *Salve Deus Rex Judaeorum*.' *Renaissance Quarterly*, 53.1: 133–79.

Lowe, A. (1992) 'Agricultural Reform and the Love-poems of Thomas Carew; with an Instance from Lovelace.' *Culture and Cultivation in Early Modern England: Writing and the Land*. Ed. M. Leslie and T. Raylor. Leicester: Leicester University Press. 63–81.

Martin, C.G. (ed.) (2004) *Milton and Gender*. Cambridge: Cambridge University Press.

Marvell, A. (2005) 'The Garden.' *Andrew Marvell: The Complete Poems*. Ed. E.S. Donno and J. Bate. London: Penguin. 101.

McColley, D.K. (1983) *Milton's Eve*. Urbana: University of Illinois Press.

——. (1988) 'Eve and the arts of Eden.' *Milton and the Idea of Woman*. Ed. J.M. Walker. Urbana: University of Illinois Press. 100–19.

——. (1993) *A Gust for Paradise: Milton's Eden and the Visual Arts*. Urbana: University of Illinois Press.

——. (1999) 'Milton and the Sexes.' *A Cambridge Companion to Milton*. Ed. D. Danielson. Cambridge: Cambridge University Press. 175–92.

McGrath, L. (2002) *Subjectivity and Women's Poetry in Early Modern England*. Aldershot: Ashgate Press.

Miller, S. (2008) *Engendering the Fall: John Milton and Seventeenth-Century Women Writers*. Philadelphia, PA: University of Pennsylvania Press.

Milton, J. (1957) *John Milton: Complete Poems and Major Prose*. Ed. M.Y. Hughes. New York: Macmillan.

Nyquist, M. (1987) 'The Genesis of Gendered Subjectivity in the Divorce Tracts and in *Paradise Lost*.' *Re-Membering Milton: Essays on the Texts and Traditions*. Ed. M. Nyquist and M.W. Ferguson. London: Routledge.

Parry, G. (1992) 'John Evelyn as Hortulan Saint.' *Culture and Cultivation in Early Modern England: Writing and the Land*. Ed. M. Leslie and T. Raylor. Leicester: Leicester University Press. 130–50.

Revard, S.P. (2008) 'Eve and the Language of Love in *Paradise Lost*.' *Culture and Cultivation in Early Modern England: Writing and the Land*. Ed. M. Leslie and T. Raylor. Leicester: Leicester University Press. 31–44.

Schoenfeldt, M. (2001) 'Obedience and Autonomy.' *Paradise Lost, A Companion to Milton*. Ed. T. Corns. Oxford: Blackwell.

Shakespeare, W. (2002) *King Richard II*. Ed. C.R. Forker. London: Arden Shakespeare.

Shepherd, S. (1985) *The Women's Sharp Revenge: Five Women's Pamphlets from the Renaissance*. London: Forth Estate.

Sowernam, E. (1617) *Ester hath hang'd Haman: or An answere to a lewd pamphlet, entituled, The arraignment of women*. London: Thomas Snodham.

Sumers, A.J. (2004) 'Milton's Mat(t)erology: *Paradise Lost* and the Seventeenth-century Querelle des Femmes.' *Milton Quarterly*, 38: 200–25.

Swetnam, J. (1615) *The araignment of lewd, idle, froward, and vnconstant women or the vanitie of them, choose you whether*. London: George Purslowe.

Theis, J.S. (2008) '"The Purlieus of Heaven": Milton's Eden as a Pastoral Forest.' *Culture and Cultivation in Early Modern England: Writing and the Land*. Ed. M. Leslie and T. Raylor. Leicester: Leicester University Press. 229–57.

Tigner, A.L. (2010) 'Eating with Eve.' *Milton Quarterly*, 44: 239–53.

Tinkham, A.E. (2009) '"Owning" in Aemilia Lanyer's *Salve Deus Rex Judæorum* ("Hail God King of the Jews").' *Studies in Philology*, 106.1: 52–75.

Wiseman, S. (2007) 'Exemplarity, Women and Political Rhetoric.' *Rhetoric, Women and Politics in Early Modern England*. Ed. J. Richards and A. Thorne. London: Routledge. 129–48.

Woodbridge, L. (1986) *Women and the English Renaissance: Literature and the Nature of Womankind, 1540 to 1620*. Urbana: University of Illinois Press.

4

Christian liberty and female rule: exegesis and political controversy in the 1550s

Adrian Streete

What is Christian liberty?[1] And is it compatible with female rule? This essay considers both of these questions as they were debated in early modern Europe, but particularly in the work of a number of English and Scottish Protestant political theologians during the 1550s. I argue that, on the one hand, writers like John Ponet, John Knox and Christopher Goodman formulate some of the most far-reaching and radical arguments for Christian liberty that can be found in the early modern period. However, on the other hand, their arguments for liberty and the freedoms of subjects are coupled with a virulent misogyny and deprecation of female rule. Building on the work of scholars such as Constance Jordan (1987), Quentin Skinner (1998), David Colclough (2009), John Witte (2010) and Ethan Shagan (2011), I want to suggest that our accounts of 'liberty before liberalism', to use Skinner's famous formulation, need to pay greater attention to the question of female liberty during the early modern period. While we can certainly understand this issue in its historical and philosophical context, Christian liberty in the early modern period is almost exclusively understood as a patriarchal phenomenon, even by those writers such as John Aylmer, who sought to defend the rule of women. As Jordan puts it: 'Whatever Renaissance feminists claimed as rights for women were not termed *rights*, nor, until the beginning of the seventeenth century, were they demanded except by way of arguing for a modification of existing domestic order' (Jordan, 1990: 28). Nevertheless, one of the most remarkable features of Ponet, Knox and Goodman's political writings is that while their biblical commitments demand a patriarchalist approach to questions of female rule, politically each man can be termed a constitutionalist, one who argued that man's primary covenantal obligation was to God, not to kings (see Jordan, 1990: 128–32). Kingship should rightly be tempered by groups such as parliament, the magistracy and even in some cases the populace themselves, since secular kingly authority derives from the consent of the people. Such arguments form the basis of the so-called monarchomach defence of popular resistance. This essay argues that in each man's discussion of female rule in the Bible, the authority of women is regularly deprecated at a patriarchal level, yet often praised in the service of a constitutional argument for Christian liberty. By looking at the examples of Deborah, Jezebel, Athalia, Judith and Jael in particular, the contradictory nature of these early modern discussions of female rule are made apparent.

The issue of Christian liberty is one that was increasingly addressed in late medieval and early modern Christian theology, and it certainly plays a central part in the writings of magisterial reformers like Martin Luther and John Calvin (see Witte, 2010). In the former's famous definition in *The Freedom of a Christian* (1520): 'A Christian is a perfectly free lord of all, subject to none. A Christian is a perfectly dutiful servant of all, subject to all' (Luther, 1989: 598). While these two propositions might be thought to be mutually exclusive, in fact, Luther argues, they correspond to a fundamental dualism in human nature: all individual subjects have, as he notes, a 'twofold nature, a spiritual and a bodily one' (598). For Luther, mankind's spiritual nature is the main locus of his liberty: it cannot be properly felt or expressed in his fallen bodily nature. As he says, 'the soul needs only the Word of God for its life and righteousness, so it is justified by faith alone and not any works' (598). However, when the Christian considers the laws laid out in the commandments, he will only 'recognize his helplessness and is distressed about how he might satisfy the law' (600). Man cannot fulfil the demands of the Decalogue, and so must rely upon faith and God's promise as expressed in the New Testament. Obedience to this promise is the first duty of the Christian subject since 'they who imagine that they are fulfilling the law by doing the works of chastity and mercy required by the law (the civil and human virtues) might not be saved' (602). As Ethan Shagan notes, these kinds of arguments offered 'a new, Lutheran solution to the problem of overlapping jurisdictions between Church and state that had plagued Europe since the eleventh century' (2011: 79). True Christian freedom is spiritual and inwards, and it cannot be constrained by secular kings or authority: 'since faith alone suffices for salvation, I need nothing except faith exercising the power and dominion of its own liberty ... this is the inestimable power and liberty and freedom of Christians' (Luther, 1989: 607).

In the case of the outer, bodily nature of man, of course he is obliged to observe the conventional interpretation of Romans 13 and to 'be subject to the governing authorities', such as they are (Luther, 1989: 621). Writing in the aftermath of the Peasants' War in central Europe during 1524/25, an event that deeply shocked the leaders of the reformed movement, William Tyndale outlines the orthodox position in *The Obedience of a Christian Man* (1528). He argues that liberty is not compatible with resistance: 'if we resiste evill rulers sekinge to sett oure selves at libertie we shall no doute bringe oure selves in to moare cruell bondage and wrappe oure selves in moch moare misery and wrechednes'. Subjects must instead 'kysee the rod' of secular authority.' (Fol. 47v). In the years that followed, many reformers retreated from their earlier political pronouncements on spiritual and secular authority. However, during that radical early period when Luther wrote *The Freedom of a Christian*, his concern was that secular obedience should never be mistaken for the spiritual work of justification. The great difficulty, as Luther sees it, are the various demands made upon subjects by the governing authorities, especially the Roman Catholic Church, whose dictates conflate the secular and the spiritual, hoodwinking the people into believing that obedience to their strictures equals salvation. As he writes: 'In this way, Christian liberty perishes altogether' (622). By defining Christian liberty as spiritual and unconstrained by the demands of secular authority, Luther identifies the radical core at the centre of reformed attitudes to prevailing power structures. Indeed, his work sets up a crucial tension, one that was to define much of the debate surrounding Christian liberty throughout the early modern period. Luther puts it this way: 'Although tyrants do violence or injustice in making their demands, yet it will do no harm as long as they demand nothing contrary to God' (622). Much rides on that conditional formulation 'as long as'. The obvious question is this: what happens when the demands of secular authority come into conflict with the laws of God?

Robert Weimann has argued that in these Lutheran debates on authority and Christian liberty, 'subordination to the state and freedom of the soul go together to such an extent that the hardness of things political is either ignored or compensated for by a new kind of *Innerlichkeit*, or interiority' (1996: 35). While the second part of this formulation is accurate, the first strikes me as somewhat overstated. As Quentin Skinner and others have shown, it was the very hardness of things political in the aftermath of the formulation of the Schmalkadic League – a reaction to the overweening imperial political power of the Holy Roman Emperor Charles V – which led to the production of the 'Magdeburg Confession' in 1550 (Skinner, 2005: 206–9). This document, intended to galvanise resistance to Charles, provided much of the impetus for later Calvinist writing on the extent of Christian liberty.[2] During the 1550s, the radical core of reformed politics was once more accessed. Turning first to Calvin, his conception very much follows in Luther's footsteps, stressing too that the law cannot be fulfilled since it 'leaves no one righteous' (1961: 834). True liberty can only be found in Christ. It then follows that 'Christian freedom is, in all parts, a spiritual thing' and that, because of this, it is incumbent upon us not to abuse, or rather misunderstand that freedom by getting mired in fleshly pleasures and failing to use such pleasures 'indifferently', a trap that Calvin sees many falling into (841).[3] As David Colclough has pointed out, liberty is a key term for Calvin and his followers, 'and they patrolled its boundaries diligently, careful of its potential for slippage into libertinism' (Colclough, 2009: 87). Even more than Luther, Calvin stresses the importance of the subject's conscience and its freedom: it can never 'be ensnared by the bonds of laws and constitutions' made by men (846–7). He realises that this is a potentially dangerous doctrine and so notes that man's twofold nature must answer to the spiritual demands of the conscience and the fleshly demands of temporal politics (847). As with Luther, the demands of the former will always trump the latter. Man must, to be sure, obey the secular authorities. Nevertheless, 'there are in man, so to speak, two worlds, over which different kings and different laws have authority' (847). Because man's conscience is only ever to subject to God, the dualism of the subject reflects the radically bifold nature of his secular and spiritual obligations. Again, what happens when the two obligations come into conflict? Obedience is (fairly) consistently enjoined throughout Calvin's writings.[4] But if a Christian finds that his conscience is intolerably constrained by authority, how might he best restore the freedom of his conscience?

The most politically radical answers to this question in Protestantism can be found in the writings of John Ponet, John Knox and Christopher Goodman during the 1550s. In the case of the former and latter, both men held prominent positions in the Protestant Church established by Edward VI. But when the King's Catholic half-sister Mary ascended to the throne in 1553, it quickly became clear that maintaining an open adherence to the Protestant faith in England was all but impossible, and both men went into exile in various centres of European Protestantism. In the case of Knox, he was working as a minister in England when Mary acceded to the throne, but his exile was also compounded by the fact that his home country Scotland was being ruled by a Roman Catholic regent, Marie de Guise, on behalf of her daughter Mary who was likely to marry a Catholic. As scholars like Dan Danner (1981), Susan M. Felch (1995), and Judith M. Richards (1997) have shown, each man had good political reason to deprecate female rule.[5] The difficulty for modern feminist critics is that the texts produced by these men have traditionally been seen as a keystone of political radicalism during the early modern period, one based on the patriarchal deprecation of women's rights in the secular sphere. For Quentin Skinner, these are 'revolutionary writings' that would find full expression in the English Civil War and the work of John Locke (2005: 233). More recently, John Witte has argued that these texts play a key part in the development of the language of liberties and rights, a narrative that pre-dates its traditional beginning in the eighteenth century (2010: 114–22).[6] From the perspective adopted in this essay, such narratives invariably invite a counter question: do the misogynistic rhetoric and patriarchal attitudes of these texts undermine their political and historical importance in the pre-history of a more capacious language of liberty and rights?

It is true that these radical writers see female rule as a hindrance to the achievement of Christian liberty. But it does not necessarily follow that there is no recognition of women's entitlement to liberty at all. The next section of this essay, therefore, argues that while the misogyny of these texts is very much a feature of their secular conception of power, their misogyny is not an absolute conception. Moreover, in the spiritual realm, women are entitled to as much freedom as men are. In keeping with the arguments found in Luther and Calvin, true Christian liberty can only ever be located in the spiritual realm and in the freedom of conscience from external constraint. But this formulation does not completely negate the need for secular political action, sometimes even by women. As Constance Jordan writes about the political and spiritual status of early modern women: 'In the language of Renaissance political thought, she is a *persona mixta*: her natural and political self balanced by her spiritual self' (1990: 23). Though early modern patriarchy often downplayed the political implications of this division, it is rarely forgotten altogether, especially in political theology. To make this point is not to downplay the misogynistic rhetoric found in the works of Ponet and the others. However, it is important to understand that such language invariably serves a fairly narrow political purpose. Felch has persuasively argued that 'although much contemporary criticism argues that such spiritual equality without concomitant spiritual power is not only illusory but coercive, it is not clear that Protestant women of the sixteenth century actually experienced it as such' (1995: 822). When we turn in particular to the radicals' discussions of female biblical rule, or to biblical women who hold some kind of political authority, a dual approach pertains: general, but not total, deprecation of female rule in the secular realm, and the assertion of female liberty in the spiritual realm.

The earliest of the texts is John Ponet's *A short treatise of politike power*. Published in Strasbourg in 1556, the title page carries a quotation from Psalm 118 that sets the tone for the rest of the treatise: 'it is better to trust in the Lorde, than to trust in Princes.' Ponet begins by referring to those guarantors of freedom in classical society: 'among the *Lacedemonians* certain men called *Ephori* were ordained to see that the kings should not oppresse the people, and among the *Romaynes*, the *Tribunes* were ordained to defende and mayntene the libertie of the people from the pride and iniurie of the nobles' (1556: sigs. A6r–7v). As Skinner has noted, discussion of ephors and tribunes in Calvinist writing of the 1550s is closely aligned with developing ideas of popular magistracy 'who are elected by the people, serve as their representatives, and remain responsible to those who have elected them' (2005: 233). Repeatedly, Ponet stresses that sovereignty is derived from the consent of the people. For instance, although certain liberties are associated with the crown, the primacy of England's parliament is affirmed. It is an institution where nothing can 'be done without the knowlage [sic] and consent of all' (sig. A7v). He also draws on the division, familiar from Luther and Calvin, between secular and spiritual authority:

> Ciuile power is a power and ordinaunce of God, appointed to certain thinges, but no general minister ouer all thinges. God hathe not geuen it power ouer the one and the best parte of man, that is, the soule and conscience of man, but onely ouer the other and the worst part of man, that is, the body, and those thinges that belong vnto this temporall life of man. (sig. D2v)

Freedom of Christian conscience is the essence of spiritual liberty, one that does not have to be predicated upon the political consent of the people in the secular realm. Moreover, the liberties supposedly guaranteed by secular authority cannot be relied upon, especially when they impinge upon the spiritual: 'thei are muche to blame, that being put in trust of Courtes and parliaments to make lawes and statutes in aduancement of Goddes glorie, and conseruation of the liberties and commonwealth of their country, neglect their office and charge' (sig. B2v).

When it comes to the issue of obedience, Ponet's understanding is similarly far-reaching. Obedience should never mean an absolute adherence to authority: 'if Obedience be to muche or to litell in a common wealthe, it causeth muche euil and disordre [sic]'. On the one hand, too much liberty 'maketh the gouernors to forget their vocacion [sic], and to usurpe vpon their subiectes'. On the other, 'to litel briedeth a licencious [sic] libertie, and maketh the people to forget their duetie' (sig. C8r). Ponet's understanding of obedience is not the absolute standard of required moral behaviour that we tend to find in the more mainstream patriarchal political texts of this period, and which typically reject the possibility of resistance and rebellion. Nor does Ponet defer obedience to lesser magistrates in the hope that they might stand against a tyrannous ruler (see Greaves, 1982). Rather, his view of obedience as a moderate mean between extremes goes to the heart of his constitutionalist model of political society, one which states that resistance against tyrants is both godly and just, even to the point of rebellion (sig. G3r ff.). Failure to oppose a wicked ruler is not only wrong; it is a derogation of Christian liberty. This is because of the secular ruler's unhappy tendency to mistake his or her own will for the rule of the law. Writing of the Old Testament female ruler Jezebel, Ponet tells the story of her commandment to Abdias to kill all the prophets. Abdias disobeys because he was 'a man fearing God, and know[s] this commaundement [sic] to be a wicked womans will' (sig. D5v). Given Protestantism's scepticism towards the human will in matters of salvation, it is hardly surprising that we should find a critique of will as misplaced law in this text.

That said, Ponet's discussion of Jezebel and Athalia in the *Treatise* brings together the related issues of liberty, consent, obedience, rebellion and female rule. Another passage concerning Jezebel relates to her husband King Achab. He is desirous of Naboth's vineyard but cannot have it since 'without his will and consent, he could not be forced to departe' (sig. F5v). Jezebel ignores Naboth's rights and his lack of consent, urging her husband to invoke his 'auncient prerogatiue' and take the vineyard. Ponet contrasts the satisfaction of Jezebel's 'will' with the tyrannous denial of proper process to Naboth: 'no laws, no equitie, no iustice might defende the poore innocent' (sigs. F5v–r). The point here is not so much the assertion of patriarchal misogyny as the critique of tyranny and the observance of the proclivity of rulers in general to trample on the rule of law and on liberty, personal and collective. Ponet's conclusion to the tale affirms this point. He notes that both King Achab and Queen Jezebel were not long after killed and 'their blood licked vp of dogges'; a warning against rulers 'that will haue their lustes a lawe, and their will to be folowed and obeyed of their subiectes as a right in dede' (sig. F5r). The will of a secular ruler does not equate to an expression of the true law. Rather, the law is 'set out by God in the boke of Deuteronomie' (sig. F6v). In an important sense, the tyranny of secular rulers like Jezebel is an affront to the covenant, the guarantee of spiritual liberty, and a further reason why wicked rule must be opposed.

The discussion of Jezebel's daughter Queen Athalia offers Ponet another striking example. Being childless after the death of her son, she determines to 'haue killed all the kynges progenye … purposing to reigne therby in securitie, and to transpose the right of the crowne to straungers' (sig. H2v). However, she fails to kill Joas who, when he is of age, returns to claim the throne. Athalia's protestations are rejected: 'they layed handes on her (for all her crieng, Treason, treason) and whan they had caried her out of the house of God, they slewe her' (sig. H2r). This act of popular rebellion is justified since it returns the nation to a proper covenantal relationship with God:

> And so was the realme ridde of a tyranne, the right enheritour possessed in his regal astate, the people made a newe bande with God to serue him syncerely according to his worde, and banished all idolatrie and false religion (which the Quene had set vp and vsed) and the common wealthe florished afreshe in her former peace and libertie. (sig. H2r)

The notion that a nation must be ruled by a legitimate inheritor and not a 'straunger' goes, of course, to the heart of England's contemporary political problem, as Ponet sees it, under Mary Tudor. Just as the Israelites' loss of the Ark to the Philistines in battle is seen as a loss of 'honour and libertie' and an adoption of 'thraldom', so Mary's Catholic rule is seen in analogous terms (sig. H7r). As a Roman Catholic monarch, her principle obedience is, of course, to the Pope, the 'Romish Antichrist […] with his miserable Masse and all popishe slauery' (sig. I6r). This kind of rhetoric may not be attractive, but it was, as many scholars have shown, central to Protestant construction of the English nation and Church in this period (see for example Tumbleson, 1998; Dolan, 1999; and Milton, 2002). Because Mary Tudor is the wife of a Roman Catholic Spanish monarch, the danger for Ponet is that the English nation will become enslaved – similar to the Israelites – as part of Spain's colonial endeavours, and 'caried in to newe Spaine, and ther not lyue at libertie, but … tyed in chaynes, forced to rowe in the galie, to digge in the mynes and to pike vp the golde in the hotte sande' (sig. L4r). Biblical exegesis and contemporary reality become intertwined here: thraldom and slavery are the antonyms of Christian liberty. Skinner has argued that for many neo-Roman constitutionalist thinkers in the early modern period, any state will 'be counted as living in slavery if its capacity for action is in any way dependent on the will of anyone other than the body of its own citizens' (1998: 49).[7] Ponet's example of Spanish slavery offers a good example of this principle in action. Mary must be opposed not because she is a woman, but because her rule engenders slavery at the expense of liberty.

Ponet's text ends with a general call for England to repent of its sins. Such a conclusion might be thought conventional and uninteresting were it not for two earlier, female examples that he draws upon from the Old Testament. The first is Judith. She is praised as a 'good and faithful woman to God and her countrey', not just for her slaying of Holofernes, but because her example shows what can happen when 'the people (against who the deuil and his kings worke) fall to repentaunce for their sinnes' and God subsequently re-affirms his covenant with the people (sig. I1v). Judith's example of resistance is more important than her status as a woman. Nevertheless, it is a remarkable moment in the text. For not only does it show that a woman's spiritual liberty is vouchsafed in the covenant, it demonstrates that female rebellion (so often associated during the period with the patriarchal condemnation of Eve) can act as an affirmation of the constitutionalist argument for political resistance and rebellion.[8] In the final example, Ponet tells of how Sisara, a general fleeing from Barak, was hidden by an Israelite woman, Jael. But because Sisara had 'long noied and hurt Israel with oppression and warres', Jael kills him by taking 'a great long spiking nayle, and driueth it with a hammer so harde in to his braines, that Sisara troubled Israel no more' (sig. H6r). Once more, Ponet affirms female agency in the face of secular patriarchal political oppression, and as a restatement of the covenant. Mary Tudor, and her biblical antecedents like Jezebel, stand as wilful deniers of Christian liberty in the secular realm. Yet certain biblical women like Judith and Jael show us that secular self-assertion by women can go beyond the mere subjective expression of 'will' if that female agency is undertaken in the service of the spiritual covenant that underpins the liberty of the populace. This is not to suggest that a more capacious feminist conception of liberty is latent in Ponet's text, but it does show that female agency is not incompatible with the (re)establishment of subjects' rights.

If Ponet's condemnation of female rule is relatively moderately expressed by the standards of the period, the same cannot be said for John Knox's 1558 text *The first blast of the trumpet against the monstrous regiment of women*. The notoriety of this tract and the negative effect that it had on Elizabeth I's attitude towards Calvinism are well known (see Felch, 1995: 815). Knox's rhetorical flourishes against 'the monstrous empire of a cruel woman' make it easy for his opponents to condemn his work (1994: 3). It also means that some of his finer points can get lost amidst the intemperate language. This is especially the case when it comes to his discussion of female biblical figures. But before turning to these sections, it is important first to note some similarities and differences between Ponet and Knox. Similar to the earlier writer, Knox is concerned to assert a collective account of Christian liberty:

> if justice be a constant and perpetual will to give every person their own right (as the most learned in all ages have defined it to be), then to give or to will to give to any person that which is not their right must repugn to justice. But to reign above man can never be the right to woman because it is a thing denied unto her by God. (30–1)

He also agrees that political enslavement and bondage is most keenly felt in the subjection of a nation to 'foreign', that is to say Roman Catholic, rule (see 3, 32, 41). In such circumstances, rebellion is both right and proper. More than Ponet, Knox's conception of Christian liberty is based upon the political centrality of the covenant: 'the office of the king or supreme magistrate hath respect to the law moral and to the conservation of both the Tables' (30). Because of this, it means that Knox is more sceptical of ideas of popular consent and custom as providing the basis for law. He notes that 'if the approbation of princes and peoples, laws made by men or the consent of realms, may establish anything against God and His Word, then should idolatry be preferred to the true religion' (42). This attitude differs somewhat from what J.G.A. Pocock famously called the 'common law mind', one that sought to establish England's ancient constitution in the common law (see Pocock, 1987: 30ff). It is not that Knox does not believe such age old freedoms exist, but that with the accession of Mary, 'the ancient liberties' that the English traditionally laid claim to have been overthrown: 'particular examples do establish no common law' (23, 27, 33). In a resonant passage, he complains of those female monarchs who share 'the spirit of Jezebel and Althaliah', who oppress 'the simple people', and whom 'by their practices and deceit, we find ancient realms and nations given and betrayed into the hands of strangers, the titles and liberties of them taken from the just possessors' (34). Because subjects give 'their suffrages, consent and help to establish women in their kingdoms and empires', this enables Knox to argue that popular consent is only really justified when it affirms the covenant (6. See also 30). His conception of the covenant is not as participatory as, for instance, many later Puritan accounts formulated during the seventeenth century (see Witte, 2010: 289). The covenant for Knox affirms the spiritual calling of God's chosen elect (1994: 31). And yet, despite this somewhat narrow conception, *The First Blast* still finds room to assert the spiritual authority of certain biblical women.

In particular, Knox singles out Deborah for extended discussion. Writing of her prophetic power and encouragement towards Barak to go into battle, Knox says that: 'she spoileth herself of all power to command, attributing that authority to God, of whom she had her revelation and certitude to appoint Barak captain' (37). The prophetic female voice is not an affront to the covenant. Indeed Deborah's female agency actively underwrites her and Barak's subsequent military victory on behalf of the Israelites. Knox amplifies the point further in this startling passage:

> Deborah did usurp no such power nor authority as our queens do this day claim, but that she was endued with the spirit of wisdom, of knowledge, and of the true fear of God, and by the same she judged the facts of the rest of the people. She rebuked their defection and idolatry, yea, and also did redress to her power the injuries that were done by man to man. But all this, I say, she did by the spiritual sword, that is, by the Word of God, and not by any temporal regiment or authority which she did usurp over Israel. In which, I suppose, at that time there was no lawful magistrate by the reason of their great affliction. (37)

The last sentence is particularly revealing. Deborah's spiritual authority has interesting parallels with the 'state of exception' described in the work of Giorgio Agamben, where sovereign power is temporarily suspended in a time of crisis and the laws governing the populace are recalibrated (Agamben, 1988: 37). The fact that this is accomplished by a woman is all the more remarkable given that Knox's main aim is to criticise female rulers who 'usurp' temporal authority. This reading also complicates Michele Osherow's argument that 'For all her victory, Deborah cannot elude the early modern presumption of feminine weakness' (2009: 82). While Knox certainly sees Deborah as weak in her sex and in the temporal realm, *spiritually* her actions affirm the values of the covenant and thus underpin the liberty and freedom of the populace, even in a 'state of exception'. It is important not to overstate the case: Knox's text remains misogynistic and it is hard to reclaim it fully for a feminist argument. Nevertheless, as Jordan rightly points out, 'dramatically misogynist literature can have a feminist dimension: by depicting women as forceful rebels, it can convey their capacity to think and to act' (1990: 19). This discussion of Deborah shows that there is more to *The First Blast* than just bone-headed patriarchal abuse: even Knox understood that the spiritual liberty promised by the covenant could not simply be restricted to men (see Felch, 1995: 821–2).

In Christopher Goodman's *How superior powers ought to be obeyed* (1558), Christian liberty is defined as a certain kind of obedience: 'If you wish for Christian liberty, come and see how easily it may be had: if you would love God above man, here you shall know how to obey God rather than men' (2004: 5). This liberty, simply expressed but hard won, is juxtaposed with England's current plight. Once more, it is claimed that the reign of Mary, the 'ungodly and unlawful Governess, wicked Jezebel', is leading the English nation 'to become slaves to a strange and foreign nation, the proud Spaniards' (14). By validating her rule, the people have forsaken their 'right title and possession of God's Laws' (73). Rather than flawed secular rulers, it is the covenant that must vouchsafe the 'inalienable' liberties of the subject (Witte, 2010: 121). Nonetheless, even the covenant is not seen as something absolutely imposed upon the people by God. Repeatedly, Goodman's discussions of the covenant stress that its adherents are limited in how far they can act: 'Moses and Aaron, God's elect and chosen servants had no more power over the people then His express commandments permits ... the people so far and no farther were bound to obey them'. Rather, the 'voice and consent' of the people are necessary for the covenant to be enacted (62).

More so than Ponet or Knox, Goodman sees Christian liberty as the spiritual enactment of God's law guaranteed in the freedom of individual conscience, one that cannot be contradicted by secular authority. This is a promise that extends to all, and that is 'plain and evident to all sorts of men and women, which profess Christ unfeignedly' (64). Passages like this, which extend the fellowship of the covenant to men and women equally, perhaps help to explain why, unlike Ponet and Knox, Goodman does not think it necessary to find 'positive' biblical examples of female rule. His focus is relentlessly on Christian liberty, a franchise that extends to both sexes. For Goodman, by anointing Mary Tudor, the English 'condemn the liberty of the Gospel' by reinstating the 'Jewish ceremonies' described in the Old Testament when the Israelites forget their covenant with God. This is a kind of spiritual and secular idolatry, one that enables a certain kind of tyranny. The nation forsakes 'the liberty of Jesus Christ and our consciences', and 'return[s] to our old vomit, much more vile then the slavery of Egypt, I mean the servitude of that Roman Antichrist' (22). To rebel against Mary is also to reject the spiritual and secular tyranny of the papacy, an important feature of Protestant claims to the political autonomy of the nation throughout the sixteenth century and key to the development of what Michael Braddick has termed the 'confessional state' (2000: 289).

However, it is Goodman's particular account of Christian liberty that is the most important feature of his text. In one of his most famous passages, he writes that:

> it is an easy matter for all manner of subjects to know what liberty belongs to them, by the word of God, which they may lawfully claim, as their own posses-sion, and are likewise bound at all times to practice: wherein also appears what things are prohibited unto them, which they may in no case exercise. If you there-fore are God's subjects and people, and He your Lord God and loving Father, who is above all powers and princes, and has made no laws, but such as are for your preservation, and singular comfort: then without all controversy there may be nothing lawful for you by any commandment of man, which your Lord God in any case forbids: and nothing unlawful or forbidden to you which He commands, whether it appertains to the first table or the second. (61)

In the face of such a radical conception of liberty, questions of gender become a secondary concern. This is why the act of political rebellion is so crucial. Consist-ently, Goodman states the right of 'the people' and 'subjects' to rebel against tyrannous rulers (68). The 'state of liberty is the natural condition of mankind'. This liberty is delegated to the state by its subjects, not the other way around, and it may be recalled by those subjects when the state acts tyrannously against that liberty (see Skinner, 1998: 19. More generally, see 17–36). The contemporary reality of Roman Catholic female rule simply crystallises for Goodman what is a much bigger problem, namely that the interests of state power should never be allowed to militate against the 'peace of your consciences' (48). This is the very essence of what Skinner has termed the constitutionalist account of liberty, one where the state 'has a duty not merely to liberate its citizens from such personal exploitation and dependence, but to prevent its own agents, dressed in a little brief authority, from behaving arbitrarily in the course of imposing the rules that govern our common life' (119). This is, for Goodman, the key point. The misogynous rhetoric found in *How superior powers* cannot be argued away. Nevertheless, it should also not blind us to what is one of the most powerful and radical political claims made during the sixteenth century. Christian liberty is, for Goodman, the basis of our 'common life', one that should be shared by men and women on an equal basis. If agents of the state threaten that liberty, then they can rightfully be resisted by all 'subjects'. When it comes to rebellion, the gender of those resisting agents is less important than the fact that they *act* and restore all subjects to their natural liberty.

Ponet, Knox and Goodman were, of course, exceptions to the general rule. Although they built upon the radical implications found in the writings of Luther and Calvin, in the main, a more restrictive, patriarchal conception of Christian liberty predominated during the sixteenth century. A good case in point is offered in the final text considered in this essay, John Aylmer's *An harborowe for faithFull and trewe subiectes* (1559), which is examined briefly here by way of a conclusion. On the face of it, we might expect that this text, which offers a defence of female rule, particularly that of Elizabeth I, might contain a similarly capacious account of liberty to the monarchomach writers. However, Aylmer's understanding is rather more constrained. For him, liberty does not emerge from the originary freedom of the subject but is instead extrinsically bestowed. Writing of Deborah, Judith and other exemplary biblical figures who represent political freedom, Aylmer notes that God

> saued his people by the hand of a woman poore Deborah. He aduanced them and ouerthrew the enemies by a poore shepherde and his sling. He cut of the head of the proud Olophernes by the hande of a weake woman. It was, in reason a poore helpe to Sampsons strenghte, a nomber of heares growing vpon his hed, or an Asses iawe bone in his hande, to destroye so many enemies and bring the people to libertie. (sig. B4v)

In this rather downbeat passage, liberty always relates back to the 'He' of the passage, God, and not to those agents whom he acts through.[9] Later Aylmer is somewhat more positive about Deborah, noting 'the happy successe of hir reigne' and that she 'iudged the people of Israell, and the people restoreth vnto hir, she delyuered them out of thraldome, and set them at libertie' (sig. D3v). But the important point here is that Aylmer sees the liberty bestowed by Deborah in secular terms. In a crucial passage, he notes that Deborah did 'al that any ruler by *civil authorite* might, or is wont to do' (sig. D3v). Spiritual liberty is in God's gift only. Indeed, the best guarantor of liberty for subjects is obedience: 'If we obey, and do our dutie: all the blessings of God shal be poured vpon vs. We shall lyue in peace bothe of bodie and mynde, with leisure and libertie to serue God freely, without feare of th ennemie to encombre vs in our possessions, or feare of Antichrist to vexe our conscience' (sig. R1v–r). This is a patriarchal conception of authority, one familiar for example from the official state homilies reintroduced under Elizabeth.

Nevertheless, this is not to say that Aylmer is an irredeemably patriarchalist theorist whose defence of Elizabeth's female rule contains no suggestive implications. It is possible to see the influence of his more radical brethren in a number of places. For one, he returns to the Old Testament covenant in his discussion of monarchy and the various checks and balances that it is subject to. As he asks: 'What could any kyng in Israell do in that common wealth, besides the pollycie appointed by Moyses? They be but ministers, obeyed for the laws sake, and not for their owne' (H3v). The suggestion that no secular ruler possesses any inherent authority would not be out of place in Ponet, Knox or Goodman. After this claim, consideration turns to the monarchy in England. Aylmer begins by arguing that a woman can rule better in England than anywhere else, not because women have a particular justification for ruling, but because the country is 'not a mere Monarchie, as some for lacke of consideration thinke, nor a mere Oligarchie, nor Democracie, but a rule mixte of all these'. This mixed monarchy is reflected in the constitution of 'the parliament hous' (H3r). And it is *this* institution, not the monarch, which underwrites the secular liberty of the people. Aylmer name-checks the authority of the Ephori and Senate like Ponet, and notes that

> [i]n like manner if the parliament vse their priuiledges: the King can ordein nothing without them. If he do it is his fault in vsurping it, and their follye in permitting it: wherefore in my iudgement those that in King Henry the viii dais, would not graunt him, that his proclamacions shuld haue the force of a statute, were good fathers of the country, and wurthy [sic] commendacion in defending their liberty. (H3r)

There are two important implications in this passage. One is the patriarchal assumption that a women is permitted to rule in England because she is subject to greater parliamentary checks than elsewhere. The other is the more foregoing constitutionalist claim that parliament inculcates and protects the liberties of subjects from overweening monarchs, for example Elizabeth's father Henry VIII. Even as he defends female rule, Aylmer opens up a radical front in his argument. The power of monarchs, female or otherwise, may potentially be checked.

Jordan has argued that 'Aylmer might not have conceded as much to Parliament had the monarch been a man', and while this is a fair point, it is necessary to acknowledge the claim of liberty in the passage quoted above (1990: 132; see more generally 129–32). Whatever side of the argument one came down on, the argument that monarchs are invariably poor defenders, or even active inhibitors, of the people's liberty can be seen in each of the texts under discussion. Yes it is true that for Aylmer, rebellion leads not to an increase of liberty but to its degradation (sig. O4r). He also prefers to stress the liberality inherent in being a true born Englishman, one made in the service of a broader militant Protestant argument for English national self-assertion against Catholic might.[10] Fundamentally, though, in each of the texts examined in this essay, no secular ruler should rightly be able to impede the liberty of subjects.

Ponet, Knox and especially Goodman go much further than Aylmer, stating that spiritual liberty is guaranteed by the covenant and available to men and women alike. The contemporary problem of female rule that these writers faced during the 1550s is of singular importance to the formulation of their political theology, and the claims of patriarchal misogyny are never far away. However, I have argued here for the importance of scholars examining the intertwined histories of misogyny and liberty during the early modern period. In the various accounts of biblical women rulers discussed in this essay, the spiritual freedom of subjects is a constant principle. It may be stressed more by some than by others. But the fact that this point is frequently made in relation to biblical exemplars of female authority like Deborah or Judith is significant. What these various biblical women show are the ways in which spiritual freedom can be a precursor to a more capacious – indeed radical – conception of secular liberty for subjects. It is therefore important that our histories of 'liberty before liberalism' do not neglect the central role of gender in formulating the radical political arguments of the 1550s.

Notes

1 As Christopher Hill notes, early modern political understandings of liberty were much more restrictive than many modern understandings of the term, and pertained largely to property rights: 'Libertas in medieval Latin conveys the idea of a right to exclude others from your property, your franchise. To be free of something means to enjoy exclusive rights and privileges in relation to it. The freedom of a town is a privilege, to be inherited or bought. So is a freehold estate. Freeholders and freemen are a minority in their communities. The Parliamentary franchise is a privilege attached to particular types of property. The "liberties of the House of Commons" were peculiar privileges enjoyed by members such as immunity from arrest, the right to uncensored discussion etc. ... The problem of early seventeenth-century politics was to decide where the king's rights and privileges ended and those of his free subjects began: the majority of the population did not come into it' (1974: 48).

2 The conditional phrasing is necessary because Skinner notes that 'we need to exercise a certain caution in speaking about the direct impact of the *Confession* ... some of the earliest Calvinist revolutionaries took their statements of the constitutional theory of resistance directly from the debates of the 1530s, rather than relying on the *Confession* as an intermediate source' (2005: 209. See more generally 206–24.)

3 Tyndale similarly criticises those princes who 'geve libertie or license vnto the spiritualitie to sinne vnpunished', saying that such rulers will be damned (1528: Fol. 34r).

4 But see Skinner (2005: 214). See more generally Greaves (1982).

5 Important recent work on these writers includes the following: Danner (1981); Jordan (1987); Felch (1995); Richards (1997); and Bowman (2007–2008).

6 It would be possible to argue that since the concept of universal human rights, one that encompasses all genders, races, and creeds, is a concept fundamentally alien to early modern political thought, it is wrong to criticise Skinner (2005) and Witte (2010) for not stressing more forcefully the fact that the most radical writings of the era advance a limited, patriarchally oriented understanding of Christian liberty.

7 Skinner notes that the issues of colonisation and slavery are not 'of great concern to the writers I am considering', playing a much more active role for eighteenth-century defenders of the American colonies (1998: 50). Ponet's text therefore offers an interesting example of a much earlier use of this argument.

8 For details on the appropriation of Eve across the seventeenth century see Hodgson's essay in this volume (Chapter 3).

9 See the passage at sig. O4r, where Aylmer (1559) likens Elizabeth to Deborah and Judith.

10 England is for Alymer a 'paradise' (1559: sig. P4r) of liberality, especially when compared with its foreign neighbours. It is in the course of making this argument that Aylmer makes his famous claim (actually in a marginal note rather than in the text) that 'God is English' (sig. Q1v.).

References

Agamben, G. (1988) *Homo Sacer*. Trans. Daniel Heller-Roazen. Chicago: University of Chicago Press.

Aylmer, J. (1559) *An harborowe for faithfull And trewe subiectes*. Strasburg [London]: John Day.

Bowman, G. (2007–2008) 'Early Calvinist Resistance Theory: New Perspectives on an Old Label.' *Journal of Law and Religion*, 23.1: 309–19.

Braddick, M.J. (2000) *State Formation in Early Modern England c.1550–1700*. Cambridge: Cambridge University Press.

Calvin, J. (1961) *Institutes of the Christian Religion*, Vol. 1. Ed. J.T. McNeill. Trans. F.L. Battles. London: Westminster.

Colclough, D. (2009) *Freedom of Speech in Early Stuart England*. Cambridge: Cambridge University Press.

Danner, D. (1981) 'Resistance and the Ungodly Magistrate in the Sixteenth Century: The Marian Exiles.' *Journal of the American Academy of Religion*, 49.3: 471–81.

Dolan, F.E. (1999) *Whores of Babylon: Catholicism, Gender and Seventeenth-Century Print Culture*. Ithaca, NY: Cornell University Press.

Felch, S.M. (1995) 'The Rhetoric of Biblical Authority: John Knox and the Question of Women.' *The Sixteenth Century Journal*, 26.4: 805–22.

Goodman, C. (2004 [1558]) *How Superior Powers Ought to be Obeyed.* Whitefish, MT: Kessinger Publishing.

Greaves, R.L. (1982) 'Concepts of Obedience in Late Tudor England: Conflicting Perspectives.' *Journal of British Studies*, 22.1: 23–34.

Hill, C. (1974) *The Century of Revolution 1603–1714.* London: Sphere Books.

Jordan, C. (1987) 'Woman's Rule in Sixteenth-Century British Political Thought.' *Renaissance Quarterly*, 40.3: 421–51.

——— . (1990) *Renaissance Feminism: Literary Texts and Political Models.* Ithaca, NY: Cornell University Press.

Knox, J. (1994) '*The first blast of the trumpet against the monstrous regiment of women.*' *On rebellion.* Ed. R.A. Mason. Cambridge: Cambridge University Press.

Luther, M. (1989) 'The Freedom of a Christian.' *Martin Luther's Basic Theological Writings.* Ed. T.F. Lull. Minneapolis, MN: Fortress Press.

Milton, A. (2002) *Catholic and Reformed: The Roman and Protestant Churches in English Protestant Thought, 1600–1640.* Cambridge: Cambridge University Press.

Osherow, M. (2009) *Biblical Women's Voices in Early Modern England.* Aldershot: Ashgate.

Pocock, J.G.A (1987) *The Ancient Constitution and the Feudal Law: A Study of English Historical Thought in the Seventeenth Century.* Cambridge: Cambridge University Press.

Ponet, J. (1556) *A short treatise of politike power.* Strasbourg: The heirs of W. Köpfel.

Richards, J.M. (1997) '"To Promote a Woman to Beare Rule:" Talking of Queens in Mid-Tudor England.' *Sixteenth Century Journal*, 28.1: 101–21.

Shagan, E. (2011) *The Rule of Moderation: Violence, Religion and the Politics of Restraint in Early Modern Europe.* Cambridge: Cambridge University Press.

Skinner, Q. (1998) *Liberty before Liberalism.* Cambridge: Cambridge University Press.

——— . (2005) *The Foundations of Modern Political Thought: Vol. 2, The Age of Reformation.* Cambridge: Cambridge University Press.

Tumbleson, R.D. (1998) *Catholicism in the English Protestant Imagination: Nationalism, Religion, and Literature, 1600–1745.* Cambridge: Cambridge University Press.

Tyndale, W. (1528) *The obedie[n]ce of a Christen man and how Christe[n] rulers ought to governe.* Antwerp: J. Hoochstraten.

Weimann, R. (1996) *Authority and Representation in Early Modern Discourse.* Ed. David Hillman. Baltimore, MD: Johns Hopkins University Press.

Witte, J. Jr. (2010) *The Reformation of Rights: Law, Religion, and Human Rights in Early Modern Calvinism.* Cambridge: Cambridge University Press.

5

Wives, fears and foreskins: early modern reproach of Zipporah and Michal

Michele Osherow

Early modern readings of biblical women are as full of variety and contradiction as the Bible itself. Margaret Fell, Aemilia Lanyer, Rachel Speght, John Aylmer and many others use biblical examples to great effect to promote women's abilities to speak, preach and rule. And yet, biblical heroines are subject to as much early modern critique as they are to praise; even those figures clearly celebrated in biblical narratives have their virtues undercut in more and less subtle ways: Thomas Bentley associates the prophetess Deborah with babbling speech (1582: Lampe 7, 137) and John Mayer wonders at Esther's immodest approach to Ahasverous (1647: 57). This grappling with the Bible's heroines demonstrates the period's difficulty reconciling the characters' activities with the well-recounted prescripts for chastity, silence and obedience that marked the feminine ideal.[1] Numerous – I would argue most – heroines of the Old Testament complicate the necessity of these prescribed virtues, which explains the staggering spectrum of early modern responses to these characters. And yet, this range of reading and interpretation diminishes significantly around Zipporah, the wife of Moses in Exodus, and Michal, David's first wife in 1 Samuel. These women, partners to biblical champions, engage in valiant activities in their own right, but to early modern readers their behaviours are beyond unsettling. Examining early modern reaction to these wives makes clear the boundaries restricting biblical women's heroics, even when those actions earn God's approval. Zipporah and Michal are unusual for the challenges they pose to masculinity in literal and metaphorical ways. Response to these characters indicates that the boldness of Zipporah's and Michal's engagement with male authority and the masculine body marks limits that even God, in his own good book, is unable to breach.

Though Jewish midrash unites Zipporah and Michal,[2] the two do not appear together in any biblical narrative or text. Still, they are routinely linked in early modern discourse and in consistently unflattering ways. In Bentley, Zipporah is ranked with Michal for 'their unsemlie upbraidings and bitter taunting, or chiding of their godlie husbands' (1582: Lampe 1, B2r), and elsewhere they are reprimanded for their 'waspish and shrewish disposition' (Gouge, 1622: 285). Characterisations such as these made about strong, decisive women, even those praised in the Bible's pages, are not surprising; but the general denial of these women's valour is. The severe disconnection between the Bible's mix of compassion and wonder toward these women and the early modern disparagement of them invites us to consider what distinguishes these biblical women's narratives from others. The contrast may depend upon a foreskin and the ease with which these women confront and subdue masculinity head-on.

Zipporah's behaviour sets the stage for women's engagement in nationalistic enterprises – an engagement that characterises the actions of several heroines in Exodus and in the biblical books that follow. In Genesis, women's heroism is largely marked by efforts toward, and in, motherhood, growing the Israelite people and fulfilling God's instruction to 'bring forthe frute and multiplie' (1:28).[3] Eve's declaration that she has 'obteined a man by the Lord' (4:1) signals the female empowerment earned by reproduction. (In Eve's telling, Adam is removed from the reproductive process altogether.) In Genesis, women do figure in Israel's politics but their stories show them as victims of political tensions (as with Dinah) or as objects for negotiation (as happens time and again with Sarah).[4] In the Book of Exodus this changes. Women assume more active roles in building, preserving and leading the Israelites.[5] From the outset a confederacy of women work to preserve the baby Moses: the midwives Shifra and Puah ignore Pharoah's order to kill all male Hebrew babies (1:17); Jocheved hides her son from Pharaoh's murdering officers, and later floats him down the Nile in an ark of her making (2:2–3); next, Pharoah's daughter draws baby Moses from the water and decides to raise him as her son. This princess knowingly defies her father's wishes: 'This is one of the Ebrewes children', she says (v. 7). In a final display of female advantage we learn that Miriam, Moses' sister, has followed her floating baby brother and offers to find a nurse for the child (vv. 7–8), thereby uniting Jocheved with her son. Moses' early history draws our attention to women's remarkable collaborative enterprises and, despite the ways they counter male authority, these women are praised for their actions in the sixteenth and seventeenth centuries. Jocheved, Pharaoh's daughter and Miriam all appear in William Barton's *A catalogue of virtuous women recorded in the Old & New Testament* (1671: 3), and Thomas Bell affirms that Shifra and Puah 'sinned not in that they feared God, and disobeyed y kings wicked commandement' (1609: 132), though he cautions elsewhere that neither were the midwives rewarded 'for the telling of a leasing' (1596: 55). Biblical commentary may at times wrestle with the extent of these Exodus women's deceptions, but by and large efforts on the young Moses' behalf are considered efforts well spent.

Moses' reliance on resourceful women extends beyond his infancy and his final feminine defender is as effective as she is unusual. Moses meets his wife Zipporah by a well in the familiar betrothal type scene established in Genesis.[6] He defends and assists her and her sisters, waters their flock, and Zipporah's father, a Midianite priest, rewards Moses with Zipporah's hand (Exodus 2:21).

Neither Zipporah's introduction nor her Midianite ties prepare us for the stunning method by which she defends Moses and exhibits the unbridled heroism that characterises the earlier Exodus women's display. As Moses began his journey back to Egypt to confront Pharaoh and achieve the Israelites' freedom, the Bible presents an unexpected scene:

> And as he was by the way in the ynne, the Lord met [Moses], and wolde have killed him. Then Zipporah toke a sharpe knife, and cut away the fore skinne of her sonne, and cast it at his fete, and saide, Thou *art* indede a bloodie housband unto me. So [God] departed from him. Then she said, O bloodie housband (because of the circumcision).[7] (Exo. 4:24–7)

Zipporah's action is undeniably effective; the 'so' in the English translation indicates that God's release of Moses stems from her performance. Still, early modern readers do not hesitate to charge her with corrupt and inappropriate conduct. Zipporah is consistently reprimanded for her actions, her attitude and her speech.

Zipporah's engagement in holy ritual is her first offence according to these commentaries. Bentley warns against her history being used as any kind of legitimising example: 'the mother ought not to baptise hir owne children', he writes. 'For though Zipporah circumcised hir owne sonne ... yet this was an extraordinarie and particular act in hir ... it is no generall example for another to follow' (1582: Lampe 6, 31). 'Extraordinary' is the word of choice when it comes to this woman – it appears in the Geneva gloss of the episode and in commentaries spanning the next 100 years (1560: 26v). Gervase Babington dismisses Zipporah's behaviour as 'meerely extraordinarie' (1604: 60), and in his description of a 'good, lawfull, and perfect baptisme', William Attersoll acknowledges Zipporah's history but considers it 'extraordinarie', reminding his readers 'we must live by laws, not by examples which have no warrant' (1606: 136). Zipporah's 'lawlessness' is marked by her interference in religious ceremony and by her foul influence upon Moses. It is because of her, some seventeenth-century readers say, that Moses chose to abandon the covenant established by Abraham. Richard Greenham argues that '*Moses* to please his wife did omit the Sacrament of Circumcision' (1612: 742). In William Slatyer's view, Moses was 'like to have ... died for the perversnesse of *Zipporah* his wife' (1643: 21). These readers resist assigning Moses responsibility for neglecting to circumcise his son – a grievous oversight by Israel's redeemer. 'It seems probable', writes Arthur Jackson, '(especially if we observe how his wife ... carries her self) that Moses had hitherto neglected the circumcising of this his youngest sonne because she was so highly displeased at the circumcising of the first' (1643: 138–9); another remarks, 'because [Moses] followed the ... Inclination of *his wife* ... he fell into this great danger' (Patrick, 1697: 76).

Zipporah's assumed disapproval of circumcision was made on the basis that she is a Midianite and Moses 'was loath to displease [her]' (Palmer, 1644: 7).

However, at this point in the biblical narrative Midianites are not Israel's enemy, nor is there reason to believe they would so object to the rite. In fact, the Midianite line stems from Abraham with whom the covenant had been established. It is more than likely that the original Midian (Abraham's fourth son by Keturah [Genesis 25:2]) was himself circumcised. The land of Midian is presented as a place of refuge for Moses; the priest Jethro embraces him literally and figuratively. When Moses and his father-in-law are reunited in Exodus 18 the men 'kiss' (v. 7) and Jethro praises and makes sacrifices to Moses' God (vv. 9–12). Although the Israelites' relationship with the Midianites will become more hostile in subsequent books, even the threat of future discord is no assurance of Zipporah's aversion to Israelite people or rituals. The Hebrew Bible features numerous foreign women who choose allegiance to Hebrew politics and practices over those of their own nations: Ruth, a Moabite, performed the duties of a loyal daughter of Israel and was great-grandmother to King David; Rahab and Jael similarly serve the Israelite cause, though their national identities would lead us to expect them to behave otherwise.[8] The point is, that while early modern commentary presents Zipporah as a barrier to Moses' fulfilling of the covenant and as one not 'thorowly acquainted with this mystery' (Willet, 1612: 45), it is she who introduces circumcision into the Book of Exodus and indicates women's readiness to enter into contracts with God.

Zipporah's venture into religious ceremony may be troublesome, but surely it is her 'physical intervention at the very locus of maleness' (Osherow, 2009: 50) that early modern commentators find so unsettling. Though early modern Christians abandoned the practice of outward circumcision in favour of an inward circumcision – a circumcising of the 'heart' or 'spirit' rather than of the flesh (Edwards, 1699: 142) – there remained a kind of uneasy fascination with the practice. Ancient, early modern and contemporary texts depict circumcision as an act symbolic of castration; it is presented even in the Bible's pages as an emasculating practice.[9] Though Zipporah circumcises her son and not her husband, her act signals Moses' failure and his desertion of masculine duty. Her language is accusatory and her gesture intense. Her aggressive behaviour is faulted by Attersoll: 'it is most probable and likely ... that Zipporah wanting discretion but not presumption, through her boldness and hastiness prevented Moses, and adventured on the worke, before the prophet could prepare himself unto it' (1606: 136). Zipporah is faulted time and again for being 'rash' (Leigh, 1654: 661) and her action is framed as usurping Moses' authority. William Shewen writes, 'you see she makes nothing to invade the Office of the Man, and that in the highest Act too' (1696: 123–4). She is accused of doing the deed 'in haste, that she might prevent her husband' (Scrivener, 1674: 201) and of performing 'a duty which belonged to her husband, and not ... to her' (Gouge, 1622: 306). In a more generous view, Thomas Weld argues that though Zipporah had 'no grounds ... to have circumcised her sonne', the upshot of her action was legitimate (1644: 57). Such a reading contrasts the more common reproof that the circumcision 'was not well done of Zipporah, because it was the office of a man to doe that she did' (Greenham, 1612: 669).

But we might read the biblical narrative as one that prepares us for a Moses who distances himself both from mannish displays and from the commitment represented by the covenant. When Moses confronts God in a burning bush he famously tries to dodge divine instruction to serve as the Israelites' redeemer (4:13). Among his self-effacing remarks is Moses' claim that he is *aral sfatayim*, one of 'vncircumcised lippes' (6:30). The Geneva glosses this statement as an example of Moses' 'disobedience' and uses his reluctance to demonstrate that Moses and the Israelites' 'deliverance came onely of Gods free mercie' (1560: 27v). Moses' odd description may reinforce his prior assertion that he is 'slow of speache and slow of tongue' (4:10) but it also signifies speech that is impure which perhaps accounts for Moses' repeated challenges and questions that so anger God (4:14). Still, Moses' description is likely more peculiar to us than it would have been to an early modern audience. To characterise something as 'uncircumcised' is to indicate that it bears the traces of original sin. The Geneva gloss of the covenant's introduction in Genesis explains, 'that privie part is circumcised to shew that all that is begotten of man is corrupt and must be mortified *Rom. 4.11*' (1560: 7r). Seventeenth-century definitions of 'mortify' include 'to cause to feel humiliated' (*OED*, 2013), which is what Zipporah conceivably does and, as Moses himself implies, what may be necessary.

The more we understand about early modern Christian perception of circumcision, the more we appreciate how disruptive Zipporah's behaviour is; for a female to engage in this 'mortification' of a male member suggests dominance over it. According to the *OED*, the primary definition of 'mortify' from the fourteenth through the seventeenth centuries was 'to deprive of life; to kill, put to death … to render insensible'; also 'to destroy or inhibit the vitality, vigour, activity, or potency of'; and later, 'to soften or tenderise' (*OED*, 2013). It will come as little surprise that in the sixteenth and seventeenth centuries women were not permitted to perform or even to attend circumcisions. Female participation was required after the ritual, however; the child's removed foreskin became the property of the mother and was to be delivered to her immediately following the ceremony (Buxtorf 1657: 51).[10] The foreskin's intended transfer underscores Zipporah's emasculating show: in throwing the fleshy bit at Moses' feet she accentuates her role as ceremonial agent and stresses his feminised position. Possible readings of this episode become even more bizarre and sexually complicated when we consider that the Hebrew term used here for feet (*regelav*, his feet, from *reglaim*) is a frequent biblical euphemism for genitals.[11] Zipporah's peculiar action is accompanied by equally peculiar language: it is when she attends to Moses' 'feet' that she refers to him as her 'bloodie housband'.

The association of blood with genitalia is perhaps the most stunning turn in Zipporah's repeated feminisation of Moses. References to menstruation appear in at least four books of the Hebrew Bible and these verses call attention more often than not to female impurity. Curious among these are the warnings directed to men because the uncleanness of women's genital blood is, biblically speaking, infectious:

> The man also that lieth with a woman hauing her disease & vncouereth her shame, & openeth her fountaine, and she open the fountaine her blood, thei shalbe euen both cut of from among their people ... Whosoever also toucheth her bed, shal wash his clothes, and wash him selfe with water, & shal be vncleane vnto the euen. And whosoeuer toucheth anie thi[n]g that she sate vpon, shal wash his clothes, & wash himself in water, and shalbe vncleane. (Lev. 20:18; 15:21–2)

The sort of gendered contamination described in Leviticus and elsewhere is wholly inverted in Zipporah's narrative.[12] Here, Moses is the bloody partner. The accusation Zipporah levels at her husband indicates her own infection by the blood she ascribes to him. It is a fair remark. The blood Zipporah confronts at the inn is just the beginning of the bloody events that will characterise Exodus.[13] We see it in the first of the plagues God visits on the Egyptians: turning water into blood. Blood reappears in the final and most severe of the plagues: the killing of the first-born. And this blood is a sign not only to Egyptian victims, but also to the Israelites who are instructed to mark their houses with it: God explains, 'and the blood shalbe a token for you' (12:13). Zipporah perceives and announces this token before God or anyone is alerted to it.

Zipporah's bloody engagement marks a shift in the Bible's portrayal of female valour. The episode by the inn underscores the transition from women's life-giving heroism in Genesis to their more violent and life-preserving acts in Exodus. Zipporah's deed, surely, is a show of wifely, national and religious duty but it is a kind hitherto unseen in the Bible. Subsequent biblical heroines who engage in violent acts direct their potency against Israel's enemies rather than at its heroes and husbands. Still, it is as a *wife* that Zipporah is identified and she underscores repeatedly that role by referring to Moses as her *chatan damim*, translated in the Tyndale, Geneva and King James Bibles as 'bloody husband'. As early modern commentators note, however, the Hebrew word *chatan* is actually closer in meaning to 'bridegroom' indicating that Zipporah's commitment to bloody engagement came with her initial vow to Moses (see Buddle, 1609: 5 and Helmont, 1685: 126). The use of *chatan* in this passage is noteworthy, too, because it appears only once prior to this episode in another narrative linking circumcision to violence when, in Genesis 34, Jacob's sons Simeon and Levi avenge their sister Dinah's rape. The brothers murder the rapist Shechem, and all the men in his community, while they are recovering from the circumcisions they have undergone in order to intermarry with Jacob's clan. Early modern commentary faults Jacob's sons for manipulating the covenant for vengeful purposes and notes Jacob's decline as a result of his sons' behaviour.[14] But unlike Simeon and Levi's enforcement of the rite, Zipporah's execution of it saves a life and appeases God. Moreover, the control she demonstrates over the male sexual organ – the source of violence in the Genesis narrative – repairs Dinah's limited agency both against her assailant-turned-bridegroom and against her brothers.

Zipporah's success is unquestioned in the biblical narrative and there are early modern readers who recognise the importance of her victory and acknowledge that, given the choice between her husband's death and her son's circumcision 'of two evills, she chuse the lesse' (Kellett, 1641: 88). Richard Hooker writes that Zipporah's circumcision of her son was 'a thing necessary at that time for her to do ... considering how *Moses*, because himself had not done it sooner, was therefore stricken by the hand of God' (1666: 240). We might wonder how those less forgiving reckon their condemnations of Zipporah's act with God's apparent approval. Such commentators often fall back on God's indulgences as a way of explaining the discrepancy between their judgement and his. There is the reminder, too, that Zipporah's lack of punishment in this world does not preclude retribution in the next: Zipporah is referenced to explain 'sins of toleration' (Scrivener, 1674: 201): '[Zipporah] ... Having no calling to doe that which shee did ... circumcised her sonne ... And yet because this fact was some manner of obedience ... God accepted the same ... and for that deferred a temporal punishment' (Perkins, 1606: 28–9). But even if God chooses to defer a penalty, early modern readers forbid Zipporah's husband to do so and much is made of the fact that Zipporah and her sons set off with Moses toward Egypt but do not actually accompany him there. Bentley writes that Moses 'seeing the great impaicence of his wife Zipporah, fear[s] ... she would be a great hinderance to his vocation' (1582: Lampe 6, 259). Greenham uses her dismissal as a warning to wives: '*Zipporah* became troublesome to *Moses* ... he left her with his fa[ther] for a time: so she depriued her selfe, by her disobedience, of his comfortable presence. [This] ought to teach wiues euer to helpe, & not to hinder their husbands' (1612: 743). In Nicholas Fontaine's view, Moses dismissed her from his company because '*Zipporah* grew outragious' (1699: 363), while Giovanni Diodati credits the decision to Zipporah's 'speaking, and thinking evill of the Sacrament' (1643: 41).

Punishment is warranted in early modern readers' estimations primarily because of the bold way Zipporah engages with Moses in deed and in word – to put it plainly, they don't like the way she talks to her husband. Women's bold speech, a perpetual problem for the early modern English, is an indisputable part of Zipporah's history. Gouge refers to her 'bitter and rayling speech' (1630: 23); Babington notes her 'bitter words ... that ... shewe but what speeches are often giuen by women that haue their tongues a little too much at liberty' (1604: 60). Josias Shute implies that Zipporah's tongue functions much the same as her knife, writing that she 'sharpeneth her tongue against her husband'; he frowns on her repeated use of the tool: 'There was too much bitterness in that speech of *Zipporah* to *Moses*, Exo. 4.25. *Surely a bloody husband thou art unto me:* and she goeth over it again: (for the clack, when it is once a going, doth not soon cease' (1649: 67). Similarly, William Thomas implies Zipporah's skilled use of weaponry describing 'the wound of [her] Tongue being more invenom'd, than of the Sword' (1678: 15), and Francis Meres comments on her 'cruell and bloody speaches' (1597: 17r).

For her bloody accusation, Zipporah is featured prominently in the section on 'anger and forwardness' in *Monument of Matrons*, and is given similar attention elsewhere in Bentley's text. Shewen refers to her as a '*Virago*' (1696: 124) and to Thomas Grantham she appears 'a terrible firie woman' (1641: 2). Nicholas Byfield stands out as one who does allow Zipporah's name on a list of holy women but this appears to be in spite of her behaviour in Exodus 4. She is held out as a cautionary example for wives:

> there is no example of a godly woman that did *customarily* live in the sinne of frowardnesse or rebellion against her husband: the instance of *Zipporah* is but of one onely fact, and the errour seemes to be as much in her judgement as in her affections. And this doctrine should light verie heavie upon many wives ... and compell them to reforme their hearts and behaviours in their carriage towards their husbands: for this Text doth import, that they want holinesse that are not subject to their husbands, and live in customarie frowardnesse and unquietnesse. (1637: 523)

In Bentley, Zipporah is listed among wives 'wicked and foolishe', described as 'rebellious ... unfaithful and disobedient' (1582: Lampe 6, 91, 98). Others call her 'vnlawfull' (Trelcatius, 1610: 351), 'deceitfull' (Attersoll, 1606: 136), 'perverse' (Slayter, 1643: 15), 'foolish' (Trelcatius, 1610: 351), 'angry' (Trelcatius, 1610: 351) 'peevish' (Marvell, 1681: 68), 'pettish' (Mason, 1626: 25), 'frantick' (Byam, 1675: 5), and 'hot' (R.A, 1662: 115). Zipporah, like Michal to follow, is presented as a foul wife who appears in stark contrast to her holy husband: 'what a sad difference there is between the holy *Law of God*, and our *base hearts*. His Law pure, we impure, that spirituall, we carnall. It was an uneven and uncomfortable match as ... between beautifull *Moses*, and black *Zipporah*' (Sheffield, 1659: 215). Moses' access to divine strength is implied by Joseph Hall who counsels, 'he had need to be more than a man that hath a Zipporah in his bosoome, and would have *true zeale* in his hart' (1612: 310). Zachary Bogan goes so far as to equate Moses' choice of Zipporah to Samson's choice of a Philistine and argues that 'marrying a wicked person, especially an Idolater ... results in strife and contention' (1653: 381).

The association of a wife with strife, contention and idolatry also surrounds Michal. Certainly, this wife stands in contrast to her husband but primarily for what biblical scholar Robert Alter describes as David's inaccessible interiority (2011: 119). Michal's emotional responses, on the other hand, are laid plain and propel her into action. After David's great victory against Goliath the narrative tells us 'Then Michal Sauls daughter loued Dauid' (1 Samuel 18:20). We read this twice within a few verses (vv. 20, 28); it is significant because it is the only instance in the Hebrew Bible in which we are told, specifically, that a woman loves a man. The explicit statement of romantic love recalls Jacob's love for Rachel in Genesis 29:18. Thus, Michal's affection sets her in the ranks of the heroic founder of Israel and prepares us for the demonstration of strength and cunning that marks both lovers' histories.

Michal's union with her beloved is not uncomplicated. Her affection is unrequited so far as we can tell. Instead, the narrative hints at David's attraction to status as he responds to the news of Michal's esteem by asking: 'Semeth it to you a light thing to be a Kings sonne in law ...?' (1 Sam. 18:23). Saul decides to use Michal 'as a snare' to David (v. 21). He tells David that he 'desireth no dowrie' (v. 25), but the narrative demonstrates that Saul and David deal in a currency of masculinity: the King asks his would-be son-in-law to deliver him a 'hundreth foreskinnes of the Philistines' (v. 25). This assemblage of foreskins goes beyond mass circumcision or conversion; Saul likes his Philistines dead. To win Michal, David must meet Saul's challenge to murder and castrate the enemy. And David does, delivering twice the number of foreskins required (v. 27). This is among the first of many masculine displays in which Saul and David vie for authority and affection from God and man. But this early example is unusual because it is triggered by a woman's desire. The fleshy denomination that constitutes Michal's bride-price extends the show of masculinity to her because the fulfilment of her love, accomplished through marriage, requires the destruction and figurative castration of 100 men. Put another way, those 100 foreskins are necessary not only to satisfy Saul, but also to satisfy Michal. David's delivering 200 foreskins signals his own uber-masculine force and at the same time sets Michal's value at a higher rate, one appraised in terms of male vulnerability.

The biblical narrative will not allow us to forget that gruesome fee or the gain that came of it. 'Deliver me my wife Michal,' David will say later in 2 Samuel, 'which I married for an hundreth foreskinnes of the Philistins' (3:14). Early modern readers do not overlook the rate of purchase either, and there are numerous explicit references to David's having 'bought' Michal 'with two hundredth foreskinnes of the philistines' (Willet, 1612: 286). Moses Vauts reads David's engagement as a sign of his ambition (1650: 62) but more common is the tendency to romanticise David's investment with 'the very great number of Foreskins' read as proof of the 'Regard [David] had for his Soverign, and [also] the Love he had for his Mistress' (Fontaine, 1699: 117). The Reverend John Murcot is extreme in this: 'Indeed *David* bought *Michal* at a dear rate, by the death of the Philistins, and afterward *two hundred foreskins of the Philistins*, it pleased him well ... *if David must have parted with his life for her*' (1657: 42).

This depiction of Michal in the narrative as one whose value is fixed to the mortification of maleness gives way to a series of distortions between masculine and feminine along the lines of those Zipporah provokes in Exodus 4. Michal's potency contrasts with male weakness and her interactions with men consistently have an effeminising effect. Though she wields no knife or stone, Michal, like Zipporah, inflicts injury to preserve her husband. In 1 Samuel 19 she learns of Saul's plan to kill David. She orchestrates her husband's escape, warning him that: 'If thou saue not thy self this night, tomorrowe thou shalt be slaine' (v. 11). The narrative details her resourcefulness: 'So Michal let David downe through a window: and he went, and fled, and escaped' (v. 12). In this episode, Michal's is the only voice heard; the narrative does not allow David a voice even to utter thanks. The majority of active verbs are hers. She directs the action while David responds obediently and in silence. After David's flight, her protection continues: 'Then Michal tooke an image and layed it in the bed, and put a pillowe stuffed with goates *heere* under the head of it, and couered it with a cloth. And when Saul sent messengers to take Dauid, she said, He is sicke' (vv. 13–14). Later, Saul demands that David be brought to him – sickbed and all – and then is Michal's deception revealed. She defends herself, as Stephen Nye notes, much as the Egyptian midwives of Exodus do, with '*Falsities* that do good to some, without doing hurt to others' (1698: 37). In both instances the women tell a king what he is prone to believe. Michal says, 'He said vnto me, Let me go or els I wil kil thee' (v. 17). Michal's effective potency is emphasised all the more because her success immediately follows her brother Jonathan's imperfect attempts to secure David's safety.

There is among early modern readers some acknowledgement of the good turn Michal does David and she is praised for preserving David at her own peril (Shute, 1649: 17). In his annotations on the Psalms, Jackson reads Psalm 59 as a response to this scene pointing out that David 'ascribes his escape to God, though it were by the device of his wife Michal' (1658: 499). Still, any praise for Michal is usually accompanied by a disclaimer: 'Michal [did well] in suffering her husband David to escape out of the hands of ... her father,' writes Gouge, though 'I justife not her manner of carrying the matter, with untruths, and false tales' (1622: 467). Roger Williams elaborates on Michal's faulty conduct:

> Michal is to be excused: as in vsing such meanes whereby ... that her husband might escape ... But in some things, shee neither deserueth commendation, nor yet can be excused: as in laying such an imputation vpon her husband, as though he threatned to kill her: for shee here three waies offended: 1. in telling an vntruth: 2. in raising a slaunder vpon Dauid, which might breede a great offence and scandall: 3. in her feare and timorousnesse, which was the cause of all this. (1652: 197–8)

Most critics recognise the benefit of Michal's assistance of David, but echo John Trapp's opinion that she 'had no great goodnesse in her' (1657: 144).[15] Salvation at this woman's hand is fraught. 'Shall I betake me to Michals wile?' asks Simon Birckbek; 'Michals wile is not for my saftey' (1647: 61–2). Though Michal rallies for her husband and not her father, her actions link her to the story's villain nonetheless: 'Who but Saul's daughter could have adventured this?' (Birckbek, 1647: 62). Michal is described as 'cunning' (Ness, 1696: 287) and as 'subtile' (Hall, 1623: 29) – the latter a particularly loaded description because it is first used in the Bible to describe the serpent in Genesis 3:1. Michal's association with subtlety potentially overshadows defences made on her behalf. Christopher Ness writes, 'her wily Wit in *deceiving deceivers* ought not too rashly to be condemned' (1696: 287), but then directly ascribes to her a '*Character* wherewith the grandest Cheats are branded' (287). Wavering between praise and condemnation, the author ultimately is unable to excuse Michal because of the lies told about David to her father 'wherein she ... notoriously scandaliz'd so good a Man' (287). Michal's 'shifts of wit' (286) are unnerving even to potential champions of her actions because she is able to lie with ease and manipulate men both good and bad; Ralph Brownrig notes that she turns men into puppets (1664: 167). In 1 Samuel 19, men do exactly as Michal directs and expects; Saul complains, 'Why hast thou mocked me so' (v. 17).

The King's response to his daughter's betrayal is to marry her elsewhere. The narrative points to the error of it by continuing to refer to Michal as 'Davids wife' (1 Sam. 25:44). Early modern readings echo charges of sin and injustice and include Michal in books such as *God's judgments against whoring* (1697). The anonymous author recognises that the problematic second marriage was Saul's doing; nonetheless, Michal's is considered 'one of the most remarkable acts of uncleanness that are to be found in sacred history' (t.p.). Henry Ainsworth describes Michal as one who 'play[s] the whore in an other mans house' (1620: 165). Reproach of the woman makes mention of her 'secret Flame' (Killigrew, 1698: 28) and faults her for 'giuing consent to be maried vnto an other' (Willet, 1612: 287). This second marriage also serves as an occasion to recall those abundant foreskins, perhaps to reassert David's masculinity though he is being cuckolded: 'David ... killed two hundred and tendered their Foreskins [as] a Dowry for *Michal*,' writes Thomas Fuller, 'And what injustice was it that he that paid her dowry double [and] should enjoy her but halfe?' (1650: 219).

There is no mention of a dowry paid by Phaltiel, but the relationship came at a cost. After Saul's death and the decline of his house in 2 Samuel 3, the new King David demands Michal's return and the narrative describes the episode: '[Saul's son] Ish-boshet sent, and toke her from her housband, Phaltiel the sonne of Laish. And her housband went with her, and came weping behind her, vnto Bahurim: then said Abner vnto him, Go, & returne. So he returned' (2 Sam. 3:15–16). Phaltiel's emotional display points to Michal's feminising effect on the men around her, particularly in this episode which stands as the only example in the Hebrew Bible of a man crying for a woman. Phaltiel's affection might appear to be a tribute to Michal – after all, why weep for an unworthy wife? – but early modern readings will not have it so. These fault Phaltiel for his fondness and use the episode to illustrate man's irrepressible attraction to corruption:

'Truly as *Phaltiel* parted with his wife *Michal* ... so unregenerate men part with their sins' (Swinnock, 1661: 104). Francis Rous connects Phaltiel more directly to desire, writing that 'even then will lust come weeping after the soule, like the false husband of Michal: hee will raise up in her remembrance the images of grosse and filthy pleasure ... [A] cruell pitty it is, when the soule pitties her owne murtherer and not her owne murther' (1631: 36–7). Phaltiel's sorrow is regarded as a show of weakness; Fuller insists that, 'all Phaltiel's tears move no pity of mine' (1650: 219). The husband's behaviour leads Oliver Heywood to liken him to 'a child follow[ing] his departing Father' (1683: 25).

Michal does appear like a father – her own – in her final scene in 2 Samuel 6. The narrative identifies her as Saul's daughter and she functions as a stand-in for the bitter, defeated, first king of Israel. The narrative indicates that she watches David through Saul's eyes: 'and Michal, Saul's daughter, loked through a window and saw King David leape and daunce before the Lord and she despised him in her heart' (2 Sam. 6:16). The love with which Michal entered the biblical narrative is replaced by her father's loathing. Her position at a window frames her distance from her husband and paradoxically recalls her earlier support. Michal approaches David in order to mock him: 'O how glorious was the King of Israel this day which was vncovered to day in the eyes of the maidens of his seruants, as a fool vncoverth him selfe' (v. 20). Michal's sarcasm and derision remind us that David is not of royal stock and her bitterness suggests her understanding of his celebration to include rejoicing over the defeat of her family. David's response confirms this: 'It *was* before the Lord, which chose me rather then thy father, and all his house, and commanded me to be ruler ouer all the people of the Lord, *even* ouer Israel' (2 Sam. 6:21–2). David's language, along with his earlier demand for Michal's return, emphasises the change in leadership from Saul's House to David's. The chapter closes: 'Therefore Michal the daughter of Saul had no childe vnto the day of her death' (v. 23). This conclusion to the narrative may appear to highlight Michal's feminine position through denial of her sexual and maternal potential, but it also suggests that she maintains her masculine presence – that she continues to represent Saul – in this closing. Michal's barrenness is presented as a punishment for a troublesome wife, but it operates even more deliberately within the narrative to confirm the devastation of Saul's line.[16]

There is a slew of charges levelled at Michal on the basis of this scene including ignorance because she 'was not able to comprehend the motions of Gods spirite' (Bentley, 1582: Lampe 6: 208–9), and sinfulness: her 'carnall eyes' are 'incompetent judges of spirituall actions' (Fuller, 1650: 304). Churchmen refer to her behaviour to illustrate a general suspicion toward the faithful: 'Thus you see what thoughts men-of-the-world have of such who fear God ... we fools and madmen ... as Michal did David, they despise them in their heart ... but with what unspeakable glory doth God honour them' (Burgess, 1658: 483).

Richard Younge uses the example of Michal's pride to educate: 'Until we be humble our selves, we are like *Michal*, who mocked *David* for his humility, and thought him a *fool*' (1660: 15). But it is as a defective wife for which Michal is most often condemned. Gouge refers to her in excess in his *Of domesticall duties eight treatises.* Her example warns women against 'an impious and envious disposition' (1622: 245). He accuses her of perversion, and of being vile and conceited (276–7). Michal's shame, as with Zipporah's, is amplified by verbal indulgences. William Strong calls her a 'scoffer' (1678: 11). John Paterson refers to her as a 'vayne precise, hypocriticall scold' (1660: 16); several times she is accused of 'frumping' (Mornay, 1599: 72; Featley, 1640: 719), 'flouting' (Slater, 1690: C2v) and 'unreverent upbraiding' (Guild, 1659: 122). There is little tolerance for mocking wives in these commentaries: 'she uttered most unreverend and vile speeches to [David], even to his face … a wife is rightly informed of a husbands superiority … it is very needful that her heart … be accordingly seasoned with the salt of good respect and high esteeme' (Gouge, 1622: 275). But by 2 Samuel, Michal's esteem is spent; her bitter speech indicative of a more bitter heart: '[Michal] uttereth her contempt by the speeches of her mouth, wherein we see Where Satan and sinne first beginnes: towit, at the spring and root of the heart, to poyson the same' (Guild, 1659: 122).

There is no need among early modern readers to indulge in punitive fantasies for Michal as they did for Zipporah. The penalty is clear: 'perpetual barrenness' (Fuller, 1650: 304). Lewis Stuckley uses Michal's history to direct women toward their obligations: 'Remember *Michal, She despised her Husband in her heart* … and she had no Child unto the day of her death. God took the Husband's part, and put a remark of displeasure upon … her sauciness. *The married Woman should care (study) to please her Husband,* by her attire, behaviour, words' (1667: 281). Michal's barrenness – the greatest curse for biblical women – is attributed in commentary to God's will, David's will or both. 'God took the matter in hand,' writes Fuller, 'so … that far in the future, Michal's daughter should never mock her husband' (1650: 304).[17] Nicholas Fontaine applauds God's punishment so '*That [Michal] might not trouble the World … with her proud Breed*' (1699: 117). Bogan sees her barrenness as David's doing: 'she were no longer worthy to bee called the wife of King David', therefore 'David never after that time us'd her as his wife' (1653: 426–7).

Michal's inability to recognise the grace to which David responds is foreshadowed, readers claim, in the earlier episode in 1 Samuel 19. Michal's distraction of Saul's officers, through use of a ready idol *(teraph)*, is troubling to many and frequent accusations of idolatry are levelled at her: John Edwards suggests that 'David's Wife, kept this piece of Idolatry in her House, to consult with upon occasion' (1692: 55).[18] The idol ties her to false religion (Williams, 1652: 90); her *teraphim* are described by Thomas Goodwin as the type used 'to consult with … as with *Oracles*, concerning things for the present vnknowne, or future to come'

(1625: 210). (Of course, had Michal engaged in such idol practice we would expect her story to have ended differently.) Idolatry is, to be sure, a weakness of Michal's but one that shows itself best in her attraction to David. That valiant son of Jesse is the closest one gets to a flesh-and-blood idol in the Hebrew Bible: he slays giants and writes and performs his own songs. The narrative itself toys with this representation. We learn that David wears a linen ephod in his celebration before the Ark (2 Sam. 6:14); the term here refers to a priestly garment but is also used in the Book of Judges to refer to actual idols (*teraphim*) (8:26–7, 17:5). In Michal's calling attention to David's ephod we are again directed to examine the male body for marks of devotion.

Both Zipporah and Michal observe male bodies and they affect them for the better. Their preservation of their husbands is unconventional; so too are the narratives in which their defences appear. Zipporah did not concoct the holy covenant; that was engineered by God and Abraham. Michal wanted David; the genital souvenirs were someone else's idea. The male vulnerability at the centre of both women's stories initially appears as the result of the imprudent behaviours of male players, including kings human and divine. Nonetheless, the reputations of these biblical women suffer for their exposure to male weakness: their bold responses are understood as cause and their aid is warped into affliction. George Hutcheson observes that 'it may be the lot of very godly men, to find very heavy afflictions in their matches' and refers to Moses and David for two of three examples (1669: 274). John Norden makes a similar observation about the trials of blessed men and his examples of trying wives (described as '*disquiet, proude, sullen, tarte and taunting*') are limited to Zipporah and Michal (1626: The Epistle, n.p.). The two women are also repeatedly compared to Delilah who, rather than preserving the biblical hero with whom she engages, betrays him for eleven hundred pieces of silver (Hieron, 1613: 14; Pack, 1673: 52). William Strong showcases Michal and Zipporah to exemplify wives who 'become a snare to a mans soul' (1678: 11).

The aversion to these women exhibited in early modern English readings is not inherited from medieval Jewish commentary. Zipporah is praised in *midrash* and stories of her preservation of Moses go beyond the events of Exodus 4 (Mikva, 2012: 102). She is described as resourceful and attractive – her beauty lasting well into old age (*Midrash Tehillim*, 1875). In *Midrash Leviticus Rabbah* (2001) Michal's chastity is preserved throughout her marriage to Phaltiel, who loved her despite their lack of physical intimacy (23:10). She also has the honour of being one of the biblical heroines directly referenced (according to midrashic tradition) in Proverbs 31, the poem describing 'the woman of valour' (*Midrash Eshet Chayil* 31:23 in *Midrash Mishley*, 1893). I think both the biblical women examined in these pages merit praise. The poem describes this woman as strong (vv. 17, 25), hardworking (vv. 13, 15, 18, 27), honourable (vv. 20, 25), and skilled with her hands (vv. 13, 16, 19). It's true that neither Zipporah nor Michal have husbands who 'praiseth her', as Proverbs 31 indicates they should (v. 28), but that speaks to the men's shortcomings more than it does to their wives'. Perhaps because they have taken a cue from these imperfect-but-heroic biblical husbands, readers of the sixteenth and seventeenth centuries fail to appreciate these heroic-but-imperfect biblical wives. Instead, such a wife is called 'a peevish piece; a cold armful' – the sort about whom it is said 'Hee had better, haply, have been married to a quartan ague' (Trapp, 1649: 9). These readers would have us believe that Moses and David succeeded in spite of these wives rather than because of them, that they chose unwisely women who are 'a constant tryal' (Hutcheson, 1669: 274) and who 'forget their womenhood' (Hooker, 1666: 240). But I'll defer to the wisdom of Proverbs that alerts us to the substance of valorous women, prizes them beyond rubies, and challenges us to know them: 'judge righteously,' the poet counsels 'and she shall rejoice in time to come' (Prov. 31:9; 25 (KJV, 2010)).

Notes

1 See for example Greene's 1587 text on 'feminine perfection' in which he identifies the 'three especial virtues' intrinsic to women of quality: chastity, silence and obedience (i).

2 Michal and Zipporah are praised variously for their beauty and for their preservation of their husbands. See *Midrash Exodus Rabbah* and *Midrash Tehillim* in *Midrash Mishley* (1893: 29, 47).

3 Unless otherwise indicated, all English biblical excerpts are taken from *The Geneva Bible*, 1560 (2007).

4 For Dinah's narrative see Genesis 34; Sarah presents herself as Abraham's sister (rather than as his wife) in Genesis 12 and 20.

5 For an examination of women's remarkable contributions to nation-building at the start of Exodus, see Osherow (2009).

6 Alter identifies these encounters, particularly at wells, as betrothal type scenes. They occur throughout Genesis and are also seen in the Books of Exodus, Judges, 1 Samuel and Ruth (see Alter, 2011: 59–62).

7 Circumcision originates in Genesis 17 where God instructs Abraham that 'Every man child among you shall be circumcised … And ye shall circumcise the flesh of your foreskin; and it shall be a token of the covenant betwixt me and you' (vv. 10–11). The seriousness of this rite is emphasised because the uncircumcised male 'shall be cut off from his people' (v. 14). See *The Geneva Bible* (2007). All italics are as the original text, unless otherwise stated.

8 Ruth's association with Moab is mentioned fourteen times within the Book's four chapters. Rahab betrays the King of Jericho in order to assist Joshua's spies in Joshua 2, and Jael is identified as a Kenite in Judges 4.

9 See Genesis 34, for example, in which the newly circumcised men of Shechem are unable to defend themselves against the attack by Jacob's sons.

10 For a complete description of the ritual see Buxtorf (1657: 46–58) and Addison (1675:

60–71). Shapiro also includes descriptions of the circumcision ritual, primarily from Thomas Coryate (1996: 114–17).

11 See Judges 3:24 and 1 Samuel 24:4. Another euphemism for male genitalia is *marge-latayv* as in Ruth 3:4.

12 For additional biblical references to menstrual impurity see Lev. 15:19–30, 18:19 and Ezek. 18:6, 22:10 and 36:17.

13 Blood is immediately linked to violence in the Bible. The word blood (*dam*) first appears when God confronts Cain with his crime against Abel: 'What hast thou done? The voyce of thy brothers blood cryeth vnto me from the grounde' (Gen. 4:10).

14 Downame writes of the 'deceitful dealing' of Jacob's sons, and explains that 'They made the holy Ordinance of God a mean to compasse their wicked purpose: It is ill to deceive … in mere civil matters, but much worse to do it under pretence of Religion, for that is to joyn impiety against God, with injury to man' (1651: on Gen. 34:14, n.p.).

15 Recognition of Michal's assistance may be found in Bentley, for example, who acknowledges that David 'by [Michal's] meanes and pollicie escaped, and fled' (1582: Lampe 6, 209). Lancelot Andrewes commends Michal's loyalty to her husband over her father (1650: 240). In a poetic telling of David's history, Robert Fleming goes so far as to describe Michal as 'a sacred gift from Heaven' (1689: A4r).

16 The narrative later reveals that Jonathan's son Mepiboshet survives, but he is identi-fied specifically as being lame and is regarded as no threat to David's victory (2 Sam. 19:26).

17 The Geneva gloss indicates divine intervention explaining Michal's barrenness as 'a punishment because she mocked y servant of God' (1560: 139v).

18 Michal's use of an idol ties her to another notable, if not problematic, wife: Rachel steals her father's idols (*teraphim*) and lies to him to cover the deed (Gen. 31:19–35). Not barrenness, but an early death awaits her for this deception. Both women's engage-ment with idols is read as weakness and as sin (see Ness, 1696: 287).

References

A., R. [Alleine, R.] (1662) *The godly mans portion and sanctuary: opened, in two sermons, preached August 17 1662*. London: s.n.

Addison, L. (1675) *The present state of the Jews*. London: J.C.

Ainsworth, H. (1620) *A reply to a pretended Christian plea for the anti-Chistian Church of Rome*. Amsterdam: Giles Thorp.

Alter, R. (2011) *The Art of Biblical Narrative*. New York: Basic Books.

Andrewes, L. (1650) *The pattern of catechistical doctrine at large, or, A learned and pious exposition of the Ten Commandments*. London: Roger Norton.

Attersoll, W. (1606) *The badges of Christianity. Or, A treatise of the sacraments fully declared out of the word of God*. London: W. Iaggard.

Babington, G. (1604) *Comfortable notes vpon the bookes of Exodus and Leuiticus, as before vpon Genesis*. London: H. Lownes and T. Purfoot.

Barton, W. (1671) *A catalogue of virtuous women recorded in the Old & New Testament*. London: W. Godbid.

Bell, T. (1596) *The suruey of popery vvherein the reader may cleerely behold, not onely the origi-nall and daily incrementes of papistrie*. London: Valentine Sims.

——. (1609) *A Christian dialogue, betweene Theophilus a deformed Catholike in Rome, and Remigius a reformed Catholike in the Church of England*. London: Nicholas Okes.

Bentley, T. (1582) *The monument of matrones conteining seuen seuerall lamps of virginitie, or distinct treatises*. London: H. Denham.

Birckbek, S. (1647) *A cordiall for a heart-qualme, or, Severall heavenly comforts for all those who suffer any worldly crosse or calamity*. London: Richard Best.

Bogan, Z. (1653) *A view of the threats and punishments recorded in the Scriptures, alphabetically composed with some briefe observations upon severall texts*. Oxford: H. Hall.

Brownrig, R. (1664) *Twenty five sermons*. London: Tho. Roycroft.

Buddle, G. (1609) *A short and plaine discourse. Fully containing the vvhole doctrine of euangelicall fastes*. London: John Windet.

Burgess, A. (1658) *A treatise of original sin ... proving that it is, by pregnant texts of Scripture vindicated from false glosses*. London: s.n.

Buxtorf, J. (1657) *The Jewish synagogue, or, An historical narration of the state of the Jewes at this day dispersed over the face of the whole earth*. London: T. Roycroft.

Byam, H. (1675) *XIII sermons most of them preached before His Majesty, King Charles the II in his exile*. London: s.n.

Byfield, N. (1637) *A commentary upon the three first chapters of the first Epistle generall of St. Peter*. London: Miles Flesher and Robert Young.

Diodati, G. (1643) *Pious annotations upon the Holy Bible expounding the difficult places thereof learnedly, and plainly*. London: T.B.

Downame, J. (1651) *Annotations upon all the books*. Vol. 1. 2nd edn. London: John Legatt.

Edwards, J. (1692) *A farther enquiry into several remarkable texts of the Old and New Testament which contain some difficulty in them with a probable resolution of them*. London: s.n.

——. (1699) *Polpoikilos sophia, a compleat history or survey of all the dispensations and methods of religion*. London: s.n.

Featley, D. (1640) *Threnoikos. The house of mourning; furnished with directions for preparations to meditations of consolations at the houre of death*. London: John Dawson.

Fleming, R. (1689) *Britain's jubilee a congratulatory poem on the descent of His Highness the Prince of Orange into England and Their Highnesses accession to the crown, and solemn coronation, April 11, 1689*. London: Randal Taylor.

Fontaine, N. (1699) *The history of the Old and New Testament extracted out of sacred Scripture and writings of the fathers*. London: s.n.

Fuller, T. (1650) *A Pisgah-sight of Palestine and the confines thereof with the history of the Old and New Testament acted thereon*. London: J.F.

God's judgments against whoring (1697) London: s.n.

Goodwin, T. (1625) *Moses and Aaron Ciuil and ecclesiastical rites, vsed by the ancient Hebrewes; obserued, and at large opened, for the clearing of many obscure texts thorowout the whole Scripture*. London: John Haviland.

Gouge, W. (1622) *Of domesticall duties eight treatises*. London: John Haviland.

——. (1630) *An exposition on the vvhole fifth chapter of S. Iohns Gospell*. London: H. Lownes, R. Young and J. Beale.

Grantham, T. (1641) *A marriage sermon A sermon called a vvife mistaken*. London: s.n.

Greene, R. (1587) *Penelope's Web*. London: T.C. and E.A.

Greenham, R. (1612) *The workes of the reuerend and faithfull seruant af Iesus Christ M. Richard Greenham*. London: Thomas Snodham and Thomas Creede.

Guild, W. (1659) *The throne of David, or An exposition of the second of Samuell*. Oxford: W. Hall.

Hall, J. (1612) *Contemplations vpon the principall passages of the holy storie*. London: M. Bradwood.

——. (1623) *The great impostor laid open in a sermon at Grayes Inne*. London: J. Haviland.

Helmont, F.M. van (1685) *The paradoxal discourses of F.M. Van Helmont concerning the macrocosm and microcosm*. London: J.C. and Freeman Collins.

Heywood, O. (1683) *Israel's lamentation after the Lord, or, A discourse, wherein every well-wisher to Zion is excited*. London: s.n.

Hieron, S. (1613) *The bridegroom*. London: M. Bradwood.

Hooker, R. (1666) *The works of Mr. Richard Hooker (that learned and judicious divine), in eight books of ecclesiastical polity*. London: Thomas Newcomb.

Hutcheson, G. (1669) *An exposition of the book of Job*. London: s.n.

Jackson, A. (1643) *A help for the understanding of the Holy Scripture intended chiefly for the assistance and information of those that use constantly every day to reade some part of the Bible*. Cambridge: Roger Daniel.

——. (1658) *Annotations upon the five books immediately following the historicall part of the Old Testament (commonly called the five doctrinall or poeticall books)*. London: Roger Daniel.

Kellett, E. (1641) *Tricœnivm Christi in nocte proditionis suæ The threefold svpper of Christ in the night that he vvas betrayed*. London: Thomas Cotes.

Killigrew, H. (1698) *Odes and elogies upon divine and moral subjects*. London: Henry Bonwicke.

Leigh, E. (1654) *A systeme or body of divinity consisting of ten books*. London: A.M.

Marvell, A. (1681) *Miscellaneous poems by Andrew Marvell, Esq.* London: s.n.

Mason, H. (1626) *The tribunall of the conscience: or, A treatise of examination shewing vvhy and how a Christian should examine his conscience, and take an account of his life*. London: George Purslowe.

Mayer, J. (1647) *Many Commentaries in One: Upon Joshuah, Judges, Ruth, 1 and 2 of Samuel, 1 and 2 of Kings, 1 and 2 of Chronicles, Ezra, Nehemiah, Esther*. London: John Legatt and Richard Cotes.

Meres, F. (1597) *Gods arithmeticke*. London: Richard Johnes.

Midrash Leviticus Rabbah (2001) Cumnor Hill, Oxford: University Press of America.

Midrash Mishley (1893) Cracow, Poland.

Midrash Tehillim (1875) Warsaw, Poland.

Mikva, R. (2012) *Midrash VaYosha: A Medieval Midrash on the Song at the Sea*. Tübingen: Mohr Siebeck.

Mornay, Philippe de (1599) *Meditations vpon Psal. 101*. London: Adam Islip.

Murcot, J. (1657) *Several works of Mr. Iohn Murcot, that eminent and godly preacher of the Word, lately of a Church of Christ at Dublin in Ireland*. London: R. White.

Ness, C. (1696) *A compleat history and mystery of the Old and New Testament logically discust and theologically improved*. London: Thomas Snowden.

Norden, J. (1626) *A pathway to patience in all manner of crosses, tryals, troubles, and afflictions*. London: E.A.

Nye, S. (1698) *An account of Mr. Firmin's religion, and of the present state of the Unitarian controversy*. London: s.n.

Osherow, J. (2009) 'Brides of Blood: Women at the Outset of Exodus.' *From the Margins 1*:

Women in the Hebrew Bible and Their Afterlives. Ed. P.S. Hawkins and L.C. Stalhberg. Sheffield: Sheffield Phoenix Press. 46–51.

Oxford English Dictionary (OED) (2013) Oxford Dictionaries Online. Oxford: Oxford University Press.

Pack, S. (1673) *Helps to the assurance of God's love whereby a true believer may with the help of Gods good spirit.* London: T.M.

Palmer, H. (1644) *The glasse of Gods providence towards his faithfvll ones held forth in a sermon preached to the two Houses of Parliament at Margarets Westminster, Aug. 13, 1644.* London: G.M.

Paterson, J. (1660) *Post nubila Phoebus, or, A sermon of thanksgiving for the safe and happy returne of our gracious soveraign.* Aberdeen: James Brown.

Patrick, S. (1697) *A commentary upon the second book of Moses, called Exodus by the Right Reverend Father in God, Symon, Lord Bishop of Ely.* London: s.n.

Perkins, W. (1606) *The whole treatise of the cases of conscience distinguished into three bookes.* Cambridge: John Legat.

Rous, F. (1631) *The mysticall marriage. Experimentall discoveries of the heavenly marriage betweene a soule and her saviour.* London: William Jones.

Scrivener, M. (1674) *A course of divinity, or, An introduction to the knowledge of the true Catholick religion especially as professed by the Church of England.* London: Tho. Roycroft.

Shapiro, J. (1996) *Shakespeare and the Jews.* New York: Columbia University Press.

Sheffield, J. (1659) *The sinfulnesse of evil thoughts: or, a discourse, wherein, the chambers of imagery are unlocked: the cabinet of the heart opened.* London: J.H.

Shewen, W. (1696) *William Penn and the Quakers either impostors, or apostates which they please.* London: s.n.

Shute, J. (1649) *Sarah and Hagar, or, Genesis the sixteenth chapter opened in XIX sermons.* London: s.n.

Slater, S. (1690) *The souls return to its God, in life, and at death. A funeral sermon, preached upon occasion of the death of Mr. John Kent, late of Crouched Friars, who departed this life Decem. 16. 1689.* London: s.n.

Slatyer, W. (1643) *The compleat Christian, and compleat armour and armoury of a Christian, fitting him with all necessary furniture for that his holy profession.* London: s.n.

Strong, W. (1678) *A discourse of the two covenants wherein the nature, differences, and effects of the covenant of works and of grace are distinctly, rationally, spiritually and practically discussed.* London: J.M.

Stuckley, L. (1667) *A gospel-glasse, representing the miscarriages of English professors, both in their personal and relative capacities.* London: s.n.

Swinnock, G. (1661) *The door of salvation opened by the key of regeneration: or A treatise containing the nature, necessity, marks and means of regeneration.* London: John Best.

The Geneva Bible: A facsimile of the 1560 edition (2007) Ed. L.E. Berry and W. Whittingham. Peabody, MA: Henderson Publishers.

The Holy Bible, King James Version 1611 (2010) 400th Anniversary Edition. Peabody, MA: Henderson Publishers.

Thomas, W. (1678) *A sermon preached before the Right Honourable, the Lords assembled in Parliament.* London: Tho. Newcomb.

Trapp, J. (1649) *A clavis to the Bible. Or A new comment upon the Pentateuch: or five books of Moses.* London: s.n.

——. (1657) *A commentary or exposition upon the books of Ezra, Nehemiah, Esther, Job and Psalms wherein the text is explained, some controversies are discussed.* London: T.R. and E.M.

Trelcatius, L. (1610) *A briefe institution of the common places of sacred divinitie.* London: T. Purfoot.

Vauts, M. (1650) *The husband's authority unvail'd; wherein it is moderately discussed whether it be fit or lawfull for a good man, to beat his bad wife.* London: T.N.

Weld, T. (1644) *An answer to W.R. his narration of the opinions and practises of the churches lately erected in Nevv-England.* London: Tho. Paine.

Willet, A. (1612) *A treatise of Salomons mariage.* London: Felix Kingston.

Williams, R. (1652) *The bloody tenent yet more bloody.* London: s.n.

Younge, R. (1660) *A Christian library, or, A pleasant and plentiful paradise of practical divinity in 37 treatises of sundry and select subjects.* London: M.I.

6

The politics of female supplication in the Book of Esther

Alison Thorne

This essay takes the form of a diptych. Starting with a brief analysis of the narrative structure of the Book of Esther, its dominant motifs and hermeneutic implications, it will examine how this Old Testament tale of persecution and redemption was understood and applied by early modern readers to the circumstances of their own cultural moment across a range of exemplary texts. The aim of this essay is two-fold: first, to assess the extent to which sixteenth- and seventeenth-century readings of events in the Book of Esther were determined both by the different generic forms they assumed and by the broader historical, cultural and religious contexts with which they resonated; and secondly, to consider the affinity between the multiple reversals of fortune that punctuate the Esther narrative and the act of supplication itself, both of which entail a rising and falling rhythm. Accordingly, this essay seeks to investigate the correspondences between the dramatic pattern of inversion that characterises the Book of Esther and the instability inherent in the process of supplication which lends itself equally to self-abasement and self-advancement in the hierarchy of power and favour. The main contention of this analysis is that the convergence of female pleading with the hidden operation of divine providence or fateful coincidences lays the bedrock for a political partnership that will ultimately deliver justice and preferment for the persecuted Jewish diaspora.

Getting to grips with the Book of Esther is a daunting task given the multiple versions of this scriptural narrative and the prolific glossing it elicited. So voluminous is the extant literature on the Esther story – a quick search of *Early English Books Online* throws up over four hundred documents featuring allusions to its biblical heroine – that it is impossible to do more than scratch the surface here. Navigating this vast archive presents the reader with a formidable challenge. Yet everything we know about early modern exegetical practices suggests that contemporary readers would have been deeply versed in Scripture and highly attuned to the recurrence of certain themes, typological parallels and topical allusions. As William Slights notes, 'just as there are no politically innocent texts, so too there are no politically neutral marginalia ... especially in cases where they were used to disguise contemporary political relevance' (1992: 258). Annotations on the Book of Esther in *The Geneva Bible* lent this text a distinctly Protestant colour and obliquely critical slant on the text, aimed at the lasciviousness of the heathen monarchs and the necessity for the wife to be 'subject to the household and at his commandment' for 'everie man shulde bear rule in his owne house' (Esth. 1:22),[1] a claim that will be repeatedly flouted in this text. These domestic annotations are inscribed in the marginalia and are used to reinforce the broader message of the invincibility of the Jews, for 'God will deliver [them] though all worldely meanes faile' (Esth. 4:14). Such comments invited topical applications and appropriation by readers.

Queen Esther among the Jews

Turning to the tale of Esther itself, readers are invited to trace the ascendancy of its eponymous heroine – a Jewish orphan, refugee and member of a marginalised community whose ethnic origins are known only to her adoptive father and leader of the exiled Judaic community, Mordecai – who will become the unlikely saviour of her people. It so happens that the Persian King Ahasuerus is in search of a new bride, having lately cast off Vashti, his former consort, for an act of insubordination when she refused to display herself before him and his guests (Esth. 1:12). In pointed contrast Esther's deferential relationship to Mordecai is emphasised throughout. Not only does she find favour with the eunuch Hege, in charge of the palace women, but with all whom she meets. Finally the King himself is smitten with her loveliness. Thus she wins the royal beauty contest and is crowned Queen (Esth. 2:1–4, 9). But while the honour and prestige conferred upon Esther should, in principle, safeguard her people from destruction, we soon learn that this can only be achieved at great hazard to herself. For despite her elevated status, Esther's position remains precarious, being wholly contingent upon the King's favour. It is further jeopardised by the animosity of Haman, his chief minister, a member of the Amekelite tribe and traditional adversary of the Israelites who is intent on wiping out their race. This sets in motion a tale of tragicomic, and sometimes farcical, reversals of fortune that will eventually culminate in the miraculous deliverance of the Jewish exiles within the Persian empire from the threat of annihilation (Esth. 9).

In his commentary on the Book of Esther, Timothy Laniak pertinently remarks that 'Esther is a story about falling and standing in which the Jews' enemies fall, and the Jewish people stand' (Allen and Laniak, 2003: 255). This is endorsed by Jon Levenson's observation that the narratological development of the story conforms to a falling and rising rhythm that is reflected in grammatical variants on the key verb, 'to fall' (*napal*), used four times in the Book of Esther (1997: 10). Not only does this prefigure the Queen's ascendancy and Haman's promotion to the rank of prime minister, it also adumbrates Mordecai's rise to power due, ironically, to his refusal to pay obeisance to his enemy by prostrating himself before him. Conversely, we discover that the honour and rewards Haman expects to reap have been conferred instead on his arch-enemy. In a scene saturated with dramatic irony Haman's wife, Zeresh, intuits that his career is about to plummet and forewarns him that 'if Mordecai before whom you have begun to fall (*linpol*) is of Jewish descent you will never overcome him. You shall collapse altogether (*napal tippol*) before him' (Levenson, 1997: 10). Her prophecy is confirmed when Haman, sensing that his machinations will backfire on him, falls on the Queen's couch in a futile attempt to beg Esther for mercy. We are thus alerted to the existence of an uncanny correspondence between the fluctuating fortunes of the Jewish exiles and the intrinsically volatile position occupied by suppliants. These structural inversions establish a chiastic pattern whereby the overrated prime minister and the despised Jewish exile exchange places. Structured around a series of ironic *peripeteia*, the story relates how Haman's genocidal conspiracy rebounds upon him, precipitating his own downfall. Consequently Haman's plot to engineer the utter ruin of Mordecai and his people is confounded when their adversary is hanged for his misdeeds on the very same gallows he had prepared for Mordecai (Esth. 7:3–10).

This retributive scheme of inversion is revealed when Haman's decree authorising the extermination of the Jews is overturned by means of Esther's timely intercession with the King and the issuing of a contrary edict permitting the Jews to defend themselves against their foes. So comprehensive is the victory of the Jewish underdogs over their oppressors that many of the gentiles converted to Judaism because 'the fear of Mordecai had, literally "fallen" on them' (Allan and Laniak, 2003: 255). The prefatory note to the Book of Esther in the Geneva Bible glosses this as a salutary illustration of how 'the ambition, pride and cruelty of the wicked when they come to honour' results in 'their sodeyn fall when they are at [their] highest' (Esth. 'The Argument'). The date appointed for their massacre is thus, contrary to all expectation, converted into victory over their enemies (Esth. 9:1–13). In true tragicomic style, the English translation of Brentius' *A right godly and learned discourse vpon the book of Ester* informs us that 'their sorrow' was 'turned into solace, their mourning into mirth, their heaviness into gladness, their darkness into light, & their death into life' (1584: 513).

From this same note early modern readers would have derived another weightier moral: that in the Jews' unforeseen triumph over their opponents 'is declared the great mercies of God towards his Church who never faileth them in their great danger, but when all hope of worldly help faileth, he ever stirreth up by some by whome he sendeth comfort and deliverance' (Esth. 'The Argument'). In spite of the notorious absence of allusions to God in the Book of Esther, these events were widely construed as testifying to the hand of divine providence, though hidden from view and enacted primarily through human agency. However, commentators such as Joseph Hall (Dean of Worcester) tended to be less cagey about rendering explicit the ineffable operations of divine justice with its promise of salvation for the righteous (1626: 476–7, 498–9). Others purveyed the comforting message that those who suffer for their faith would find solace in the assurance of God's protection. The message is also reinforced *within* the text by Mordecai's strong admonition to Esther that should she refuse to plead on behalf of her countrymen in their time of need: 'comfort and deliverance shall appear to the Jewes out of another place, but you and thy father's house shall perish' (Esth. 4:14). More auspiciously, Mordecai's rhetorical question – 'who knoweth whether thou art come to the Kingdome for such a time?' (Esth. 4:14) – reminds Esther of the magnitude of the challenge confronting her while also hinting at the providential role she is destined to play in saving her people from obliteration. This reflects a pervasive tendency to elide the tribulations of the Israelites with the suffering inflicted on the Marian martyrs and other non-conformists whose resistance came to personify 'the courage of the reformed church' (Wiseman, 2006: 46) as extensively chronicled in Foxe's *Acts and monuments* (1583).

Although, as Christopher Hill points out, the Old Testament is principally 'concerned with the indiscriminate collective elimination of God's enemies and with the salvation of the Jewish people, rather than with individuals' (1993: 74–5), Esther's personal courage, prudence and political sagacity play a decisive role in the outcome of this story. Nowhere is this more clearly demonstrated than by her participation in multiple supplication scenes – there are five scenes, all told, in which Esther performs the role of suppliant, and another three in which she is supplicated, in turn, by Ahasuerus, Mordecai and Haman. All of them are left wondering what Esther's intentions might be until she reveals Haman's ruthless plan to exterminate his foes. Each time she puts her own life at risk in her determination to rescue the Jewish community from the calamitous fate awaiting them. Once informed of Haman's plot, she overcomes her initial reluctance to intervene on behalf of her co-religionists and takes the bold step of violating the law prohibiting her from entering the King's presence unbidden on pain of death. Fortunately, the King promptly pardons her transgression. That she evades Vashti's fate despite having committed a seemingly comparable act of disobedience is due to Esther's wise discretion in neutralising her offence by adopting the self-deprecatory posture and diplomatic language expected of suppliants. Evidently, the rhetoric of self-abnegation may, ironically, serve as a front for self-assertion. This chimes with Lillian Klein's contention that the only way women could achieve 'honour' or authority in the ancient world was through a display of feminine 'shame' or modesty (2004: 149–75). The reader is thus invited to reassess Esther's pleas, obliquely phrased in the subjunctive mood, as a tactical manoeuvre. In her final petition she appeals directly to the King in ways that deftly manipulate his desire for her while also retaining her deferential use of the conditional tense, beseeching him that '[if] I have found favour in thy sight, O King, and if it please the King, let my life be given me at my petition and my people at my request' (Esth. 7:3). This is the prelude to Esther's shocking disclosure that she and her co-religionists are to be 'sold, I and my people to be destroyed, to be slain & to perish', adding that 'if we were sold for servants and handmaidens I would have held my tongue' (Esth. 7:4), knowing that a submissive approach is more likely to succeed in currying favour with the monarch. The Queen's eloquence, combined with her performance of feminine abjection and her apologetic violation of the silence enjoined on women, are aimed at pre-empting objections to the audacity of her demands. However, the possibility of the Queen and her people being annihilated on a regal whim persists, since the original edict against the Jews has still to be revoked. Moreover, the risk is compounded by the intrinsic volatility of supplicatory acts that may easily tip either way – whether against or in favour of the petitioner. In short, Esther finds herself embroiled in a case of double jeopardy. Only through her canny use of pleading strategies is the threat to herself and her people averted.

A surfeit of supplication scenes

Modern and early modern commentators alike have accused Esther – unfairly, I would suggest – of dithering in carrying out Mordecai's commands and, worse, of a disinclination to come to the aid of her compatriots. Nevertheless, I would argue that Esther's cautious handling of this crisis is in keeping with her politically circumspect approach to this perilous situation. This is evidenced by the deferral of her suit and the gradual revelation of her demands over the course of the supplication scenes in what might – facetiously – be described as a rhetorical striptease. Almost imperceptibly, her demands escalate. Initially, Esther merely requests that the King and Haman attend a banquet prepared by her. On the morrow this invitation is renewed. Only on the third such occasion does Esther raise the stakes by exposing Haman's true identity as the would-be nemesis of her people. On the fourth she pleads for, and is granted, her life and the right of self-defence for the Jewish exiles, before finally reprising her role as suppliant in a successful bid to persuade the King to issue a new edict countermanding his original order for the extermination of the Jews. Ironically, the Queen's policy of withholding information repeatedly compels the King to turn suppliant himself by imploring Esther to disclose her petition. This leads to the prompt and unconditional granting of her request even before he knows what it is – each time triggering the refrain: 'What is thy petition … that it may be given thee? And what is thy request? It shall be even performed to the halfe of the kingdome' (Esth. 7:2). Ahasuerus' characteristic rashness in pledging his consent without ascertaining what is at stake gives Esther a decisive advantage over him. Power relations between suppliant and supplicated are thus inverted to the benefit of the Jews. As Levenson notes, 'with the King's immediate acquiescence, Esther is now effectively stage-managing the scene, commanding both Ahasuerus and

Haman just as she successfully commanded Mordecai in the previous chapter'
(Esth. 4:15–17; Levenson, 1997: 90). Moreover, another unexpected reversal is
enacted here, this time regarding the King's ill-considered demand that every
man should be master in his own household, for now it is his ostensibly meek
consort who is calling the shots. This marks the final stage of the Queen's
remarkable transformation from a passive figure to a woman secure in her influence over the King and her capacity to wield power by issuing commands and
edicts in her own right. By the end of this process Esther's politically risky tactics
have placed herself and her kinsman Mordecai firmly in control of the situation.

Esther's resolve in putting her life on the line in a desperate bid to save her
people was seized upon by early modern commentators as indicative of her
selfless concern to preserve the Jewish people and their faith. The Queen's
loyalty to her community is consistently presented as overriding her personal
trepidation at the prospect of interceding with the King with no concern for
her 'owne private profit and commoditie' (Brentius, 1584: 491). The emphasis
placed on Esther's willingness to sacrifice herself for the greater good of the
commonwealth – encapsulated in her famously stoical comment, 'so I will go
to the King, which is not according to the Law: and if I perish, I perish' (Esth.
4:16) – led to her recruitment as a paragon of courageous womanhood. The
'godly Queen Esther's' integrity had already earned her a resounding tribute in
Aemilia Lanyer's poem, *Salve Deus Rex Judaeorum* (1611) where she is extolled as
a paragon of godliness, determination and purity of heart:

> Though virtuous Hester fasted three dayes space,
> And spent her time in prayers all that while,
> That by Gods powre shee might obtain such grace,
> That she and hers might not become a spoyle
> To wicked *Hamon*, in whose crabbed face
> Was seen the map of malice, envie, guile;
> Her glorious garments though she put apart,
> So to present a pure and single heart. (Lanyer, 1993: 115–16)

Such sentiments were to be echoed in a hagiographic sermon preached before
Parliament in May 1646, entitled *Queen Esthers resolves: or, A princely pattern of
heaven-born resolution, for all the lovers of God and their country*, wherein Esther is
lauded as a model of 'Wisedome and Courage', 'Heroicke Virtue' and 'Religious
Fortitude' as well as a staunch defender of the faith, more fit for emulation than
the example of heathen men (Heyrick, 1646: 1–3). The sermon was probably
timed to coincide with a critical juncture when the royalist cause hung in the
balance, with the implicit aim of stiffening the resolve of Members of Parliament to defend their constitutional rights. The author of this sermon relentlessly
drives home the patriotic message that 'all owe more to their Country than to
themselves; this *Ester* knew which thus strengthened her resolution, together
with the preservation of her Religion' (8), being duty-bound to lay down their

lives for their brethren. The Deity, it is claimed, 'honours them that are of publike Spirits, that will lay out themselves and what they have for God' (15).

Esther is of course one such public spirit, albeit cast in a less aggressive mould than the virulent rhetoric of the Puritan lobby by virtue of her sex. The crisis confronting her people forces her to exchange her reclusive life for a more active role in the public domain. Following Haman's downfall, we learn that the King delegates much of the business of state to his Queen and Mordecai. Indeed in alternative recensions of this story – for example in Thomas Heywood's *The exemplary lives and memorable acts of nine the most worthy women* (1640) – they are jointly credited with Mordecai for 'guiding the whole state', while we learn that Esther wrote 'with all authoritie' to confirm the establishment of the festival of Purim as well as issuing and revoking decrees in her own right and celebrating 'Gods great providence [that] turneth the joy of the wicked into sorrow, and the teares of the godly into gladnesse' (64). As a symbolic protector and typological figure of the true Church, her image was, by the 1640s and 1650s, firmly associated with the interlocking themes of piety, self-sacrifice and concern for the welfare of the body politic.

Generic transmutations

Early modern receptions of the Book of Esther depended, to a great extent, upon the generic form it took, since each retelling was shaped by a distinctive set of ideological, political and religious conventions and priorities. Matters were further complicated by the tendency of these genres to overlap or merge with each other in ways that might make it difficult for modern-day readers to assign them definitively to a specific category, as is manifested most clearly in the coalescence of biblical exposition, petitionary texts and scriptural exegesis with conduct literature, all of which were primarily authored by Protestant Divines. As will become evident, these heterogeneous categories generated markedly different interpretations.

Discussion thus far has demonstrated how the Old Testament constantly reiterates God's pledge to deliver the devout and god-fearing 'Saints' from extermination at the hands of their adversaries 'when as all help and deliverance seemeth to be furthest off' (Brentius, 1584: 525). One inevitable consequence of this was the subsumption of the individual within an overarching providential scheme. Hence Esther's pivotal role in the various recensions of the Old Testament acquired a quasi-allegorical or exemplary significance. This generalising propensity is established in Brentius' *A right godly and learned discourse vpon the book of Ester* where 'Ester' is taken to signify all those whom God has blessed with extraordinary enlightenment, while 'Mordecai' comes to stand for 'grave, learned and godly magistrates' and 'Haman' for corrupt and ungodly counsellors everywhere (1584: 502). As Tom Furniss notes, *The Geneva Bible* and its editorial apparatus 'encourage[d] its readers to make direct connections between what they read about the Old Testament Jews or early Christians and their own contemporary situation in England' (2009: 8). This hermeneutic approach invited readers to seek out typological parallels between their own struggles to resettle the reformed Church in the wake of the Marian regime and the tribulations of the Israelites as a captive people suffering persecution under idolatrous pagan rulers. To that end, historical distinctions were intentionally blurred, using the glue of scriptural idioms and religious imagery to elide the biblical past with what seemed, to radical Protestants, to be an equally precarious foothold within the Elizabethan settlement.

The topical applications generated by such reading strategies were potentially innumerable, reflecting the fact that '[t]he Bible could mean different things to different people at different times in different circumstances' (Hill, 1993: 5). There is only sufficient space here to discuss one of the more noteworthy readings of the Book of Esther. Brentius implicitly identifies Esther as a prefiguration of Elizabeth I (a marginal gloss directs us to 'Read [Foxe's] *Acts and Monuments* in the life of Queen Elizabeth' [502]) on the presumptive grounds that just as the Israelites were subjugated to a despotic ruler who did not share their faith and were exposed, along with their Jewish queen, to the threat of death, so Elizabeth was unjustly incarcerated in the Tower of London and in danger of being executed by her half-sister whose name among Protestants had become a by-word for idolatry, tyranny and persecution. More specifically, Elizabeth was widely regarded as having been appointed by God in order to fulfil her destiny as a staunch defender of her English subjects and their Protestant creed against anti-Christian agents; Judaism is being tacitly conflated here with the Puritan wing of the reformed Church. The role ascribed to Queen Elizabeth in these commentaries reflects her loyal subjects' hopes and aspirations that she would prove to be a just and godly ruler (in contrast to her unpopular predecessor), capable of unifying a commonwealth riven by sectarian divisions (not unlike the scattered and beleaguered Jewish community) in the face of continuing internal and external threats to the nation's survival from Catholic activists.

Contrastingly, Brentius' commentary on Esther represents Haman as the anti-type of the devout Esther who is a 'worthy … [precedent] for all noble men and great personages' that instructs them to use their positions for the preferment and renovation of God's Church (1584: 489). We are thus conditioned to see in him 'a most perfect paterne of a malicious and subtile enimie unto the Church and people of God' who '[b]ends all his studie, labor, travel, and policies to seeke the utter ruine' of the true Church (493, 496). The demonization of Haman was later ratified by Thomas Cooper who specifically characterised him as the archetypal papist in his polemical disquisition on *The Churches deliuerance contayning meditations … and short notes vppon the booke of Hester* (1609: 3). By the 1580s Haman, as the personification of Jesuitical malice and treachery, was strongly linked with the suffering inflicted on the godly by Mary's ministers, just as it would be aligned retrospectively with the 1605 gunpowder plot. Nevertheless the focus fell to a lesser extent on specific individuals than on the promise of divine salvation from oppression, for which Elizabeth's accession and the fortunate discovery of Guy Fawkes' conspiracy supplied welcome corroboration. Thus Cooper finds in the downfall of all such 'Hamans' confirmation of divine favour and protection of the elect in 'that the wonderful deliverance of our Church and State, from that horrible plot of poulder-treason; [w]herein every true harted Christian and Subject ... may see in the same a ful assurance of whatsoever blessings of GOD are yet laid up in store for him' (1609: 2). In this miraculous turn of events 'the deliverance of the Jewes from Haman's malice' becomes 'a most lively glass [in which] to behold our deliverance from the bloody Papists' (3). Historical evidence was manipulated to reinforce the notion that Englishmen and women were a covenanted race and therefore the natural inheritors of the Israelites' title as God's chosen people (Greenfeld, 1992: 60–5 and Hill, 1993: 264–70).

While scriptural exegesis was fixated on the broader scheme of God's interventions on behalf of the righteous, it was also prone to merging biblical exposition with the homiletic discourse of conduct literature and petitionary tracts, creating new hybridised genres. Consequently, it was necessary to reconfigure the characters' roles in the Book of Esther in order to construct a model against which conformity to, or deviation from, an ideal standard of behaviour (in terms of gender, social status and religious conviction) could be measured. This generic template produced a more ambiguous appraisal of Esther than the salvific heroine of the Old Testament. On the one hand, she is eulogised in a sermon on *Queen Esthers Resolves* as a female Worthy, an undaunted defender of her religion and countrymen, a paragon of 'Wisedome and Courage' whose 'Resolution did breath an Heroick Virtue, the Execution a Religious Fortitude, [and] the Successe Honour and Glory' (Heyrick, 1646: 1). Such language hints, rather coyly, at the masculine qualities imputed to this heroine who was thought to surpass the bravery of Pagan men. Characterised as 'a virtuous woman more than manfully wrestling with publike danger and destruction' (Heyrick, 1646: 3), she is enlisted as an exemplary model capable of galvanising others into action. However, this only served to throw her sex into sharper relief by presenting such qualities as all the more admirable for being embodied in the 'weaker vessel'. The equivocal nature of such tributes is underlined by the author's invitation to view Esther as embodying 'strength in weaknesse, vertue in infirmity, resolution in constancy' (Heyrick, 1646: 3).

Conversely, the insistent privileging of male authority and concomitant inculcation of female subservience in the prescriptive debates about conduct during this period inevitably led to the sidelining of Esther and devaluation of her role from that of a key policy-maker to an instrument for implementing male-authored plans. Significantly, one of the most influential contributions to this genre, Thomas Bentley's *The Monument of Matrones* (1582), directed squarely at a devout female readership, places much greater onus on feminine weakness than either the Hebrew scriptures (Masoretic Text) or *The Geneva Bible*. Esther's subordination, as shown in her unquestioning obedience to her guardian Mordecai, is stressed throughout, as is the latter's impatience with her 'too womanly tymerousnes and feare' (Bentley, 2005: 150) at the lethal prospect of venturing into the King's presence unbidden. Equally notable is the decision to incorporate the non-canonical additions to the Septuagint (the Greek translation of the Hebrew Bible) which exaggerate, in baroque style, her womanly frailty and the pathos of her predicament when confronted with the King's ire, 'which so daunted her womanly courage that it made her presently for feare to fall downe ... being very pale and faynt' (152).

Dislodged from the centre of her own eponymous narrative, Esther's role as an articulate, active and successful political operator was reduced by conduct book writers, such as William Gouge, to a state of mute acquiescence. Indeed Gouge's *Of Domesticall Duties* (1622: 1 ff) goes so far as to erase Esther's voice altogether. As Michele Osherow has demonstrated, this is in itself a consequential act, given that the eloquence of the Old Testament heroines functioned as a vector of spiritual authority and political power (2009: 3–5). Yet Esther features in this text not as a vocal presence but only as a silent recipient of the Persian King's condescension; Ahasuerus' decision to extend royal protection to his wife by touching her with his sceptre is described by Gouge as a gesture of 'courtesie' that 'commeth of a superior ... [that] is no abasement of himself, but an advancement of his inferior: a great grace to her, no disgrace to him' (1622: 210). Continuing in this disparaging vein, other commentators opted to strike an uneasy balance between Esther's virile prowess and her more traditional feminine attributes. Attention is drawn in Nicholas de Hannapes' *The ensamples of vertue and vice, gathered oute of holye scripture* (1561) to her womanly humility, piety, obedience, reticence and compassion, while seeking to counterpoise this by paying homage to her redoubtable fortitude, presence and courage. Hence the magnitude of Esther's achievements is briefly restored in Hannapes' tribute to her bravery in 'having compassion on those that were addicte and appointed to dye, [she] put her selfe in great peryll, and yet shee obtained of "Ahaswerus" the Jewes advauncement and pardon' (1561: A3r). Nevertheless the overall effect is to diminish Esther's heroic feats by a process of domestication aimed at accommodating her high-profile role to the docile, self-deprecatory conduct laid down for early modern women.

Petitionary matters in an era of civil conflict: the 1640s and beyond

For all his many faults, Ahaseurus shared with his early modern equivalents a wish to uphold justice via the process of petitioning as shown in his impartial willingness to reconsider his position regarding his treatment of the Jews. Indeed it is in relation to the key matter of petitioning that Esther's importance as an emblematic figure imbued with political, allegorical and spiritual meaning underwent a resurgence in the polemical literature produced by women who lobbied Parliament in their droves during the civil wars and their immediate aftermath (c.1648–53) when the struggle over civil rights was at its height. More than just a hortatory appeal to reason, Esther's exemplary courage acted as a spur to direct political action. Consequently, female petitioners, mindful of the strong civic and religious associations informing the Book of Esther, appropriated her spiritual image and reputation as a precedent in order to license their own forays into the political arena. In one of the earliest petitions addressed as *A true copy of the petition of the centlewomen, and tradesmens-wives in and about the city of London* (1642) to the House of Commons, it is noted that

> when the State of the Church, in the time of King *Abasuerus* was by the bloudy enemies thereof sought to bee utterly destroyed, wee find that *Ester* the Queene … petitioned to the King in the behalfe of the Church: and though shee enterprised this duty with the hazard of her owne life, being contrary to the Law to appeare before the King before she were sent for, yet her love to the Church carried her thorow all difficulties, to the performance of that duty. (5)

What is being revived here is a collective sense of the body politic being at risk – a threat that alludes more perhaps to the political upheavals around Westminster than to the plight of an imperilled Jewish minority. Yet even when political agitation waned, Esther's iconic status continued to be mobilised by interested parties. Arguably, the passage cited above was a rallying cry for Parliament to press on with its agenda for an increasingly militant reformation of the Church and suppression of Popish rituals, whatever difficulties might lie ahead.

It is important, though, not to underestimate the fluidity and complexity of the stance adopted by the female petitioners lobbying for radical change. As Susan Wiseman has argued, the civil war petitioners occupied an ambiguous position somewhere between compliant suppliants pleading for an alleviation of their socio-economic distress, and civic-minded petitioners asserting their readiness to lay down their lives in defence of their ancient rights (2006: 45–9; see also McEntee, 1992: 92, 108). This is reflected in the fluctuating tone of the women's overtures to the Members of Parliament. Initially, the petitioners' appeals to the House of Commons were tentatively phrased and limited in the scope of their demands. Pre-emptive attempts were clearly being made to defuse the inflammatory content of petitions by conceding that it 'may bee thought strange, and

unbeseeming our sex' for women to petition alongside men while simultaneously defending the shared 'right and interest wee have, in the common and
publique cause of the Church' (*A True Copie of the Petition of centlewomen*, 1642:
4). Another petition addressed *To the supreme authority, the Commons of England*
(1649) also sought to press their case alongside men while robustly maintaining
their right to 'an equal interest with the Man of this Nation in those liberties
and securities contained in the Petition of Right, and other good Lawes of the
Land'. They forcibly reminded the Commons that

> since we are assured of our Creation in the image of God, and of an interest in
> Christ, equal unto men, as also of a proportionable share in the Freedoms of this
> Common wealth, we cannot but wonder and grieve that we should appear so
> despicable in your eyes, as to be thought unworthy to Petition or represent our
> Grievances to this Honourable House. (n.p.)

Adopting the abject speech and lowly persona of the suppliant in one of their
earlier interventions, the petitioners deferred to parliamentary authority 'with
all thankfull humility' while also appealing to familiar gender stereotypes,
stressing their 'fraile condition', their timidity and fear of violence (*A true copy
of the petition of the centlewomen*, 1642: 1, 2). Disclaiming any 'wish to equall
our selves with Men ... either in Authority or wisedome' they professed to be
acting 'not out of any selfe-conceit, or pride of heart', but merely 'following
herein the example' of their husbands 'which have gone in this duty before us'
(*A true copy of the petition of the centlewomen*, 1642: 5). Yet, for all their protestations to the contrary, the women's demands became more openly assertive as
they grew in confidence through their involvement in collective action. Such
defiance of authority perpetrated under the guise of humility can be seen, in its
uneasy mixture of brashness and deference, as a typically paradoxical feature of
petitionary acts that brought their feminine submissiveness into conflict with the
more aggressive attitudes they espoused. Nevertheless they persisted in dramatising their humility, frailty and distress *as women* while relentlessly pressing their
demands for further reformation of the Church, the abolition of the prelacy and
the purging of 'both the Court and Kingdom of that great Idolatrous service of
the Masse' (*A true copy of the petition of the centlewomen*, 1642: 4).

Of far greater consequence was Esther's action in breaching the notional
boundary between the private and public spheres by assuming the hazardous
role of spokesperson for the Jewish community. Her enforced involvement in
political activism was exploited by hard-line Protestant agitators as a means
of authorising their self-arrogated right to influence ecclesiastical matters and
the direction of the Church. Various reasons were used to justify their incur-
sions into the public sphere. Of particular relevance here are the two Leveller
petitions printed in 1649, comprising *To the supream authority of this nation ...
and places adjacent* written in response to the arrest of the Leveller leaders and

their growing disillusionment with Parliament; and *To the supreme authority, the Commons of England.* The latter boldly lays claim to an 'equal interest with the men of this Nation, in those liberties and securities, contained in the Petition of Right and other the good Laws of the Land' (n.p.), thereby asserting their parity of status while glossing over gender issues.

Earlier petitions had deployed a range of exculpatory arguments as a means of authorising the female petitioners' incursion into the public domain. But meanwhile the Leveller leaders had stepped up their demands for toleration, gender equality and a say in the government of Church policy. The author(s) thereof depict themselves as being so overwhelmed by 'the grievous weight of the publick Calamity and distress' that they can no longer suffer in silence or confine themselves to their domestic abode, but are forced to make themselves heard in the political arena (*To the supream authority of this nation ... and places adjacent,* 1649: 3). Such attitudes were broadly commensurate with the Leveller vision of the commonwealth as part of a single unbroken continuum between familial and political life (Amussen and Kishlansky, 1995: 162–88). Conscious of challenging social and gender conventions head-on, the women sought to legitimise their collective interventions in affairs of state on the grounds that extraordinary times called for extraordinary measures. Just as Esther had been compelled to violate ancient laws for the sake of a higher cause, so – it was implied – female petitioners had no choice but to quit the relative safety of their homes for the rougher (but intoxicating) environment of Westminster. For them, the survival of their husbands, families and the body politic itself was at stake:

> We are so over-prest, so over-whelmed in affliction that we are not able to keep in our compass, to be bounded in the custom of our sex; for indeed ... it is not our custom to address our selves to this House in the Publick behalf, yet considering, That we have an equal share and interest with men in the Common-wealth, and it cannot be laid waste (as now it is) and not we be the greatest & most helpless sufferers therein. (*To the supream authority of this nation... and places adjacent,* 1649: 4)

Here too we are confronted with contrarieties. For while these women crafted an image of themselves as 'helpless sufferers' – victims of lawlessness, oppressive taxation, food shortages and parliamentary indifference – they brazenly defied orders from parliamentary leaders, such as John Pym, to confine themselves to domestic issues. Instead the female petitioners confronted the matter head-on, contesting the men's claim that 'the matter you petition about is of higher concernment than you understand, that the House gave you an answer to your Husbands; and therefore you are desired to go home, and look after your own business, and meddle with huswifery' (McEntee, 1992: 99), rather than dabbling in political matters of which they were ostensibly ignorant. Attempts to reinscribe the image of female petitioners as adopting an apolitical stance reflects a deeper anxiety among the ranks of both Houses of Parliament over the potential disruption they posed to the social and gender hierarchy. However, this view only encountered sardonic derision when the women inquired whether they should be deemed 'so sottish or stupid, as not to perceive, or not to be sencible when dayly those strong defences of our Peace and welfare are broken down, and trod under-foot by force and arbitrary power' (*To the supream authority of this nation ... and places adjacent*, 1649: n.p).

In the twilight years of the Leveller movement (c.1648–53) the primary focus was on concerns over the abuse of parliamentary privileges and the encroachment of state tyranny that was countered by using print, notably petitions, pamphlets and persecution narratives, to 'make extreme cases for toleration and religious liberty' (Smith, 1994: 130–42). This was accompanied by the pillaging of authority vested in biblical heroines such as Deborah and Jael who had figured prominently in the earlier petitions. Within this broader context the subject's entitlement to petition became a major issue in its own right, eclipsing specific grievances. Parliament's repeated dismissal of the women's complaints and their denial of what many regarded as the inalienable right of petition, enshrined in the 'Nation's ancient Rights and Liberties' (1628) provoked outrage among the citizenry. That Esther resurfaces in the polemical literature of the early 1650s cannot be fortuitous when civil liberties were, once again, perceived as in danger of being eroded, this time by parliamentary statutes. A subsequent petition addressed to the House of Lords as part of the campaign for the release of the Leveller leader John Lilburne, and his associates, seized on this key issue. It protested that 'we cannot but be much sadde[n]d to see our undoubted Right of Petitioning with-held from us ... although it is the known duty of Parliaments to receive Petitions: and it is ours and the Nations undoubted right to petition, although an Act of Parliament were made against it' since 'God is ever willing and ready to receive the Petitions of all, making no difference of persons' (*Unto every individual Member of Parliament*, 1653: n.p.). Appropriately, the women's grievances were aired under the banner of Esther's reputation, who as a 'righteous woman being encouraged by the justness of the Cause (as we at this time are, through the justness of Mr. *Lilburn*'s Cause, and the common Cause of the whole Nation) did adventure her life to petition against so unrighteous Acts obtained by *Haman* the Iews enemy' (*Unto every individual Member of Parliament*, 1653: n.p.). A set of typological parallels were thus instituted in which the justice of Lilburne's cause was compared with the infamous acts of that arch-enemy 'Haman'. Disaffected female petitioners scathingly insinuated that they looked for no better treatment from the Houses of Parliament than from foreign infidels, 'judging that you will not be worse unto us, then the Heathen King was to *Esther*, who did not onely hear her Petition, but reversed that Decree or Act gone forth against the Iewes' (*Unto every individual Member of Parliament*, 1653: n.p.). For those aware of the irony that Esther herself was denied the automatic right of petition under Persian law – a fact widely brandished as a marker differentiating heathen from Christian regimes – this could have been taken as a gibe at Parliament's failure to respect freedom of speech among other civil liberties.

To the modern reader it may seem highly improbable that the fictionalised world of the Book of Esther, governed by a capricious monarch whose subjects were exposed to multiple reversals of fortune, would have failed to strike a chord with the political vicissitudes experienced by so many English citizens in the turbulent era of the late 1640s and early 1650s. Interpretations of this biblical narrative also underwent many permutations, being conditioned by the various generic forms they assumed. Their meaning, too, depended on hermeneutic strategies that scanned texts with a view to their 'use and application' in relation to their own historical circumstances and inherited past. Esther's fortunes waxed and waned accordingly. But, ultimately, it was as 'a patron saint of Civil War women's petitions', to borrow Susan Wiseman's phrase (2006: 46), that this biblical heroine scored her greatest impact. A paradoxical figurehead who managed to combine masculine and feminine qualities and who straddled the spheres of public and private life, Esther made it permissible, for a brief period, for women from all walks of life, not solely the gentry and aristocracy, to vocalise their opinions freely on the religious upheavals, domestic tribulations and regime changes they had to endure

Note

1 All biblical citations are from *The Geneva Bible* (1561), unless otherwise stated.

References

A true copy of the petition of the centlewomen, and tradesmens-wives in and about the city of London Delivered, to the Honourable, the knights, citizens, and burgesses, of the House of Commons in Parliament, the 4th. of February, 1641. (1642). London: s.n.

Allen, L.C. and Laniak, T.S. (eds) (2003) *New International Biblical Commentary: Ezra, Nehemiah, Esther.* Carlisle: Hendrickson Publishers.

Amussen, S.D. and Kishlansky, M.A. (eds) (1995) *Political Culture and Cultural Politics in Early Modern Europe.* Manchester: Manchester University Press.

Bentley, T. (2005) *The Monument of Matrones*, 3. Ed. C.B. Atkinson and J.B. Atkinson. Aldershot: Ashgate.

Brentius, J. (1584) *A right godly and learned discourse vpon the book of Ester.* London: John Wolfe.

Cooper, T. (1609) *The Churches deliuerance contayning meditations ... and short notes vppon the booke of Hester.* London: G. Eld.

Foxe, J. (1583) *Acts and monuments.* London: John Daye.

Furniss, T. (2009) 'Reading the Geneva Bible: Notes Towards an English Revolution?' *Prose Studies*, 31.1: 1–21.

Gouge, W. (1622) *Of domesticall duties eight treatises.* London: John Haviland.

Greenfeld, L. (1992) *Nationalism: Five Roads to Modernity*. Harvard: Harvard University Press.

Hall, J. (1626) *Contemplations upon the historicall part of the Old Testament: the eighth and last volume*. London: M. Flesher.

Hannapes, N. de (1561) *The ensamples of vertue and vice, gathered oute of holye scripture*. London: J. Tisdale.

Heyrick, R. (1646) *Queen Esthers resolves: or, A princely pattern of heaven-born resolution, for all the lovers of God and their country*. London: J. Macock.

Heywood, T. (1640) *The exemplary lives and memorable acts of nine the most worthy women in the vvorld three Iewes. Three gentiles. Three Christians*. London: Tho. Cotes.

Hill, C. (1993) *The English Bible and the Seventeenth-Century Revolution*. London: Allen Lane.

Klein, L. (2004) 'Honour and Shame in Esther.' *A Feminist Companion to Esther, Judith and Susanna*. 2nd edn. Ed. A. Brenner. New York: T&T Clark International. 149–75.

Lanyer, A. (1993) *The Poems of Aemilia Lanyer: Salve Deus Rex Judaeorum*. Ed. S. Woods. Oxford: Oxford University Press.

Levenson, J.D. (1997) *Esther: A Commentary*. London: SCM Press Ltd.

McEntee, A.M. (1992) '"The [Un]Civill-Sisterhood of Oranges and Lemons": Female Petitioners and Demonstrators, 1642–53.' *Pamphlet Wars: Prose in the English Revolution*. Ed. J. Holston. London and Portland: Frank Cass. 92–109.

Osherow, M. (2009) *Biblical Women's Voices in Early Modern England*. Aldershot: Ashgate.

Slights, W.E. (1992) '"Marginal Notes that spoile the Text": Scriptural Annotation in the English Renaissance.' *Huntington Library Quarterly*, 55: 254–78.

Smith, N. (1994) *Literature and Revolution in England, 1640–1660*. New Haven, CT: Yale University Press.

The Geneva Bible. (1561) Geneva: s.n.

To the supream authority of this nation, the Commons assembled in Parliament: the humble petition of divers wel-affected women inhabiting the cities of London, Westminster, the borough of Southwark, hamblets, and places adjacent; (affecters and approvers of the late large petition) of the eleventh of September, 1648. (1649) London: s.n.

To the supreme authority, the Commons of England assembled in Parliament The humble petition of divers well-affected women of the cities of London and Westminster, the borough of South-wark, hamblets, and parts adjacent. Affecters and approvers of the petition of Sept. 11. 1648. (1649) London: s.n.

Unto every individual member of Parliament The humble representation of divers afflicted women-petitioners to the Parliament, on the behalf of Mr. John Lilburn. (1653) London: s.n.

Wiseman, S. (2006) *Conspiracy and Virtue: Women, Writing and Politics in Seventeenth-Century England*. Oxford: Oxford University Press.

7

Gender and the inculcation of virtue: the Book of Proverbs in action

Danielle Clarke

In one of many commentaries in the early modern period, the virtuous woman of Proverbs 31 is praised

> for the wise, fruitfull and gracious speeches of her lips ... she talketh not rashly, undiscreetly, or unreasonably of matters; but prudently and soberly ... she speaketh not of toyes, or of trifles, but of faith, of repentance, of the feare of God, and of such other duties and points of religion, and she laboureth as much as she can to provoke unto liberalitie, mercie, and weldoing. (Cleaver, 1615: 553)

Perhaps surprisingly, the virtuous woman is not characterized by silence, but by her actively virtuous eloquence, a type of work or labour in itself (akin to her economic productivity – spinning, tilling, making cloth, buying and cultivating land – as outlined earlier in the same book). Her 'gracious speeches' are a form of eloquence, as they 'provoke' her household to morality and good works through example and persuasion. Robert Cleaver's commentary highlights the virtuous woman of Proverbs as a model for emulation within the household, and is aimed at husbands and wives alike (Larson, 2011). Through the powerful example of the Book of Proverbs, I shall suggest that Reformation thought re-invigorates the reading, interpretation and application of feminine precursors to be found in the Bible, by advancing these both as suitable examples for emulation and as standards by which contemporary women might be judged. In reading of exemplary women, however restrictive the model of behaviour to be imitated, women readers are intended to participate directly in *applicatio* ('the application of a text to action in the world' (Hampton, 1990: 10)).

The history of biblical exegesis is complex and contested, particularly in relation to *how* its lessons should be understood and applied, and a stark debate between literal and figurative signification still structures theological discussion today (Dunn, 1998; Loades, 1998). The early years of the Reformation witnessed lengthy debates about the merits of the translation of the Bible into the vernacular, often presented in terms of the sheer complexity and difficulty of the text, and hence its suitability for the unlettered and the uneducated. Particular books of the Bible were deemed to be suitable for female (and by extension other uneducated) readers, as Vives outlines:

> Nowe what bokes ought to be redde / some every body knoweth: as the gospelles
> / and the actes / the epistoles of the apostles / and yᵉ olde Testament ... But as
> touching some / wyse and sad men must be asked counsayle of in them. Nor the
> woman ought nat to folowe her owne iugement / lest what she hath but a liyght
> entryng in lernyng / she shuld take false for true / hurtful in stede of holsome /
> folishe and pevyshe for sad and wyse. (Vives, 1529: F2r)

Other authors point women readers specifically in the direction of the Book of
Proverbs, which will be my focus here, such as Samuel Torshell in *The womans
glorie*, who also argues that parts of the Bible should not be off-limits to women
readers:

> They say again, that many places are too *hard* for *women* to understand. But there
> are other places, *plaine* and *easie*. And if the Scriptures were not to be read at all;
> because all cannot be understood by women, then *none* may reade them, for *no
> man* can perhaps understand all he reades. (1645: 212–13)[1]

Torshell's position might appear to be a form of deference to his dedicatee
(Princess Elizabeth, daughter of Charles I, to whom he was tutor (Eales, 2004)),
but it reflects a widespread view about the capacity of women to read, understand and apply the scriptures to their spiritual and daily lives. Giovanni Bruto
similarly sees women's exposure to Scripture (and other exemplary texts) as a
means to virtue: 'I will not that shee should bee debarred from the commodities
of reading and understanding, because it is not onely commodious to a wise and
virtuous woman, but a rich and precious ornament' (1598: G4r–v).

The prescription of the Book of Proverbs as a suitable text for women to
read is not purely a matter of consumption; despite the book's heterogeneous
nature, it is clear that female readers are to adopt a particular hermeneutic in
their reading of it, one that links an ancient text to contemporary conduct to
the end of inculcating virtue. Women in the Book of Proverbs are sources of
authority, but they are also exemplary models to be followed and emulated in
the here and now, as Thomas Gataker's exposition suggests, in response to the
question, 'how may *a Woman* know then whether shee be *a Wife* or no?':

> I answer: Reade over the *Rules* that *S. Paul* and *S. Peter* prescribe *Maried Women*; and
> examine thy selfe by them. Reade over the *Description* that *Salomons Mother* maketh
> of *a good Wife*; and compare thy selfe with it. There is set downe *a Paterne* and *a
> Precedent* for thee. There is *a Looking Glasse* for thee ... to see thy selfe in, and to
> shew thee what thou art. (1623: F3r)

The metaphor of texts as mirrors is relatively common in writing on exemplarity in the Renaissance, and might be understood to suggest a relatively simple
two-way process of reflection and imitation, where the reader endeavours to
bring herself into conformity with the model that she finds in the text, just as
the infant ideally learns pure and uncorrupt (the terms carry both moral and
linguistic value) language from the lips of his mother.[2] For Gataker, the process

of self-scrutiny is closely allied with the Protestant practice of self-examination, which here entails a constant engagement and re-engagement with the biblical text which both allows the reader to view herself through the prism of the exemplary conduct outlined in the text ('*a Looking Glasse* for thee') and to position herself in relation to it ('to shew thee what thou art').

The Book of Proverbs was adapted and recycled in multiple versions in early modern England, primarily because it was easy to break down into digestible units. One of the more popular approaches to the book is to reorganise it for the 'ordinary' reader using methods and techniques derived from the commonplace tradition. The biblical proverbs are treated in a similar fashion to those deriving from the confluence of the popular and the classical proverbial traditions – where adages and saws are mingled together on the basis of topic rather than textual, historical or cultural origin. Robert Allen's 1596 text *An alphabet of the holy proverbs of King Salomon* reveals its indebtedness to an oral tradition that placed a high value on memory, and on textual recall, alongside the continuing importance of rote learning both in formal pedagogy and in informal domestic contexts. The title page announces that the collection is '[f]or the helpe of memorie and for a more ready finding out of any whole sentence, if onely the beginning be called to mind' (Allen, 1596: t.p.). The verses are set out in alphabetical order by topic, a de facto acknowledgement of the indebtedness of Allen's method to the classical commonplace tradition, whilst arguing that these sayings are superior, being characterized by 'plainnes, brevitie, and varietie' (A6v). There was a ready market for pre-digested units of handy scripture: Allen compiled a further volume, *Concordances of the Holy Prouerbs* in 1612, a text which is presented specifically in the context of the rhetorical tradition: 'reduced … to as many and sundry kindes of *Heads* or *Common Places*, as any *Concordance* would conveniently admit' (A2v). Allen deliberately mobilizes the conventional language of literary value, stressing 'their good and profitable use' (B2r), and emphasising the mnemonic potential of his text: 'which for the helpe of memorie, and to the furthering of the holy and religious use of them, you have in this familiar maner, sorted out unto you' (B2r). Allen is emphatic on the superiority of the Book of Proverbs to classical texts: 'What *Rhetorician* or *Orator*, could have beautified these with so great and delightfull a variety of *tropes* and *figurative speeches*, as he hath done?' (B2v).

One of the reasons for the popularity of the Book of Proverbs – and consequently, for the many different forms in which it was presented to the reading public – was the fact that it was easily assimilated into the commonplace tradition, or as the anonymous author of *Solomon's remembrancer* notes: 'every verse comprehends almost a whole point in itself, without *dependency* of that which goeth before, nor doth it minister the occasion of that which cometh after' (1672: 15). They are particularly valued for their style, and thus for their propensity to be easily memorized: 'short *Sentences*, and notable Sayings, sometimes setting them down in plain and open termes, sometimes in *Obscure* and *Figurative* Expressions, that this *brevity* and *variety* might the better imprint the sayings in the *minds* and *memories* of men, to be for common use' (15). This text, like many others, is less a text to be learned than a series of interpretations to be applied, and a lack of exegetical certainty is no object to drawing clear contemporary parallels. Commenting on Proverbs 7:21 ('With her much fair speech she caused him to yield, with the flattering of her lips she forced him'), the author writes: 'it is uncertain whether this be a true History, or merely a Parable to represent the Arts and proceedings of a Whorish Woman; but it aptly suits with the practice at this day of debauched persons of both Sexes' (36).[3] The emphasis here on both sexes is relatively unusual, although the negative exemplar of the whore is paraded for the benefit of male readers too, in a way that reinforces the homologies between 'fair speech', femininity and immorality. The whore of the Book of Proverbs fails to observe and maintain the power hierarchy signalled by linguistic conservatism and deference; thus her speech is not only immoral, it is actively corrupting of the male's normative virtue.

The alliance between the Book of Proverbs and other types of wisdom, adages and commonplaces is underlined in the more conventional Protestant commentaries, most of which are designed for use and consumption within the household. Peter Moffett presents his book as 'a nosegay', and 'a looking glasse' (1592: A6v), allying both Proverbs and commentary with a populist anthologising tradition, and with a more élitist exemplary model, underlined by the application of the language of literary value to the scriptures:

> Even as then the busie bee, when she flieth into some faire and pleasant garden, and lighteth sometimes here and sometimes there as it falleth out, sucketh out some sweetnesse out of everie floure and herbe whereon she sitteth: so your Lordship [the Earl of Bedford] looking into the volume of the sacred Scripture, and reading sometimes this parcel thereof, sometimes that, shall receive by everie booke therein such comfort and profit, as will cause you to preferre the same before the hony and the honie combe. (A3v–4r)

The Book of Proverbs is 'a garland of heavenly flowers' (A4r), and a knowing and committed Protestant female readership is specifically alluded to when Moffett thanks the Earl's aunts, the Countess of Warwick and the Countess of Cumberland (A6r). The high status of these literate scions of Protestant dynasties does not seem to affect Moffett's approach to the relationship between language and gender as expressed in the Book of Proverbs and later commentaries. Indeed, his stated method serves to augment the authority of the book, which is 'to be used by those who intend to *apply* some frutefull instruction, then by those whose onely drift is to open and cleare hard and darke places of Scripture' (A5v, emphasis added). In other words, the commentary is not a mere exegetical exercise, but aims to turn the scriptures into an exemplary text prompting moral action, and for female readers, this entails controlling and curbing speech. Indeed the interpellation of the two Russell sisters serves to set the seal on the virtuous containment of female speech; Moffett's earlier work, *The excellencie of the mysterie of Christ Jesus* (1590) was dedicated to the Countesses (who presumably helped obtain the patronage of their nephew, the Earl of Bedford, for the later work) in terms that suggest their status as living exemplars:

> as Paragons preferred in degree above the rest, & Countesses of excellent and high account; me thinketh, if any have gathered an heape of sweet and pleasant flowers out of the Scripture, for the use or comfort of the professors of the gospel, that such a garland is first to be proffered unto your right honorable heads, & must needs best fit, & most seemely become your noble temples. (A5v–6r)

Moffett's commentary on Proverbs is broken down chapter by chapter, verse by verse. Read cumulatively it creates a series of cross-references and commonplaces within the Book of Proverbs, as well as a network of references to other parts of the Bible, and establishes a productive method of non-linear reading alongside apparently punctilious and precise linguistic scholarship. Moffett frequently refers his reader to the *topos* from which particular statements derive; commenting on Proverbs 2:22 (*But the wicked shall be cut off from the earth, and the transgressors shall be rooted out of it*) he writes: 'see the roote of these sentences in the II Deut. 8 and Psal 37.2' (1592: 22). Marginal commentary glosses both the semantics and the grammar of the scriptural text; thus Proverbs 25:23, '*the whispering tongue*' is glossed '*or secret,' and '*a lowing looke*: as '*or sad.' Elsewhere, the marginalia explicitly assign given verses to topics, like 'Eloquence' (214) or link the topic to other examples, as with 12:20 on evil counsel where Moffett notes '[a]s for example Achitophel who for griefe hanged him selfe. Thus Mardoches advise which he gave to Hester, rebounded into his heart with joy' (107). This apparatus creates a powerful authority for the various statements about the effect and status of women's speech, statements that can then assume an exemplary status. The biblical text is repeatedly appropriated in support of an anachronistically narrow view of the proper scope and potential of women's language, even as Moffett's own text gestures at a virtuous female readership that transcends the kinds of binaries that his own commentary repeatedly reinforces. His commentary on 5:3–6, for example ('For the lips of a strange woman drop as an honeycomb ... But her end is bitter as wormwood, sharp as a two-edged sword'):

> yea they are verie plausible, soopling [sic] the vains and sinews with flatteries and smooth shewes ... her speeches, gestures, and dealings are so craftie and crooked, as that like by-pathes full of turnings, they will leade thee hither & thither, & cause thee to stray in such sort, as that thou art sure to misse the kingdome of God. (48–9)

Moffett's choice of metaphor here is particularly revealing, because it alludes to a stylistic ideal troped in terms of masculine muscularity, transferred from the homosocial sphere of classical Latinity, to the hetero-social sphere of the vernacular, threatened by the 'soopling' effect of female speech ('verie plausible'), a process that is posited here as being moral in its influence.[4] As Patricia Parker's arguments suggest, such figurations reveal a cultural anxiety related to virility and speech, where the term 'sinew' (*nervus*) is 'the "keyword" of an entire tradition of masculine or virile style linked to a metaphorics of the male body in its prime' (1996: 203). The opposition between effeminate and soft, and virile and vigorous, that Moffett finds from this particular scriptural verse, suggests the kinds of contestations that surround female utterance, and the sorts of paradigm shift that the adaptation of historical traditions can suggest (and veil). What is posited here entails considerably more than the temptations of female speech. The Book of Proverbs, with the exception of Chapter 31, generally envisages female speech as inevitably leading to, or embodying, sexual entrapment, because the women that the reader is warned against are precisely those who operate outside of direct patriarchal control, although they certainly function within its terms.

Moffett's commentary on Proverbs, along with those of other Protestant divines, repeatedly calls upon a demotic misogyny which deploys a discourse that allies female speech not only with the domestic, but also frequently with the infantile. The harlot of Chapter 7, for example, is re-presented to the reader in the homeliest of terms: 'she is not sparing of words, but very talkative ... she is not a house-dove, but a gadder to and fro' (Moffett, 1592: 66). The term *house-dove* is used ironically in North's translation of Plutarch's life of Coriolanus, where it operates as a thinly veiled insult to cowards; elsewhere it implies an ideal of virtuous, but passive femininity (*OED*, 2013). The term *gadder* is not gender-specific, although it is frequently used derogatively to denigrate a woman who strays from her proper place. Moffett's dilation upon the efficacy of female speech is revealing.[5] He states: 'the force or issue of the straunge womans oration, is declared in these verses. First of all, herein she is resembled to a schoolemistresse, which leadeth and draweth her novices and scholers, to follow her and do what she prescribeth or perswadeth' (1592: 68). Her speech is described as an 'oration', which draws the son away from virtue and towards vice; but the analogy with 'schoole-mistresse' uncomfortably combines the literal and figurative senses of this word (the figurative tending to be a female figure who tempts an innocent to vice). The metaphor gestures at an unwarranted and potentially immoral incursion into the male-coded territory of education. Hidden beneath this statement may well be a degree of anxiety about the role played by women in teaching children basic literacy skills, and the degree to which such activities were both unregulated and beyond the reach of both Church and state. Negative female speech models are repeatedly associated with terms that carry some degree of social denigration: 'so brawling women, by their scoulding, greatly and continually molest their families & their husbands' (Moffett, 1592: 162); 'the mouth of such strumpets, is compared to a pit' (178). Whilst these terms are not exclusively used of women, they are strongly and persistently associated with them, and in each case the inference is of the speaker exceeding the social norms laid down for where, when, how and to whom she may speak.

Robert Cleaver's *A briefe explanation of the whole booke of the Prouerbs of Salomon* reveals a similar investment in derogatory terminology to present his commentary on the Book of Proverbs. Commenting on 7:11–12 ('She is loud and stubborn; her feet abide not in her house: / Now is she without, now in the streets, and lieth in wait at every corner'), Cleaver (with Dod) writes: 'her unwomanly disposition, and properties: she is a babler, and full of tattle, she is *stubborne*, perverse, and rebellious to God, and her husband, she is a gadder abroad' (1615: 115). There is much in this vein, in Cleaver, and in other scriptural commentaries; on 19:13, 'The other is *a contentious wife*, whose brawlings offend the eares, and vexe the heart'; 21:9 reveals 'a woman given to brawling and chiding' (329); for Jermin, 7:10–12 represents 'a tonguish woman'; '[f]rom her own house she goeth to the houses of others, and there her tongue is tatling, as at home it was brawling', and in general, for a woman, 'wantonnesse of apparel, a brawling stubbornnesse of speech, an idle gadding abroad, are no signes of a good mind' (Jermin, 1638: 140). T.W.'s *A short, yet sound commentarie* (1589) was dedicated to Lady Anne Bacon – herself a learned translator and exemplar of virtuous eloquence (Magnusson, 2004) – with praise for her 'sundrie like holie and heavenlie gifts' (A2v). He deploys the same kind of vocabulary when, describing the harlot of Proverbs 7, verses 11 and 12, he argues '[t]each us, that these bee two things that womankind specially should avoide: vz. tatling and loud speach: and also much gadding abroad' (f.29v). The recurrence of the terms 'babbling', 'tattling',' gadding' and 'brawling' in response to the negative representations of female speech in the Book of Proverbs suggests that early modern England had a set of relatively fixed images or stereotypes for transgressive language, particularly when uttered by women. Whilst these terms are not specifically gendered, it certainly is the case that their gendered associations are powerful. 'To babble', for example, is to be inarticulate, indistinct, and allies the user of such speech with marginal speech communities: children, old men, those who cannot control their tongues, those of other faiths (Catholics, particularly) and speakers of foreign tongues (*OED*, 2013).[6] 'Babbling', by definition, positions the speaker on the margins of eloquence and articulacy, and by extension, provides a sign of the failed efficacy of speech against which later efforts might be measured (Mazzio, 2009: 19–55). For women, to 'babble' aligns them with the world of children, with the infantile, and removes them from the public world, from the exercise of subjectivity, and requires that they submit to the authority of a masculinist language regime, whilst not fully participating in it.

The existence of these forms of speech, coded as disruptive both linguistically and morally operating outside the limits of pedagogic literacy or eloquence, also serves to mark particular kinds of language use as socially and culturally

privileged. The entire project involves the moral resolution of a wide range of
speech styles for women into a simple binary that could be mapped onto the
other structuring binaries of early modern England in ways that contain or
conceal powerful linguistic and cultural forces. This involves, in particular, the
movement of the 'mother tongue', the vernacular, from being seen as low-status,
domestic, spoken by children, women and the uneducated to being the main
language of state, religion, law and eloquence. As Margaret Ferguson argues, an
uneven and dispersed process of standardisation is under way in early modern
England, where 'standard' English (like French) is being formed into

> prestige dialects that were, like Latin, *not* accessible to a great many historical subjects.
> These people, because of their gender, their class status, and/or their geographical
> distance from the places where the new, national vernaculars were chiefly taught and
> modeled, found themselves in the odd situation of not knowing what some of their
> countrymen referred to as their mother tongue. False mothers were multiplying ...
> as were bastard speakers of the language(s) of the land. (2003: 85–6)

Despite the attempts of these accounts to drive a wedge between virtuous and
vicious female speech, in practice the distinction is not so easy to maintain;
indeed, this is the point of the advice circulated to the normative male reader
and the assumption upon which the circulation of causal relationships between
types of speech and morality (or lack of it) is based. Proverbs 9:16, for example,
suggests the difficulty of distinguishing between moral and immoral speech.
It '[t]eacheth us, not to beleeve all words; for harlots many times will labour
to allure with the same words that holie wisedome doth, and all to make her
perswasions more plausible' (T.W., 1589: f.29v).

By a process of deduction, readers of Proverbs, and the various commentaries
and sermons that it gives rise to, can also find positive models of female speech,
that Protestant commentators adapt and apply in order to produce an exemplary
ideal – a woman who instructs her household (and her children in particular) in
virtue and religion through both example and her knowledge of the word of
God. These positive valuations of female speech rest heavily on the precondi-
tions supplied by situation, audience and context, and surface at various points
throughout Proverbs. Frequently the model of the virtuous woman involves
referring the reader to the catalogue of exemplary biblical women; thus Moffett
urges readers of 11:16 ('a gracious woman retaineth honour') to '*see examples in
Hester and Abigail*' (1592: 95). They are largely articulated in relation to Proverbs
31, where Lemuel, using the words taught to him by his mother Bathsheba, gives
an encomium to the good wife. It is particularly interesting in the context of a
discussion about the status and authority of female speech, that this ostensibly
female-authored piece of mother's advice to a son on choosing a good wife is
mediated by a male speaker.[7] It is fascinating that readers and interpreters of the
text tend to acknowledge, and thus recuperate, Bathsheba's voice only for the
purposes of rendering her portrait of the ideal wife all the more persuasive. It

is an often overlooked but culturally central piece of female voicing to a specific ideological end, where the authority of the message is finally seen to reside in the male term: 'a *prophecie*, an holie and excellent doctrine, which had a better author then *Lemuels* mother, or *Lemuel* himselfe, the holie Ghost, who was pleased to use only their tongue and pen, for the publication of it to the Church' (Cleaver, 1615: 536).

Proverbs 31 is a frequently cited text where praise of an exemplary contemporary woman is required, usually in the context of a marriage sermon, or more commonly, a funeral sermon. In Dod and Hinde's *Bathshebaes instructions*, dedicated to William Fiennes, Lord Saye and Sele and his wife Elizabeth (née Temple) in 1614, Bathsheba is held up as the type of godly maternal love and instruction:

> the duety of Parents in generall, and in speciall of mothers; which is, to bring up and intrust their Children, even their sonnes in the feare of God, and to endewe them with lessons and precepts, which may bee of use unto them, not onely whilst they are under their nurturing, government, and oversight: but also may bee necessary and profitable until them for the framing and governing the whole course of their life: and that even from their cradles; which appeareth by her loving manner of speech toward him. (3)

Bathsheba's authority depends upon the good conduct of her son, 'such plentifull fruit of the mothers instruction ... as they by that meanes may through Gods blessing have a sonne excelling both in piety, wisdome, and glory' (7). The model of a good wife outlined in Proverbs 31 feeds directly into Protestant ideologies of marriage and household governance, but what is striking here is the degree to which one of the axes around which a judgement may be made about the good wife is her speech – and as commendatory texts make clear – it is not silent submission that is required. Dod, like other Protestant commentators, places wifely obedience below obedience to godliness (28), but maintains the sexual hierarchy within the household – the wife allots work to 'her maidens' but not to the men servants (37). A primary index and signifier of virtue is to be found in the wife's use of language; it is typical of many such statements, and is therefore worth quoting at length:

> honour or comelinesse ... where in the first place commeth, that shee doth not use speach, but wisely, and warily, which is very fitly applied unto this woman. For it is commonly knowne and growne to a Proverbe, that women by nature are more talkative, so as a greater care is to be had, and straighter watch to be kept least at any time the lockes and barres of wisdome and modesty being broken, the tongue before being silent, doe wander and stay abroad here and there. Whereunto it is a great helpe, that a woman be constant and continuing in her labour; for even as the Apostle doth define idlenesse, & sloathfulnesse to be the seede of much talke in younger widdowes, so continuance in labour, is a singular remedy again rashnesse and forwardnesse of the tongue. (Dod and Hinde, 1614: 60)

The good wife is both example and exemplar, simultaneously a reflection of feminine ideals and the embodiment of them. The extended metaphor adopted here is commonly found in relation to the need to control speech in general, as well as in the particular instance of women. Questions of linguistic legitimacy reside as much in *how* things are said, as in *what* is said (see Waswo, 1987: 134–212). As Dod and Hinde themselves go on to assert:

> shee is not onely a hearer and reader of the word of God, but also shee conferreth thereof with her children, with her maides, and with her husband, instructing her children and maidens, as we reade of *Hester* … and asking her husband those things whereof shee standeth in doubt. (1614: 61)

The concern here is the maintenance of proper social and spiritual order, rather than any sense of innate intellectual weakness based on gender, indicated by their judicious selection of vocabulary; she 'conferreth' with her children and maidens (her social inferiors on the basis of age and status respectively) in her own right; she is envisaged as 'instructing' them 'with her husband', and seeking his resolution of questions that she is uncertain of. This final point, of course, is indebted to Pauline theology, which Dod and Hinde splice into their commentary, with a marginal reference to 1 Corinthians.[8] The example thus appears not as singular and incontrovertible, but intertextual, and multiple in its sources, a fact that not only gives rise to instability but encodes it within the example itself.

This is made quite clear when Dod and Hinde produce a kind of typology of examples by linking a series of otherwise unrelated biblical and early Christian women through their relationship to the Word – Anna, Hester, Mary and Priscilla:[9]

> Whereby appeareth how carefull godly women have been for true knowledge out of the word of God: Whereas hee sayth that doctrine & c. resteth in her tongue, hee doth thereby plainly declare, how often she used speech, and how plentifully it dwelt in her house … and yea her often talking of the word [of] God, is an undoubted argument of the same written in her heart. (62)

What is finally asserted here is an exemplary ideal of virtuous female speech, an outer manifestation of spiritual devotion, based on an unequivocal homology of tongue and heart; the breach, or potential breach, between tongue and heart is central to early modern anxieties about how language signifies its moral value, and to questions of status, place and gender. The good wife of Proverbs 31 is asserted in strongly Protestant terms, with the virtue of her speech as the key signifier of both female virtue and reformed knowledge (and dissemination) of the Word, as part of a process of elevating productivity in the domestic sphere to spiritually significant status:

> for the wise, fruitfull and gracious speeches of her lips … she talketh not rashly, undiscreetly, or unreasonably of matters; but prudently and soberly … she speaketh not of toyes, or of trifles, but of faith, of repentance, of the feare of God, and of such other duties and points of religion, and she laboureth as much as she can to provoke unto liberalitie, mercie, and weldoing. (Cleaver, 1615: 553–4)

The Book of Proverbs, and chapter 31 in particular, is a frequent and popular choice for female encomia in the seventeenth century. Proverbs 31:29 ('Many daughters have done virtuously, but thou excellest them all') provides clergymen with a good deal of scope when praising the virtuous lives of their recently departed female parishioners or patrons, or wives, mothers, sisters or daughters of local male figures who (presumably) control their livings. What is interesting about these funeral sermons is their investment in turning the well-lived spiritual life to rhetorical account, not only from the pulpit, but also through print circulation (Carlson, 2000). Just as classical examples are stretched, extended and modified through generic experimentation and a widened class of readers, so too biblical examples undergo some metamorphosis during the course of the early modern period, particularly as they are applied to contemporary examples. This is not to imply that the 'living exemplar' does not have a purchase well before this – texts like Foxe's *Book of Martyrs* played a key part in the construction and circulation of types of virtuous Protestant resistance and piety. The figure of Lady Jane Grey, for example, was explicitly packaged to this exemplary end in *The life, death and actions of ... Lady Iane Gray*, her writings revealing the 'never enough to be imitated virtues of that most admirable, wise, learned, and religious lady' (Grey, 1615: A2r). What is particularly engaging about the exemplary women commemorated in sermons is that they are praised for the proper exercise of reading and writing; they are held up for emulation not purely and simply in terms of their virtue, charity and piety, but in the exercise of these as manifested in, and symbolized by, their use of literacy both in the home and in the parish and community.

Proverbs provides a springboard, or a framework, within which the exemplary life of Frances Hobart, the daughter of the Countess of Bridgewater, can be placed. Rather than Proverbs 31:29, 30, and 31, which is John Collinges' text in his funeral sermon, *The excellent woman* (1669), being the authoritative model to which woman should aspire, the biblical text is presented as a prefiguration of the recently living woman who is its embodiment. This shift to the central use of real exemplars in outlining feminine, pious and domestic ideals perhaps represents a relatively simple extension of rhetorical practice into the realm of new material; most of these sermons combine the conventional funeral sermon on a text with a description of the life and achievements of the deceased, a kind of domesticated version of the tradition of *gestae* within epideictic rhetoric. Many of these printed texts are written by theologically partisan clergymen, often the beneficiaries of female patronage, keen to capitalize on their (usually) privileged access to, and direction of, the spiritual development of the deceased. This is undoubtedly the case with John Collinges, a clergyman with Presbyterian leanings, whom the Hobarts engaged as their chaplain. After Lord Hobart's death, Lady Hobart appears to have gone to considerable lengths to protect Collinges, and to enable him to continue his (by then) controversial ministry in Norwich (Allen, 2004). The difficulties encountered by Collinges after the Restoration account for the fact that *The excellent woman* appeared only in 1669, despite the fact that its subject died in 1664. This gives the text additional weight, as it powerfully suggests the longevity of the exemplary power of the figure that it memorialises, and Collinges leaves the reader in no doubt that the text is intended both to proselytise and to provide a model of active, literate piety for the emulation of others. Collinges presents the text 'that others may learn the steps of holiness' (1669: A3v); like many other writings in this vein, the text is metaphorically conflated with its subject, suggestively hinting at, or accomplishing, the transformation of individual into authoritative exemplar. The text, the 'sheets' of the book, are envisaged as 'her *Picture*', and Collinges comments: 'it might indeed have deserved a better hand, but as it is, I dare say your *Ladiship* will see many a *line* in her *countenance*, which you will remember' (A4v). The presentational trope of the text is that of conversion, with the key term being the example of its subject; addressing the self-indulgence of the archetypal Restoration figure ('Who at a Sermon, think an *hour*, an *age*', A5v), Collinges urges them, '[t]urn here your wanton eyes, here you may spy / A true *Exemplar of Nobility*' (A5v). Structured according to the traditional division of a woman's life into the roles of virgin, wife and widow, *The excellent woman* supplements conventional accounts of Lady Hobart's virtuous accomplishment as a wife and mother with a considerable amount of precise detail as to her literate and spiritual activities. Her early education is seen as crucial to her later development; her Huguenot governess is credited not only with her flawless fluency in French, but also with her strong inclination towards the more radical wing of Protestantism. The trope of conversion is mobilised once more to underline Lady Hobart's rejection of the conventional pursuits associated with her privileged upbringing, and her regret at 'mispending part of many *Lords dayes*, in *masks*, and other *Court pastimes*, according to the fashion of others in her circumstances' (6). The idea of the virtuous wife is authorised by repeated reference to Proverbs, including 'those which were more extrinsical, and ordinarily no womens imployment' (10).

The remainder of the 'short Account of the *Holy Life* and *Death*' is devoted to a detailed description of the spiritual activities of the household, and Lady Hobart's role in directing these, and in exemplifying its key tenets and principles, which, as Collinges suggests (like other encomiasts of pious women) is an argument of force in itself. These activities typically revolve around prayer, meditation and the reading of scripture:

> a *Course of Prayer* (in conformity to *Davids* Copy, *Morning* and *Evening* and at *Noontime*; *Reading some portion of Scripture*, twice each day, and *expounding it*, as my leisure would allow me) *Catechizing* once every week, or *stricter observation* of the Lords dayes, and *Repetitions* of *Sermons* both on that, and other dayes, when we had attended upon the publick Ordinances. (18)

Lady Hobart's religious practice is something more than the kind of virtuous occupation envisaged as proper activity by the earlier generation of humanists, such as Vives. Its positive representation here is testament to the ideological interventions that might be made through patronage, as well as ultimately reflecting well on Collinges' own ministry – the scheme quoted above is of his devising. Whilst Collinges does not directly cite biblical texts to frame Lady Hobart's exemplary practice, the discourse that he employs is indebted to the kinds of conventions that structure Scripture, the Pauline epistles in particular. Thus, following a lengthy description of her daily activities ('the private Devotions and retirements of her Closet'; reading, meditation (25)), she is described as '*spinning or sowing* with her Maids' (25), an indirect allusion to the domestic activity of the ideal wife of Proverbs 31. Likewise, the account of Frances Hobart's reading activity alludes tangentially to the injunction in 1 Corinthians 14:35 to women to consult an authority higher than herself on points of uncertainty:

> she was rarely to be found alone with her Bible before her, she had drawn up for her self a method for reading the Scripture ... that she might want no satisfaction to any doubt arising upon her reading the Scripture, she had furnished her self with a large library of English Divines, which cost her not much less that 100 *l.* of which she made a daily use. (26)

A number of such sermons survive, mostly from the post-1600 period; interestingly, most of the women commemorated in this way were born in the Elizabethan or Jacobean period, and thus could be assumed to have been the recipients of the kind of godly instruction that they themselves are enjoined to practice in their own households.[10] Thus exemplary texts are repositioned in relation to textual, and actual, practice, and followed through into 'action' – it is relatively easy to see in this context why Proverbs 31 was such an appealing text to the household chaplains and spiritual advisors who normally delivered, wrote and published these sermons. Spiritual leadership – of a kind – becomes another central part of the activities of a good wife, and not just for women as socially elevated as Lady Frances Hobart. William Gouge, who spent a good part of his writing career communicating an accessible version of the godly household, also deployed the sermon to similar ends. His *A funerall sermon* (1646) is directed to Mrs Margaret Ducke, who lived under Gouge's ministry in his Blackfriars parish.[11] The sermon is presented as an example to her daughters, in the hope that it will 'raise in them by Gods grace, a desire of imitation of the piety and vertues of their Mother' (Gouge, 1646: A2v). Not coincidentally, the sermon incorporates the idea of the mother's advice manual into its generic frame – a form which has a related set of exemplary functions in relation to the transmission of virtues and ideals normally inculcated within the household – where the text and the remembrance of its writer substitute for the individual herself. The exemplary function of the printed sermon is made clear by its use of Proverbs 31:29 as its text; referencing a text which is itself part of an exemplary description inevitably partakes of the intended function of the original. Gouge employs a series of textual metaphors that position his subject's virtue beyond the power of expression; in fact, to ally them doubly with the divine exemplar of the Bible:

> upon these grounds, and for these causes, I have broken this box of Spickhard over this deceased Gentlewoman, which her own Name left behind her. I shall be but the Eccho to her true voice, and accordingly repeat truly, though very brokenly and short of what she deserved, the rest, her worth and deeds will speak for her in the gate. (22–3)

Her virtue is indexed by her devotion to her home, and by implication she is the polar opposite of the wandering temptress of much of Proverbs: 'she was so farre from the gadding disposition of the talking, walking woman, that she was for the most part as a Snail *Domi-porta*, within her own shell and family' (27). Like other exemplary women, her spiritual activities are central to her role as a model for others:

> her constant and unfailing practice was, besides daily publike Prayers in the family, to betake herself in the morning and at other times, to her constant private devotions in her closet, and then allotting some time … in the education of her Children … the rest of the day she spent in reading bookes of Piety and Devotion, most willingly of Dr. *Gouges*, by which she made her heart *Bibliothecam Christi*, a Library of Christ, and furnished her self with such a stock of Christian knowledge and devotion, as carried her with much comfort and chearfulnesse through all her afflictions. (28)[12]

Proverbs is a popular, if obvious, choice of scriptural text for the praise of exemplary women; this is an indication of early modern culture's ways of contextualising women's speech and, increasingly, female literacy. John Kettlewell's *A funeral sermon for … the Lady Frances Digby* uses a textual metaphor to mark his subject's transition from living to written exemplar: 'since it has pleased him to take away the Original, 'tis pity the World should want the Copy too, and lose the Benefit of her Example' (1684: A2v). He draws upon Proverbs both for his text (14:32) and for his discourse of pious but active virtue; of the deceased Kettlewell he writes, 'the Character of whose Virtues will give life to all that I have said, and be the best, and most useful thing in all my Sermon' (15). John Birchall's *The non-pareil, or, The vertuous daughter* commemorates Elizabeth Hoyle, the wife of a York alderman, again using Proverbs 31:29 as the text, where a continuity between biblical model and the sermon's subject is strongly emphasised: 'when I looke into those examples in the Scripture of rare persons, even of godly women, as *Sarah* and *Deborah a Mother in Israel*, and the like, may not we say, that the name indeed differs, but the practise doth not' (1644: 10). Like her more socially elevated peers, Elizabeth Hoyle is renowned both for her virtue *and* her spiritual literacy, and her daily practice of these:

as for private performances what shall I say for reading the Scriptures from the first, unto the last, she was a constant dayly reader of Gods word ... for that same duty of Meditation (oh, that too much neglected duty) it was her constant course one [sic] or twice a day to run over what she had heard on the Lords-Day, even on the weeke day, and I my self have seen her many a time retire her self to walk in a place commonly called the Garth, or in some other place in a speciall manner ... for this very end, to presse upon her soule in secret, what she had heard in publique. (12–13)[13]

Philip Horneck's sermon on Lady Guilford uses the final verse of the final chapter of the Book of Proverbs as its text ('let her own works praise her in the gates');[14] its terms are mostly familiar, citing her religious and moral education at the hands of Lord Brooke and his 'Pious Lady' (1699: 5), and her constant habit of self-scrutiny and moral examination: 'All her thoughts came under Correction; and as she kept Minutes of her Life, so nothing of the least importance could escape her Knowledge' (7). Horneck also suggests that exemplary subjects assisted Lady Guilford in her attempts at spiritual improvement. Her prayer time was habitually from 6 to 8am:

part of which time was spent in Reading the *New-Testament*, with Annotations upon it; and wherever she lighted on a passage applicable to her self, or fell in with relations of Great and Exemplary Men, she would pitch on them for Subjects of her ensuing Meditation. (8)

The implication here is that her topics are derived from her biblical reading, but Horneck's phrasing ('Great and Exemplary Men') suggests that historical texts may also have been used, and he later notes that '*Essays, History, Morality*, with the like, took up all the vacancies she could spare from the stricter Duties of *Religion*' (12–13).

Examples like these, linking the biblical *topos* – often, although by no means universally, derived from the Book of Proverbs – with the literate practice of an exemplar whose authority is augmented by the fact that she exists in the collective memory of family, parish and community, abound in seventeenth-century writing. They appear not solely in the rather predictable form of the funeral sermon, but in other emergent forms, forms that might loosely be grouped under the anachronistic heading of 'life-writing' – diaries, collections of exemplary lives, mothers' advice manuals. Samuel Clarke's *A collection of the lives of ten eminent divines* (1662) includes the lives of several middle-ranking women renowned for their pious virtue; Mrs Margaret Corbet is eulogized for her reading, her catechizing and for her charity, and these good works are framed by references to the Book of Proverbs, 31:29 in particular (507) along with other scriptural texts and biblical figures. Evidently, the funeral sermon is highly significant as a vehicle for the formation of ideologies relating to women's speech, and their exercise of articulacy within and beyond the household. This has to do with the simple fact of circulation, namely the sermon's double existence as an oral performance and as written text. Additionally, the sermon's importance derives both from the authority of its source and its author / speaker, and from its unique ability to move across social and cultural boundaries – from church to home, from the public arena to the domestic, from the realm of kin and family to that of recipients of instruction and charity. Finally, the almost universally encomiastic tone of such sermons reinforces their status as enactments of the exemplary, however heavily troped and conventionalized their terms turn out to be; indeed, it is those very conventions that make these kinds of text such powerful cultural and ideological forces.

Notes

1 Unless otherwise stated, the italics used in quotations from early modern texts appear in the original.

2 For more on the image of the mirror and its role in the representation of gender relations, see Clarke (1998).

3 All biblical citations have been taken from the *Holy Bible: King James Version* (1611, rev. edn. 2011).

4 See Jonson: 'There be some styles, againe, that have not lesse blood, but lesse flesh, and corpulence. These are bony, and sinnewy: *Ossa habent, et nervos*' (1947: VIII: 627), and the discussion of this by Parker (1996).

5 Proverbs 7:21: 'With her much fair speech she caused him to yield, with the flattering of her lips she forced him'.

6 The kinds of meaning that I am positing for 'babble' and its cognates run from the late medieval period through to the end of the seventeenth century, with a few stray survivals after that; post-1700 its meanings are largely figurative. See also 'tattle' v. and its various cognates, which track a similar process.

7 See Collinges: 'whether these also were the words of *Bathsheba* (as some think) instructing *Solomon* her Son in the choice of a wife, and by him recorded for our *instruction*: Or whether they *Originally* be the words of *Solomon* from the pattern of his excellent Mother, describing a desirable woman … is as unprofitable to dispute, as difficult to be determined' (1669: 45), and T.W., *Short...Commentarie*: 'she speaketh wisely, and frameth his selfe to speake not of toyes and vaine things, as women commonly use to doo, but of grave matters, as of wisdome and virtue … shee dooth ever propounde the doctrine, and shew the way how to doo good unto others' (1589: f. 204v).

8 The reference is to 1 Corinthians 5, but the verse that the authors have in mind is 1 Corinthians 14:35 'and if they will learn anything, let them ask their husbands at home: for it is a shame for women to speak in the church'.

9 See also Moffett on 31:26, 'the right guiding of her speech' and his marginal comment, '*See examples in Abigaile, Sarah, Hester, the Queene of Sheba, Mary Elizabeth and Priscilla*' (1590: 317).

10 As such, they are the first generation to have been educated in this way; for this point I am indebted to discussions with Dr John McCafferty of UCD.

11 Margaret Duck, the daughter of a London merchant, was the wife of Arthur Duck, a civil lawyer (see Stein, 2004).

12 Both of the passages quoted here are reproduced, without acknowledgement in Clarke (1662: 491, 492).

13 On women and meditation practices, see Coolahan (2007).

14 The text is cited as Proverbs 33:33, but the verse is that found in KJV 31:31.

References

Allen, E. (2004) 'Hobart, Lady Frances (1603–1664).' *Oxford Dictionary of National Biography*. Oxford: Oxford University Press.

Allen, R. (1596) *An alphabet of the holy proverbs of King Salomon*. London: Robert Robinson.

———. (1612) *Concordances of the Holy Prouerbs of King Salomon*. London: William Hall and John Beale.

Askew, A. (1996) *The Examinations of Anne Askew*. Ed. E.V. Beilin. Oxford: Oxford University Press.

Barton, J. (ed.) (1998) *The Cambridge Companion to Biblical Interpretation*. Cambridge: Cambridge University Press.

Birchall, J. (1644) *The non-pareil, or, The vertuous daughter*. York: Tho. Broad.

Bruto, G. (1598) *The necessarie, fit, and convenient education of a yong gentlewoman*. London: Adam Islip.

Carlson, E. (2000) 'English Funeral Sermons as Sources: The Example of Piety in Pre-1640 Sermons.' *Albion*, 32: 567–97.

Clarke, D. (1998) '"This domestical kingdome or monarchy": Cary's *Mariam* and Resistance to Patriarchal Government.' *Medieval and Renaissance Drama in England*, 10: 179–200.

Clarke, S. (1662) *A collection of the lives of ten eminent divines*. London: William Miller.

Cleaver, R. (1615) *A briefe explanation of the whole booke of the Prouerbs of Salomon*. London: Felix Kyngston.

Collinges, J. (1669) *The excellent woman discoursed more privately from Proverbs 31. 29, 30, 31*. London: s.n.

Coolahan, M.L. (2007) 'Redeeming Parcels of Time: Aesthetics and Practice of Occasional Meditation.' *Seventeenth Century*, 22: 124–43.

Dod, J. and Hinde, W. (1614) *Bathshebaes instructions to her sonne Lemuel*. London: John Beale.

Dunn, J. (1998) 'The Pauline Letters.' *Cambridge Companion to Biblical Interpretation*. Ed. J. Barton. Cambridge: Cambridge University Press. 276–89.

Eales, J. (2004) 'Torshell, Samuel (1605–1650).' *Oxford Dictionary of National Biography*. Oxford: Oxford University Press.

Ferguson, M.W. (2003) *Dido's Daughters: Literacy, Gender, and Empire in Early Modern England and France*. Chicago: University of Chicago Press.

Gataker, T. (1623) *A good wife Gods gift and, a wife indeed. Tvvo mariage sermons*. London: John Hauiland.

Gouge, W. (1646) *A funerall sermon preached ... At the funeralls of Mrs Margaret Ducke wife of Dr Ducke*. London: A.M.

Grey, J. (1615) *The life, death and actions of the most chast, learned, and religious lady, the Lady Iane Gray*. London: G. Eld.

Hampton, T. (1990) *Writing from History: The Rhetoric of Exemplarity in Renaissance Literature*. Ithaca, NY: Cornell University Press.

Horneck, P. (1699) *A sermon occasioned by the death of the Right Honourable the Lady Guilford*. London: Edmund Rumball.

Jermin, M. (1638) *Paraphrasticall meditations, by way of commentarie, upon the vvhole booke of the Proverbs of Solomon*. London: R. Badger.

Jonson, B. (1947) *Timber, or Discoveries. Ben Jonson*, Vol. VIII. Ed. C.H. Herford, P. Simpson and E. Simpson. Oxford: Clarendon Press.

Kettlewell, J. (1684) *A funeral sermon for ... the Lady Frances Digby*. London: Robert Kettlewell.

Larson, K.R. (2011) *Early Modern Women in Conversation*. Basingstoke: Palgrave Macmillan.

Loades, A. (1998) 'Feminist Interpretation.' *The Cambridge Companion to Biblical Interpretation*. Ed. J. Barton. Cambridge: Cambridge University Press. 81–94.

Lyons, J.D. (1989) *Exemplum: The Rhetoric of Example in Early Modern France and Italy*. Princeton, NJ: Princeton University Press.

Magnusson, L. (2004) 'Bacon [Cooke], Anne, Lady Bacon (c.1528–1610).' *Oxford Dictionary of National Biography*. Oxford: Oxford University Press.

Mazzio, C. (2009) *The Inarticulate Renaissance: Language Trouble in an Age of Eloquence*. Philadelphi, PA: University of Pennsylvania Press.

Moffett, P. (1590) *The excellencie of the mysterie of Christ Jesus*. London: Thomas Orwin.

——. (1592) *A commentarie vpon the booke of the Prouerbes of Salomon published for the edification of the Church of God*. London: Robert Robinson.

Oxford English Dictionary (OED) (2013) Oxford Dictionaries Online. Oxford: Oxford University Press.

Parker, P. (1996) "Virile Style". *Premodern Sexualities*. Ed. L. Fradenburg and C. Freccero. London: Routledge. 199–222.

Solomon's remembrancer to transgressors of both sexes (1672) London: T.N.

Stein, P. (2004) 'Duck, Arthur (1580–1648).' *Oxford Dictionary of National Biography*. Oxford: Oxford University Press.

The Holy Bible: King James Version (1611, rev. edn. 2011) London: Collins.

Torshell, S. (1645) *The womans glorie a treatise, asserting the due honour of that sexe, and directing wherein that honour consists*. London: G.M.

Vives, J.L. (1529) *A verie fruitfull and pleasant booke, called the instruction of a christian woman*. London: Thomas Bertholet.

W., T. (1589) *A short, yet sound commentarie*. London: Thomas Orwin.

Waswo, R. (1987) *Language and Meaning in the Renaissance*. Princeton: Princeton University Press.

PART II

Women and feminine archetypes of the New Testament

8

Overview: Reading New Testament women in early modern England, 1550–1700

Victoria Brownlee and Laura Gallagher

The New Testament is not as populated with female figures as the Old, and many of the women found within its pages are only partially depicted. Indeed, it is commonplace in early modern literature to find a string of Old Testament female exemplars with what can sometimes seem like a token few New Testament names tacked on. In *The glory of women* (1652), Heinrich Cornelius Agrippa lists countless Old Testament women who assert pre-eminence over men, but the New Testament compilation is slight by comparison. It includes, however, Elizabeth, who 'beleeved faithfully', 'the blessed Virgin … *Anna* the Prophetesse' and the 'foure Daughters' of Philip who are termed 'Virgin Prophetesses' (21–2). While numerically smaller, Agrippa's list of New Testament women advances a powerful pattern of effective female faith, and illuminates a series of women whom the Bible marks as profoundly significant because of their relationships with, and faith in, Jesus. Certainly, it seems that the limits of biblical record do not hamper the cultural significance afforded to New Testament women in early modern writings.

Arguably, it was Jesus' mother Mary who was among the most discussed, and debated, New Testament women of the early modern period. Like Eve, the discussion she generated was disproportionate to her scriptural presence. Only Matthew and Luke record the birth narrative, and the latter alone recounts the visitation by Gabriel and Annunciation; yet, each of the Gospels acknowledges, if only in brief, Mary's role as Jesus' mother.[1] As such, although the reformers may have disagreed with the intercessory role afforded to Mary in the Roman Catholic tradition, and rejected any suggestion that she was involved in the atonement of sins, Mary's scriptural presence ensured that her virgin mother-hood and centrality within the Christian narrative were broadly accepted. As the mother of Christ, Mary continued to have a literary presence in England throughout the sixteenth and seventeenth centuries, even after reformers destroyed the Marian statues and other physical reminders of her medieval cult. Indeed, she was explicitly appropriated by Protestant writers including John Donne (1633) and John Milton (1671: 31–6).[2] The controversy generated by the Anglican writer Antony Stafford's work, *The femall glory: or, The life, and death of our Blessed Lady* (1635), demonstrates that Mary remained an important, yet contentious, subject in Protestant circles. Exemplifying a brand of Marian devotion that had by the 1630s become associated with Henrietta Maria, the Catholic wife of King Charles I, Stafford's work attracted criticism for its courtly, Neoplatonic and Laudian overtones.[3] More broadly, however, various features of this text – including the title page note ('A treatise worthy the reading, and meditation of all modest women'), dedication to Lady Theophila Coke and primary address 'to the feminine reader' – signpost Mary's perceived importance as a model for women. Indeed Stafford terms her 'a Mirrour of Femall perfection' (B3r). Mary's significance among (Protestant) women is also evident in Dorothy Leigh's maternal advice book *The mothers blessing* (1616), where, alongside Old Testament women, she demonstrates the spiritual, as well as practical, importance of motherhood. Her maternal example is similarly central to Elizabeth Clinton's encouragement of women to breastfeed: 'take notice of one example more, that is, of the *blessed Virgin:* as her womb bare our *blessed Saviour*, so her pappes gave him sucke. Now who shall deny the own mothers suckling of their owne children to bee their duty, since every godly matron hath walked in these steps before them' (1622: 5).

Mary's motherhood was not, however, the only aspect of her character that attracted the attention of early modern readers. She was also appropriated in debates about female authority and queenship, as demonstrated by texts including N.N.'s *Maria Triumphans* (1635), Francis Lenton's *Great Britains Beauties* (1638), and *The life and death* (1669) which draw links between Queen Henrietta Maria and Mary as queen of heaven.[4] This understanding of Mary as a queenly intercessor emerges more overtly within early modern rosary texts that were written for, and circulated among, an English Catholic audience as a means of encouraging recusants to continue in their faith in Mary despite risk of persecution (Bucke, 1589; DeVos, 1600; Loarte, 1597 and 1613). Mary also remained a prime devotional subject in Catholic prose and poetry, as Rist's focus on Henry Constable and Richard Verstagen suggests (see Chapter 10).[5] Yet, as Gallagher's essay (Chapter 11) considers, such texts were rarely a straightforward reiteration of a medieval Mary but are inflected by reformed sensibilities.

Mary's maternity of Jesus is not the only miraculous conception recounted in the Gospel of Luke. The motherhood of Elizabeth, wife of Zachariah and cousin of Mary, is also attributed to God's care (Luke 1:11–25).[6] Despite being of 'great age', Elizabeth conceived and 'broght forthe a soone' who was named John, as the angel Gabriel instructed (Luke 1:18, 57).[7] With direct and sustained reference to Elizabeth, Christopher Hooke's puritan sermon *The child-birth* (1590), which reflects on Luke 1:57–8, considers the concept of God's mercy in the safe delivery of children. For Hooke, Elizabeth's story 'teacheth women especially ... what account they haue to make of the conception and bearing of their Children, and from whence it doth proceede: namely that they haue to account of it as of a great mercy, and as proceeding from the great mercy of God' (Div). Elizabeth's pregnancy also garnered comment because of what occurred during the Visitation (Luke 1:39–56); Elizabeth explains that 'as soon as the voice of [Mary's] salutation sounded in mine ears, the babe leaped in my womb for joy' (Luke 1:44). Biblical commentators disagreed over the significance of the baby's movement, as well as Elizabeth's declaration of Mary as 'blessed' (Luke 1:42). Within the Roman Catholic tradition both examples were cited to prove that Mary possessed intrinsic grace; yet, Protestants were quick to assert that the child's movement was, as Stafford explains, 'not an effect of the Virgins vertue, but of the Word incarnate' (1635: 108).[8]

Another famous Mary – Mary Magdalene – appears frequently across the pages of the New Testament.[9] She was a fluid and composite figure in the early modern period and, although sometimes associated with vanity and wanton sexuality, her emotive lamentations (for Jesus at the cross and sepulchre), repentance (exemplified by washing Jesus' feet), and faith (demonstrated in her encounter with the risen Jesus) attracted interest and praise.[10] In addition, as Hopkins' essay (Chapter 12) reveals, the Magdalene image could be mobilised to offer social and political commentary. Although Mary Magdalene's association with the assumed prostitute who washes Jesus feet (Luke 7:36–50) meant that there were limitations to her exemplary function, she remained, as Christine Peters explains, important to early modern writers because she 'offered a powerful image of the redemption of the sinner through faith' (2003: 6).[11] Mary Magdalene's faith was understood to be visibly manifested in her tears, and her weeping emerges as a significant devotional trope across a spectrum of confessionally diverse writings. The prose text *Marie Magdalens funeral teares* (1591) and poems including 'Mary Magdalens blvsh' and 'Marie Magdalens complaynt at Christes death' (1595: F1r–3v), both written by the Jesuit Robert Southwell, evocatively centre on the sensory manifestation of Mary's faith and the resulting edification of her spirit. Mary's tears and 'signs of shame' are presented as physical markers of her remorse and function as a deep-seated expression of her sorrow at Christ's death (1595: F1r).[12] This Magdalene-focused example of the literature of sorrow is also evident in Richard Crashaw's 'Sanite [sic] Mary Magdalene or The Weeper' (1652) where Mary's tears make her a model of the penitent sinner: 'We are taught best by thy tears and thee' (86). But Mary's tears were not only the concern of Catholic poets. An interest in this outward sign of her sorrow and faith also emerges within Protestant poetry. George Herbert's 'Marie Magdalene', for example, questions the significance of the tears Mary sheds while washing Jesus' feet asking 'Why kept she not her tears for her own faults, / And not his feet?' Yet, in spite of this questioning, the movement of the poem sanctions her tears as evidence of her washed soul for 'in washing one, she washed both' (1633: 168). Mary's weeping similarly preoccupies the tellingly named 'Eyes and Tears' (1681) by Andrew Marvell which luxuriates in Mary's 'liquid chains', 'those seeing tears' to consider the beauty of sorrow (9). Across religious divisions, then, Mary Magdalene had a specific function as an example of remorseful repentance.

Closely linked to the figure of Mary Magdalene is Martha.[13] Her character is revealed in two encounters with Jesus: on the occasion of her brother Lazarus' death, where she exhibits faith in Christ's healing powers and openly declares her belief in his status as Son of God (John 11:21–7); and when her practical, hospitable response to Jesus' presence in her home is compared unfavourably to her sister Mary's attentiveness to his teaching (Luke 10:38–42). Jesus explains that Martha is 'careful and troubled about many things', whereas Mary has 'chosen that good part' (Luke 10:41–2). The distinction drawn between the sisters' response to Jesus reverberates in early modern appropriations of Martha. *The Memorandum of Martha Moulsworth* (1632), for example, opens with the author recounting her birth and a digression on her name 'Martha' spurs the comment:

> My Name was Martha, Martha tooke much payne
> our Sauiour christ hir guesse to entertayne
> God gyue me grace my Inward house to dight
> that he with me may supp, & stay all night.
> (Evans and Wiedemann, 1993: 4–5)

The author's identification with Martha reworks the biblical emphasis by suggesting that hospitality and housekeeping can have an inward, spiritual dimension: the home Martha is concerned with is her soul, into which she welcomes Jesus. The role of housekeeper is thus elevated and esteemed as spiritually relevant by Martha's biblical example.[14]

The faithful domesticity of Martha makes for a pointed contrast with the sexuality of another woman in the Gospels, Salome.[15] The Gospels of Matthew (14:6–12) and Mark (6:21–8) relate how Salome danced sensuously before King Herod at his birthday feast and, having pleased the King and been granted a request, asks for the head of John the Baptist on a platter.[16] Early modern discussion of Salome tends to ruminate, however, on the political machinations of her mother, Herodias.[17] Typically, it is the actions of the mother, rather than daughter, that are censured: Thomas Bentley absolves Salome of some of the blame by explaining that she asks for the head of John 'to please her mother' (1582: 230) and, upon receiving it, 'straight wayes brought it vnto her bloodthirstie mother for a present' (230). This emphasis on Herodias is also a distinguishing feature of Joseph Hall's (1661) discussion of the beheading of John the Baptist (see also Hall, 1654: 54–6). Yet, Hall goes further than Bentley by categorising Salome's actions as those of a dutiful child rightly obeying her parent: 'so much good nature and filial respect was in this wanton Damsel, that she would not carve her self of her option, but takes her Mother with her ... It is both unmannerly and unnatural in the Child to run before, without, against the will of the Parent' (1661: 97). Hall even employs Salome to exemplify the obedience that the Christian should show to God, as their Father: 'Oh that we could be so officious to our good and Heavenly Father, as she was to an earthly and wicked Mother' (1661: 97). Therefore, Salome's obedience is at once her downfall and her duty. Her actions were not routinely condemned and instead, as this example suggests, she could be used to exemplify ideal parent-child relationships and, in turn, the proper connection between the Christian and God.

The use of New Testament women to consider the relationship between an individual and God is more forcefully revealed in early modern readings of Anna. Anna's scriptural presence is slight. Luke 2:36–8 terms her 'a prophetess', offers brief comment on her ancestry, remarks on her 'great age' and marital status (she is a widow of 44 years), and reveals that she resides permanently in the Temple in continual fasting and prayer, and offers instruction to all 'that looked for redemption in Jerusalem' (v. 38). She is frequently praised for her gift of prophecy (Agrippa, 1652; Fell, 1667),[18] but commentators more often remark on her fasting, reading it as an indicator of her closeness to God. Henry More argues that 'this holy woman receive[s] the spirit of prophecie' because she is in 'constant chastitie, and continued fasting' (1656: 38), and Richard Allestree explains that Anna's example shows that fasting 'is reckoned as a service of God, fit to be joyned with *prayers*' (1659: 132). For Downame, however, Anna's example is used to illustrate the particular value of prayer over fasting: 'Not that fasting in it selfe is a worship of God, as prayer is, but onely is a meanes and helpe to further vs in the worship of God, & to make our prayers more feruent & effectuall: to which purpose *Anna* ioyned fasting with her prayers' (1604: 10).[19] In addition to modelling fervent commitment to God, Anna became a point of reference for early modern writers debating the merits of fasting and prayer.

Another biblical woman who makes a brief, but notable, cameo in the Gospels is Pilate's wife: she appears in a single sentence in the Gospel of Matthew. Pilate rests to consider his judgement of Jesus and his wife urges 'have thou nothing to do with that just man: for I have suffered many things this day in a dream because of him' (Matt. 27:19). Because of the advice she offers to her husband, Pilate's wife is, generally, positively appropriated. Lanyer, for example, cites her alongside the Daughters of Jerusalem in *Salve Deus* as one of a number of women whose actions and words contrast with those of the narrative's sinful men (see 1993: 87). Two other peripheral, but significant, women appear in the Gospel of John. A 'woman of Samaria', who encountered Jesus while attempting to draw water at Jacob's well (John 4:1–38), is diversely appropriated on matters of faith, but she also emerges in anti-Catholic rhetoric. William Allen, as part of a condemnation of Roman Catholic devotion compiled by William Fulke, uses the Samaritan woman to denounce blind devotion that is not focused on the word of God (Allen in Fulke, 1577: 21). John 8:1–11 recalls another unnamed woman who, having been accused of adultery, is saved from stoning by Jesus' challenge to her accusers: 'He that is without sin among you, let him first cast a stone' (John 8:7).

This woman is often used in early modern religious writings to discourage the condemnation of sinners (Richardson, 1617; Adams, 1619); yet, she also remains fundamentally tied to her adulterous past. She is invoked as example of adultery by Thomas Wilson (1612), and titled an 'Aduoutresse' by Bentley who, in a richly elaborate account of the event, carefully clarifies that 'Iesus spake not to abolish the law against Adulterie, but ... onely to bring sinners to repentance' (1582: 261). Evidently, it is the Samarian woman's deviant sexuality, as opposed to Christ's mercy or the Pharisee's hypocrisy, which remains paramount.

Beyond the Gospels, women from other books of the New Testament also receive attention from early modern writers, including Sapphira, Dorcas (Tabitha), Lydia and Priscilla who appear in the Book of Acts. In Acts 5:1–11, Sapphira and her husband Ananias die suddenly when they lie to the apostles about withholding profit obtained from the sale of their property. Reflecting the biblical record, Sapphira is consistently condemned in early modern texts for her deceit, hypocrisy and disregard of God's laws, and and her punishment of death is frequently cited as an example of God's power and anger (Gostwick, 1616). As Roger Gostwick's commentary reveals though, Ananias' example tends to take precedence in condemnations of the pair and could be used to illustrate that a wife's obedience should primarily be to God (see also Gouge, 1622). In distinction, Dorcas, or Tabitha as she is sometimes termed (Acts 9:36), is commonly extolled in religious writing as an example of 'good works and almsdeeds' in accordance with the biblical record; not least in Bartholomew Parsons' full sermon on Dorcas entitled *A perfect patterne of a true disciple* (1631).[20] Dorcas is also extolled for making and donating garments to the poor in Acts 9:36 (Dent, 1607; Younge, 1655), and her resurrection by Peter (Acts 9:40) unsurprisingly attracted considerable comment (see Bentley, 1582; Donne, 1640; Oliver, 1663). Many of the qualities and roles for which Dorcas was typically celebrated by early modern readers are summarised in a funeral sermon for Mary Rich, Dowager Countess of Warwick. The Countess is favourably remembered as 'Another Dorcas she was (Acts 9.36) doing good, / She cloath'd the Naked, gave the Hungry Food. / The Sick She visited; in their condition, / Was Alm'ner, Surgeon, and Physician' (*A Funeral elegy*, 1678). Dorcas' example operates, then, as another biblical marker against which appropriate female behaviour could be judged.[21]

But as our previous discussion (see Chapter 2) of Hannah has suggested, the Bible's female figures could operate as exemplars for men as well as for women. In the New Testament, Lydia is one such example. She appears in Acts 16 (vv. 13–15; 40) and is routinely praised by early modern readers for her open heart, listening skills and faith (Smith, 1629; Downame, 1647; Guild, 1658; Horton, 1679). These virtues mark her as a model for *all* Christians, as William Perkins explains: 'Wee must therefore like godly Lydia, Act. 16. stirre vp our dull and heauie spirits, and with all diligence marke the things wee heare' (1606: 47).

Because Lydia's belief is celebrated by baptism (Acts 16:15), her narrative is also deployed in theological discussions on the importance of being baptised and, more specifically, in debates on the merits of adult baptism (Robinson, 1624; Rutherford, 1644; and Norcott, 1694).

Lydia's example was, however, also cited among those who sought to counter cultural restrictions on female silence in worship. Thomas Taylor, for instance, deploys her to prove that women, 'as well as men' 'must worship God: Lydia, Act. 16.14' (1612: 362). A concern with the roles occupied by women in the Book of Acts also emerges in early modern theological considerations of Priscilla. Priscilla appears in Acts 18 with her husband Aquila, as a companion to Paul and instructor of Apollos in matters of faith.[22] The order in which 'Priscilla and Aquila' (Acts 18:18) are introduced in the biblical text piqued the attention of several early modern commentators. Edward Leigh, for example, notes that 'Priscilla is here named first ... she was a very vertuous woman; and perhaps to be preferred before her husband for piety' (1650: 228), but Andrew Willet dismisses any suggestion that the biblical sequence indicates the primacy of the wife over the husband (1611: 720). Nevertheless, Priscilla and Aquila's relationship is offered as an example of the holiness of marriage and was also turned to counter the Roman Catholic belief that marriage was an impediment to holy orders (Cowper, 1609; Willet, 1611). A number of seventeenth-century writings also mobilise the couple's example to promote the benefits of private (rather than public) preaching and teaching (Bewick, 1642; Cotton, 1650) and, as a woman, Priscilla could be powerfully deployed to authorise female instruction and ministry (Byfield, 1626; Hall, 1651). Her teaching of Apollos is used by Nicholas Byfield, within a list of scriptural women, to argue 'that the word of God, and the instructions of the ministery of the word, belong to women as well as men' (1626: 7). Similarly, Margaret Fell also calls on Priscilla's example to illuminate the disparity between early modern and biblical attitudes towards female speech: 'we do not read that [Apollos] despised what *Priscilla* said, because she was a Woman, as many now do' (1667: 8). Yet, just as Priscilla could be used by some writers to confound gendered expectations, she was used by others to inform restrictions on women's use of cosmetics and ornamentation. As Willet advises, from Priscilla women can learn 'the true ornaments' of piety and zeal (1611: 746).

That New Testament women were implicated in the debates around female teaching and authority is further revealed in the appropriation of Phoebe. Described in Romans 16:1–2 as a sister, servant of the Church, saint and 'succourer of many', early modern writings commonly extend Phoebe's example of Christian duty and holiness to women and use her narrative to teach on the importance of good works (Willet, 1611; Wilson, 1614). Yet, this biblical woman was also deployed to rebuke those men who failed to recognise the sincerity and power of female faith and teaching (Wilson, 1614: 1238–40), and could be used to argue against the cloistering of nuns. As Willet explains: 'This Phebe ministred vnto the whole Church of her substance, and so was a seruant vnto it: but these [cloistred and inclosed Nunnes] serue no[t] the Church, beeing sequestred from the publike companie and societie of men' (1611: 718–20, 740). In this instance, it is the public nature of Phoebe's teaching that is foregrounded and, although Willet reveals in subsequent discussion an anxiety about how her role has been interpreted to support women speaking, his words remind that the biblical text situates this woman in an authoritative role within the 'whole' church. Thomas Hall similarly notes that while Priscilla's example seems to permit women to teach in a 'private way', Phoebe proves that 'not only men, but women also may instruct their families' (1651: 3). Nevertheless, Hall too is cautious about the potential application of Phoebe's narrative and asserts that, ultimately, she 'was a Diaconess to minister to the sick, and not a Praedicantess to preach, or have Peters keys jingling at her girdle' (1651: 60). It seems that, as is the case so often with early modern male readings of biblical women, the Bible prescribes a role for women that is at odds with early modern expectations of female behaviour.

The final book of the New Testament, the Book of Revelation, contains two evocative female figures: the Whore of Babylon and the Woman Clothed with the Sun. The Whore, a vividly feminine yet grotesque personification of the city of Babylon (14.8; 17:1–5, 16), was ubiquitously interpreted in Protestant religious and polemical writings as a representative of the Roman Catholic Church. And, as Brownlee's essay (Chapter 13) discusses, she is also powerfully evoked in the literary writings of the later Elizabethan and early Jacobean period to warn of the perceived threat Catholicism posed to the individual believer and the English state. However, as Elaine Hobby has shown, this politicised appropriation of the Whore gives way to her re-figuration as a symbol of male learning and selfish wealth in the later female-authored prophecies of the 1650s and 1660s (2002: 274). The Book of Revelation draws a pointed contrast between the Whore and the Bride of Christ – the New Jerusalem (Rev. 21:2, 9–10)[23] – and also with the Woman Clothed with the Sun (Rev. 12:1). Among early modern Protestants, the Woman Clothed with the Sun was widely read as 'the Church … persecuted of Antichrist' (Rev. 12:1, Geneva note). Yet, among Catholics, this woman, as a mother who 'brought forth a man childe' (Rev. 12:5), was commonly understood as a type of the Virgin Mary, as is suggestively revealed in the imagery of Mary on the title page of Henry Hawkins' emblem book (1633).

The alternative, and shifting, readings of the women of Revelation 12 and 17 attest to the fact that homogenising assessments of early modern readings of New Testament women are impossible to make. While typical readings can be discerned, and exegetical commonalities may be traced, there exists no uniform appropriation of the New Testament's female figures. What unites these biblical women is their diversity, fluidity and enduring relevance to a host of contemporary debates. Despite the limited detail of their scriptural accounts, the characters and roles of New Testament women can be amplified, extended and even altered by early modern readers so that any individual woman can be at once sinful and virtuous, powerful and constrained, vivacious and passive, a cautionary example and a positive model. The aspects of a biblical woman's character or narrative that are emphasised depend on her rhetorical usage; she might be employed as a model of faith, to debate theological issues, or to exemplify or confound gendered constraints. Although, like many of the female figures of the Old Testament considered earlier, New Testament women – as women – are to some degree always subject to the conventions of early modern gender, their narratives, as subsequent essays attest, resonated strongly with men as well as with women. Indeed, the women of the New Testament, as we shall see, evoked a vivacity and imaginative power that frequently extends beyond the Bible's words.

Notes

1 The Gospel of Matthew records Mary's role in the birth of Jesus (1:18–25) and the flight to Egypt (2:13–21). Mark's Gospel refers to Christ's mother being present as he teaches (3:31–5) and identifies the family of Jesus (6:3). The Gospel of Luke features Mary most prominently: it includes the Annunciation (1:26–38), Visitation (1:39–56), Jesus' birth (2:1–7), Jesus' presentation in the temple (2:21–38) and Jesus going missing in Jerusalem (2:41–52). John's Gospel includes the wedding at Cana (2:1–12), information on Jesus' origins (7:41–2; 8:41) and records Mary's presence at the crucifixion scene (19:25–7). Acts 1:14 mentions Mary as part of a community at prayer after Jesus' ascension to heaven, and, in the Catholic tradition, the Woman Clothed with the Sun in Revelation (12:1–6) is often interpreted as Mary. Many supplementary details about Mary's early life and her perpetual virginity originated in the New Testament Apocrypha. In addition, the belief in Mary's Immaculate Conception (see Boss, 2007) and Assumption (see Shoemaker, 2002) has its own particular history.

2 Studies by Spurr (2007) and Waller (2011) discuss these appropriations. Mary also appears less explicitly in other writings, such as Shakespeare's plays (see Buccola and Hopkins, 2007; and Espinosa, 2011).

3 Stafford's text, authorised by the Bishop of London, William Juxon, was denounced by other Protestant ministers for what they viewed as its Catholic elements. As part of a sermon, the Puritan Henry Burton, for example, meticulously references page numbers and quotes passages from *The femall glory* which he finds particularly distasteful. He suggests that Stafford 'mightily deifies the Virgin Mary', and overall presents 'a Metamorphosis of our Religion' (1636: 123, 126; see 123–6 for his full commentary). For further detail see Parry (2009).

4 For further discussion of the links between Queen Henrietta Maria and the Virgin Mary in 1630s texts see for example Veevers (1989) and Gallagher (2012).

5 Devotional prose that took Mary as the main subject includes: C.N (1595); Lodge (1596); Shaw (1618); A.G. (1619); Taylor (1620); Sweetnam (1620); Falconer (1632) and Hawkins' emblem book (1633). Mary also appears in Catholic poetry (Crashaw, 1957; I.B., 1632).

6 This follows the tradition of Old Testament barren women thanking God for their pregnancy. See for example Sarah (Genesis 15–21).

7 Unless otherwise stated, scriptural references have been taken from *The Geneva Bible* (1560, rpt. 2007).

8 To illustrate and add credence to this interpretation, Stafford lists other examples of biblical figures (including Abraham, Lot, Laban, Elisha and Zachary) whose house was also conferred with God's grace and, in doing so, negates the (Roman Catholic) interpretation that the child moving signifies Mary's intrinsic virtue (1635: 108–11). Mary and Elizabeth's conversation was also used by some writers as model of appropriate female speech. See for example Stafford (1635: 124–5) and Fell (1667: 6). For more on how biblical women influenced early modern attitudes towards female speech, see the essays by Osherow, Thorne and Clarke in this volume (Chapters 5, 6 and 7).

9 Mary Magdalene is explicitly mentioned in Luke 8:2 where she is healed of evil spirits. She also appears as a follower of Jesus (Mark 15:40–1); at the cross (Matt 27:56; Mark 15:40; John 19:25); watching Joseph of Arimathaea place Jesus' body in the sepulchre (Mark 15: 42–7); going to anoint Jesus' body; hearing news of his resurrection and informing the Apostles (Matt. 27:61; 28:1–10; Mark 16:1–8; Luke 23:55–24:11; John 20:1–2); and as a witness to the risen Christ (Mark 16:9–11 and John 20:11–18). Other biblical women – Joanna, the Wife of Chusa, and Susanna – are mentioned alongside Mary Magdalene, as supporting the group of disciples (Luke 8:3) and Joanna also reports the evidence of the risen Jesus according to Luke 24:10. In addition to these references, Mary Magdalene has been conflated with the penitent sinner who washes and anoints Jesus' feet (Luke 7:37–50), and with Mary, sister of Martha and Lazarus (Matthew 26:6–13; Mark 14:3–9; John 12:1–8), who is praised by Jesus for choosing to sit and listen to his words. This Mary also appears in the story of the raising of Lazarus (John 11). For studies of Mary Magdalene's significance in the early modern period see Jansen (2001); Badir (2009); and Erhardt and Morris (2012).

10 Mary Magdalene is appropriated in Protestant texts such as Wager (1566); Breton (1595 and 1601); Markham (1601); White (1618); Andrewes (1620); Walkington (1620); Hodson (1639); and Bunyan (1688). She also features in Donne's 'To the Lady Magdalen Herbert, of St. Mary Magdalene' (1839) and in Catholic prose by I.C. (1603); Sweetnam (1617); and Robinson (1899).

11 As Peters notes, 'included in the list of saints in 1549, she was omitted in 1552 and, even more strikingly, from the longer list in 1559, despite her symbolic importance as testimony to the saving power of faith' (2003: 212). See Peters (235–6) for further details on Mary Magdalene's gradual omission from the Elizabethan Prayer Book.

12 Badir (2009: 59–90) explores the idea of an absent Christ in various texts that centre on Mary Magdalene and illuminates how they interrogate the concept of 'Christ's presence'.

13 Martha's sister Mary anoints the feet of Jesus (John 11:2 and 12:3) and this conflated character is traditionally understood to be Mary Magdalene (see above).

14 For further reading of this text see Tancke (2010: 45). Martha Moulsworth's funeral sermon also compares her to the biblical Martha (see Becker, 2003: 134–5). For another example of female self-identification with Martha, see the spiritual diary of Mary Rich (written 1666–1678) in which she compares herself to both Martha and her sister Mary (Rich, 1847). This comparison was also employed in Rich's funeral sermon (see

Walker, 1678) and, as Mendelson (2004) identifies, 'by the time she died, the countess had attained almost legendary status as a pattern of the saintly life' (for Rich's autobiography see Rich, 1848).

15 Although not directly named in the New Testament, the 'daughter of Herodias' (Matt. 14:6) is identified as Salome by Josephus (1602: 472).

16 Mark's Gospel places particular emphasis on Herodias' involvement in Salome's decision to ask for John's head and, in both Gospel accounts, she delivers the head to her mother.

17 Herodias seeks vengeance on John the Baptist because of his earlier condemnation of her marriage to Herod. John tells Herod, 'It is not lawful for thee to have thy brother's wife' (Mark 6:18; see too Matthew 14:3–5).

18 In both of these texts Anna's example of prophecy is also linked to the prophet Philip's four daughters described in the Book of Acts as 'virgins, which did prophesy' (21:9).

19 Breton (1597: 21–2) uses the devotion of Anna to illuminate 'the comfort of prayer'.

20 For more on her role as female disciple see Williams (1644).

21 See the essay by Clarke in this volume (Chapter 7) that reveals how the female figures in the Book of Proverbs were appropriated in funeral sermons to celebrate early modern women (7).

22 Paul's appreciation is recorded in Romans 16:3–4. For a neat summary of the respect she inspired in Paul, see Bentley (1582: 214–5).

23 For detail on the feminised portrayal of Jerusalem in the New Testament see Groves' essay (Chapter 9) in this volume.

References

A Funeral elegy upon the much lamented death of the right honourable and eminently virtuous lady and exemplary pattern of piety, charity and humility, Mary, Dowager Countess of Warwick who died April 12, 1678 (1678) London: s.n.

Adams, T. (1619) *The happines of the Church*. London: G.P[urslowe].

Agrippa, H.C. (von Nettesheim) (1652) *The glory of women*. London: s.n.

Allestree, R. (1659) *The whole duty of man laid down in a plain way for the use of the meanest reader*. London: s.n.

Andrewes, L. (1620) *A sermon preached at White-hall, on Easter day the 16. of April. 1620*. London: Robert Barker and John Bill.

B., I. (1632) *Virginalia, or Spirituall Sonnets in Prayse of the most glorious Virgin Marie*. Rouen: N. Courant.

Badir, P. (2009) *The Maudlin Impression: English Literary Images of Mary Magdalene, 1550–1700*. Notre Dame, IN: University of Notre Dame Press.

Becker, L.M. (2003) *Death and the Early Modern Englishwoman*. Aldershot: Ashgate.

Bentley, T. (1582) *The sixt lampe of virginitie conteining a mirrour for maidens and matrons*. London: Thomas Dawson and Henry Denham.

Bewick, J. (1642) *An antidote against lay-preaching*. London: s.n.

Boss, S.J. (2007) 'The Development of the Doctrine of Mary's Immaculate Conception.' *Mary: The Complete Resource*. Ed. S.J. Boss. London: Continuum. 207–35.

Breton, N. (1595) *Marie Magdalens loue*. London: John Danter.

——. (1597) *Auspicante Iehoua Maries exercise*. London: Thomas Este.

———. (1601) *A diuine poeme diuided into two partes: the rauisht soule, and the blessed vveeper*. London: R. Bradock.

Buccola, R. and Hopkins, L. (eds) (2007) *Marian Moments in Early Modern British Drama*. Aldershot: Ashgate.

Bucke, J. (1589) *Instructions for the use of the beads*. Louvain: I. Maes.

Bunyan, J. (1688) *Good news for the vilest of men*. London: George Larkin.

Burton, H. (1636) *For God, and the King .The summe of two sermons preached on the fifth of November last in St. Matthewes Friday-streete. 1636*. Amsterdam: J.F. Stam.

Byfield, N. (1626) *Sermons upon the ten first verses of the third chapter of the first Epistle of S. Peter*. London: H. Lownes.

C., I. (1603) *Saint Marie Magdalens conuersion*. England: English Secret Press.

Clinton, E. (1622) *The Countesse of Lincolnes nurserie*. Oxford: John Lichfield.

Cotton, J. (1650) *Singing of Psalmes a Gospel-ordinance*. London: s.n.

Cowper, W. (1609) *Three heauenly treatises vpon the eight chapter to the Romanes*. London: Thomas Snodham.

Crashaw, R. (1652) *Carmen Deo nostro, te decet hymnus sacred poems*. Paris: Peter Targa.

———. (1957) *The Poems, English, Latin and Greek*. 2nd edn. Ed. L.C. Martin. Oxford: Clarendon Press.

Dent, A. (1607) *The plaine mans path-way to heauen*. London: Melchiside Bradwood.

DeVos, M. (1600) *The Rosarie of Our Lady*. Antwerp: Apud Ioannem Keerbergium.

Donne, J. (1633) *Poems*. London: Miles Flesher.

———. (1640) *LXXX sermons preached by that learned and reverend divine, Iohn Donne*. London: Miles Flesher.

———. (1839) *The Works of John Donne*. Ed. H. Alford. London: John W. Parker.

Downame, G. (1604) *The Christians sanctuarie*. London: Adam Islip.

———. (1647) *The covenant of grace*. London: John Macock.

Erhardt, M.A. and Morris, A.M. (eds) (2012) *Mary Magdalene: Iconographic Studies from the Middle Ages to the Baroque*. Leiden: Brill.

Espinosa, R. (2011) *Masculinity and Marian Efficacy in Shakespeare's England*. Farnham: Ashgate.

Evans, R.C. and Wiedemann, B. (eds) (1993) *'My name was Martha': A Renaissance Woman's Autobiographical Poem*. West Cornwall, CT: Locust Hill Press.

Falconer, J. (1632) *The Mirrour of Created Perfection*. Saint-Omer: English College Press.

Fell, M.A. (1667) *Womens speaking Justified, proved and allowed of by the Scriptures*. London: s.n.

Fulke, W. (1577) *Tvvo treatises written against the papistes*. London: s.n.

G., A. (1619) *The widdoves mite cast into the treasure-house of the prerogatiues, and prayses of our B. Lady, the immaculate, and most glorious Virgin Mary, the Mother of God*. Saint-Omer: English College Press.

Gallagher, L. (2012) 'The Virgin Mary in the Early Modern Literary Imagination.' PhD thesis, Queen's University Belfast.

Gostwick, R. (1616) *The anatomie of Ananias: or, Gods censure against sacriledge*. Cambridge: Cantrell Legge.

Gouge, W. (1622) *Of domesticall duties eight treatises*. London: John Haviland.

Guild, W. (1658) *Loves entercours between the Lamb & his bride, Christ and his Church*. London: W. Wilson.

Hall, J. (1654) *Cases of conscience*. London: R.H. and J.G.

——. (1661) *The contemplations upon the history of the New Testament*. London: James Flesher.

Hall, T. (1651) *The pulpit guarded with XVII arguments proving the unlawfulness, sinfulness and danger of suffering private persons to take upon them publike preaching, and expounding the Scriptures without a call and compiled by a friend to truth and peace*. London: J. Cottrel.

Hawkins, H. (1633) *Partheneia Sacra*. Rouen: John Cousturier.

Herbert, G. (1633) *The temple Sacred poems and private ejaculations*. Cambridge: Thom. Buck and Roger Daniel.

Hobby, E. (2002) 'Prophecy.' *A Companion to Early Modern Women's Writing*. Ed. A. Pacheco. Oxford: Blackwell. 264–81.

Hodson, W. (1639) *The holy sinner a tractate meditated on some passages of the storie of the penitent woman in the Pharisees house*. London: s.n.

Hooke, C. (1590) *The child-birth or womans lecture*. London: Thomas Orwin.

Horton, T. (1679) *One hundred select sermons upon several texts fifty upon the Old Testament, and fifty on the new*. London: s.n.

Jansen, K. (2001) *The Making of the Magdalen: Preaching and Popular Devotion in the Later Middle Ages*. Princeton: Princeton University Press.

Joseph, F. (1602) *The famous and memorable works of Iosephus, a man of much houour and learning among the Iewes*. London: Peter Short.

Lanyer, A. (1993) *The Poems of Amelia Lanyer: Salve Deus Rex Judaeorum*. Ed. S. Woods. Oxford: Oxford University Press.

Leigh, D. (1616) *The mothers blessing*. London: John Budge.

Leigh, E. (1650) *Annotations upon all the New Testament philologicall and theologicall*. London: W.W. and E.G.

Lenton, F. (1638) *Great Britains Beauties or, The Female Glory epitomized*. London: Marmaduke Parsons.

Loarte, G. de (1597) *Instructions and advertisements*. London: W. Carter.

——. (1613) *Instructions and advertisements*. Rouen: Cardin Hamillon

Lodge, T. (1596) *Prosopopeia containing the teares of the holy, blessed, and sanctified Marie, the Mother of God*. London: s.n.

Markham, G. (1601) *Marie Magdalens lamentations for the losse of her master Iesus*. London: Adam Islip.

Marvell, A. (1681) *Miscellaneous poems by Andrew Marvell*. London: s.n.

Mendelson, S.H. (2004) 'Rich, Mary, countess of Warwick (1624–1678).' *Oxford Dictionary of National Biography*. Oxford: Oxford University Press.

Milton, J. (1968) *The poems of John Milton*. Ed. J. Carey and A. Fowler. London: Longmans.

More, H. (1656) *The life and doctrine of ovr Savior Iesvs Christ*. Ghent: Maximiliaen Graet.

N., C. (1595) *Our Ladie hath a new sonne*. England: English Secret Press.

N., N. (1635) *Maria Triumphans*. Saint-Omer: English College Press.

Norcott, J. (1694) *Baptism discovered plainly & faithfully according to the word of God*. London: Widow Norcott.

Oliver, J. (1663) *A present for teeming vvomen*. London: Sarah Griffin.

Parry, G. (2009) 'High-Church Devotion in the Church of England, 1620–42.' *Writing and Religion in England, 1558–1689: Studies in Community-Making and Cultural Memory*. Ed. R.D. Sell and A.W. Johnson. Aldershot: Ashgate. 239–52.

Parsons, B. (1631) *Dorcas: or, A perfect patterne of a true disciple.* Oxford: William Turner.

Perkins, W. (1606) *A godly and learned exposition or commentarie vpon the three first chapters of the Reuelation.* London: Adam Islip.

Peters, C. (2003) *Patterns of Piety: Women, Gender, and Religion in Late Medieval and Reformation England.* Cambridge: Cambridge University Press.

Rich, M. (1847) *Memoir of Lady Warwick: Also her diary, from AD 1666 to 1672.* London: Religious Tract Society.

——. (1848) *Autobiography of Mary Countess of Warwick.* Ed. T. Crofton Croker. London: Percy Society.

Richardson, C. (1617) *The price of our redemption A sermon preached at Paules Crosse.* London: W. Iaggard.

Robinson, J. (1624) *A defence of the doctrine propounded by the synode at Dort against Iohn Murton and his associates.* Amsterdam: Successors of G. Thorp.

Robinson, T. (1899) *The life and death of Mary Magdalene: a legendary poem in two parts about A.D. 1620.* London: K. Paul, Trench, Trübner & Co.

Rutherford, S. (1644) *The due right of presbyteries, or, A peaceable plea for the government of the Church of Scotland.* London: E. Griffin.

Shaw, J. (1618) *The blessednes of the Virgin Marie the Mother of our Lord Jesus Christ.* London: Richard Field.

Shoemaker, S.J. (2002) *The Ancient Traditions of the Virgin Mary's Dormition and Assumption.* Oxford: Oxford University Press.

Smith, J. (1629) *Essex doue, presenting the vvorld vvith a fevv of her oliue branches.* London: Adam Islip and George Purslowe.

Southwell, R. (1591) *Marie Magdalens funeral teares.* London: John Wolfe.

——. (1595) *Saint Peters complaynt With other poems.* London: I[ames] R[oberts].

Spurr, B. (2007) *See The Virgin Blest: The Virgin Mary in English Poetry.* Basingstoke: Palgrave Macmillan.

Stafford, A. (1635) *The femall glory: or, The life, and death of our Blessed Lady, the holy Virgin Mary.* London: Thomas Harper.

Sweetnam, J. (1617) *S. Mary Magdalens pilgrimage to paradise.* Saint-Omer: English College Press.

——. (1620) *The Paradise of Delights, Or the B. Virgins Garden of Loreto.* Saint-Omer: English College Press.

Tancke, U. (2010) *'Bethinke Thy Selfe' in Early Modern England: Writing Women's Identities.* Netherlands: Rodopi B.V.

Taylor, J. (1620) *The Life and Death of the most Blessed amoung Women.* London: G. Eld.

Taylor, T. (1612) *A commentarie vpon the Epistle of S. Paul written to Titus.* Cambridge: Cantrell Legge.

The Geneva Bible: A facsimile of the 1560 edition (2007) Ed. L.E. Berry and W. Whittingham. Peabody, MA: Henderson Publishers.

The life and death of that matchless mirrour of magnanimity, and heroick vertues Henrietta Maria de Bourbon (1669) London: Sam. Speed.

Veevers, E. (1989) *Images of Love and Religion: Queen Henrietta Maria and Court Entertainments.* Cambridge: Cambridge University Press.

Wager, L. (1566) *A new enterlude, neuer before this tyme imprinted, entreating of the life and repentaunce of Marie Magdalene.* London: John Charlewood.

Walker, A. (1678) *Eureka, Eureka the virtuous woman found, her loss bewailed, and character examined in a sermon preached at Felsted in Essex, April 30, 1678.* London: Nathanael Ranew.

Walkington, T. (1620) *Rabboni Mary Magdalens teares, of sorrow, solace.* London: Edw. Griffin.

Waller, G. (2011) *The Virgin Mary in Late Medieval and Early Modern English Literature and Popular Culture.* Cambridge: Cambridge University Press.

White, H. (1618) *The ready way to trve repentance: or, A Godly, and learned treatise, of the repentance of Mary Magdalen.* London: G.E.

Willet, A. (1611) *Hexapla, that is, A six-fold commentarie vpon the most diuine Epistle of the holy apostle S. Paul to the Romanes.* Cambridge: Cantrell Legge.

Williams, R. (1644) *The blovdy tenent, of persecution.* London: s.n.

Wilson, T. (1612) *A Christian dictionarie.* London: W. Iaggard.

——. (1614) *A commentarie vpon the most diuine Epistle of S. Paul to the Romanes.* London: W. Iaggard.

Younge, R. (1655) *The prevention of poverty.* London: R. & W. Leybourn.

9

Christ's tears and maternal cannibalism in early modern London

Beatrice Groves

No Chronicle that shal write of Ierusalems last captiuitie, but shall write of mee also. (Nashe, 1958: 2:76)[1]

Early modern English preachers and writers were obsessed by the Roman siege of Jerusalem, a siege which was recorded by Josephus in his *Jewish War* and which culminated in the fall of the city to Titus and desolation of the Temple in AD 70. The biblical text which lies behind this event, for both the Gospel writers and my early modern authors, is Lamentations (a text about the first destruction of the city, in 587 BC). This biblical book performs Jeremiah's lament over Jerusalem in which the sinful, suffering city is insistently female. Lamentations opens with the famous words – 'Howe doth the citie remaine solitarie that was full of people? she is as a widowe' (1:1)[2] – and it consistently casts urban sorrows as feminine ones. Gail Kern Paster's (1993) influential formulation of the female form as presented as a leaky vessel is evident in the feminine persona of the invaded city of Lamentations who weeps without ceasing (1:2) and 'is as a menstruous woman in the middes of them' (1:17). The two most common feminine symbols for the city – that of virgin and mother – have failed to fulfil their symbolic role, for the city walls are no longer intact and the mothers of the city have turned from protective to predatory. Implicit within Lamentations is the idea that just as the defilement of the virgins within the city finds its analogue in the breaching of Jerusalem's walls, so these cannibalising mothers are the literal embodiment of a metropolis which no longer protects but destroys: 'in the day of the Lordes wrath none escaped nor remained: those that I haue nourished and brought vp, hath mine enemie consumed' (2:22). 'Mine enemie' distances the city itself from this aggression, but the fact that the Babylonian sacking is called 'the day of the Lordes wrath' is a reminder that Lamentations sees God as the author of this destruction: as the Geneva edition notes somewhat nervously in the marginalia: 'This declareth that we shoulde acknowledge God to be the author of al our afflictions, to the intent that we might seeke vnto him for remedy' (note to Lamentations 13). In the darkest interpretation of the text, the mothers who eat their own children find disturbing parallels in both the city whose besieged walls no longer save but starve her citizens and a deity who now appears not as a protector but, as Lamentations states, 'as an enemie' (2:4; 2:5).

Lamentations was a layered and complex text in the early modern period, because it was read as referring not simply to the Babylonian fall but also to the crucifixion (as the Church had traditionally identified the sufferings of Jerusalem described here with those of Christ on the cross)[3] and to the Roman fall which was held to have been figured by this first destruction (Drant, 1566: 18r). The Roman fall had been read by the medieval Church as Christ's vengeance on his crucifiers and hence this double typology of Lamentations figures Christ simultaneously as the feminised, suffering city and as its punitive God, revenging himself on the place of his crucifixion. The failed maternal love of Lamentations ultimately encodes anxiety about the protection afforded by both the fortified cities man has built for himself and by the loving divinity believed to preside over them.

The most infamous event in Josephus's narrative of the Roman siege is Miriam's cannibalisation of her child. The sufferings endured by the citizens of Jerusalem are encapsulated by this act which simultaneously breaks the ultimate taboo of eating human flesh and the closest human bond. Miriam's act became an enduring image of the unimaginable horror of life trapped within the city. While classical examples of parental cannibalism always involve a father consuming their child, Josephus, influenced by the maternal cannibalism of Lamentations, has a mother perform the act. Lamentations says that: 'The hands of the pitifull women haue sodden their owne children, which were their meate in the destruction of the daughter of my people' (4:10). The 'pitifull' nature of the women here can be understood either as a natural compassion that they have overcome (as in Thomas Drant's translation: 'The mothers (els much pitifull) / did boyle their sucklings small' (1566: K8r)) or, as their loving execution of their children to save them from the horrors of starving to death. The latter is the interpretation given in the most extraordinary text about Miriam's cannibalism – a 1593 plague-pamphlet by Thomas Nashe entitled *Christ's Tears over Jerusalem*. Nashe's Miriam says: 'Ile bind thee to me againe, in my wombe Ile beare thee againe, and there bury thee ere Famine shall confounde thee' (1958: 2:72). In the Josephean source, however, Miriam is not pitiful but swept up in an enraged powerlessness: 'while hunger was eating her heart out and rage was consuming her still faster, she yielded to the suggestions of fury and necessity, and in defiance of all natural feeling laid hands on her own child, a baby at the breast' (353). In a distasteful but striking detail, while the lachrymose mothers of Lamentations boil their infants, Josephus's fiery mother roasts hers (Josephus, 1981: 354). While medieval accounts of the cannibalism always follow Josephus in having Miriam roast her infant (Deutsch, 1986: plates 144–7), early modern narratives bring together the roasting of Josephus with the boiling of Lamentations. This distinctive detail suggests a larger point about the way that early modern writers, believing that Josephus is recording history as patterned out by the prophecies of Jesus and Jeremiah, thought that history was a composite of these sources. Miriam is not a biblical figure, but her early modern incarnation is a synthesis of the suffering women, and the metaphors of perverted mother-hood, which congregate around the fall of Jerusalem in scriptural texts.

Reformed early modern theologians were proud to believe that they had excised from biblical history the mythic accretions of Catholicism that had no basis in scriptural history; but Miriam is a cogent example of the way that such stories did persist. Josephus's history is a biblical paratext which continued to form a midrash to the story of the fall of Jerusalem long after the Reforma-tion. (The most extreme example of this is Sebastian Castellio's (banned) 1554 biblical translation which included sections from both Josephus's *Antiquities* and *Jewish War*).[4] Not only was Miriam's story read as foretold by the Bible, in her embodiment of failed maternity she incorporates the scriptural tropes for the fall of Jerusalem. In Lamentations Jerusalem is a city that weeps into the night but cannot save her children, and in the Gospels she is a city who is presided over by a weeping deity figured as a mother-hen whose wings cannot gather in her offspring (Luke 13:34). The early modern Miriam synthesised the violence of Josephus with the weeping of Lamentations to create a maternal figure who wept lovingly over her child before killing him. Preaching during the plague epidemic of 1593, Adam Hill recounted Miriam's story and told how 'when she had wept and kissed him often, she put her child behind her and killed it with a dagger' (1595: D8v). This image of the loving yet violent mother finds its apogee in Nashe's Miriam, whose weeping self-justification finds a disturbing analogue in that of Christ. As Crewe has written: 'The effect of Nashe's "sophistication" of the naïve form is to make it both self-advertising and self-questioning ... Christ becomes the ultimate victim of his own self-incriminating rhetoric. He protests far too much, thus betraying his own sense of impotence, his own guilt, and his own violent resentment' (1982: 56, 61). Christ's monologue is directly followed by Miriam's even more problematic address, which retrospectively colours Christ's words so that the city's destruction seems (like her murder of her son) an act of pre-meditated violence.

The medieval approach to the fall of Jerusalem as the 'Vengeance of Our Lord' is revisited in the early modern period with a new, and biblical, emphasis on the terror and horror of envisaging a loving God as attacking his once-beloved children. England was proud to think of herself as the new Sion and, inflected by both this identification with Jerusalem and the renewed emphasis on the historicity of the Old Testament and Josephus, the fall of Jerusalem became an event which no longer symbolised the triumphant ascendancy of Christianity so much as the shared sinfulness and vulnerability of humankind.

The retelling of Miriam's cannibalism tended to proliferate around years of plague. Thomas Dekker's plague-pamphlet *The Wonderful Year* (1603), for example, opines that the sufferings of Londoners in 1603 were comparable to those of the Jews at the destruction of Jerusalem (1967: 47–8). Dekker makes Miriam into the horrific counterpoint of his carnivalesque treatment of the plague-time city in which graves await their 'breakfast' of corpses and Londoners walk 'with rue and wormewood stuffed into their ears and nostrils, looking like so many boars' heads stuck with branches of rosemary, to be served for brawn at Christmas' (59, 47). The high death-rates of urban communities were exacerbated by epidemics to the extent that, as Paul Slack (the most important historian of early modern plague) has put it, 'towns were above all places where people died' (1985: 188). Plague was described as cannibalistic rather than simply predatory in Dekker's pamphlets because it was believed to have been mankind's sinful behaviour which had caused God to send the plague as punishment. The claustrophobic closeness of life in London was thought to lead to a break-down of conventional morality. Preachers, pamphleteers and playwrights warned that people who left their families to search for wealth in the metropolis would find a mother whose protective embrace would instead be a choking hold of poverty and plague.

It was plague which gave towns their reputation as consumers of men; it is estimated that one-third of all plague deaths between 1570 and 1670 occurred in London (Slack, 1985: 174–5). In Dekker's early plague pamphlets London is a loving mother – one 'Whose soft brest thousandes nourisheth' – who watches in helpless misery as her children die in their thousands: 'thou hast wept / Thine eyes out, to behold thy sweete / Dead children heapt about thy feete' (1925: 90). But by the plague of 1625 she has become complicit in the death of her children: 'thou with *Ierusalem*, didst feele as grieuous a Desolation: eating vp, with *Mariam*, thine owne children' (Dekker, 1925: 176). Miriam's action, the touchstone of suffering for the exigencies of a city under siege, came to figure the dangers of the city itself. Early modern Miriams embody the equivocal early modern city whose nurturance turns violent as it consumes its citizens in times of plague.

In panegyric the City is always figured as feminine: a virgin or mother wearing a coronet of battlements, her unbreached walls bolstered by the cultural value placed on the intact female body (Rosenau, 1983: 12–14; Paster, 1985: 4). London is described as impregnable in her purity: 'And here is now the Maiden toune, that keepes her self so cleane, / That none can touche, nor staine in trothe, by any cause or meane' (Churchyard, 1580: D4r). Latent in virginity's prestige, however, is the ubiquity of its opposite. The implicit vulnerability which is encoded in the image of the city as an intact female body is made explicit in the ubiquitous equation of sacked cities and violated women. The fates of cities are inscribed on female bodies: Lucrece's rape enables the change of power structures in Rome, and Troy falls after Cressida has given herself to the besieging Greek forces. In the seventeenth century the story of Berenice – the Jewish princess who falls in love with Titus the Roman conqueror – was likewise woven into dramatisations of Jerusalem's fall.[5] The connection between sacked cities and violated woman suggests the unreliability of the city herself, as through the misogyny of traditional discourse the city invites her own rape. In *A Larum for London*, for example, the leader of the invading Spanish forces says of Antwerp: 'Oh she is amorous as the wanton ayre, / And must be Courted ... mary her selfe inuites, / And beckons vs vnto her sportfull bed' (Gascoigne, 1602: A3r). The city is not only vulnerable – she is also complicit in her vulnerability. Nashe in his *Christs Tears over Jerusalem* describes Jerusalem breaking from Christ 'to runne rauishtlie into [Satan's] rugged armes' (1958: 2:22): 'ravishtly' is a neologism that equates sinning with self-rape. The same anxieties over unruly female desire and inherently unreliable, feminine cities can be heard when Chapman (in his continuation of Marlowe's famous epyllion) compares Hero's voluntary, desired union with Leander, to the sack of Cadiz (Marlowe, 1973/81: 2:462–3).

The image of the city as a virgin marks it as vulnerable, but it does at least have a symbolic clarity: the *virga intacta* signifying the city's unbreached walls. Existing in tandem with the image of the virginal city, however, was that of city as mother: the classical city goddesses, for example, personify the city as the *Magna Mater* who encircles and caresses her children.[6] It is not simply, however, that virgin and mother are categories which are in conflict, but that the maternal is in itself an inherently problematic trope for the city: city walls are figured as impregnable, but the maternal body has been breached from both within and without. The early modern preoccupation with the female body as 'effluent, overproductive, out of control' (Paster, 1993: 21) found its parallel in England's capital city which would not stay inside its borders. The walls of the early modern city, like the boundaries of the maternal body, were under threat from internal growth as well as from external forces. The uncontrolled expansion of the metropolis imitated the unruly swelling of the pregnant body, as Dekker's London notes: 'I swelled vp in greatnes, euer since haue I bin loued of our kings' (1963: 4:75).

In Middleton's 1613 mayoral show *The Triumphs of Truth* the figure of London says 'A woman's counsel is not always weak. / I am thy mother; at that name I know / Thy heart does reverence to me' (Middleton, 2007: 969). Lawrence Manley has suggested that the 'attribution of a feminine persona to the city' was intended to diminish fears of economic domination, providing 'a gender-based model of obedient submission' (1988: 349). The status of Middleton's London as a mother makes her worthy of respect but her use of traditional misogynist discourse ('A woman's counsel is not always weak') supports Manley's suggestion that her female persona presented her as reassuringly docile: her wisdom is exemplified by her acceptance that it is not usually woman's place to give advice. The submissive 'reverend mother' of Middleton's mayoral show, however, shows her darker side in this playwright's city comedies in which London is a 'man devouring' city (Middleton, 2007: 347). In Miriam, these two faces of the metropolis become one. The spectre of maternal cannibalism in the pamphlets of Dekker and Nashe, and the frequent presence of Miriam in London's ballads, sermons and pamphlets, is evidence of the fear that behind a gendering of London which tries to keep her submissive, the metropolis is in fact rapacious in its uncontrollable growth and unrivalled power.

The growth of London is one of the most important events of early modern English history (Slack, 2000: 161). The sharpest increase in London's population came at between 1580 and 1640 (Beier, 1986: 11) and it was at this time that Londoners began to describe their city as a 'metropolis'.[7] The literal meaning of metropolis – 'mother city' – belongs to the New Jerusalem: 'the mother of us all' according to St Paul (Galatians 4:26, KJV, 1611). Imagining London as a mother, therefore, brings forward the image of the holy city of milk and honey:

> And thou (the mother of my breath)
> Whose soft brest thousandes nourisheth ...
> Thou Fownt, where milke and hony springs:
> *Europs* Iewell; *Englands* Iem:
> Sister to great *Ierusale.* (Dekker, 1925: 89)

Early modern Protestants were keen on speaking of themselves, their nation and their metropolis as the New Jerusalem, and phrases such as 'our Ierusalem' (King, 1599: 660) and *'our Sion'* (Knell, 1648: C2r) abound as early modern designations for England and its capital. For Richard Niccols, in a work dedicated to the city's mayor, London was both 'the Nurse of pietie and pious men' and the place God had chosen 'for his Sion' (1616: 76). Jerusalem, queen of the promised land, flowing with milk and honey, is the zenith of the maternal, lactating city who feeds her children, and London had become likewise 'a blessed Mother' from whom 'the sonnes of England ... suck wealth' (Dekker, 1963: 4:9–10, 15) and 'the daughters will sucke their instruction' (Lawrence, 1624: 38). But Dekker's pamphlet continues, disturbingly: 'thou hast wept / Thine eyes out, to behold thy sweete / Dead children heapt about thy feete' (1925: 90). London as a metropolis or mother city is a version of England's confident claim that its reformed capital was a New Jerusalem, but such an assertion invited uneasy reminiscences of the cataclysmic fate of old Jerusalem: 'thou with *Ierusalem,* didst feele as grieuous a Desolation: eating vp, with *Mariam,* thine owne children' (Dekker, 1925: 176). London in plague time, like the Jerusalem of the Roman siege, is a city that consumes its young.

The child whom Miriam murders is noted by Josephus as being 'a baby at the breast' (1981: 353) and maternal cannibalism is an almost exact inversion of the lactating mother: she consumes where she should nourish. This inversion would have been more striking in the early modern period due to the quasi-cannibalistic understanding of breastfeeding in which milk was 'whitened' blood. A seventeenth-century manual on nursing, for example, writes of how a child 'sucks & draws' his mother's 'own blood' (Guillemeau, 1635b: I3r). Maternal nurturance was therefore suggestive of the sacrificial giving of the pelican who was believed to feed its young with its own flesh and blood (see Guillemeau, 1635a: D2r; Guillemeau, 1635b: Ii2r, Kk4r, Ll2v; and Joubert, 1989: 192, 201). The image of Miriam builds on and inverts this traditional language. Instead of a sacrificial mother, she is a predatory mother who desires to replenish the blood she lost in nurturing her children. Miriam becomes the focus of early modern accounts of the fall of Jerusalem because it is the nature of the city itself which is at the heart of these narratives. In panegyric, London was a fountain, a heart or a lactating mother who produced nourishing streams of water, blood and milk, but in plague-time texts she becomes a 'Sea that sucks', a greedy spleen and a cannibalising parent hoarding the benefits she had once appeared to confer. London, like the famine-haunted Rome in *Coriolanus*, might at any moment turn from 'our dear nurse' into 'an unnatural dam' who 'eat[s] up her own!' (Shakespeare, 1986: 5.3.111, 3.1.294–5). As noted by Mervyn Nicholson, 'In literature, cannibalism is not anthropological (still less gustatory); it is a metaphor for power relations' (1991: 198). The mother who eats her own children flouts every gender expectation, inverting the traditional conceptions of feminine nurturance and submissiveness.

London, and especially its suburbs, ingested the people of the realm, alarming Parliament and Crown with its unbridled growth.[8] Numerous ineffectual laws were passed under Elizabeth and James to try to halt the spread of London (Rasmussen, 1934/82: 63–75). By the end of the seventeenth century, the metropolitan population (which at the beginning of the sixteenth century had stood at fewer than 50,000) exceeded half a million (Ward, 1999: 24). Most of these people resided in the suburbs and liberties, rendering redundant the traditional fortification of the city walls as London expanded beyond them and began swamping the surrounding villages such as Deptford, Islington and Newington-Butts (Defoe, 2001: 2:66). As Defoe wrote in his *Tour of England* (1724): 'Whither will this monstrous city then extend?' (2001: 2:66). This swamping of other settlements by London is an objective correlative to the danger to individuals of losing their contours in the city: the press of people is both claustrophobic, and alienating. Jerusalem prior to its fall was a perfect analogue to the alarmingly crowded status of early modern London, for Josephus's astonishing estimates of casualties during the siege meant that Jerusalem had been crowded with over a million people (Josephus, 1981: 371). Defoe's *Journal of the Plague Year* (1722) is one among many texts which connects London on the eve of a plague epidemic with Jerusalem on the eve of its siege. As W. Austin Flanders suggests, Defoe's *Journal of the Plague Year* recognises 'the anxieties generated by a sense of the precariousness of individual life in the midst of rapid urban expansion' and 'the creeping moral and psychological malady which Defoe chronicles' is not just the plague but the 'universal fear of human contact' (1976: 152–3, 155) engendered by crowded urban spaces.

Plague was a metaphor for the dangers of urban living as well as the greatest danger of city life. In Nashe's plague pamphlet *Christ's Tears over Jerusalem* Miriam's cannibalism is a dominant motif both because plague has transformed London into a predatory metropolis and because plague has been caused by the heartless predation of citizens upon each other: 'the Vsurer eateth vp the Gentleman, and the Gentleman the yeoman, and all three being deuoured one of another, do nothing but complaine one vpon another' (1958: 2:159, ft.). Nashe's text is repetitive in both form and lexis to the extent that the reader is encouraged, almost forced, to see the connections on which the work is predicated: sin is the cause of London's suffering, just as it was of Jerusalem's. The text's structural repetitions, however, cause the question which underlies Lamentations to surface with a new force. The oration of Miriam over the child she is about to devour forms a parallel to the oration of Jesus over the soon-to-be-destroyed Jerusalem. The connections between the two speeches places Christ in both a feminine, and a disturbingly predatory, position.

The feminisation of Jesus as he foretells Jerusalem's destruction is not Nashe's invention. The Gospels not only describe Jesus as taking the traditionally feminine role of the tearful mourner as he approaches the city and weeps over it; but likewise describe Jesus as a mother hen: 'howe often would I haue gathered thy children together, as the henne gathereth her brood vnder her wings, and ye would not!' (Luke 13.34). In Jesus' only explicitly feminine image of himself he is a mother hen whose chicks have rejected his nurture. His image draws explicitly on Old Testament images of God's maternal love and in particular Deuteronomy's description of God as a mother bird who cares for his flock 'as an eagle stereth vp her nest, flootereth ouer her birdes, stretcheth out her wings, taketh them and beareth them on her wings' (Deut. 32:11. See also Isa. 49:15, 66:11–13; Psalm 41:3). In this lone New Testament instance of a maternal image for divine love, the tender protectiveness of the Old Testament trope has been evacuated of its comforting power. The safety inherent in the strength of maternal love – a love tender and tenacious, the eagle who will defend her brood to the death – has been infected by the discourse of feminine weakness: Jesus' maternal wings are unable to gather his brood and, in Nashe's extraordinary version of this moment, they have even been broken by sin: 'My wings her gray-headed sturdy disobedience hath now cleane vnpinioned and broken, so that (though I would) I cannot *gather* her' (1958: 2:57).

Debora Shuger has suggested that Calvinist Passion narratives are interested in the fall of Jerusalem because of issues surrounding masculinity (1994: 126). Shuger may be right that an unease at the apparent emasculation of Christ's body at the crucifixion and the fundamentally feminised message of the Gospel of non-violence is legible in the narratives of the fall of Jerusalem. The biblical account of the destruction of David's city, however, is linked not so much with unsuccessful masculinity as with failed maternity, and this is exacerbated in Protestant Passion narratives in which the figure of maternal love, Mary, the *stabat mater* has been largely excised (Shuger, 1994: 99–100).[9] She has been replaced by the daughters of Jerusalem who weep for the wrong things and long to be barren; the mothers of Lamentations who eat their children; the mother hen who cannot protect her young; and Miriam. The failed civic ideal of the fallen city finds its parallel in the failure of the feminine ideal – the violated virgin and the predatory mother – at Jerusalem's fall.

The maternal joys of Jerusalem and the maternal care of God are entwined and ecstatically celebrated at the end of Isaiah, where God declares:

> Reioyce ye with Ierusalem, and be gladde with her, all ye that loue her: reioyce for ioy with her, all ye that mourne for her, That ye may sucke and be satisfied with the brests of her consolation: that ye may milke out and be delited with ye brightnes of her glorie. For thus saith the Lord, Beholde, I will extend peace ouer her like a flood, and the glorie of the Gentiles like a flowing streame: then shall ye sucke, ye shall be borne vpon her sides, and be ioyfull vpon her knees. As one whom his mother comforteth, so will I comfort you, and ye shall be comforted in Ierusalem. (Isa. 66:10–13)

Miriam is the perversion of this ideal, and as such she articulates the fear that just as the maternal protection of the city has failed in siege and plague, so likewise may the maternal love of the ultimate protector. The recurrence of Miriam's image in plague-time texts suggests that, if only unconsciously, the questions of Lamentations surfaced in Londoners' plague-embattled consciousness: has God become an enemy?

The question of God's complicity in the destruction of the city is at its most visible in Nashe's lurid pamphlet, *Christ's Tears over Jerusalem*, written and published during the epidemic of 1592/93. In this text Christ's lament over Jerusalem is suffused with the anxiety voiced by Calvin – 'Some thinke it an absurditie that Christ should bewaile that mischiefe, which he could haue remedied' (Calvin, 1584: 561) – and Jesus' pity – the explicit meaning of his biblical tears – is swallowed up in his desire to exculpate himself from the vengeance that follows. Miriam's oration, which follows in uneasy juxtaposition, is likewise a speech of self-justification for the violence she is about to inflict. Nashe brings the two closer by expanding on the Gospel's image of Jesus-as-mother, and finding in Christ, as in Miriam, a site of failed maternity: 'At my breastes *Ierusalem* hast thou not suckt, but bitte off my breastes' (1958: 2:53). This is a shocking inversion of the usual Christ-as-mother trope (common for example, in twelfth-century Cistercian writing) in which Christ's breasts are emblems of the nurturing compassion and strength of God's love (Bynum, 1982: 151). Nashe's image is not as much at odds with medieval writing as might at first appear, however, and seems in fact an heir to the evolution of this imagery in thirteenth- and fourteenth-century literature when greater stress was placed on Christ's suffering and, as Caroline Bynum has shown, 'nursing tends to become nursing with blood, not milk; giving birth in great agony is emphasised along with cuddling and suckling' (1982: 151–2). Maguerite D'Oingt, for example, a thirteenth-century Carthusian prioress (died 1310), wrote of Christ as a mother who is in perpetual labour: '*Ha! Pulcher Domine dulcis, quam amare laborasti pro me tota vita tua!*' (D'Oingt, 1965: 78) ('Ah! beautiful, sweet Lord, how bitterly you laboured for me your whole life!'). In a highly Nashean image in which the confining of cosmic love within the human form necessarily inflicts violence on the latter, she writes: '*Et certe non erat mirum si vene tue rumpebantur quando totum mundum pariebas pariter una sola die*' (78) ('and truly it is no surprise that your veins ruptured when in only one day you gave birth to the whole world').

The fundamental difference, however, lies not in the violence of the image but that Nashe, uniquely, stresses failure: 'So penetrating and eleuatedly haue I prayd for you, that mine eyes woulde fayne haue broke from theyr anchors to haue flowne vp to Heauen, and myne armes stretcht more then the length of my body to reach at the Starres' (1958: 2:37). 'Woulde fayne' – the grotesque mangling of Christ's body in Nashe does not achieve redemption. Nashe's creation of a maternal, feminised Christ is the evocation not so much of a nurturing but of a weak body, lacking the redemptive power that lay at the heart of its medieval construction. While the maternal images of God in the Old Testament were images of strength – the strength of love – here, through the ubiquitous equation of femininity with weakness, they have become images of powerlessness. In Nashe's text God's love has, astonishingly, actually been disabled by sin: 'Mee would not *Ierusalem* heare, when with sweet songs I haue allur'd, cluckt, & wooed her to come vnder my wings ... My wings her gray-headed sturdy disobedience hath now cleane vnpinioned and broken, so that (though I would) I cannot *gather* her' (1958: 2:57). Nashe has found an unorthodox response to the problem of why Christ allows the destruction of the city: he feminises him to the extent that he becomes powerless: 'One crosse alone (cruel *Ierusalem*) is not able to sustaine the weight of thine iniquities: tenne times I must be crucified ere thou be clensed ... It is too monstrous a matter for my mercie or merites to work on' (1958: 2:35). This is heresy (the Book of Common Prayer, for example, reiterated at each Eucharist that the crucifixion was a 'full, perfect and sufficient sacrifice for the sins of the whole world') and it is heresy which finds its root in anxiety: if Christ *could* have saved Jerusalem, why did he not?

The primary connection between Christ and Miriam's orations are their endless self-justifications. In both cases plentitude undermines itself, making each justification less convincing. Christ's persona seems plagued by doubts about his own reasoning; his oration is performed in a strikingly interrogative voice: he asks fifty-three rhetorical questions in under forty pages of text. Some of his justifications are singularly inauspicious: Nashe's Christ says he is entitled to use violence against men in curbing them to his will, for men do likewise with horses 'you tame and spurre, and cut their mouthes with raining, and finally kil with making carry heauy burdens' (2:31). Such parallels with the worst examples of human behaviour render Christ liable to human infirmity: 'No friende so firme but by oft ill vsage may be made a foe' (2:34). The main human parallel the text forms for Christ, however, is with Miriam. Their orations share both imagery[10] and empty hyperbole: before killing her child, Miriam protests that she would have laid down her life for it: 'O my deere Babe, had I in euery limbe of mee a seuerall life, so many liues as I haue lymbes to Death wold I resigne, to saue thine one life. Saue thee I may not, though I shoulde giue my soule for thee' (2:72–3). Christ makes similar 'if only' pronouncements of how 'I wold quite renounce and for-sweare mine owne safety, so I might but extort from thee one thought of thine own safety' (2:35). Christ likewise expresses his impossible desire 'that myne armes were wide enough to engraspe the walls of *Ierusalem* about, that in myne amorous enfoldment (vnawares) I might whyrle her to Heauen with me!' (2:52). The awkward physicality of the image is recalled when Miriam, gruesomely, tells her son that having eaten him: 'Ile beare thee in my bosome to Paradise' (2:74). The similarities between Christ's words and Miriam's can work to make Christ appear, like Miriam, as one whose protestations are thinly veiled self-justifications for an act of horrific violence. Nashe's text obliquely presents Miriam (the mother turned killer) as a terrifying analogue to God's inability to defend his children from his own anger.

Christ's Tears' serious theological stance makes it unique in Nashe's oeuvre, and literary critics have long suspected that it contains an undercurrent of satire (Groves, 2011: 239–42). As Jonathan Crewe comments: 'it is difficult to avoid the suspicion that *Christ's Teares Over Jerusalem* is a gigantic hoax sprung, not without malicious pleasure, on the God-fearing citizens of London' (1982: 59). While I do not believe this, I think the signs of Nashe's usual creative acuity are visible in this, as in his more congenial writing. Despite the hysterical violence of this text and its claustrophobic intimation of a cataclysmic future, there are times when Nashe seems to undermine the tub-thumping piety of his personae. Nashe has not only committed an act of narrative audacity in putting words into Christ's mouth, he has done so by taking scriptural phrases about the infinite nature of God's love and mercy and twisting them to suit his depiction of a Jesus who is 'a jealous god in a newly deceptive – even effeminate – guise' (Crewe, 1982: 56). In the pursuance of his rhetorical goal of scaring his readers into goodness, Nashe (like many a Calvinist preacher) has twisted the gospel of love, but he has also drawn attention to this strategy through his misquotation of well-known biblical texts. It is a technique which keeps Nashe's Christ separate from the Christs of Calvinist Passion narratives whom he might otherwise be seen to be emulating.

Christ's Tears over Jerusalem is, in fact, a sustained polemic against bad preachers (Hill, 2006), particularly those 'hotte-spurd Diuines' who 'deafe mens eares, but not edifie. Scripture peraduenture they come of thicke and three-folde / with, but it is so vgly daubed, plaistred, and patcht on, so peeuishly speckt & applyde, as if a Botcher (with a number of Satten and Veluette shreddes) should cloute and mend Leather-doublets & Cloth-breeches' (1958: 2:124). Patching with different fabrics causes the material to warp, and yet this twisting of meaning by puritan divines, of which Nashe complains, could likewise be levelled against his own personae. Nashe's Christ takes famous texts of consolation – such as Psalm 23's 'thy rod and thy staffe, they comfort me' (4) – and turns them into texts of vengeance: 'my Rodde and my staffe of correction' (2:27). He inverts the meaning of the crossing of the Red Sea, for example, so that the dry feet of the Israelites – a sign of their chosen status as God has moved the waters for them ('let the children of Israel goe on drie ground thorow the middes of the Sea' (Exo. 14:16)) – become a sign of their indifference to Christ's suffering: 'ouer the waters of my Teares and tribulation, shee [Jerusalem] passeth as driefoote as once they past ouer *Iordan*' (2:46). Nashe's Christ inverts his own parables: the story of the unjust judge and the widow which is a parable about the power of prayer (as Luke explains: 'And he put foorth in a parable vnto them, to this ende that men ought alwayes to pray, & not to be weery' (Luke 18:1, Bishops' Bible)) becomes a tale of the ineffectiveness of prayer, because Christ now puts himself in the position of the powerless widow: 'Neuer did the Widdow in my Parrable so follow and tyre the wicked Iudge wyth fury-haunting instancie, as I haue doone' (2:56). This changing of the subject position is frequent in *Christ's Tears*. Instead of the traditional medieval image of Christ as the pelican who selflessly feeds his children with his own flesh, Nashe makes Jerusalem into both aggressor and victim: '*Ierusalem*, euen as the Pellican in the Wildernesse, so (by thine owne progenie) shalt thou haue thy bowels torne out: by ciuill warres shalt thou be more wasted then outwarde annoyance' (2:58).

The inverted eucharistic image of the Pelican follows another, when Christ complains: 'Neuer could I gette them to flocke vnder my *wing*, or come vnder my roofe' (2:43). Once again the subject positions are reversed: for the final phrase is from a passage in Matthew: 'Master, I am not worthy that thou shouldst come vnder my roofe: but speake the worde onely, and my seruant shall be healed' (Matt. 8:8). Nashe is alluding to a passage which had long been used as a pre-communion prayer: 'Lord, I am not worthy that thou shouldest come under my roof: but speak the word only and my soul shall be healed'.[11] Nashe's Christ's strange reversal of this eucharistic text is repeated, more shockingly, by Nashe's preaching persona who shatters the word 'healed' into 'hel' and 'had': 'speake but the word, and to Hel shal you be had' (2:104). In a similar vein, Nashe's preaching persona rewrites Paul as he declares: 'As no eye hath seene, no eare hath heard, no tongue can expresse, no thought comprehend, the ioyes prepared for the Elect, so no eye hath seene, no eare hath heard, no thought can comprehend, the pains prepared for the reiected' (2:140). This passage is a version of Paul's famous affirmation of God's love ('The eye hath not seene, and the eare hath not heard, neither haue entered into the heart of man, the things which God hath prepared for them that loue him' (1 Cor. 2:9, Bishops' Bible)) as radically unknowable by the heart of man because it is infinite and hence more generous than man could comprehend, let alone imitate.[12] Paul's famous phrase comes at a moment when he is explaining the authority on which he preaches: which makes it particularly noticeable that the first half of Nashe's sentence has the authority of Scripture, the second half has no authority at all.

Nashe's uniquely lurid take on the story of Miriam and the fall of Jerusalem is neither as simplistic nor as Calvinist as at first appears. These explicitly misapplied or misquoted scriptural examples can, I would argue (especially given the slippery and satiric nature of Nashe's authorial persona), be seen as a parody of the scare-tactics of hot-gospellers rather than a simple imitation of them. Shuger puts *Christ's Tears* in the context of Calvinistic Passion narratives but she does not note how fundamentally opposed its theology is to theirs. Nashe's text for example is vociferous in support of good works, saying that one cannot be saved without them: 'If in your bodies you haue done no good works, of God you shall receiue no good words' (2:104). It seems at least possible that Nashe's violent hyperbole throughout *Christ's Tears* registers an awareness with the problem inherent in the idea of the vengeance of a loving God. The figure of Miriam, like Nashe's effeminate and bible-twisting Christ, embodies the new complexity with which early moderns approached the fall of Jerusalem. The maternal figure once used as simple evidence for the extremity of God's punishment of his chosen people, and hence of Christianity's ascendancy over Judaism, became a complex sign bearing the weight of anxiety about suffocating cities and the failure of past certainties in the ravages of plague time.

Notes

1 Unless otherwise stated, the italics that appear in quotations from early modern texts are preserved from the original. I gratefully acknowledge the assistance of Imogen Black and Mark Burnett who provided me with information for this essay.

2 All biblical references are to the Geneva Bible, unless otherwise stated.

3 Lamentations was part of the lessons for the first nocturn of Matins on Maundy Thursday, Good Friday and Holy Saturday. In the 1549 Prayer Book, Lamentations was read for evensong on the Wednesday before Easter, Matins on Maundy Thursday, and Matins on Easter Evening (Brightman, 1915). The Improperia, or Reproaches, drawn from Lamentations and performed as spoken by Christ during the Good Friday liturgy of Creeping the Cross, were an important part of medieval liturgy (Tuve, 1952: 32–4, 43–7) and many of these texts remained available for sixteenth- and seventeenth-century readers (204–10). The connection between Lamentations and Christ on the cross remained strong into the seventeenth century: see for example George Herbert's 'The Sacrifice' and Cockburn's sermon: 'The Words of the Prophet are applicable to him; and as they were spoken prophetically of him, so in him only they were fully accomplished. *Is it nothing to you all ye that pass by? Behold, and see, if there be any sorrow like unto my sorrow*' (Cockburn, 1697: 140–1).

4 As Castellio notes in his 'Admonition to the Reader' the gap between the Old and New Testaments is knitted together with passages from Josephus's *Antiquities* and *Jewish War* (1554: A5v).

5 Racine's *Bérénice* (1670) was translated into English by Thomas Otway (*Titus and Berenice* (1677)) and John Crowne's *The destruction of Jerusalem by Titus Vespasian* (1677) is an account of the fall of the city into which Berenice's history – and other love-plots – are woven.

6 In Virgil's famous description of Rome: 'septemque una sibi muro circumdabit arces, / felix prole virum: qualis Berecyntia mater' (1999: 6:783–4). See also Hawkins (1981); and Rosenau (1983: 12–14).

7 The earliest example I have found is: 'ye citie of London beareth oddes, and preroga-tiue ouer other cities in England, being the *Metropolis* or mother Citie therof' (*A Breefe Discourse*, 1584: 10). This has now been entered into the on-line *Oxford English Dictionary* (which had previously given 1636 as the first reference to London as a metropolis (s.v. 'Metropolis')). For other citations in this period, see Taylor (1625: A4v); *Lachrymae Londinenses* (1626: 23); Dekker (1963: 4:21); and Marlowe (1973/81: 2:497).

8 London grew from 50,000 souls in 1530 to 225,000 in 1605. This growth alarmed Parliament and Crown to the extent that Elizabeth issued a proclamation in 1580 forbidding 'any new buildings of any house or tenement within three miles from any of the gates of the City of London' (Morris, 1994: 249. See also Rasmussen, 1934/82).

9 For further details on Mary as the *stabat mater* see Gallagher's essay (Chapter 11) in this volume.

10 Miriam and Christ also use the same striking, and odd, image of adamant's magnetic attraction, which form a rhetorical chiasmus across fifty pages of text: Christ says 'with thyne yron breast drawest vnto thee nothing but the Adamant of GODS anger' (Nashe, 1958: 2:23); Miriam says to her hands, in preparation for their murder, 'Embrawne your soft-skind enclosure with Adamantine dust, that it / may drawe nothing but steele vnto it' (Nashe, 1958: 2:72–3).

11 This had been a pre-communion prayer since the eleventh century, and entered the official rite in the thirteenth century (Jungmann, 1959: 503). For an awareness of it in a eucharistic context in the early modern period, see Groves (2002).

12 The familiarity of this biblical passage is made clear by the fact that Shakespeare could make humorous capital out of Bottom getting it wrong when he wakes from his adventures in fairyland in *A Midsummer Night's Dream*: 'The eye of man hath not heard, the ear of man hath not seen, man's hand is not able to taste, his tongue to conceive, nor his heart to report what my dream was' (4.1.202–13). For more detail see Groves (2007).

References

A breefe discourse, declaring and approuing the necessarie and inuiolable maintenance of the laudable custeme of London (1584) London: Rafe Newberie.

Beier, A.L. (1986) 'The Significance of the metropolis.' *London 1500–1700: The Making of the Metropolis*. Ed. A.L. Beier and R. Finlay. London: Longman. 1–33.

Brightman, F.E. (1915) *The English Rite: Being a Synopsis of the Sources and Revisions of the Book of Common Prayer*. London: Rivingtons.

Bynum, C.W. (1982) *Jesus as Mother: Studies in the Spirituality of the High Middle Ages*. Berkeley: University of California Press.

Calvin, J. (1584) *A harmonie vpon the three Euangelists, Matthew, Mark and Luke, with the commentarie of M. Iohn Caluine: faithfullie translated out of Latine into English, by E. P. [Eusebius Paget] whereunto is also added a commentarie vpon the Euangelist S. Iohn, by the same authour*. London: Thomas Dawson.

Castellio, S. (1554) *Biblia Interprete Sebastiano Castalione*. Basel: J. Oporinus.

Churchyard, T. (1580) *A light Bondell of liuly discourses called Churchyards Charge*. London: John Kyngston.

Cockburn, J. (1697) *Fifteen sermons preach'd upon several occasions, and on various subjects*. London: William Keblewhite.

Crewe, J.V. (1982) *Unredeemed Rhetoric: Thomas Nashe and the Scandal of Authorship*. Baltimore, MD: Johns Hopkins University Press.

Crowne, J. (1677) *The destruction of Jerusalem*. London: James Magnes and Richard Bentley.

Defoe, D. (2001) *A Tour Thro' the Whole Island of Great Britain*. London: Pickering & Chatto.

Dekker, T. (1925) *The Plague Pamphlets of Thomas Dekker*. Oxford: Clarendon Press.

——. (1963) *The Non-Dramatic Works of Thomas Dekker*. New York: Russell & Russell.

——. (1967) *The Wonderful Year etc. and Selected Writings*. London: Edward Arnold.

Deutsch, G.N. (1986) *Iconographie de l'illustration de Flavius Josephe au temps de Jean Fouquet*. Leiden: Brill.

D'Oingt, M. (1965) *Les Oeuvres de Marguerite D'Oingt*. Paris: L'Institut de Linguistique Romane de Lyon.

Drant, T.H. (1566) *A medicinable morall ... The wailyngs of the prophet Hieremiah, done into Englyshe verse*. London: Thomas Marshe.

Flanders, W.A. (1976) *Defoe's Journal of the Plague Year and the Modern Urban Experience*. Englewood Cliffs, NJ: Prentice-Hall.

Gascoigne, G. (1602) *A Larvm for London, or The Siedge of Antwerpe*. London: William Ferbrand.

Groves, B. (2002) '"Temper'd with a sinners tears": Herbert and the Eucharistic Significance of the Word "temper".' *Notes & Queries*, 247.49: 329–30.

——. (2007) '"The Wittiest Partition": Bottom, Paul and Comedic Resurrection.' *Notes & Queries*, 252: 277–82.

——. (2011) 'Laughter in the Time of Plague: A Context for the Unstable Style of Nashe's Christ's Tears over Jerusalem.' *Studies in Philology*, 108.2: 238–60.

Guillemeau, J. (1635a) *The Happy Delivery of Women*. London: Joyce Norton and Richard Whitiker.

——. (1635b) *The Nursing of Children*. London: Joyce Norton and Richard Whitiker.

Hawkins, P.S. (1981) 'From Mythography to Myth-making: Spenser and the Magna Mater Cybele.' *Sixteenth Century Journal*, 12: 51–64.

Hill, A. (1595) *The Crie of England*. London: B. Norton.

Hill, C.A. (2006) 'Thomas Nashe's Imitation of Christ.' *Prose Studies*, 28: 211–21.

Josephus, F. (1981) *The Jewish War*. London: Penguin Books.

Joubert, L. (1989) *Popular Errors*. Tuscaloosa, AL: University of Alabama Press.

Jungmann, J.A. (1959) *The Mass of the Roman Rite: Its Origins and Development*. London: Burns & Oates.

King, J. (1599) *Lectvres vpon Ionas, delivered at Yorke in the yeare of our Lorde 1594.* Oxford: Joseph Barnes.

Knell, P. (1648) *Israel and England Paralelled, In a Sermon preached before the honorable society of Grayes-Inne, upon Sunday in the afternoon, Aprill 16. 1648.* London: s.n.

Lachrymae Londinenses: or Londons lamentations and teares (1626) London: H. Holland and G. Gibbs.

Lawrence, J. (1624) *A golden trvmpet, to rowse vp a drowsie magistrate: or, a patterne for a governors practise, drawne from CHRISTS coming to, beholding of, and weeping ouer Hierusalem.* London: John Haviland.

Manley, L. (1988) 'From Matron to Monster: Tudor-Stuart London and the Languages of Urban Description.' *The Historical Renaissance: New Essays on Tudor and Stuart Literature and Culture.* Ed. H. Dubrow and R. Strier. Chicago: University of Chicago Press. 347–74.

Marlowe, C. (1973/81) *The Complete Works of Christopher Marlowe.* Cambridge: Cambridge University Press.

Middleton, T. (2007) *Thomas Middleton: The Collected Works.* Oxford: Oxford University Press.

Morris, A.E.J. (1994) *History of Urban Form: Before the Industrial Revolutions.* New York: Longman.

Nashe, T. (1958) *The Works of Thomas Nashe.* Oxford: Basil Blackwell.

Niccols, R. (1616) *Londons Artillery.* London: William Welby.

Nicholson, M. (1991) 'Eat – or Be Eaten: An Interdisciplinary Metaphor.' *Mosaic,* 24: 191–210.

Otway, T. (1677) *Titus and Berenice.* London: Richard Tonson.

Paster, G.K. (1985) *The Idea of the City in the Age of Shakespeare.* Athens, GA: University of Georgia Press.

——. (1993) *The Body Embarrassed: Drama and the Disciplines of Shame in Early Modern England.* Ithaca, NY: Cornell University Press.

Rasmussen, S.E. (1934/82) *London: The Unique City.* Cambridge, MA: MIT Press.

Rosenau, H. (1983) *The Ideal City: Its Architectural Evolution in Europe.* London: Methuen & Co.

Sedgewick, W. (1648) *The spirituall madman.* London: s.n.

Shakespeare, W. (1986) *William Shakespeare: The Complete Works.* Ed. S. Wells and G. Taylor. Oxford: Oxford University Press.

Shuger, D.K. (1994) *The Renaissance Bible: Scholarship, Sacrifice and Subjectivity.* Berkeley: University of California Press.

Slack, P. (1985) *The Impact of Plague in Tudor and Stuart England.* Oxford: Clarendon Press.

——. (2000) 'Perceptions of the Metropolis in Seventeenth-Century England.' *Civil Histories: Essays presented to Sir Keith Thomas.* Ed. P. Burke, B. Harrison and P. Slack. Oxford: Oxford University Press. 161–80.

Taylor, J. (1625) *The fearefvll svmmer: or Londons calamity, the countries courtesy, and both their misery.* Oxford: John Lichfield and William Turner.

The Bible: Translated according to the Ebrew and Greeke, and conferred with the best translations in diuers languages: with most profitable Annotations vpon all the hard places, and other things of great importance, as may appeare in the Epistle to the Reader (1583) London: Christopher Barker. [Geneva Bible].

The Holi Bible (1569). London: R. Jugge. [Bishops' Bible].

THE HOLY BIBLE, *Conteyning the Old Testament, AND THE NEW* (1611) London: Robert Barker [King James Version].

Tuve, R. (1952) *A Reading of George Herbert*. Chicago: University of Chicago Press.

Virgil (1999) *Eclogues. Georgics. Aeneid I–VI*. Cambridge, MA: Harvard University Press.

Ward, J.P. (1999) 'Imagining the Metropolis in Elizabethan and Stuart London.' *The Country and the City Revisited: England and the Politics of Culture, 1550–1850*. Ed. G. Maclean, D. Landry and J.P. Ward. Cambridge: Cambridge University Press. 24–40.

10

Mary of recusants and reform: literary memory and defloration

Thomas Rist

> HAile *Mary*, full of grace, it once was said,
> And by an Angel, to the Blessed Maid,
> The Mother of our Lord: why may not I,
> (Without prophannesse) as a Poët, cry
> Haile *Mary*, full of Honours, to my Queene,
> The Mother of our Prince? When was there seene
> (Except the joy that the first *Mary* brought,
> Whereby the safety of the world was wrought)
> So generall a gladnesse to an Isle,
> To make the hearts of a whole Nation smile,
> As in this Prince? let it be lawfull so
> To compare small with great, as still we owe
> Our thankes to God: then haile to Mary, spring
> Of so much health, both to the Realm, and King! (Jonson, 1965: 238)

For an essay that focuses on the fate of the Virgin Mary after 1559, Ben Jonson's 'An Epigram to the Queen' is an evocative reminder that, although she presented a 'self-evident' problem to an officially Protestant England, the Virgin was not forgotten (Peters, 2003: 212). From the start, Jonson evokes by direct quotation the opening of the 'Hail Mary', developed from Luke's Gospel into a formal prayer.[1] Yet the final clause of line one, 'it once was said', throws this remembrance into ironic, historical relief since 'the last official Hail Mary was heard in the wake of the death of Queen Mary I' and Marian veneration was 'outlawed in consciously protestant practice' (MacCulloch, 2004: 214; Peters, 2003: 228).[2] Before becoming a panegyric to the Queen, then, Jonson's poem opens with a reflection on the loss of the Hail Mary prayer in formal English religion.

The reflection on this prayer colours the analogy between the Virgin Mary and Henrietta Maria to follow. Line four, thus, is not just concerned with the profanity of comparing the sacred Virgin to a human being – a comparison already suggesting a catholic definition of profanity since, rejecting Mary as Queen of Heaven, Protestants reconfigured her as plainly, if gracefully, human (Peters, 2003: 224).[3] It also recalls the outlawed Hail Mary of line one, that too being 'prophanness' in Protestant England, thereby extending the Marian transgression with which the poem began. The nature of that transgression develops again at line eleven, where the allusion to what is 'lawfull' refers not only to the profanity or otherwise of analogies between the Queen and the Queen of Heaven, but also to the unlawful status of the Hail Mary prayer itself. Recalling the prayer to Mary that opened the poem, 'let it be lawfull' is a thinly disguised demand for the return of the Hail Mary in official religion. Concluding 'then haile to Mary' in the same vein, the final couplet leaves open the possibility that it is Henrietta Maria being hailed, while establishing the Hail Mary prayer with a defiance of tone characteristically Jonsonian. Having re-established the outlawed prayer, Jonson presents an ambiguous scenario where, as well as to Charles I, the 'King' of the final line refers to God the Father or Christ; so that the wider 'health ... to the realm' (in earlier elaborations the 'gladnesse to an Isle, / To make the hearts of a whole Nation smile' and the 'safety of the world') suggests a transformed Christianity, English but also universal and 'catholic', with Mary at its heart.

This is not to say that a catholic – indeed Roman Catholic – sense of profanity is not also present. In celebrating the birth of the future Charles II to Queen Henrietta Maria in 1630, the poem links the notoriously Roman Catholic Queen and her son with the Virgin Mary and her Son; Maria with Mary; the Queen of England with the Queen of Heaven. Yet sensitive to 'prophannesse', Jonson sidesteps it by emphasising that these are comparisons of 'small with great', pointedly making Henrietta Maria full of 'honours' rather than grace. Rather than producing catholic profanity, therefore, Jonson's equation of Henrietta Maria with the Virgin, in which each reflects on the other, reinforces the Roman Catholic in both. It is a linking strategy common at the court of Henrietta Maria and one which writers deployed under Mary Tudor.[4] No doubt Jonson recognised the increased sympathy for Rome at court and indeed elsewhere in England under Henrietta Maria. Even as Jonson's poem testifies to the historical lessening, over time, of Marian veneration since the reign of Mary Tudor, it attests to authors and readerships ready to recognise and venerate the Virgin in older ways.[5] Most obviously, these included those recusants who 'refused' England's Protestant solutions, in whose number Jonson counted himself for a time, and whose complex influence on Jonson Ian Donaldson has now brought to life (see Donaldson, 2011). To discover how traditional salutations to Mary did *not* disappear in the era, to discover their marginal persistence up to and beyond Jonson's poem, and to observe in any detail how they adapted to straitened circumstances, we begin with such authors.

Recusant Marys

Since venerating Mary was outlawed after 1559, subsequent poetry exalting her is in a sense recusant by default because it refuses Elizabethan conformity.[6] Not that recusancy equates wholly with subversion. 'Though I am passionately affectionate to my Religion', Henry Constable wrote to the Earl of Essex, 'yet am I not in the number of those who weh [wish] t[h]e restitution thereof w[it]h the servitude of my country to a forrein Tyranny' (1960: 37).[7] Although his conversion to Roman Catholicism meant forfeiting his lands, loss of powerful friends, including Essex and Sir Francis Walsingham, and a life spent largely abroad, and despite being imprisoned at various points including in the Tower of London in 1604, Constable (1562–1613) had qualities of open-mindedness and moderation. The opening chapter of his *The Catholike moderator*, 'To All the Kings Faithful Subjects And Principally to those Faithful Catholikes, that are desirous of the Quiet of the Church and State', gives a taste of the outlook of this gentleman who found his convictions a 'hard hap'; the full title of the work gives somewhat more:

> The Catholic Moderator: Or A Moderate Examination of the Doctrine of the Protestants. Proving against the too rigid Catholikes of the times, especially of the book called, *The Answere to the Catholike Apologie*, That We, Who are Members of the Catholike, Apolstolike, and Roman Church, ought not to Condemn the Protestants for Heretikes, until further proof be made. (1623: t.p.)

Not condemning Protestants out of hand; deferring judgement until matters of doctrine are ascertained through reason; even condemning 'too rigid' Romanists from the off: these matters exemplify *The Catholike moderator*'s aim to moderate and be moderate in the wake of the murder of Henri III of France. How fully the text is a response to those circumstances or a more general statement of belief is debatable (Grundy, 1960: 33–4; Kuchar, 2006: 71); but being too radical for most English Protestants and Counter-Reformation authorities, it shows a recusant's ability to rise far above the 'charitable hatred' of the day (Walsham, 2006).

The saints being legally proscribed, Constable's *Spiritual Sonnetts to The honour of God and hys Sayntes* (c.1593, see 1960 edn), including a sequence of three poems 'To our blessed Lady', shows that he rose above such religious hostility without compromising his beliefs.[8] Alison Shell has noted the 'autobiographical bitterness' of these poems: 'not to mankind, nor to women in general, but specifically to queens', the 'primary monarch suggested' being Elizabeth I, who blocked his advancement following his conversion (1999: 123–5). In contrasting Mary with Elizabeth I, Constable used the Virgin to critique a perceived injustice at the very heart of English political life and at its highest echelon, while implying there are more significant loyalties than those even to a monarch. As the poems express it, those loyalties are to the Virgin. But Mary's contrast with the Protestant Queen makes the Virgin a locus for religious contrasts and controversy, so that political commentary comes to entail critiques that are both theological and religio-political. The poems fulfil various religious functions, the first of which is to render Mary visible in a landscape where her traditional role and image had formally disappeared and where Marian images raised the deepest Protestant hostility (Peters: 2003: 212). Intensely concerned with religious imagery, 'To our blessed Lady (1)' follows its request to see Christ with an emphatic expression of the poet's need to see the Virgin: 'shewe me thy lovely face; / whose beams the Angells beuty do deface; / and even inflame the Seraphins with love' (Constable, 1960: 189). All three poems envisaging the Virgin are expressions of this longing for her un-defaced image.

Each poem also foregrounds the mediation of Mary which English Protestants rejected on the ground that her mediation with God detracted from that of Christ with his Father (Peters, 2003: 219). With tact, therefore, Constable makes Mary mediate between himself and Christ, rather than directly to the Father, so that Christ is unequivocally above His mother in a chain of being where He, not she, is the necessary link to the Father, and avoids the contemporary suggestion that 'Mother Mary' might have authority over her Son (Ray, 2012). 'Sovereigne of Queenes', the first poem begins, approaching Christ through Mary: 'shewe me thy sonne in his imperiall place, whose servants reigne, our kinges & queens above' (189). This Marian role as 'mediatrix' to Christ is still more explicit in the third poem in the sequence:

> Sweete Queene: although thy beuty rayse upp mee
> from sight of baser beutyes here belowe:
> Yett lett me not rest there: but higher goe
> to hym, who tooke hys shape from God & thee. (190)

This address to the Virgin carefully balances its appeal for help from her with an unambiguous picture of heavenly hierarchy in which Christ is above Mary, and God is the ultimate Father. Constable thus accommodates Protestant anxieties that Catholics make Mary into God by ensuring the Virgin does not threaten Him, while nevertheless ensuring that her mediating role continues.

The second poem in the sequence combines the foci on Marian mediation and Marian imagery with lovely complexity. The sestet opens by contrasting sights of the Virgin with 'earthly sight':

> An earthlye syght doth onely please the eye,
> and breedes desire, but doth not satisfye:
> thy sight, gives us possession of all ioye,
> And with such full delyghtes eche sense shall fyll,
> as harte shall wyshe, but for to see thee still,
> and ever seyng, ever shall inioye. (190)

In an era of Marian iconoclasm, the poet wants to see the Virgin, but he also wants to see as through her eyes (with 'thy sight'). One implication of this play on 'seeing' is that it is through Mary's eyes that one finds the 'all ioye' of God: Constable again makes Mary a mediator. Besides this ambiguity, there is a more problematic meaning. So far we have seen the phrase 'thy sight, gives us possession of all ioye' interpreted to mean that the eyes of Mary are those through which we see God; yet the phrase might also be taken to imply the image of Mary is itself 'all joy', suggesting, since treating Mary as 'all' joy equates her with God, the kind of idolatry with which reformers regularly charged Romanists. There is, then, a paradox: Mary may be the vehicle to the divine or the divine itself.

The suggestion that Mary actually is the divine is still stronger in the opening octave:

> Why should I any love O queene but thee?
> if favour past a thankful love should breede?
> thy womb dyd beare, thy brest my saviour feed;
> and thou dyddest never cease to succour me.
> If Love doe followe worth and dignitye?
> Thou all in [thy] perfections doest exceed:
> if Love be ledd by hope of future meede?
> what pleasure more then thee in heaven to see? (190)

Presenting Mary in her role of Mother of God, bearing Jesus in the womb and suckling Him at her breast, shows Christ at his most infantile and vulnerable, and shows Mary at her most powerful. According to Ray, such Madonna-and-Child imagery offended reformers for the seeming implication that Mary could dominate Christ, relegating him to a position of dependency (2012: 9).[9] Further-more, with its query as to whether there is any greater pleasure in heaven than Mary, the final line of the octave verges on a blasphemy. Blasphemy is also suggested in the insistent claims that not God but rather Mary ('thy womb … thy brest … thou …') does the work of salvation; this has been implied from the opening question and it is latent in the statement that Mary exceeds 'all … perfections'. Opening 'Why should I any love O queene but thee?' no doubt has Elizabeth I in mind. But in championing the Virgin over Elizabeth so that the English Queen comes to stand for 'any' and 'all' other loves, every other love, including perhaps that for God, becomes less than love for the Virgin. Of course, the claims that the poet loves Mary above both 'any' and 'all' are conditional – the first is part of a hypothetical question and the second is predicated on an 'if' clause. But creating a hierarchy where the Virgin looks down on an Elizabeth, herself associated with God (even if only implicitly), especially amid images of the Mother of God, is flirting with two blasphemies: that the Queen of England and God can be identified; and that the Virgin is therefore above God.

Constable thus presents both striking and problematic illustrations of Mary after 1559. He offers direct, poetic venerations of Mary extant after 1559, and provides a glimpse into continuing contemporary beliefs about her which official policy sought to undermine. By the same token, however, he is problematic because it is difficult to assess how widely representative his attitudes were. As we have seen, the very particular circumstances of Constable's Roman Catholicism and alienation from Elizabeth help create his near-idolisation of the Virgin in the first 'To our Blessed Lady'; but should we infer from such circumstances that the attitude of that poem was unusual, or does it warrant us to imagine other recusant devotees of Mary idiosyncratically diverging from correct theology – and if so, in what numbers? In Constable's case, a clear concern to explain correct veneration of Mary merges with hints of incorrectness that a sensitive reader of the era might easily have taken exception to. Since much Reformation polemic hinges on whether Roman Catholic saints were venerated or idolised, these questions deserve a wider response.

The poetry to Mary of Richard Rowlands or Verstegan, as he later became, is less known than that of Constable, and their backgrounds seem initially rather different. While Constable was a nobleman with apparent leanings towards ecumenism who fell from grace, Rowlands was a printer who, in the wake of Edmund Campion's execution, became a leading Counter-Reformation publicist on the continent. However, there are parallels between the two men. Both were university-educated, converts to Catholicism and sought by the law, and spent large portions of their lives in exile. Rowlands converted to Catholicism while at Oxford and as a result left the university. He printed an account of the martyrdom of Campion in 1581, was arrested, escaped, and then left the country. He eventually settled in Antwerp, where he died in 1640. Rowlands was an important smuggler of recusant books – and also people – into England, and his works circulated widely on the continent. It is likely that his poetry also found readerships in England and the *Odes*, published in English in 1601, certainly anticipates English readers.[10]

On the twenty-fifth page of the *Odes*, there begins a sequence titled 'The Fifteen Mysteries of the Rosary, to our Blessed Lady. Whereof the First are Joyful. The Second Sorrowful. And the Third Glorious' (Verstegan, 1601). Although it may sound stodgy, Rowlands introduces the collection in verses emphasising their poetic innovation and sophistication:

> The vaine conceits of loues delight
> I leaue to *Ouids* arte,
> Of warres and bloody broyles to wryte
> Is fit for *Virgils* parte.
> Of tragedies in doleful tales
> Let *Sophocles* entreat:
> And how vnstable fortune failes
> Al Poets do repeat.
> But vnto our eternal king
> My verse and voyce I frame
> And of his saintes I meane to sing
> In them to praise his name. (1601: A3r)

This scan of the contemporary literary scene reveals a poet who knows his voice. 'All poets' are doing Ovid, Virgil and Sophocles, Rowlands notes, showing his literary credentials; so avoiding cliché, Rowlands will do otherwise. The difference is not writing religious poetry (hardly a new activity) but rather honouring the saints in English, which English law prohibits; this creates room not only for a literary novelty but also for an anti-establishment aesthetic under-scored by Rowlands' status as an exile. This is no mouldy verse (to adapt Jonson), but self-consciously marginal poetry, advertising itself as of the moment.

Establishing an appropriate mood before her entrance, the sequence approaches Mary through seven odes based on the Penitential Psalms and a sequence on the 'Sybyllaes Prophesies of Christ'. The last of these gives our first glimpse of the Virgin, in what is clearly an end-of-section, transitional moment in the text. She appears as both Mother of God and *Madonna lactans*:

> **Sibylla Tiburtina.**
> THow Bethlem arte the birth-place of thy Lord,
> That doth from Nazareth assume his name,
> O blessed moother, blis doth thee affoord,
> His loue, that leaues himself pledge of the same
> O blessed bee that sweet milk-yeilding brest,
> To no wrish [nourish] God, right happely adre. st
> FINIS. (25)

What follows is a lengthy rosary sequence concluding with three stanzas under the heading 'Ave Maria', followed by further sections of similar length titled 'Epithets of Our Blessed Lady', 'Our Blessed Ladies Lullaby' and 'A Reprehen-sion of the Reprehending of our Ladies Praise'. Structurally, thus, Mary is the first and most prominent of the saints that the sequence honours, in a collection that is carefully integrated to showcase her importance.

The integrated design is visible in Mary's place in the collection. Appearing, as described, at a transitional moment, where the sequence moves from the pre-Christian (Psalms and Prophesies) to the Christian (beginning with the Virgin herself), Mary is also the 'door' and 'way' to later, sacred topics, including Christ crucified and in the sepulchre. She is thus not only the mediator to whom we pray, but also the mediator of Christian history. Linked epithets suggest the self-conscious pivoting of the sequence around such mediation. This is Mary as 'Porta Caeli' and 'Scale Caeli':

> **Porta Caeli.**
> WHen grace came from aboue, then wa'st thou made the gate,
> By which it entred heer, & brought the hope of blis,
> Which hope in hartes of men, remaineth stil in state,
> And stil through faith and loue, aliue preserued is:
> Then since thow wa'st the dore, for grace this to relate,
> So art thow heauens gate, and wel accordeth this,
> That as God vnto men, did thee his entrance make,
> Men entrance vnto God, againe by thee may take.

Scale Caeli.
HOw may our heauy load, enclyning to descend,
Ascend vp in the ayre, beyond the egles flight,
Except by such a guyde, as wil assistance lend,
And can from step to step, direct the passage right:
Or rather her owne self, vs better to defend,
The ladder wil become, that scaleth heauens height,
By whose degrees of grace, to blis we may attaine,
And in our mounting vp, not to fall downe againe. (42–3)

Whether as a stairway to heaven or as its gate, Mary appears here as what she is in the sequence as a whole: the approach to the sacred. *En route*, her humanity is important. Images such as the Virgin breast-feeding humanise and render accessible the theological subject-matter, or would have done so for traditionalists. Calvin, who sneered that frequent renderings of the breastfeeding Mary made her into a milk-cow, was as put off by the image as he was by the implications of Marian power and mediation (Waller, 2010: 125–6). The recusant's Catholic identity is clearly illuminated, but identity and politics are inseparable here, making this a religio-political and even proto-feminist intervention by the standards of the day. In one respect, too, Calvin might not have objected to the *Odes* because, although Mary is its foremost personality, readers of the sequence move through the poems about her towards those about Christ. It is His mediating sacrifice that is the reader's ultimate goal. Here, then, is the kind of theological correctness one might expect of an active counter-reformationary;[11] and evidence that – despite Constable – Catholic Mariolatry in the period is not synonymous with idolatry.

Mary deflowered

Besides its theological content, the movement of Rowlands' sequence towards Christ through the Virgin carries penetrative connotations which are also sexual in view of Rowlands' intensely physical depictions of Mary. Mary's body is highly visible in the *Odes*: in her 'sweet smelling breath' ('Quasi Cypressus', 47), in her 'womb' ('Ave Maria', 41), and in the maintained 'maiden' that closes the gynecologically inflected 'Conteyning the Birth of Christe' (28). Her sensuality in relation with Christ is tangible in the opening of 'Our Blessed Ladies Lullaby':

Vpon my lap my soueraigne sits,
And sucks vpon my brest,
Meane whyle his loue sustaines my lyf,
And giues my body rest.(50)

Here the lap, the breast, the body, the sucking and sitting all give Mary a highly physical existence. In 'Lillium inter Spinas' (Lily among Thorns) and 'Nauis Instituoris' (Merchant Ships), that physicality is sexual. Here is 'Nauis Instituoris':

> IF certitude of gaine, may stit the searching mynde,
> To venter in the ship, from whence misfortunes flee,
> That gouerneth the tyde, and doth comaund the wynde,
> And speedely returnes, with goodes that pretious bee,
> The barck of blis is shee, and fortunate by kynde,
> With grace shee fraighted is, and is of custome free,
> Taking but for her hyre, and her inritching trade,
> Loue of deuoted myndes, that rich by her are made. (45)

The 'bark of bliss' is a Mary we penetrate into to find grace – something with which Mary has been 'freighted', implying she receives it from elsewhere to maintain Rowlands' mediating theme. Yet seeking to 'styt' (that is, fish) 'the searching mind' is an uncertain business. The seventeenth century knew the 'stit' as the 'stittle bag', 'stickle bag' or 'Prick-fish',[12] and because this last meaning has obvious sexual connotation, Mary becomes in the poem as freighted with sexual suggestion as she is with grace. Associating her 'bliss' with free custom, hire and the 'enriching trade' of love, the final four lines even sustain analogies with prostitution, though the return to 'devoted minds' of the final line ensures that we understand such Marian intercourse metaphorically. The controversial point, then, is that Mary is available to us; that her availability is the height of pleasure; and that we need only devote our minds to appreciating her to have such happiness. As a sensual reflection on Mary, the poem delivers on the kind of pleasure it promises.

'Lilium inter Spinas' takes Mary's sexuality a stage further:

> AMiddes a gard of thorne, this goodly lilly grew,
> Defended from the foe, that would it faine deface,
> Who neere it to aproche, the entrance neuer knew,
> With poison to infect, where filth had neuer place,
> Yet such might bee the hate, that heeron did ensue,
> That hee reseru'd reuenge, vnto succeeding space,
> What tyme a crowne of thorne, the sonnes head did sustaine,
> To make the mothers hart, be pricked with the payne. (46)

If the innocent reader might miss the eroticism of the opening eight lines praising Mary-the-Lily, the final view of her being 'pricked' should give reason to pause. The word renders the phallic already latent in line one's 'thorn' explicit; so that with hindsight, the garden of Mary whose 'entrance never knew / ... poison'– a well-established garden originating in the marriage hymn of the Song of Songs (Stewart, 1966) – is seen to have faced a sexual threat from the start. Once again, of course, there is a theological point. Mary's garden becomes deflowered by the thorny 'prick' of the crucifixion, experienced here through the mediation of Mary's motherhood and given vibrant poignancy because her person is so sensuously appreciated.[13]

In the poetry of Rowlands, then, Mary is virginal, sensual and deflowered, but her defloration is a sign of the ultimate Christian tragedy, Christ's death, as well as perhaps of our redemption, though Rowlands does not dwell on that. What is absent from his treatments of the Virgin's sexuality is any real anger, bitterness or sense of permanent damage done. Even in 'Lilium Inter Spinas', where Mary's defloration expresses the Christian tragedy of Christ's crucifixion, the horror is offset by the neatness of the conceits linking garden to thorn, thorn to Christ's death, Christ's death to Mary's defloration, and that defloration to the garden-setting once again. The poem is thus organised with an extreme artful congruence proclaiming its author not struck down by tragedy, but in full control of his faculties, even as its congruent arrangement of disparate items and ideas (gardens, Christ's Passion, Mary's defloration) teases rather than mourns.[14] To encounter Mary's defloration with truly mournful connotation, one must turn to an event of genuine, iconic destruction. The unsurprisingly anonymous 'The Wracks of Walsingham' records such a cataclysm.

Medieval Walsingham was one of Europe's two leading sites of Marian devotion: a cultural hub which the anonymous 'The Wracks of Walsingham' celebrates by lamenting its destruction:

> Level, level with the ground
>   The towers do lie,
> Which with their golden glittering tops
>   Pierced once to the sky.
> Where were gates no gates are now,
>   The ways unknown
> Where the press of peers did pass
>   While her flame far was blown. (Jones, 2002: 550)[15]

Though intrinsically tied to a Marian iconoclasm these lines lament a cultural loss: of a centre whose towers 'Pierced … the sky', attracting from faraway lands a 'press of peers'. This alliteration conveys the vibrancy of grandees rubbing shoulders in a packed and bustling shrine, rather than the destruction of a Marian locus: a reminder that what was at stake in the era's changing devotion were not just points of religious preference or theological abstraction, but of the fabric and habits of traditional ways of life. Making that idea of life central to the poem by contrasting it with a death repeatedly 'bitter', the destruction of the shrine entails 'seely sheep / Murdered' by reformers and complacent Catholics. The result is a landscape of 'ways unknown': a wasteland starkly contrasting with the former bustle:

> Bitter was it, O, to view
> The sacred vine
> (While gardeners played all close)
> Rooted up by the swine.
> Bitter, bitter, O, to behold
> The grass to grow
> Where the walls of Walsingham
> So stately did show. (550)

'Swine' simultaneously evokes the iconoclastic reformers who created the ruin, and the pigs left rooting in its grounds after the destruction. With a contrasting metonymy, the gardeners playing 'all close' in those grounds connotes not only the unresisting Catholic leaders, earlier criticised as 'shepherds [who] did sleep' (line 12), but also, via the image of gardeners devoted to its upkeep, the magnificent gardens of the Walsingham estate. Yet all this is a kind of defloration. Contrasting the wild 'grass' of the ruin with the 'sacred vine' of the cultivated site, the passage juxtaposes rival ideas of flowering, so that the flowering of the wilderness comes with the deflowering of the sacred.[16]

At the centre is Mary, the 'rose' of the rosary, the traditional 'Lilium Inter Spinas' and famed bloom of Walsingham. As the *raison d'être* of the pilgrimage site, she stands in metonymic relation to Walsingham's gardens, whose undefiled *floruit* express her inviolate self.[17] The destruction of the gardens, contrarily, entails her defloration. The idea is all but explicit as the closing poem turns, in Dominic Janes and Gary Waller's phrase, 'from mournful plaint to increasingly direct invective' (2010: 9):[18]

> Weep, weep O Walsingham, Whose dayes are nightes,
> Blessing turned to blasphemies, Holy deedes to dispites
> Sinne is where our Ladye sate, Heaven turned to helle;
> Sathan sittes where our Lord did swaye, Walsingham oh, farewell. (551)

As part of this pattern of ruin in which 'Heaven [is] turned to helle' and Satan replaces 'our Lord', a personified Sin – normally a corrupt sexual woman[19] – replaces the Virgin. Though Sin and the Lady are allegorically different persons, the sitting Lady (that is the Virgin) gives way to sin with stark sexual suggestion. Focusing on 'where our Ladye sate', indeed, makes the contest between the two figures a competition over Mary's 'seat'. The seat giving way, Mary and her seat in Walsingham – the two are by now synonymous – are violated.

The Mary of 'The Wracks', then, raises with an intensity not to be ignored the question of what the Reformation really was.[20] Containing meanings of construction, building and form, 'Reformation' certainly does not reflect the historical testimony of 'The Wracks'. Deformation, perhaps, catches the mood better. Defloration, recalling the emotively charged flowering metaphors underlying much Marianism of the period, might be better still. Reading literature as historical evidence in this way, though, brings with it problems parallel to those that micro-historians discover when seeking to generalise from their findings: it takes a micro-history as big as *The Stripping of the Altars* (Duffy, 2005) to become persuasive. All that is possible in this piece is to notice that the association of Reformation with rape, and indeed rape with Marian connotation, is not confined to 'The Wracks of Walsingham'. Bearing in mind the 'powerful and long-standing' identification of Mary with the Christian Church (Rubin, 2009: 168), a deeply-embedded tradition originating in St Paul's designation of the

Church as Christ's virgin bride (2 Corinthians 11:2), the rape of churches found in numerous literary representations in early modern England testifies not only to a pervasive anxiety about the Reformation as violation, but also to the more specific anxiety that it was a Marian violation. Significantly, this anxiety appears in Protestant writings of the period, and indeed among Protestant writers of very different kinds.

Protestants, as I have in part observed, had not forgotten Mary but reconfigured her into a model for emulation, 'primarily, but far from exclusively, for women' (Peters, 2003: 243). The Sorrows of the Virgin were adopted 'as the appropriate metaphor for the godly' and Protestant women found in Mary a 'chaste and godly partner for the godly minister or martyr' (Peters, 2003: 234, 226). Poetic versions of Mary in this mould include 'The salutation and sorrow of the Virgin Marie', in Aemilia Lanyer's *Salve Deus Rex Judaeorum* (1611), where she receives ninety-six lines (twelve stanzas) and *Paradise Regained* (Milton, 1671), where she speaks for 39 lines.[21] Both of these texts represent a suffering parent in whom, in Milton's words 'Motherly cares and fears got head, and rais'd some troubl'd thoughts' (1671: II, 64–5), but these thoughts bring out the exigencies of a Mary of the biblical past and the easily transforming and a-temporal Mary seen previously in this essay is gone. The tiny exceptions amid such restriction are Lanyer's allusion to Mary not just as 'Servant, Mother, Wife' but also as 'Nurse / To Heavens bright King' (1611: E2r): a brief moment of Mother Mary's subversive revival; and the very facility with which Milton's Mary expresses her sorrow, which gives just enough sense of an unusual mind in anguish, perhaps, as to make one wish for more. Yet if these small hints have significance, it is in their suggestion that the authors knew Mary could be greater than their depictions for the most part allow.[22] Whether on such internal evidence or by contrast with the Marys we have noticed previously, the prevailing sense is that the authors' enhanced biblical adherence comes at a very considerable imaginative price.[23]

Equating Mary with the Christian Church – both its entirety and its parts – meant that contemporaries expressed this loss to the religious imagination through the language of Marian violation. A considerable precedent is in Spenser's *The Faerie Queene*, whose Kirkrapine emerges in a depiction linking the dissolution of the monasteries with church-robbery, so that rape and abusing a church become synonymous.[24] Similarly, Anna Swärdh detects the motif of 'rape as iconoclasm' in Shakespeare's *Titus Andronicus* and *The Rape of Lucrece* (2003: 223), and I have extended such reading in regard to *Titus* and Marston's *Antonio's Revenge* (Rist, 2008: 50–1, 94–5). Later examples associating the Christian Church with rape in order to express its reformations include the accomplished poem of 1649 *The presbytery: A satyr*. Writing with an entirely different religious perspective from the author of 'The Wracks' or for that matter Shakespeare, in the midst of civil war the anonymous poet condemns continuing popery in the English Church (equated by the author with the Christian Church) concluding:

Religion, which a blind man well might call
Immense, but one that's deafe, not finde at all,
That which the world doth generally disguise,
That stamp by which all knavery currant is;
Art thou thy selfe, great Nymph? or else doe some
Deflowre thee, nay force thee away from home,
And make thee doe their drudgery? O spleen,
Couldst thou but rise as some lungs stretch'd ha been,
Thou mightst boil out more hot, then ere one brother
Could to pronounce damnation on another. (n.p.)

The polemical targets of this poem are entirely different from those of 'The Wracks', but here the Christian Church is explicitly feminine and her abuse – not by reformers, as in 'The Wracks', but principally through popery – again takes the form of a defloration or rape. Further on in the century, in 1679, the royalist debunking of the Popish Plot known only as *A ballad upon the Popish Plot, written by a lady of quality*, presents the same idea: 'If our English Church (as he says) be a Whore / We're sure 'twas Jack Presbyter did her deflower.'[25] Implying how definitions of 'Reform' are contingent on the speaker, this time the true Christian Church (as understood by this author) receives satire from a ceremonialist rather than puritan standpoint. Yet despite the gulfs between their ideals of religion, these poets of 1649 and 1679 share the key idea with the 'The Wracks': despoilers of the Christian Church (which they invariably equate with their version of it) are her rapists. Moreover, in evoking the feminine Church as ideally inviolate, each author recalls the Marian connotations in St Paul's Virgin Church; as, indeed, 'scriptural references to Mary, not by name, but as "woman" [that] acknowledge her as the personification of the messianic people' (Spurr, 2007: 5). Recalling these deeply inscribed, indeed scriptural, Marys, the poets present the Church as a seventeenth-century Mary without name: thereby acknowledging a loss of memory metaphorically, but with maximum sadness and horror, termed defloration.

Notes

1 For a useful discussion of the history of the 'Hail Mary' prayer, see Thurston (1910).
2 For discussion of the 'eradication of all invocations of the Mother of God' in the King's Primer accompanying the Book of Common Prayer of 1552, and in the re-issued Primer of 1559, see Tavard (1996: 135).
3 I consider this matter further below.
4 Wizeman observes that praise of Mary Tudor frequently linked her with the Virgin so that 'one Mary possessed an essential role in salvation' and the other possessed 'an essential role in England's participation in salvation' (Wizeman, 2004: 245). Su Fang Ng discusses the promotion of associations between the Virgin and Henrietta Maria as a significant feature of the Queen's court (2007: 41–2). In these pages she

also recalls Erika Veevers' association of masque-culture – in which Jonson was the leader – with Marian veneration (see Veevers, 1989).

5 Peters (2003: 229) alludes to the generally 'more favourable environment [to 'strongly catholic authors'] of the 1630s'. For discussion of Catholic court culture in this period, see Shell (1999: 146–68).

6 See definition 1a of 'recusant' in *Oxford English Dictionary (OED)* (2013).

7 For wider discussion of Catholic loyalism see Shell (1999: 107–68)

8 There is in fact a fourth poem 'To the Blessed Virgin', but I do not consider it in this essay. In what follows I therefore refer to the three poems of the sequence as the first, second and third poems 'To our blessed Lady'.

9 Ray (2012: 9) notes that Calvin was 'particularly opposed' to this Madonna-and-Child imagery.

10 For a fuller biography of Rowlands (a name I retain as it was the English one with which he was born), see Arblaster (2004).

11 Such sensitivity especially emerges with the reformers but was not restricted to them. Wizeman describes the exclusive direction of Marian veneration towards Christ as an 'imperative' of the Counter-Reformation, though having roots in the fourteenth century (Wizeman, 2004: 247–8).

12 See under 'Stickleback' in *OED* (2013).

13 I have commented, above, on the theological importance of Mary as mediator for Rowlands, but he repeatedly deploys the literary technique of approaching the Passion through Mary's particular, feminine relation to Christ: see, most strikingly, the magnificent sub-sequence of poems 'The Fifteen Mysteries of the Rosary, of Our Blessed Lady' (Verstegan, 1601).

14 For further information on recusant portrayals of Mary's mourning at the cross see the essay by Gallagher (Chapter 11) in this volume.

15 I prefer the title 'The Wracks of Walsingham' because the poem as we have it today has no title; 'The Ruins' is an editorial interpolation, while 'In the wracks of Walsingham' is the poem's first line.

16 Such contrasts between nature and the sacred are not unusual in the period. I discuss one example of the phenomenon in *Titus Andronicus* (see Rist, 2008: 54).

17 For wider illustration of Mary as a garden in the period (indeed by Ben Jonson) see Spurr (2007: 94–7). For recent discussion of the ways Renaissance gardens entailed symbolic meanings more generally, see Tigner (2012).

18 For discussion of the poem's dating, see Janes and Waller (2010: 8).

19 For sin being allegorised as feminine in this way since early Christianity, see Milton (2007: 146–7).

20 The question has become standard among Reformation historians of the last two decades, including a number cited in this essay.

21 Lanyer's 'Salutation' is in fact thirteen stanzas long, but the last stanza does not address Mary, so I discount it here. Hodgson's essay in this volume (Chapter 3) considers the figure of Eve in Lanyer's *Salve Deus* and Milton's *Paradise Lost*. For further detail on Lanyer see also the introduction to this volume and Thorne's essay (Chapters 1, 6).

22 Lanyer, notably, is considerably more subversive in her prose address 'To the Virtvovs Reader' prefacing the poetry, than she is in the poetry itself: 'It pleased our Lord and Saviour Jesus Christ, without the assistance of man ... to be begotten of a woman,

borne of a woman, nourished of a woman, obedient to a woman' (1611: A1v). Here, unlike in the poetic depiction, the subversive potential of Mother Mary is writ large.

23 Historians disagree on how fully the Protestant restriction of Mary was felt by contemporary women (see Peters, 2003: 244–5 and MacCulloch, 2004: 215–16), but restriction, as much as the feeling of it, is the key point here. Spurr (2007) rightly emphasises that the 'conservative cast' of Lanyer's Virgin Mary stands out the more for its contrast with *Salve Deus Rex Iudaeorum*'s more general feminism. He is also right that the Mary of *Paradise Regained* is more striking than the stereotype of a Milton 'supposedly convinced of the inability of women to engage in cerebral activity' allows. Nevertheless, by the standards of Marian representation of the day, even as illustrated in this essay, the depiction of Milton's Mary is restricted. The claim that Lanyer's conservative Mary 'most likely' arises because Mary did not need feminist enhancement, having a role in salvation, is unconvincing; because in Lanyer's poetry Mary becomes, especially by comparison to Lanyer's Eve, dull; and because far less restricted, but more catholic, depictions of Mary were, as we have seen, available in the era. It is Lanyer's Protestantism, this last implies, that restricts her Virgin Mary. See Spurr (2007: 83–4, 113–16) for his views on this matter.

24 Mary Robert Falls argued against allusion to the monasteries, which she took to be the prevailing reading, and in favour of an allusion to church-robbery; however, she acknowledged that Kirkrapine 'can, in one sense, be interpreted as a condemnation of the dissolution' (1953: 457), so her argument's either/or procedure is reductive. Her insistence elsewhere that Kirkrapine refers exclusively to church-robbery fails to deal with Spenser's most striking objection to him: 'The holy Saints of their rich vestiments / He did disrobe, when all men careless slept, / And spoild the Priests of their habilliments' (I.3.5–7). This objection is not just to robbery, but also to iconoclasm. Finally, the premise of Falls' argument – that alluding to the monasteries would entail a 'startling anachronism' since they had been dissolved under Henry VIII (1953: 459) – no longer looks persuasive, since we now know monasteries were still much in reference in Elizabethan England (Shell, 2007: 23–54).

25 This is a single-leaf document. Although, the document does contain the number 104 on the left-hand page, and 105 on the right-hand page (the passage cited here comes from the right-hand page), these numbers are in a different hand from the rest of the text, and I am not convinced they are an original part of this one-leaf document.

References

A ballad upon the Popish Plot, written by a lady of quality (1679) London: s.n.

Arblaster, P. (2004) *Antwerp and the World: Richard Verstegan and the International Culture of Catholic Reformation.* Leuven: Leuven University Press.

Constable, H. (1623) *The Catholike moderator.* London: Eliot's Court Press.

——. (1960) *The Poems of Henry Constable.* Ed. J. Grundy. Liverpool: Liverpool University Press.

Donaldson, I. (2011) *Ben Jonson: A Life.* Oxford: Oxford University Press.

Duffy, E. (2005) *The Stripping of the Altars: Traditional Religion in England, c.1400–1580.* 2nd edn. New Haven, CT: Yale University Press.

Falls, M.R. (1953) 'Spenser's Kirkrapine and the Elizabethans.' *Studies in Philology*, 50.3: 457–75.

Grundy, J. (ed.) (1960) 'Introduction.' *The Poems of Henry Constable*. Liverpool: Liverpool University Press. 1–105.

Janes, D. and Waller, G. (2010) 'Walsingham, landscape, sexuality and cultural memory.' *Walsingham in Literature and Culture from the Middle Ages to Modernity*. Ed. D. Janes and G. Waller. Farnham: Ashgate.

Jones, E. (ed.) (2002) *The New Oxford Book of Sixteenth-Century Verse*. Oxford: Oxford University Press.

Jonson, B. (1965) *Ben Jonson: The Prose Works*. Ed. C.H. Herford, P. Simpson and E. Simpson. Oxford: Clarendon Press.

Kuchar, G. (2006) 'Henry Constable and the Question of Catholic Poetics: Affective Piety and Erotic Identification in the *Spirituall Sonnettes*.' *Philological Quarterly*, 85: 69–90.

Lanyer, A. (1611) *Salue Deus Rex Judaeorum*. London: Valentine Simmes.

MacCulloch, D. (2004) 'Mary and Sixteenth Century Protestants.' *The Church and History*. Ed. R.N. Swanson. Woodbridge: Boydell Press.

Milton, J. (2007) *Milton: Paradise Lost*. Ed. A. Fowler. 2nd edn. Harlowe: Longman.

Ng, S.F. (2007) *Literature and the Politics of Family in Seventeenth-Century England*. Cambridge: Cambridge University Press.

Oxford English Dictionary (OED) (2013) Oxford Dictionaries Online. Oxford: Oxford University Press.

Peters, C. (2003) *Patterns of Piety: Women, Gender and Religion in Late Medieval and Reformation England*. Cambridge: Cambridge University Press.

Ray, S. (2012) *Mother Queens and Princely Sons: Rogue Madonnas in the Age of Shakespeare*. Basingstoke: Palgrave Macmillan.

Rist, T. (2008) *Revenge Tragedy and the Drama of Commemoration in Reforming England*. Aldershot: Ashgate.

Rubin, M. (2009) *Mother of God: A History of the Virgin Mary*. London: Allen Lane.

Shell, A. (1999) *Catholicism, Controversy and the English Literary Imagination, 1558–1623*. Cambridge: Cambridge University Press.

———. (2007) *Oral Culture and Catholicism in Early Modern England*. Cambridge: Cambridge University Press.

Spurr, B. (2007) *See the Virgin Blessed: The Virgin Mary in English Poetry*. Basingstoke: Palgrave Macmillan.

Stewart, S. (1966) *The Enclosed Garden: The Tradition and the Image in Seventeenth-Century Poetry*. Madison, WI: University of Wisconsin Press.

Swärdh, A. (2003) *Rape and Religion in English Renaissance Literature: A Topical Study of Four Texts by Shakespeare, Drayton and Middleton*. Uppsala: University of Uppsala Press.

Tavard, G. (1996) *The Thousand Faces of the Virgin Mary*. Collegeville, MN: The Liturgical Press.

The presbytery. A satyr (1649) s.n. (see Wing P3229A).

Thurston, H. (1910) 'Hail Mary'. *Catholic Encyclopedia*. New York: Robert Appleton Company.

Tigner, A.L. (2012) *Literature and the Renaissance Garden from Elizabeth I to Charles II: England's Paradise*. Farnham: Ashgate.

Veevers, E. (1989) *Images of Love and Religion: Queen Henrietta Maria and Court Entertainments*. Cambridge: Cambridge University Press.

Verstegan, R. (1601) *Odes*. Antwerp: A. Conincx.

Waller, G. (2010) 'The Virgin's "pryvities": Walsingham and the late medieval sexualization of the Virgin.' *Walsingham in Literature and Culture from the Middle Ages to Modernity*. Ed. D. Janes and G. Waller. Farnham: Ashgate.

Walsham, A. (2006) *Charitable Hatred: Tolerance and Intolerance in England, 1500–1700*. Manchester: Manchester University Press.

Wizeman, W. (2004) 'The Virgin Mary in the reign of Mary Tudor.' *The Church and History*. Ed. R.N. Swanson. Woodbridge: Boydell Press.

11

Stabat Mater Dolorosa: imagining Mary's grief at the cross

Laura Gallagher

Despite the Gospels providing no explicit insight into the suffering of the Virgin Mary during the Passion, from the mid-thirteenth century onwards a developing interest in the humanity of Christ, and Mary's privileged and unique intimacy with her son, inspired multiple visual and textual representations that drama-tized Mary's motherly pain and sorrow.[1] Such imagery was indebted to the *Stabat Mater Dolorosa* tradition ('the sorrowful mother was standing') that originated from a thirteenth-century Latin sequence. Often set to music, it explored the Virgin's grief at the cross and strategically employed the first-person narrative voice.[2] The mournful Latin reads:

> Stabat mater dolorosa,
> Iuxta crucem lacrymosa,
> Dum pendebat filius.
> Cuius animam gementem,
> Contristantem et dolentem,
> Pertransivit gladius.
>
> (At the cross her station keeping,
> Stood the mournful mother weeping,
> Close to Jesus at the last.
> Through her heart, his sorrow sharing,
> All his bitter anguish bearing,
> Now at length the sword has passed).[3]

In accordance with the *Stabat Mater Dolorosa* tradition, the Virgin was frequently imagined in the medieval period as present at, and involved in, the crucifixion scene, openly grieving and sharing in Jesus' agonies in both a physical and spiritual sense, as the sword of sorrows prophecy foretold.[4] She was typically depicted in positions of extreme grief, including swooning, leaning, agitated gesturing, weeping, wailing, pulling at her clothes and the *pietà*.[5] Frequently, Mary was also represented as engaging in dramatic speech acts testifying to her agony and such signs of her sorrow were commonly interpreted as the delayed experi-ence of child-birthing pains.[6] This portrayal of the Virgin's anguish coincided with a graphic representation of Jesus' agony, which established her as the chief mediator of his pain and as a partner in redemptive suffering. As such, the Virgin could be imitated by Christians who sought to share in and meditate on the suffering of Jesus (the process of *imitatio*).

However, such physical manifestations of the Virgin's motherly suffering 'did not typify the modest, restrained and disciplined religious life' sought by Protestant and Catholics alike after the Reformation (Ellington, 1995: 254). As Ellington (2001) and Kuchar (2008) assert, Mary was generally refigured in the early modern period as a sorrowful but silent and controlled witness (the *lo spasimo* controversy).[7] This re-reading remained faithful to scriptural accounts; it also highlighted Mary's knowledge and faith in the resurrection; emphasised the inner spiritual communication and unique relationship between mother and son; and focused greater attention on the death of Christ and his redemptory sacrifice, rather than Mary's role alongside it. Furthermore, imagining a stoic Mary ensured that she could not be considered to be an active participator in the scheme of salvation and as such, this de-authorised her intercessionary-influence.[8]

Despite this re-interpretation of Mary's role at the cross, this essay argues that early modern Catholic accounts of Marian grief continued to nostalgically present Mary using the medieval motif of the *Stabat Mater Dolorosa*.[9] Yet, in doing so, such texts refigure the significance of the trope in light of the new historical and religious context so that the traditional conventions associated with the Virgin's mourning provide a means of ruminating on the performativity, gender and significance of grief in the early modern period. The presentation of the Virgin's suffering – her voice, tears, and other 'aesthetics of mourning' (Rist, 2008: 15) – are thus infused with profound significance. Her performance of grief simultaneously embodies and undermines communal memory: it tests the 'presentness of the [Catholic] past' (Goodland, 2005: 3)[10] and illuminates the continued importance of Mary's intercession to the Catholic community in England.

Grief, and the gestures which signify it, may be a broadly universal trope but its significance alters in particular historical circumstances and is defined by culturally conditioned (linguistic, artistic and religious) conventions.[11] In the wake of the religious and cultural developments of the Reformation, grief and its associated signs underwent considerable alterations. Whether changes to mourning practices were welcomed or whether they imbued mourners with a sense of fear and 'powerlessness' is open to debate, but the reformation certainly forced a significant reconceptulisation of grief and the grieving process.[12] Medieval Catholic activities that engaged with the fate of the dead were condemned by reformers and particular scrutiny was given to the doctrine of purgatory: the belief in an interim realm between heaven and hell.[13] With ritual and liturgical reform, new and unfamiliar mourning rites were created (abolition of purgatory, elimination of prayers of intercession to Mary and the saints to assist dead relatives, removal of indulgences, compression of funeral rites), which eradicated the concept of 'assistance' for the dead and negated the importance of these particular frameworks of collective memorial and memory.

This is not to say that acts of commemoration and memory were completely eradicated in Protestantism. Rather, as various studies into early modern death rites have shown, alternative and increasingly worldly acts of commemoration emerged, including sermons, elegies, poetry, secular funeral displays, elaborate funeral monuments and emotive tombstone inscriptions (see Neill, 1997: 38–41 and Gittings, 1999: 156–69). Nevertheless, under Protestant 'rigorism', grief was prohibited for all those who died virtuously because they were (presumably) in heaven and in any case, for many (particularly Calvinists), predestination ensured no human influence was possible over the fate of the soul (Pigman, 1985: 27). Indeed, Rist notes that although reformed opinion on mourning divided into two broad types – 'rigorism' and '*de facto* rigorism' – the only difference between them was that 'of emphasis' (2008: 27).[14] As mourning for the dead no longer had a tangible effect on the soul in the afterlife (according to rigorists), and measured grief rites were advised by *de facto* rigorists, expansive demonstrations of sorrow came to have Catholic overtones in the early modern period. At the crux of this controversy surrounding mourning rites was the performativity of grief – the style, enactment and manner of devotion to the dead. Reformed prescriptions stressed limited, moderate grief and as such present a guide for the staging of mourning. Diverse studies, including those by Huston Diehl (1997), Michael Neill (1997), Frances E. Dolan (1999), Stephen Greenblatt (2001), Katherine Goodland (2005), Tobias Döring (2006) and Thomas Rist (2008), highlight how the early modern theatre negotiated and accommodated the cultural angst associated with mourning changes.[15] Although this essay does not consider mourning on the early modern stage, it is nonetheless concerned with the performance controversy surrounding Mary's grief at the cross.

Thomas Lodge's *Prosopopeia containing the teares of the holy, blessed, and sanctified Marie, the Mother of God* (1596) directly engages with the performative nature of the Virgin's grief.[16] Lodge's Catholicism was long suspected but this pious tract (printed in London) 'confirmed' his heresy, and forced his exile to France.[17] The text emerged during a period in which a series of high-profile public executions of Jesuit priests took place (across the 1580s and 1590s) and, as such, its focus on Mary's grief upon witnessing the corporeal suffering of Jesus and her lamentations over 'her sonnes most tragike martyrdome' would have had particular and profound significance to the Catholic community who viewed such priests as martyrs for the faith (B1v).[18] The introduction 'To the readers' acknowledges both the controversy Lodge's work will generate and the general debate that surrounded the figure of Mary in the period: 'Some there bee that will not onely gybe at this complaint, but impaire the person, drawing from *Maries* demerite all that which the fathers in her life helde maruelous' (A6r). Although the contemporary reaction and some features of Lodge's text signal its Catholic overtones, the prose resists such labels. Instead, the text actively engages with particular early modern concerns surrounding the performance of grief – as is immediately signalled by the title *Prosopopeia*.

Although Gavin Alexander has dismissed Lodge's text as 'a school exercise on a grand scale', his discussion of the term prosopopoeia actually reveals the text's significance (2007: 105). Alexander outlines that 'the Greek word *prosōpon* means a face or mask and from those core meanings derive subsidiary meanings of a dramatic part or character' (99). In turn, literary prosopopoeia 'learns from rhetorician interest in what is involved for the performer of the voice, how that performer can become absorbed in the role he plays, can only move his audience by moving himself' (102). If the Virgin Mary's grief is a prosopopoeia, a role or mask that can be assumed, the reader can also be urged to 'put on the mask' and perform her grief so that 'we then take over the prosopopoeia' (111). To encourage this prosopopoeia, the text employs various performative strategies, and various cues attempt to control the reader's response. Although this is a prose text,

> performance and performativity are also central issues when analysing texts not meant for stage production. There are several strategies by which printed texts engage performative powers: apostrophes, appellative moves, perlocutionary effects, dialogical orientation towards an implied audience, foregrounding the speaking persona, simulating physical presence, corporality and voice, showing self-awareness and self-consciousness. (Döring, 2006: 19)[19]

These performance gestures are designed to provoke the reader's identification with Mary, compassion for her, and even move them in *imitatio* of her sorrow.[20]

That Lodge expressly intends for his text to be used as a tool for devotional meditation and to elicit an emotional response emerges in his address to the female dedicatees Margaret Stanley, Countess of Darby and Margaret Clifford, Countess of Cumberland. He urges them to 'accept these teares in their nature, and ... weepe many times with Iesus and Marie'; and he asserts that involved reading will produce tears: 'if giue what you owe, you shall grieue when you reade' (A3v). Not only is this affective reading mode commended to these female dedicatees, but encouraging the reader to share in Mary's grief in this way can also be understood as a performance of gender.[21] As mourning rituals were profoundly associated with the feminine in the period, imitating the sorrows of Mary constructs any reader as feminine by identification. But even more significantly, imagining the Passion from the mother's perspective compels the reader to imitate Mary's maternal response to the death of her son.

Combining several of Döring's performance features and focusing on the maternal response, Lodge's text invites the reader to contemplate a dual perspective: to view the suffering physical body of Mary, and to appreciate the Passion scene from her perspective:

Ahlasse, what seest thou? Nay, what seest thou not to bewaile? If thou seest the virgines lappe, it is bloudied with the streames that fall from her Sonnes wounded head. If thou seest her modest eies, they are almost swolne and sunke into hir head with teares. If thou looke for her pure colour, it is decaied with extreame sorrowe, her breasts are defaced with often beating of her handes, her handes are wearyed by often beating of her breasts.

   If shee looke on the one side, shee sees Marie the sinner washing her sons feet with her tears: if on the other, she beholdeth Ioseph wofully preparing his funeralls: if on the other, she seeth virgins mourning: if on the other, she beholdeth soldiers mocking. (D5r–6r)

This itemisation of the Virgin's body parts (lap, eyes, skin, breasts and hands) operates as a tragic-blazon, dismembering her mourning body as tragically beautiful and allowing the reader to appreciate its emotive power. The focus on these particular parts, as well as the repetitious detail about beating her breasts, reveals the specific significance of her female body to the reading of the scene. Mary is at the interpretative centre of the action; she demarcates the surrounding activities. Through Mary's encouragement, the Passion becomes an interactive, visual experience for the reader: the reader sees what *she* invites us to notice and interprets the scene as *she* would have it read, especially through the affective employment of verbs and adverbs ('woefully', 'mocking'). Submerging the reader in a sensory experience mediated by an attentive Mary ensures that he / she is also pierced by the sword of sorrow: 'shall not the swoorde of afflictions pearce your entrayles to beholde this tragedie?' (C2r). In this way, Lodge's text recalls typical medieval appropriations that interpreted the crucifixion scene through the experience of Mary. However, Lodge's focus on Mary's sight as a tool of individualisation, communication and spirituality is at odds with the growing distrust surrounding the body, and in particular the sight, as a means of religious experience in the early modern period. As Ellington highlights, by the sixteenth century 'only a purely spiritualised apprehension of the divine could be considered authentic' (2001: 201). Yet, employing the 'eye' to understand the Passion, in this example, signals the continued importance and value placed on Mary's individualised experience.

   Mary's gaze on the crucified body of Christ is also shown in Lodge's text to have an erotic potential. She is imagined saying: 'I wold kisse thee seuentie times seuen, & seeme more thy louer than thy mother' (G2r). This perceived relationship change is further exposed by evoking Mary Magdalene: 'if thy wounds fell new a bleeding, I would wash them with my teares; my hairs should dry them, my lips should suck them, thou shouldest make me more than a mother, in recouering mee an absent sonne' (G2r).[22] Despite the controversy surrounding the identity of the woman who washes Jesus' feet, in *this* context (which has already been signposted as erotic and because of the earlier reference to Magdalene washing Jesus' feet (as cited above)) it is evident that the Virgin's predicted actions are intentionally meant to recall Mary Magdalene.[23] In doing so, the Virgin's imagined act of wound washing (and sucking) has added erotic charge, and the line 'thou shouldest make me more than a mother, in recouering mee an absent sonne' is particularly revealing because the 'absent' Jesus is a typical feature of Mary Magdalene sepulchre scenes, as Shuger explores (1994: 167–91). In *Abandoned Women and Poetic Tradition*, Lawrence I. Lipking highlights that 'abandonment' has two meanings: to be forsaken by a lover and to violate norms, conventions and respectability (1988: xvii). Like Magdalene narratives, Lodge's text characterises the Virgin's abandonment under these conventions. The Virgin perceives a violation of respectability in noting her shifting status from mother to lover, and constructs herself as the abandoned woman in relation to Jesus, the absent and insensitive lover. Her mournful countenance is directly caused by his prolonged absence. Mary articulates: 'my eies long fore for thy sight, oh when wilt thou comfort me?'; 'in flesh whilest thou art absent, & dwellest with death, let mee bewaile thee'; and 'I cannot leave weeping teares, untill thou come and wipe awaie my teares.' (Lodge, 1596: 52, 57, 60; among other examples).[24] Jesus' absence is to blame for her suffering and his presence is constructed as intrinsic to her happiness.

The Virgin's concerns also manifest general anxieties about an absent, distant God. Although she assumes Jesus will eventually return (demonstrating her faith in his resurrection), her disquiet hints at a lack of complete confidence. In this sense, the Virgin's bewilderment mirrors that typically ascribed to Magdalene. As Peters notes: 'Mary Magdalene's persistence in grief matched that of the believer who lost assurance of Christ's presence and promise' (2003: 237). The Virgin Mary's doubts in this instance (in contrast to the stoic confidence generally shown in the period) thus enable her to be a more relatable and personal model, providing hope and comfort to ordinary Christians struggling with their faith. Moreover, as Badir (2009) suggests is true for Magdalene texts that focus on the absent Christ, Mary's pain could represent that of early modern Catholics struggling to come to terms with perceived religious abandonment and the removal of the doctrine of transubstantiation: Christ is absent to Mary, as his body is now absent from communion rites.[25] In addition, Shuger identifies a third type of religious abandonment as Jesus' lonely experience on the cross (1994: 182), and this aspect emerges in Lodge's text too by including details of Christ's direct speech on the cross (even though the text is predominantly concerned with Mary's dialogue): 'Hee cryed, My God, my God, why hast thou forsaken me? and was not succored' (F3r). Drawing attention to Jesus' desertion by God and his followers implicitly links Jesus to Mary, the abandoned women (as in Magdalene texts). Christ's Passion is therefore associated with Mary's erotic passion: their sorrows are equivalent, since both are founded on a profound sense of abandonment.

As these various examples have indicated, the employment of Mary's first-person voice powerfully communicates her pain and individualised experience;

it is another indicator of the performative powers of the prose (Döring, 2006: 19). Elsewhere in the text, Mary directly urges the reader to contemplate their loss and 'feede with poore *Marie* on the bread of tribulation, for I haue lost a sonne, and you lost your Sauiour' (B4r). The assignment of the name 'Marie' to the speaking persona, the adjective 'poore' to describe her and the appellative move of calling Jesus son and saviour attempt to incite the audience to mourn. Mary even explicitly implores the reader to cry alongside her: 'Let your faces bee swolne with weeping, for I wil water my couch with teares' (B5v). Here too, the co-ordinating conjunction links the reader's pain with Mary's grief, which indicates the expected, shared emotional response. Throughout the text, the Virgin Mary also rails furiously and incessantly at the reader – in the first-person and present tense, giving it particular impact – to recognise their role in the death of Christ: 'you haue crucified this Christ with your sinnes, & slain him by your offences' (E6v). The reader is urged to weep and grieve with her in the understanding of their shared loss and the reader's particular guilt: 'come, come and weepe bitterly with mee, for you haue much cause of lamentation' (E5v). Through repetition, apostrophes, rhetorical questions, brutal details of Christ's suffering, considerations on the nature of sin, and the speaker Mary's mounting distress, the reader is coerced into lamentation as the text progresses. Employing the mother of God's voice to insist that the reader acknowledge and grieve for their saviour and her son is evidently a highly emotive and gendered strategy. It evokes empathy between the reader and the sorrowful mother, and in turn an affected response.

The Virgin's first-person speaking voice is also 'fictively' appropriated in a meditative text contemporary to that of Lodge, C.N.'s *Our Ladie hath a new sonne* (1595), and it is likely that this text was similarly informed by the Jesuit executions.[26] Despite a later reference to Jesus being moved by Mary's 'inward speeches' (suggesting the spiritual and emotional connection between them that transcends verbal communication), the text implies that the Virgin's speech acts are audible and have both personal and public audiences: 'with sorrowfull sighes began to bewaile her selfe, somtime to him [Jesus], other times to S. John, & sometimes to the Jewes, who seeing her excessiue griefe coulde not but take compassion upon her' (47). This reference to the Jewish people will be further explored below, but it is important to note first that another intended audience is, of course, the reader. Adopting the performative powers typical of grief, Mary asks rhetorical questions, a perlocutionary effect designed to elicit guilt: 'Who will give water vnto my head (saith she) and a Fountaine of teares vnto mine eyes, to bewaile both day & night the murther, not of any other then mine owne and onlie sonne?' (48). Assigning Christ the title 'son' is an appellative move that justifies her own sorrow as his mother, and works to shame the reader into a shared sorrow. Moreover, Mary outlines the reader's specific guilt: they should weep 'since that life itselfe, by whome ye all haue life, leaueth to liue any longer among you' (48). The repetition of 'life' (and its forms) for different meanings works to persuade the reader of their role in Christ's death. Employing similar methods to Lodge's, then, C.N.'s text attempts to persuade the reader to share in Mary's grief performance.

C.N.'s text distinguishes itself, however, in its attention to the people at the crucifixion scene. After coercing the reader, Mary, in an apostrophe, turns her attention to an implied audience of Jewish people and condemns them as culpable in her son's death: 'O who of you all (once his chosen people, now his chiefest enemies) can accuse him of the least sin, that ye cause him to die with great shame?' (48–9). Despite the above-mentioned reference to Jewish pity for Mary's plight, several pages of the text are dedicated to Mary denouncing the actions of the Jewish people (48–53). Mary's invective is interspersed with various performative effects: most notably, rhetorical questions intended to elicit guilt; the appellative move of discussing the actions of Pilate in particular; and the citing of the crowd's words 'Let him be crucified' and 'Crucifie him', with the incriminating biblical evidence recorded in the margins (John 19). Emphasising the role of the Jews in Christ's death and the terrible impact this had on his mother assigns Jewish guilt. As Rubin notes, the sorrow of Mary generally worked as a 'particularly poignant … statement against Jews' and calls for reader revulsion and anger (2009a: 68). Mary's voice in this text actively works to accuse and incite shame, sadness and rage; so that rather than compassion, Mary affects compunction in the reader. In addition, the text concludes with the burial of Christ, without reference to his resurrection, which strategically heightens the guilt that the reader should feel.[27]

This sense of guilt is compounded by imagining the Virgin as suffering physically alongside her son. Lodge's *Prosopopeia* takes a grim, almost misogynistic, satisfaction from simulating the Virgin's physical body and tracing her physically manifested sorrows. Lodge imagines Mary experiencing the trials of the Passion with Jesus, exhaustively focusing on the pains induced by the nails and thorns over a couple of pages (G6r–v). To briefly illustrate the conjectured violence, the Virgin is imagined saying: 'those nailes which nailed thy handes and feete to the crosse, shall nail my soul & thoughts to thy crosse … my flesh is torne with thornes, because thy forehead is rent wyth thornes' (G6r). Although the Virgin is speaking metaphorically, it can be inferred that her body is ravaged like Jesus' body. Aside from the possible erotic reading of such piercing, the focus on the injuries done by the nails and thorns (and their physical shape) also recalls the 'sword of sorrow' prophecy, a typical feature of the *Stabat Mater Dolorosa* tradition. The prophecy is realised and performed by Mary vocalising her physical torment.

C.N.'s *Our Ladie hath a new sonne* recalls another tradition of the *Stabat Mater*, a vivid performative gesture, the *pietà:* Mary physically holding and lamenting over the crucified Jesus in her arms. The text reads: 'so sate she at the foote of the Crosse, with the dead bodie in her lap, offering it all bloodie to Almightie God ... everye one which see her, might easily judge hee was her sonne and shee his mother' (80–1). The static, arresting image operates as a tableau, evoking Mary's longing and loss for her dead son. Notably, this is a non-biblical devotional image, one that was highly popular in the medieval period, and thus its employ-ment explicitly recalls medieval Catholicism.[28] The relatable, human grief on display also works to undermine the Protestant erasure of such mourning rituals, and highlights the emotive power of such images. Its power and pathos derives from its simultaneous evoking of comfort and pain, love and sacrifice, birth and death. Mary's holding of her dead son instinctively recalls his birth and infancy, and the text plays on this evocation:

> thou broughest forth thy first begotten Son, thou swadlest him in cloutes, & laidst him downe in a maunger [Luke 2] ... insteed of swaddling him in cloures, and ioyfill laying him downe, and tending him, thou art constrained to swaddle thy first begotten Sonne againe, and with sorrow to lay him downe in a Monument [John 19]. (81–2)[29]

Juxtaposing Mary's tender care for the infant with her burial of her adult son emotively suggests the depth of the mother's loss. The terms 'swaddle' and 'lay down' are repeated, but their meaning suggestively alters depending on whether the context is one of birth or of death, so that Mary's emotion shifts from joy at the sleeping baby to sorrow as she lays Jesus in his tomb. The antithetical contrast between Mary's previous joys and present grief intensifies the pathos so that, again, Mary's motherhood emerges as a powerful means to appreciate the mystery of the Passion.

So too, another dominant feature of the medieval trope was to interpret Mary's experience at the cross as the delayed experience of childbirth. *Our Ladie hath a new sonne*, in keeping with the text's overarching theme, imagines Mary's birthing pains at the cross as her delivery of her 'new son', John. These newly felt pains meant 'that thou shouldest be a comfort vnto others, thou hast experience what that saying meaneth, a. *thou shalt bring forth in griefe* (a. Gen. 3).' (75). Significantly, Mary's labour pains enable her to (newly) operate as a gendered model to childbearing women: they render her more applicable and consoling,[30] just as her mourning over the absent Jesus makes her increas-ingly relevant as an exemplar of faith. The torment and pain Mary suffers at the cross is thus understood to help increase her appeal. Despite the insistence to mourn alongside the mother of God in these Marian texts, the mournful reader's signs of grief are typically imagined as lesser than Mary's. In Lodge's *Prosopopeia* the readers are to be 'partners in [her] grief', 'associats in bewailing', yet Mary stresses that her relationship with Jesus is privileged and anomalous, thereby befitting her particular sorrow (B6r). She asserts: 'I will then weepe for thee as my father, sigh for thee as thy da[u]ghter, die for thee as thy spouse, and grieue for thee as thy mother: & as thou art wonderfully mine, so will I weepe such a labyrinth of teares, as no mortall mourner shalbe able to tract them' (B6r). Establishing her unique relationship with Jesus helps justify the Virgin's mourning and, moreover, distinguishes it from that of the 'mortall mourner'.[31] Her tears are posited as a 'labyrinth' to highlight their bewildering complexity: she is losing her son, husband, father and saviour. Her loss is simultaneously public and private, and her tears embody both her personal loss and that of the Christian community.[32] Despite contemporary concerns over 'appropriate' mourning, such strategies posit the Virgin's sorrow and visual expression of that pain – her tears – as human, relatable, and sympathetic.

As well as evidence of Mary's humanity, Lodge's *Prosopopeia* makes explicit the rhetorical and spiritual power of tears:

> Come, come and learne what tears be, that you may know their benefites. The sinners teares are Gods mirrours: their penitent sighs, his incense: God heareth praiers, but beholdeth tears: praiers moue God to heare, tears compell him to haue mercie. Silent teares are speaking advocats. (C5r)

This passage implicitly comments on some of the major theological debates in the period: iconography, the distinction between the word/image, and the comparative rhetorical power of listening and sight. In Lodge's reading, tears operate as a sign and their significance is linked to their visual status. Tears are a literal object, 'God's mirrours', in which devotion to God can be observed and, thus, tears are demonstrable of faith. The act of 'beholding' associated with the mirror also highlights how tears harness the sight to influence; the verb 'compel' denotes the forceful, visual impact tears have on God. Tears are understood to be more persuasive than prayers in influencing God: God favours the sight of faith over the sound of faith. The reader is therefore encouraged to visually testify to their sorrow and faith when seeking God's intercession, as 'silent teares are speaking advocats'. This legalese language also evokes Mary's intercessionary powers – the belief that she could petition Jesus on behalf of sinners – so that it can be understood that Mary's intercession can be sought by following the example of her tears. Indeed, Mary explicitly attests to the influence of emotion: 'teares are sweet weapons to wound and to winne harts, I will vse them, I will inuite them, I will maintaine them, I will triumph in them' (D6r–v). Rather than operating as a sign of the Virgin's submission, then, tears are deliberately and influentially harnessed by her for a specific purpose and, in turn, can be utilised by the reader. Although the critical studies cited above which explore mourning in early modern drama suggest that the *effect* of performance is generally intangible, in such accounts of Marian grief her tears have an explicit function and intention – they affect the reader and in turn, this appeals to Mary's intercessionary compassion.

In addition, Mary's reference to her tears as a 'triumph' highlights how they were understood to help facilitate the resurrection. Lodge imagines Mary explaining:

> There are two teares ... the one of ioy and praise, the other of sorow and lamen-
> tation: I wepte the teares of ioye when thou blessedst my wombe, I weepe the
> tears of sorow, because the hope of my daies is decaid ... so let mee recouer him
> with comfort ... and behold him in his resurrection, and triumph in his ascension,
> that pleasing in either sort of teares, I maye praise thee for both sortes of mercie.
> (H6r–7v)

The Virgin's tears, whether of joy or of sorrow, evidence her maternal faith in,
and love for, her son. Additionally, her tears register her belief and confidence
in her saviour, and allow her to participate in his saving work. Tears, unlike
other bodily effluvium, are not considered polluting or revolting; instead, as
water, tears are linked to the complex symbolism of the baptismal waters of
birth, death and rebirth; so the Virgin's tears are also often paralleled to Jesus'
blood: 'let teares drop from thine eyes to recompence the bloud pouring from
his wounds' (F3v). Like Jesus' blood, tears symbolise the death and rebirth made
possible by his sacrifice. Not simply, then, are the Virgin's tears those of sorrow;
they also symbolise 'the purifying sacrifice of the Cross, which washes sinners
of all stain and gives them new life' (Warner, 1978: 223). They reveal Mary's love
for her son and her understanding of his ministry.

The Virgin at the cross is thus understood, in the *Stabat Mater Dolorosa* tradition, to be poised between grief and happiness; sorrow and exaltation; agony
and triumph. Kuchar identifies that sacred sorrow (*penthos*) is 'complexly bound
up with conflicting emotions of joy and sorrow, emotions which counter-
intuitively coexist at one and the same moment' (2008: 5–6). The Virgin's
paradoxical experiencing of joy-sorrow (*charmolypi*) extends from her position as
sorrowful mother, but hopeful believer in the resurrection.[33] In C.N.'s *Our Ladie
hath a new sonne*, for example, Mary celebrates 'O happie Crosse! O Holy nailes!
O sweete instrumentes of a sorrowfull death!' (52). The cross is understood as
simultaneously a symbol of Jesus' death *and* resurrection. The paradoxes of
Mary's joyful sorrow and her understanding of Jesus' resurrection means that
she can be rendered a co-redemptrix, participating in and facilitating her son's
sacrifice to ensure salvation. Lodge's text proposes Mary as a full participant
in the scheme of salvation. She is metaphorically rendered an altar, a site of
religious offering: 'Behold two altars raised by one massacre, one in the bodie
of Christ, the other in the heart of the virgin: on the one is sacrificed the flesh
of the sonne, on the other the soule of the mother: such a death no creature
hath suffered, such a sorrowe no heart hath contained' (D6v). The formulation recalls medieval interpretations and actually mirrors the twelfth-century
theologian Arnauld Bonnaevallis' interpretation of 'two altars, one the body
of Christ, the other in the breast of Mary' (Ellington, 2001: 91). Although both
are presented as willing participants, a distinction is made between the type
of offering and suffering involved: Jesus 'suffered' in 'body' and 'flesh'; Mary
'contained' in 'heart' and 'soul.' Christ is represented as a high priest, offering

his body for the people, but depicting Mary as an altar also evokes her priestly assistance. She is imagined as receptively participating in the scheme of salvation, thus her performance of grief is understood to have another tangible effect – Jesus' resurrection. To extend this further, because the reader is also invited to suffer alongside the mother of God, their tears can also be understood to help effect the resurrection.

Although the traditions of the *Stabat Mater Dolorosa* may have been undermined by the early modern concern with appropriate, rational mourning, they emerge in these Catholic texts as a cultural tool to ruminate on the significance of grief generally, and Marian grief particularly. Mary's grief at the cross does not simply operate as a static image of medieval Catholicism; instead, that legacy is negotiated in these texts to reveal what the Virgin represented to the particular historical moment. Lodge and C.N.'s meditative prose imagine Mary performing a variety of self-conscious grief gestures that are interpreted as having deliberate effects: they make Mary sympathetic, move the reader into imitation of her sorrows, and in turn promote Mary's intercession, and force them to recognise and help facilitate the saving work of Christ. Mary's performance of grief is demonstrated to have an actual, tangible effect – facilitating the resurrection – and within the context of contemporary executions of Jesuits, such a perspective would have provided hope and confidence to the embattled English Catholic community and legitimised their outward grief. Mary's participation at the cross was also understood to authorise her intercessionary powers, reasserting her significance in an era coming to terms with the eradication of purgatory from Protestant doctrine. The imagery thus suggests the Virgin's continued significance to conceptualising death and the fate of the soul. Evidently, through a process of accommodation and negotiation, the mournful Virgin of the Catholic past could still be utilised in the emerging Christocentric early modern devotion to highlight the immense significance of her son's death and provide a tool for meditation and affective piety. Appropriating the voice, tears, visual experience and bodily pains of the mother enables the early modern reader to fully appreciate and share in Jesus' sacrifice. However, the return to affective piety could operate as a mechanism of compensation: it attempts to counter the visual erasure of the Virgin and her perceived significances, reaffirm her centrality to the Passion narrative and assert her ability to intercede. The surplus of affective representation could indicate an attempt to bolster the Virgin's wavering influence and power. Indeed, the relatively infrequent deployment of Marian grief suggests that it remained deeply problematic and divisive in early modern England.

Notes

1 John 19:26–7, which details Jesus' address to the Virgin and his disciple John, is the only biblical evidence that confirms Mary's presence at the crucifixion scene but it gives no insight into her emotion. See Rubin (2009a) for an overview of representations of the Passion in art until the Reformation.

2 See Pelikan (1996: 125–36) on the *Stabat Mater Dolorosa* tradition.

3 Translation is traditional. The translation and the original Latin are sourced from Miola (2007: 257).

4 Simeon prophesised that the Virgin's soul would be pierced by a sword of sorrows: see Luke 2:34–5.

5 The *pietà* – Mary lamenting Jesus, his dead body limp in her lap – emerged in the fifteenth century as a new and arresting way of representing Mary's sorrow and their shared sacrifice (see Rubin, 2009b: 313–4).

6 See Neff (1998: 254–73) for detail on the widely perceived connections between Mary's swoon and her physical experience as a mother.

7 The *lo spasimo* controversy considered the merits of the Virgin's swoon at the cross (as depicted from the mid-thirteenth century). Reformers debated whether Mary's exemplarity was evidenced in her capacity to restrain human emotion and transcend grief, or whether her capacity to feel and express sorrow was intimately related to Christ's agony on the cross.

8 Catholics believed she could mediate between Christ and penitent. For further discussion of Mary as mediatrix see Rist's essay (Chapter 10) in this volume.

9 Martz's comment that 'meditative treatises of [the early modern] period were attempting to develop the spiritual life through utilising all the rich and various resources of medieval religion' seems particularly pertinent in this respect (1954: 113).

10 If, as Goodland argues, the image of the mourning woman generally 'embodies the cultural trauma of the Reformation in England', then the religiously loaded sorrowful Virgin Mary is rendered particularly symbolic of the religious change (2005: 123).

11 See Phillippy: 'if emotions are at once physiologically experienced and culturally conditioned, their expression is partially reflective of an individual's interiority and partially determined by conventions, including linguistic and artistic conventions, in which they are cast' (2002: 5).

12 Houlbrooke (1998) speculates that the rejection of Catholic mourning rituals decreased fear of suffering in the afterlife; while Phillippy notes the 'widespread powerlessness' of mourners with no memory framework (2002: 8).

13 Catholics believed that continual prayers of intercession and other liturgical practices (including memorial masses and indulgences) by living relatives could help ensure the soul's onward movement to heaven. Living relatives could therefore continue to have an involved and influential connection with the dead, providing a constructive outlet for their grief. For early modern funeral practices see Gittings (1984); Houlbrooke (1998); Cressy (1999: 379–474) and Marshall (2004). The 1552 *Order for Burial* shortened the funeral service and forbade prayers for the dead and the twenty-second of the *Thirty-Nine Articles* of 1563 outlined that 'the Romish doctrine concerning purgatory … is a fond thing, vainly invented, and grounded upon no warranty of scripture, but rather repugnant to the word of God' (Article 22 'Of Purgatory.' See Cressy and

Ferrell (eds), 1996: 65). Archbishop Grindal's *Injunctions for the Laity in the Province of York* (1571) written to impose Protestantism on the northern province of York, makes such concerns explicit. It stresses 'no month-minds or yearly commemorations of the dead, nor any other superstitious ceremonies, be observed or used, which tend either to the maintenance of prayer for the dead, or to popish purgatory' (Injunction 8 as cited in Cressy and Ferrell, 1996: 92). For a detailed consideration of the significance of the abolition of purgatory see Greenblatt (2001).

14 The phrase '*de facto* rigorism' is cited from Pigman (1985: 39).

15 The studies connect the curtailment of Catholic mourning and the mass to the emergence of the theatre generally, and revenge tragedy particularly.

16 There are multiple spellings of 'Prosopopoeia' which is reflected in the various versions of the word in this essay. The *OED* (2013) spelling is used, except when the original text adopted an alternative spelling, for example, the spelling of the title of Lodge's text.

17 Linton (1998: 48–9) comments on Lodge's Catholicism and cites Edward Tenney's 1935 study of Thomas Lodge which suggests early Catholic leanings. Kuchar (2008: 130) states that the text is 'implicitly Catholic'; however, this reserved statement is somewhat undermined by the contemporary reaction.

18 Lodge's attention to such contemporary events is evident in his use of nine variations of the term 'martyr' throughout the text. Nuttall (1971: 193) claims that there were 86 Catholics executed between 1586 and 1591. This spate of executions claimed the highest numbers across the period 1535–1680. (The second highest was the period 1535–1539, during the reign of Henry VIII, when there were 44 executions.)

19 To clarify three, perhaps unfamiliar, terms: an apostrophe in rhetoric is 'a figure of speech, by which a speaker or writer suddenly stops in his discourse, and turns to address pointedly some person or thing, either present or absent; an exclamatory address'; an 'appellative move' is the process of naming and a 'perlocutionary effect' is 'an act of speaking or writing that is intended to persuade or convince.' (See *OED*, 2013). For further information on how plays affected weeping in early modern audiences see Steggle (2007). These performative strategies also directly recall the particular narrative themes, rhetoric and poetic conventions in classical and medieval accounts of (female) grief (as outlined by Goodland, 2005), which draws further attention to the concept of grief's performativity.

20 Rubin's claim that 'the Italian confraternities probably developed the most affective techniques for imitation of the Passion … Such styles of collective devotion never developed in England' (2009a: 103) is undermined by Lodge's text.

21 Lodge's dedication indicates that women engaged in affective reading and piety (as Molekamp's recent study (2013) has also illuminated, especially 119–50). For an example of Lodge anticipating a tearful response in all readers, see the 'Epistle to the Reader' (A7r).

22 For further consideration of Mary Magdalene's appropriation and relevance in the period see the New Testament Overview and Hopkins' essay in this volume (Chapters 8, 12).

23 For detail on the ambiguity of Mary Magdalene's identity see the New Testament Overview (Chapter 8).

24 Mary also compares herself to other biblical weepers including Hannah (Lodge, 1596:

57). C.N.'s, *Our Ladie hath a new sonne* similarly dwells on Mary's perceived abandonment: 'Why sufferest thou mee to languish and pine away with griefe? Why hast thou separated thy selfe so far from me?' (1595: 54).

25 For a full discussion of Magdalene's links to a variety of concepts of abandonment see Badir (2009: 59–90).

26 'C.N.' signs the preface 'To the Reader'. The title page claims the text was printed in Douai, but it was in fact printed in England by the secret press (as the EEBO note explains). Although the text's title refers explicitly to Mary 'birthing' John at the cross, in light of the context, it could also implicitly suggest that the Catholic martyrs are Mary's 'new sons' in suffering and dying for their faith as Jesus did. Given such circumstances, the focus on Mary's grief (orally and visually communicated), and the descriptions of Christ's crucified body, become even more emotive.

27 This anti-Semitic rhetoric in relation to the Virgin's suffering is also apparent in a variety of Marian appropriations in the (medieval and) early modern period (see Rubin 2004: 7–39; 2009a: 53–69 and 2009b: 161–188, 228–242).

28 Goodland (2005: 2) and Peters (2003: 75–6) both identify the popularity of the *pietà* statue in the medieval period and its depiction in medieval English Passion plays. It appealed to male and female parishioners alike as it evoked mankind's shared grief at the death of Jesus (see Peters, 2003: 76–7).

29 The bracketed Bible verses appear in the margins of the text. The reference to Jesus as 'first begotten Son' relates to the text's reading of John as Mary's second son (because of Jesus' words to both at the cross).

30 Mary as a particular model for women is explored by Peters (2003) and Gallagher (2012), as well as in this volume's New Testament Overview (Chapter 8).

31 Highlighting the relationship with the dead is a typical theme of lamentation, as Goodland notes (2005: 18).

32 Similarly, C.N. (1595) identifies the multiplicity of the Virgin's loss: 'O true sonne of God, thou wert a father unto me, thou wert a mother to mee, thou wert my sonne, thou wert my spouse, thou wert my soul, now am I become an orphant, without Father or Mother, a spouse without a mate, a Mother without a sonne, a body without sence, and soule, and inconc'usió when thou art gone, all that I have and all that I am is gone' (53–4). Mary's loss is devastating in its totality.

33 As Kuchar (2008: 5–6) explains, 'this combination of opposing feelings in one state led the late fifth-century commentator John Climacus to coin the neologism *charmolypi* or joy-sorrow as a way of denoting *penthos*.' The paradoxes of *charmolypi* also recall the contradictions inherent in the Virgin's own persona: virgin/mother, spirit/flesh. Her *charmolypi* is symptomatic of her simultaneous position as earthly mother and spiritual believer.

References

Alexander, G. (2007) 'Prosopopoeia: The Speaking Figure.' *Renaissance Figures of Speech.* Ed. S. Adamson, G. Alexander and K. Ettenhuber. Cambridge: Cambridge University Press. 97–114.

Badir, P. (2009) *The Maudlin Impression: English Literary Images of Mary Magdalene, 1550–1700.* Notre Dame, IN: University of Notre Dame Press.

Cressy, D. (1999) *Birth, Marriage, and Death: Ritual, Religion, and the Life-Cycle in Tudor and Stuart England*. Oxford: Oxford University Press.

Cressy, D. and Ferrell, L.A. (eds) (1996) *Religion and Society in Early Modern England: A Sourcebook*. London: Routledge.

Diehl, H. (1997) *Staging Reform, Reforming the Stage: Protestantism and Popular Theatre in Early Modern England*. Ithaca, NY: Cornell University Press.

Dolan, F.E. (1999) *Whores of Babylon: Catholicism, Gender, and Seventeenth-Century Print Culture*. Ithaca, NY: Cornell University Press.

Döring, T. (2006) *Performances of Mourning in Shakespearean Theatre and Early Modern Culture*. Basingstoke: Palgrave Macmillan.

Ellington, D.S. (1995) 'Impassioned Mother or Passive Icon: The Virgin's Role in Late Medieval and Early Modern Passion Sermons.' *Renaissance Quarterly*, 48.2: 227–61.

——. (2001) *From Sacred Body to Angelic Soul: Understanding Mary in Late Medieval and Early Modern Europe*. Washington, DC: Catholic University of America Press.

Gallagher, L. (2012) 'The Virgin Mary in the Early Modern Literary Imagination.' PhD thesis, Queen's University Belfast.

Gittings, C. (1984) *Death, Burial and the Individual in Early Modern England*. London: Routledge.

——. (1999). 'Sacred and Secular: 1558–1660.' *Death in England: An Illustrated History*. Ed. P.C. Jupp and C. Gittings. Manchester: Manchester University Press. 147–73.

Goodland, K. (2005) *Female Mourning in Medieval and Renaissance English Drama*. Aldershot: Ashgate.

Greenblatt, S. (2001) *Hamlet in Purgatory*. Princeton: Princeton University Press.

Houlbrooke, R. (1998) *Death, Religion, and the Family in England, 1480–1750*. Oxford: Oxford University Press.

Kuchar, G. (2008) *The Poetry of Religious Sorrow in Early Modern England*. Cambridge: Cambridge University Press.

Linton, J.P. (1998) *The Romance of the New World: Gender and the Literary Formations of English Colonialism*. Cambridge: Cambridge University Press.

Lipking, L.I. (1988) *Abandoned Women and Poetic Tradition*. Chicago: University of Chicago Press.

Lodge, T. (1596) *Prosopopeia containing the teares of the holy, blessed, and sanctified Marie, the Mother of God*. London: s.n.

Marshall, P. (2004) *Beliefs and the Dead in Reformation England*. Oxford: Oxford University Press.

Martz, L.L. (1954) *The Poetry of Meditation: A Study in English Religious Literature of the Seventeenth Century*. New Haven, CT: Yale University Press.

Miola, R.S. (ed.) (2007) *Early Modern Catholicism: An Anthology of Primary Sources*. Oxford: Oxford University Press.

Molekamp, F. (2013) *Women and the Bible in Early Modern England: Religious Reading and Writing*. Oxford: Oxford University Press.

N., C. (1595) *Our Ladie hath a new sonne*. [England]: English Secret Press.

Neff, A. (1998) 'The Pain of Compassio: Mary's Labour at the Foot of the Cross.' *Art Bulletin*, 80.2: 254–73.

Neill, M. (1997) *Issues of Death: Mortality and Identity in English Renaissance Tragedy*. Oxford: Clarendon Press.

Nuttall, G.F. (1971) 'The English Martyrs 1535–1680: A Statistical Review.' *Journal of Ecclesiastical History*, 22.3: 191–7.

Oxford English Dictionary (OED) (2013) Oxford Dictionaries Online. Oxford: Oxford University Press.

Pelikan, J. (1996) *Mary through the Centuries: Her Place in the History of Culture*. New Haven, CT: Yale University Press.

Peters, C. (2003) *Patterns of Piety: Women, Gender, and Religion in Late Medieval and Reformation England*. Cambridge: Cambridge University Press.

Phillippy, P. (2002) *Women, Death and Literature in Post-Reformation England*. Cambridge: Cambridge University Press.

Pigman, G.W. (1985) *Grief and the Renaissance English Elegy*. Cambridge: Cambridge University Press.

Rist, T. (2008) *Revenge Tragedy and the Drama of Commemoration in Reforming England*. Aldershot: Ashgate.

Rubin, M. (2004) *Gentile Tales: The Narrative Assault on Late Medieval Jews*. Philadelphia: University of Pennsylvania Press.

——. (2009a) *Emotion and Devotion: The Meaning of Mary in Medieval Religious Cultures*. Budapest: Central European University Press.

——. (2009b) *Mother of God: A History of the Virgin Mary*. London: Allen Lane.

Shuger, D.K. (1994) *The Renaissance Bible: Scholarship, Sacrifice and Subjectivity*. Berkeley: University of California Press.

Steggle, M. (2007) *Laughing and Weeping in Early Modern Theatres*. Aldershot: Ashgate.

Warner, M. (1978) *Alone of all her Sex: The Myth and Cult of the Virgin Mary*. London: Quartet Books.

12

St Helena of Britain in the land of the Magdalene: *All's Well That Ends Well*

Lisa Hopkins

In this essay, I want to suggest that we should read the pilgrimage-minded Helena of *All's Well That Ends Well* in the light of two holy women, St Helena of Britain and Mary Magdalene. First, however, I want to pause on one of the most promi-nent of many problematic moments in this strange, difficult play, when Helena sends her mother-in-law the countess a letter informing her that *'I am Saint Jaques' pilgrim, thither gone'* (Shakespeare, 2007: 3.4.4). J.C. Maxwell observes that 'the first point which I regard as beyond controversy is that Saint Jaques le Grand must be the famous shrine at Compostella' (1969: 190); however, if this is the case, the same geographical vagueness that led Shakespeare to endow Bohemia with a sea coast seems to be at work again here. Helena is setting out from her mother-in-law's house in Roussillon, giving her a relatively simple journey through the passes of the Pyrenees from France to Spain, but when we next see her she is in Florence, making it unsurprising that 'she writes / Pursuit would be but vain' (3.4.24–5). Certainly, John Weever says of Rome in *Ancient funerall monuments* that 'whoo that visite the Chirche of saint *Poule* two sondayes doth as moche as he went to *Iames* of Compostela in Spaine Saint *Iames* and come geyne' (1631: 161–2), which might be taken to suggest that one could, in a sense, go to Compostela without actually visiting it. Yet, the editor G.K. Hunter's note on 3.4.4 is: 'It is true that Florence is (as Johnson remarked) "somewhat out of the road from Roussillon to Compostella" but it is more probable that Shakespeare would make this mistake than refer to other shrines of merely local celebrity'; Hunter is, therefore, confident that Compostela is the shrine meant. Grace Tiffany agrees: she argues that, both in this play and also in *Cymbeline* and *Othello*, Shakespeare reveals himself to be well informed about the traditions associated with the Compostela pilgrimage, declaring that he 'borrows from the specific legend of Santiago de Compostela' (2000: 87).

Furthermore, Helena persistently gestures at one of the most famous attrib-utes of the road to Compostela: its status as 'the way of the stars'. Revealing, in soliloquy, the true reason for her distressed state at the beginning of the play, which the Countess supposes to be due to her father's death, she muses: "twere all one / That I should love a bright particular star / And think to wed it, he is so above me' (1.1.87–9). She classes herself as one of 'we the poorer born, / Whose baser stars do shut us up in wishes' (I.i.178–9), and convinces herself to go to Paris because

> There's something in't
> More than my father's skill, which was the great'st
> Of his profession, that his good receipt
> Shall for my legacy be sanctified
> By th'luckiest stars in heaven. (1.3.237–41)

She later promises that she

> ever shall
> With true observance seek to eke out that
> Wherein toward me my homely stars have fail'd
> To equal my great fortune. (2.5.73–6)

Helena also transfers this language to Parolles: she tells him 'Monsieur Parolles, you were born under a charitable star' (1.1.185–6); Parolles subsequently tells Bertram that the lords at court 'move under the influence of the most receiv'd star' (2.1.53–4). Thus, as Richard Wilson points out, 'Stellar imagery reinforces the connection between Helena and Compostela', and indeed Wilson even suggests that '*All's Well* has the programme of St James's Day' (2004: n.p.), that is, the day associated with the saint venerated at Compostela.

If, as regularly assumed, Helena really does mean Compostela, why does she go to Florence, and is her route as odd as it appears? In *The Golden Legend*, the popular medieval collection of saints' lives which includes an account of St Helena of Britain and her invention of the True Cross, Jacobus de Voragine recounts an even odder journey: 'Pope Callixtus … relates that about the year 1100 a certain citizen of Barcelona went in pilgrimage to Saint James, and besought him for one favour, namely that he should never be taken captive. Returning by way of Sicily, he was captured at sea by the Saracens, and sold as a slave; but the chains wherewith he was bound broke' (1969: 376). This does suggest that there is a certain amount of latitude to the parameters of the journey, and certainly Shakespeare does not invite us to perceive a problem as the characters in the play are not particularly surprised to see Helena in Florence. They easily recognise her as a pilgrim, though Judith Champ suggests that this would not have been difficult: she notes the example of Mary Ward, who was advised by the Spanish Infanta to travel as a pilgrim for safety reasons, rather as Rosalind in *As You Like It* proposes to Celia that they should do:

> A nearly contemporary portrait of Mary Ward exists of her in dark brown dress and cloak, topped by a broad-brimmed hat and carrying a staff. If her dress is anything like authentic the portrait – and there was presumably something identifiable as 'pilgrim's garb' – this suggests that the traditional dress of the pilgrim had survived the Reformation. (2000: 81)

The existence of this garb is presumably why the Widow instantly recognises Helena's pilgrim status:

> WIDOW
> Look, here comes a pilgrim. I know she will lie at my house; thither they send one another. I'll question her: God save you, pilgrim! Whither are bound?
> HELENA
> To Saint Jaques le Grand.
> Where do the palmers lodge, I do beseech you?
> WIDOW
> At the Saint Francis here beside the port. (3.5.30–6)

Entirely indifferent to the information Helena proffers, the Widow simply says:

> Come, pilgrim, I will bring you
> Where you shall host; of enjoin'd penitents
> There's four or five, to Great Saint Jaques bound,
> Already at my house. (3.5.92–5)

Of course, it may be that the Widow thinks initially that Helena is making the journey in the other direction, but it does seem clear that Florence is understood by Shakespeare as a credible, and possible, stop on a pilgrimage route associated with Compostela. In fact, Kathy Gower notes that Paris, Helena's point of origin,

> has been known for centuries as a gatherings point for pilgrims making their way on the Camino de Santiago. The Chemin du St. Jacques, as it is known in France, is particularly marked by both a starting point, the Tour St. Jacques ... and the rue St. Jacques itself, which extends kilometers from the center of Paris. (2002: 1)

The Chemin du Saint Jacques would indeed be the route that a pilgrim from Paris would take, but pilgrims from England had usually followed the Via Francigena, the main pilgrimage route from France into Italy, which English pilgrims started from Canterbury.

The Via Francigena goes through Siena and Lucca and many pilgrims took a detour via Florence, where there was a pilgrims' hospital of the company of Saint-Jacques d'Oltrarno, which could, I suggest, be the source of Shakespeare's association of Saint Jacques with Florence. The initial road from Paris formed part of the Via Turonensis. At either Puente la Reina or just before the Pyrenees, pilgrims could turn off from this onto the Via Francigena. Either bifurcation brought pilgrims close to Roussillon, where *All's Well That Ends Well* is very unusually set, and Richard Wilson suggests that

> one cue for the play is ... the yarn about Gerard of Roussillon who built the abbey of Vézelay, at the start of the Road [to Compostela], as penance for refusing a bride chosen by Charlemagne. There he enshrined relics of Mary Magdalene, who supposedly died at Marseilles: from where Helena returns as if from the dead. (2004: n.p.)

Wilson's association of Helena with Mary Magdalene is suggestive, because I shall be suggesting that *All's Well* actually works to establish just such a connection. Moreover, I shall further suggest that this connection is inflected by the fact that the story of the play's Helena may also invite the play's audience to think of the story of another saint, Helena of Britain, who, like Mary Magdalene, would be a particularly apt comparator for the Helena of the play because she too was associated not only with France but with a dubious sexual reputation. John Eliot's *The suruay or topographical description of France with a new mappe* makes it clear that the Magdalene was indeed associated with the territory of *All's Well That Ends Well*:

> Between Aix and Marseilles lieth Baulme a solitarie place and an Oratorie where Magdalen doing her penaunce died: this Mount is craggie, being 3000 paces high, and 1000 long. It is as it were euen hewen, and is inaccessible, resembling a wall, at the foot whereof is Magdalens caue raised as high as a man maye cast a stone. (1592: sigs A4r–v)

Eliot subsequently goes on to mention 'Narbone' (73–4) and Montpellier (76), which might have been of interest to Shakespeare because his son-in-law John Hall, the husband of his daughter Susanna, may well have studied there.[1]

Other places in the vicinity also have connections with Mary Magdalene. Montpellier itself is not far from Les-Saintes-Maries-de-la-Mer, at which Mary Magdalene had supposedly landed and from which it takes its name. I have suggested elsewhere that the motif of the doctor's daughter Helena restoring health to the king, whose wound had such obviously sexual connotations, closely recalls the marriage between Catherine de' Medici, whose name meant literally 'of the doctors', and Henri II, who was unable to produce offspring for the first ten years of their marriage (2003: 369–81). It may therefore be worth noting that Catherine de' Medici's mother was Madeleine de la Tour d'Auvergne, which suggests a familial affinity with the biblical figure. Catherine de' Medici also had personal similarities with Mary Magdalene: she first landed at Marseilles, where the Magdalene too was said to have made her first landing in France, and, more significantly, she was, in her own person, a link between France and her birthplace Florence, a city which had been personified in art as the Magdalene. Katherine Ludwig Jansen highlights this in her commentary on Botticelli's *Mystic Crucifixion* (c.1497), explaining that 'critics agree unanimously that the prostrate Magdalen personifies the city of Florence, which Pius II had punningly called the meretricious city' (1999: 196), which makes it an uneasily apt destination for Helena, whose virtue is repeatedly called into question.

In *All's Well That Ends Well*, Lafew's daughter is called Maudlin (5.3.68), and other aspects of the play are also pertinent to the story of the Magdalene, not least the fact that Mary Magdalene's emblem in art was an ointment jar (Attwater, 1983: 230), and Helena explains that the reason she expects to be able to cure the king is that her father 'left me some prescriptions / Of rare and prov'd effects'

(1.3.216–7), so that both are associated with medical imagery. In the case of the Magdalene, this imagery is evident in a medieval Resurrection play in which she says of Christ 'Of ilka mischief he is medecine' (Cawley, 1974: 178) and refuses to leave 'till I see that faithful friend, / My lord and leech' (182), 'leech' being a standard term for doctor. In most dramatic versions of her story, Mary Magdalene was the sister of Lazarus,[2] and thus she, like Helena, was also associated with narratives of death and miraculous or quasi-miraculous recovery. Katharine Goodland observes of the Towneley and York *Resurrection* plays that 'both plays focus upon Mary Magdalene's search for Christ's body' (2005: 19) and notes that 'although the Lazarus episode in the Digby *Mary Magdalene* differs markedly from the Towneley in its characterization of the Magdalene, it embodies similar disapproval toward mourning for the dead' (51).[3] Finally, in Lewis Wager's *The Life and Repentaunce of Mary Magdalene*, Mary Magdalene, like Helena, is first introduced with reference to her late father: Infidelitie says to her 'I knew your fathers state and condition' (1567: sig B1v).

Alison Findlay has already suggested reading Helena within the paradigm of the Virgin Mary, arguing that

> Diana's confident proclamation that she is still a maid, never gave Bertram her ring, and yet knows her bed 'defiled' re-presents the familiar mystery of the Incarnation embodied by the Virgin Mary. The male courtiers' reactions to Diana ... replay the Nativity's illegitimate subtext in Matthew's Gospel ... Joseph's discovery that Mary is with child of the Holy Ghost and his unwillingness to make a public example of her draws attention to a story of cuckoldry that threatens patriarchal authority in the very fulfilment of divine will ... Helen is, similarly, introduced as the Marian matrix in which purity and knowledge, divinity and human flesh, mortality and resurrection combine. (2007: 40)

I think, however, that the paradigm of the Magdalene is more directly evoked within Shakespeare's play. Despite the official marginalisation of Catholicism, there were many cultural uses made of Mary Magdalene in the late sixteenth and early seventeenth centuries. Patricia Badir argues that 'English writers "gathered" ... the bits and pieces of the medieval Magdalene and used them, within the unfolding drama of the Reformation, as sanctioned resources for thinking about the commemorative form and mnemonic function of religious art' (2009: 3–4); she suggests that the figure of the Magdalene was particularly resonant in such a context because she encoded 'a feeling lost to all latter-day Christians: the feeling of being close enough to Christ to reach out and touch him' (57). Among various cultural uses of the Magdalene, her name occurs a number of times in connection with exploration of the New World: Juan González de Mendoza notes that Father Custodio carried with him 'the Image of Marie Magdalen made of feathers', which he later gives as a gift to the captain general of the city of Aucheo (1588: 281). In 1571 an English ship travelling to Moscow was named the Magdalene, and Hakluyt several times dates events in relation to the feast of Mary Magdalene: 'vpon the day of *Marie Magdalene* we arriued at the court of *Cuyne* the Emperour elect' (1599: 67); 'at the length, a fewe dayes before the feast of *Saint Marie Magdalene*, we arriued at the bank of the mightie riuer *Tanais* which divideth *Asia* from *Europa*' (103); and Jaques Noel reports that he hopes that his two sons will return from Canada 'about Magdalene tyde' (237). Obviously these are essentially coincidental, but they do show that Mary Magdalene was still a figure in the cultural consciousness.

She was also found in other contexts. Lesel Dawson, for instance, suggests that Gervase Markham's *Marie Magdalens lamentations for the losse of her master Iesus* should be read as a lament for the recently executed Earl of Essex, arguing that 'by adopting the voice of Mary Magdalene, Markham is able to accentuate his personal devotion to Essex' (2002: 351). Particularly pertinent to Shakespeare, who may have been Robert Southwell's cousin, is *Marie Magdalens funeral teares*, published in 1591.[4] In this long devotional work, Mary Magdalene fails to recognise the risen Christ and he asks her 'Quem quaeritis?' – a resonant question since, as Elizabeth Williamson notes, 'the reenactment of Christ's resurrection, which appears in various dramatic forms, has long been associated with the origins of modern drama in England' (2009: 40). Later, Southwell's Magdalene laments: 'He is now too bright a sunne for so weake a sight' (1591: 64v), which may perhaps foreshadow the idea of Bertram as 'a bright particular star' (1.1.88) in *All's Well*. Setting the drama in the land of the Magdalene, and naming a minor character after her, Shakespeare might be remembering this biblical woman in the play.

Mary Magdalene is not, though, the only saint possibly suggested by *All's Well*. For Laurie Maguire, Helena's name is a clear and unequivocal pointer, for 'Helen meant only one Helen – Helen of Troy':

> Other historical or mythological Helens – the virtuous St Helena, mother of the Emperor Constantine, for example, whose church in Bishopsgate made her part of the Elizabethan cultural landscape – never displaced the Lacedemonian or Spartan (as Helen of Troy was also called), and this despite a pre-Reformation predilection for hagionymy. Camden's glossary of names in his *Remains* (1605) does offer St Helena as the name's primary referent; but his view is unusual and does not seem to be shared by literary texts, even when the association is specifically invited, as in the case of the pilgrim Helen in *All's Well That Ends Well* ... When the Shakespeare canon invokes St Helen, she requires appositive explanation: "Helen, the mother of great Constantine" (*1 Henry VI* 1.2.142). (Maguire, 2007: 75)

Maguire reads *All's Well* firmly within this Graeco-Trojan paradigm, seeing it as resembling Euripides' *Helen*, with the king as a Menelaus figure (75–7). However, Richard Wilson argues that

> for a play about 'holy wishes' which starts with Helena's joke: 'I wish well ... That wishing well had not a body in it' (I.i.52; 166–8), [it cannot] be incidental to *All's Well* that the largest number of all well-dedications is to the Yorkshire mother of

Emperor Constantine, who united Britain and Rome, the first English pilgrim, Saint Helena herself. (2004: n.p.)

St Helena was certainly associated with wells: for instance, John Leland visited St Helen's Well on the Wharfe, West Yorks, c.1540 (see Jones, 2001) and Maguire notes the presence of well imagery in the play when she suggests that 'In one respect ... the name Diana is a repetition of Fontibell, not a correction. Fontibell means "beautiful fountain", and fountains are invariably associated with chaste women, with the goddess Diana ... and with the virgin queen Elizabeth' (2007: 104–5).[5] Moreover, Winifred Joy Mulligan notes that 'later legends lauded St Helena as a beautifier of cities, a restorer of walls, the builder of highways in Wales, and the architect of the promontory at Land's End' (1978: 260), and the Helena of the play also evokes the idea of Land's End, albeit a different one, since the Compostela pilgrimage customarily ended at Finisterre. Equally, Helen Wilcox suggests that 'medical science seems to have been put in its place by supernatural influences, and a new Saint Helen appears to be in the making, with her power to effect miracles and her almost sacral embodiment of a "heavenly effect in an earthly actor" (2.3.33)' (2007: 144).

The story of St Helena, mother of the Emperor Constantine and supposed finder of the True Cross, was well known in Britain – where, according to many versions of her story, she was born – and people may well have been fairly regularly reminded of it since Camden notes that: 'Hellens mony many oftentimes found under the walles' of London (Hingley, 2008: 34). Antonina Harbus explains that St Helena was being claimed as British as early as the eighth century (2002: 3), and that she was also sometimes mentioned in the same breath as the Blessed Virgin Mary: 'Eusebius, in his widely emulated comparison of Constantine and Helena to Christ and Mary, calls her "the God-beloved mother of the God-beloved emperor"' (19). She figured in Jacobus de Voragine's hugely popular *The Golden Legend*, where she was said to be the daughter of King Coel (the old King Cole of the rhyme) and where, faced with three crosses which have all been found at Golgotha, Helena identifies the true one when a dead man is laid on it and returns to life.[6] (Thus, it is not surprising that Richard Wilson observes that 'when Helena states that it were better "I met the ravin lion" than stay at home, "although / The air of paradise did fan the house / And angels officed all" (3.2.116–26), the narrative expectations she prompts by her quest are those of *The Golden Legend*' (2004: n.p.).)

St Helena's is the first story in a manuscript compilation of *The Lives of Women Saints of our Contrie of England*, compiled c.1610 (Horstmann, 1887: 30–6), and her search for the True Cross was also the first story in Hakluyt's *Principal Navigations*; indeed she, like Mary Magdalene, was often associated with the exploration of the New World. The island of St Helena was so named because it was discovered by the Portuguese on St Helena's Day, 21 May, in 1502, but it later figured in English exploration narratives: Thomas Cavendish landed there on 8 June 1588; Abraham Kendall in 1591, with a crew suffering from scurvy who subsequently recovered; and in 1592, Philip II warned his fleet that English captains were lying in wait for them at St Helena (St Helena Foundation, 2010). The first settlement on the American mainland, founded by Cortés in 1519, was Villa Rica de Vera Cruz, better known as Vera Cruz; the derivation of its name from the True Cross, allegedly found by St Helena, would have been obvious to all. Thus, St Helena too remained in the general cultural consciousness.

Above all, though, the story of St Helena encoded a complex set of associations about class, religion and background, and the roles they could or could not play in the founding of dynasties and determining the identities and loyalties of future generations. Harbus notes that 'the concept of a British Helena acquired new political resonance when Henry VIII sought a direct imperial connection with ancient Rome through his supposed descent from a British Constantine' (2002: 120). Thus, there is a statue of Helena in the Henry VII chapel in Westminster (Mancall, 2000: 17), visually reinforcing the idea that she was related to the Tudor dynasty. Mulligan notes that 'in 1533 ... Henry VIII discarded King Arthur in favor of the British Constantine' and argues that Constantine and his progeny became distinctively associated with Britishness (1978: 269). Thus Richard Harvey claims, in *Philadelphus, or a defence of Brutes*, for instance, that '*Constantine* the third' was buried at Stonehenge (1593: 96), which in the sixteenth century was understood as an icon of the true nature of 'Englishness' since it supposedly marked the burial place of true-born Britons slain by treacherous Saxons.

Henry's 1533 adoption of Constantine was a direct result of the publication of an argument impugning the veracity of the so-called 'Donation of Constantine', the grant by which Constantine had supposedly ceded ultimate authority over the Roman Emperor to the Pope (Koebner, 1953: 32). Once it was possible to claim that Constantine did not necessarily emblematise imperial submission to papal authority, he became suddenly attractive to Henry. Harbus suggests that 'when Henry VIII styled himself as the possessor of the "imperial Crown" of the realm of England in 1533, he was claiming imperial authority for himself as British monarch on the basis of Constantine's legendary dual position as both emperor of Rome and King of Britain', though she observes that 'Henry never claims personal genealogical descent from Constantine, but rather the acquisition of the monarch's status in relation to the Church through Constantine's position: ecclesiastical sovereignty of the English Church from Rome' (2002: 121, 122). However, she also notes that 'the manifestation of the Constantine legend in the Welsh genealogies also implicitly linked Brutus and Arthur with the Tudors' (2002: 121–2), and that 'the notion that Constantine had a British mother was deployed within the Protestant discourse of England as an "elect nation" of the late sixteenth century, especially in the writings of the Reformation propagandist John Foxe' (125). Even the notorious sceptic Polydore Vergil allowed the truth of the Helena story, and hence of Constantine's British descent. Mulligan lists numerous sixteenth-century supporters for a British Constantine including the fact that 'Maurice Kyffin, on the occasion of Elizabeth I's birthday, referred to her imperial descent from Constantine' (1978: 272), and observes that the idea was particularly topical in 1604, the probable year of composition of *All's Well That Ends Well*:

> In 1598, Lipsius ... argued that when Eumenius proclaimed that Britain 'first saw Constantine Caesar,' the panegyrist did not refer to his birthplace but to Constantine's assumption of the imperial dignity there ... In 1604 Camden responded to Lipsius in a letter ... Later in 1604 Lipsius wrote to Camden, asking why Bede, that famous English historian, had not mentioned that Constantine was British. (275)

Richard Koebner argues that the idea of the imperial crown, supposedly derived from Constantine, 'underlies some moving passages in Shakespeare's *Histories*, where the diadem appears as a challenge to reproach, to ambition, and to regret' (1953: 49), and also draws attention to Helena's reference to 'imperial Love, that god most high' (2.3.75) (52).

St Helena was, then, associated with Britishness, with patriotism, and with Protestantism, and in all these respects it should not be surprising to find her being evoked in the work of a dramatist whom a number of recent critics have identified as very carefully avoiding any kind of public adherence to a Catholicism to which he may well have had familial ties and a personally sympathetic attitude. Indeed for Richard Wilson, '*All's Well* turns away from the Pyrenees to disavow the ultramontanes' (2004: n.p.), that is to make a symbolic gesture of refusal to commit to the idea that support for Catholicism should translate into support for Spain. However, St Helena was an inherently ambiguous figure. Jeanne Addison Roberts points out that

> Geoffrey of Monmouth called her a queen and identified her as the daughter of King Coel of Britain and wife of Constantius, father of Constantine. Other historians claimed, however, that she was a public courtesan and that Constantine was born of a union consummated without benefit of clergy. (1991: 145)

The precise nature of Helena's marital status was a question in which a great number of early modern writers were interested. For some of them, Helena was unquestionably married, royal and virtuous. Richard Hakluyt, for instance, referred to her as 'Helena Flauia Augusta, the heire and onely daughter of Coelus sometime the most excellent king of Britaine, the mother of the emperour Constantine the great' (1599: 2). In the manuscript *Lives of Women Saints of our Contrie of England*, she is the daughter of King Cole and the legitimate wife of Constantius, and Polydore Vergil too says that Helena was married to Constantius (Horstmann, 1887). John Bridges, the Dean of Sarum, spoke of 'Constantine the great ... beeing the sonne of Constantius Chlorus, by the most noble and Christian Queene Helena' (1587: 1356). John Gordon, in his *Enotikon or A sermon of the vnion of Great Brittannie, in antiquitie of language, name, religion, and kingdome*, declared that 'God did conciliate a marriage, betwixt *Constantius Chlorus* (who had to his part of the Romane Monarchie, Germanie, France, Spaine, and great Brittaine) and *Helena* daughter to *Coilus* or *Coelus*, who was King ouer that part of Brittaine, that did resist the Romans' (1604a: 45). He sees their son Constantine as uniting the two parts of Britain which represented his parents' inheritance, and he tells much the same story in his *England and Scotlands happinesse in being reduced to vnitie of religion, vnder our invincible monarke King Iames* (1604b: 24).' However, Michael Drayton in *Poly-Olbion* speaks of '*Constantius* worthy wife – That is *Helen*, wife to *Constantius* or *Constans Chlorus* the Emperour, and mother to *Constantine* the great, daughter to *Coile* King of *Britaine*, where *Constantine* was by her brought forth', but he also feels the need to add that those who dispute this version of events are wrong (1612: 129).

In the counter-tradition to which Drayton alludes, St Helena was sometimes said to have been an innkeeper's daughter. Mulligan notes that

> the unsympathetic Zosimus branded her 'an ignoble woman who bore Constantine out of wedlock,' and the anonymous Valesianus cited her 'very common origin.' St. Ambrose addressed her as a *stabularia*, or serving wench at an inn, which caused medieval writers much consternation. An even thornier problem for medieval writers was the status *concubina* given her by Eutropius and Orosius. (1978: 259)

Though this early version of her history tends not to register much during the Renaissance, a faint whiff of unease still attaches to her: Mulligan records that 'Holinshed observed that "S. Ambrose following a common report, writeth that this Helen was a maid in an inne: and some againe write that she was a concubine to Constantius, and not his wife"' (1978: 273), and Harbus notes that Camden 'reacted to the growing doubt in the legend by promulgating and defending it' (2002: 126–7). Unease of a slightly different sort is detectable in Richard Harvey's *Philadelphus, or a defence of Brutes, and the Brutans history*, where he reports that

> Feare amazed *Coil*, till marriage ioined *Constantius* a Roman Duke with his daughter *Helen*, the fayrest mayd aliue: then Contentment setled them both in the kingdome, and Loue brought them foorth into the world *Constantine* the first, whom Excellency lifted vp to the Roman Empire. (1593: 71)

Harvey does not leave it here, however; he goes on to note that '*Helen* the daughter of *Coil* the third married *Constantius*, a Roman by the agreeme[n]t of the *Brutans*, not on her owne head, lesse she should seeme incontinent: she was but a part of hir countrey, not aboue it, or out of it' (74), where the always latent pun on 'country' may well be active.

What difference does it make to our understanding of Shakespeare's Helena to read her in terms of these paradigms and with these associations in mind? I want at this point to return to Southwell's *Marie Magdalens funeral teares*. A foreword, signed 'Your louing friend. S.W.', declares that

Passions I allow, and loues I approue, onely I would wishe that men would alter their obiect and better their intent ... Loue is but the infancy of true charity, yet sucking natures teate, and swathed in her bandes, which then groweth to perfection, when faith besides naturall motiues proposeth higher and nobler groundes of amitye. (1591: sigs A3v–4r)

It is, it seems, acceptable to write of secular love insofar as it is stepping stone to a higher and more spiritual emotion. Therefore, the writer suggests,

shal I thinke my indeours wel apaide, if it may wooe some skilfuller pennes from vnworthy labours, eyther to supply in this matter my want of ability, or in other of like piety (whereof the scripture is full) to exercise their happier talents ... sith the finest wits are now giuen to write passionat discourses, I would wish them to make choise of such passions, as it neither should be shame to vtter, nor sinne to feele. (sigs A5v–6r)

Southwell's own address to the reader reiterates much the same sentiments. The remark that Southwell's work may 'wooe some skilfuller pennes from vnworthy labours' seems to echo Southwell's injunction in *St Peter's Complaint* to his 'worthy good cousin, Master W.S.', often understood to be a reference to Shakespeare, to write sacred verse. Many critics have suggested that such comments were prompted specifically by the recent publication of *Venus and Adonis*, whose verse form *St Peter's complaint* imitates (see for instance Shell, 2006: 85–112). If he was indeed the target of that injunction, Shakespeare signally failed to act on it, and *All's Well* might conceivably be seen as a miniature version of that refusal: the pilgrimage route is not followed to its end, and Bertram chooses conformity rather than martyrdom. In this context, the idea of St Helena as a paradigm would become especially interesting, since her husband Constantius Chlorus had become central to the debate about religious and secular authority, a crucial question for contemporary English Catholics, being cited in this connection by authors including Francis Hastings (1598: 64 and 108–9), Robert Parsons (1602: 78–9) and John Gordon (1603: 24–5).

Southwell's emphasis on love is equally interesting, though, and may help us to understand some of the ways in which *All's Well* may be working. It is sometimes argued that *All's Well That Ends Well* does not offer any examples of true love, but it is possible to see the future marriage of Bertram and Helena as genuinely companionate.[8] What Bertram ultimately promises with respect to Helena, whom he has been trying to get rid of for most of the play, is that 'If she, my liege, can make me know this clearly / I'll love her dearly, ever, ever dearly' (5.3.309–10). Initially, Bertram crudely dismissed Helena on the grounds that 'I know her well', with a clear sexual slur; now, he finds that he does *not* know her, nor indeed very much else. He recognises here that Helena can teach him the things which he has finally learned that he needs to know. This would certainly be a different kind of love from that found in *Romeo and Juliet* and in the early comedies, but, by the same token, it is also far less dangerous, because it is founded not on passionate emotion but on esteem and on a wish to buy into a shared value system.

Both Mary Magdalene and St Helena of Britain went on long journeys in search of truth and salvation, and both, as we have seen, were also associated with more contemporary forms of voyaging and exploration. It is not, I suggest, too far-fetched to see Bertram as also having been on a long journey, albeit one of the spirit rather than of the flesh, in the course of which he has, at last, acquired some of the wisdom he so sadly lacked. Moreover, rather as St Helena of Britain had come to be understood in early modern England as primarily a dynastic figure, so a Bertram who is genuinely prepared to settle down with Helena and resume the reins of his life in Roussillon could be seen as doing so for what are essentially dynastic reasons, to secure the comfort of his mother and guarantee the continuation of his family name.

Most notably, the twin associations with both St Helena of Britain and the Magdalene can help us with the figure of Helena, who has often struck critics as troublingly knowing and sexual. That the king's dysfunction may be sexual is hinted at in his opening negotiation with Helena:

> KING
> Upon thy certainty and confidence
> What darest thou venture?
> HELENA
> Tax of impudence,
> A strumpet's boldness, a divulgèd shame;
> Traduced by odious ballads my maiden's name. (2.1.169–72)

It is is not, at first sight, obvious what *his* health has to do with *her* sexuality. The two appear to be linked on some deeper level, in a way more reminiscent of the leaps and hidden connections of myth than of logical thought:

> KING
> Thou knowest she has raised me from my sickly bed.
> BERTRAM
> But follows it, my lord, to bring me down
> Must answer for your raising? (2.3.110–12)

The language here, with its talk of raising things up and then causing them to go down, is wildly suggestive, and so too is Lafew's remark that

>   I have seen a medicine
> That's able to breathe life into a stone,
> Quicken a rock, and make you dance canary
> With sprightly fire and motion; whose simple touch
> Is powerful to araise King Pippen, nay,
> To give great Charlemain a pen in's hand
> And write to her a love-line. (2.1.72–8)

There is clearly innuendo in this talk of pens, stones and raising, but, in the cases of both Helena of Britain and Mary Magdalene, similar associations could be safely recuperated into a narrative of sanctity. So too they may well be for Helena, especially since in the source narrative, the Helena figure bears Bertram twin sons and then shows them to him. However, Shakespeare's pregnant Helena becomes simply an icon of maternity per se, and in this role, she also recalls Mary Magdalene: Katherine Ludwig Jansen notes that, despite not being a mother herself, Mary Magdalene 'came to be regarded symbolically as both a mother-figure and a saint who specialized in issues relating to motherhood' (1999: 294). This twin set of associations with St Helena of Britain and St Mary Magdalene, then, allows for a genuine sense that sinners can repent and that even low-born women can contribute to the building of a community and a dynasty. The play may be one of the darkest of Shakespeare's comedies, but after all, all's well that ends well.

Notes

1 Lane (1996) suggests that Hall was living in Stratford by 1607, but Schoenbaum argues that Hall had already settled in Stratford around 1600 (1977: 287), which was before the likely composition date of *All's Well*. Arthur Gray notes that James Cooke, who edited John Hall's notebook in 1637, observed 'that Hall had travelled and "was acquainted with the French tongue"' (1939: 3) and Gray himself recounts that 'he studied medicine, apparently at a French university' (10), later identified as 'almost certainly Montpellier' (14–15), which he suggests Hall attended from 1597–1599/60. Further highlighting Shakespeare's links to Montpellier, Gray points out that its medical professor was Rabelais, and traces Shakespeare's interest in Rabelais (17–19). Indeed, there is an obvious sign of Shakespeare's medical interest and knowledge when Parolles mentions 'Galen and Paracelsus' (2.3.11), which might conceivably suggest the influence of Hall.

2 Mary Magdalene is referred to as the sister of Lazarus and Martha in John 11:1–2. She is also mentioned among Jesus' named followers in Luke 8:1–2 and is named in the New Testament resurrection narratives (Matthew 28:1; Mark 16:1; Luke 24:10; John 20:10–18).

3 Elizabeth Williamson similarly suggests that this feature of Mary Magdalene plays might have been particularly remembered, in that she thinks that 'one of the most notable inheritances from guild-sponsored drama were technologies for staging resurrection scenes' (2009: 33)

4 On the connection between Southwell and Shakespeare, see for instance Wood (2003: 153–4 and 162) and Brownlow (1987: 27–30).

5 Richard Wilson identifies Fontibell specifically as 'the name of the public fountain in London that featured a statue of Diana' (2004: n.p.).

6 Jacobus de Voragine also notes the existence of an alternative account in which it is a very sick woman who is healed by the cross (see 1969 edn).

7 See also Lloyd (1590: 283); Spenser (1596: 541–2); Clapham (1606: 135); and Warner (1597: 85).

8 For a good summary of the generally unenthusiastic response to the play as a love story and to the character of its hero in particular, see Waller (2007: 1–56).

References

Attwater, D. (1983) *The Penguin Dictionary of Saints*. 2nd edn. Harmondsworth: Penguin.

Badir, P. (2009) *The Maudlin Impression: English Literary Images of Mary Magdalene, 1550–1700*. Notre Dame, IN: University of Notre Dame Press.

Bridges, J. (1587) *A defence of the gouernment established in the Church of Englande*. London: John Windet and T. Orwin.

Brownlow, F. (1987) 'Southwell and Shakespeare.' *KM 80: A birthday album for Kenneth Muir*. Ed. P. Edwards. Liverpool: Liverpool University Press. 27–30.

Cawley, A.C. (ed.) (1974) *Everyman and Medieval Miracle Plays*. London: J.M. Dent and Sons.

Champ, J.F. (2000) *The English Pilgrimage to Rome: A Dwelling for the Soul*. Leominster: Gracewing.

Clapham, J. (1606) *The historie of Great Britannie declaring the successes of times and affaires in that iland, from the Romans first entrance, vntill the raigne of Egbert, the West-Saxon prince*. London: Valentine Simmes.

Dawson, L. (2002) 'The Earl of Essex and the Trials of History: Gervase Markham's *The Dumbe Knight*.' *Review of English Studies*, 53: 344–64.

Drayton, M. (1612) *Poly-Olbion*. London: Humphrey Lownes.

Eliot, J. (1592) *The suruay or topographical description of France with a new mappe*. London: John Wolfe.

Findlay, A. (2007) '"One that's dead is quick": Virgin re-birth in *All's Well That Ends Well*.' *Marian Moments in Early Modern British Drama*. Ed. R. Buccola and L. Hopkins. Aldershot: Ashgate. 35–45.

González de Mendoza, J. (1588) *The historie of the great and mightie kingdome of China, and the situation thereof togither with the great riches, huge citties, politike gouernment, and rare inuentions in the same*. Trans. R. Parke. London: I. Wolfe.

Goodland, K. (2005) *Female Mourning and Tragedy in Medieval and Renaissance English Drama*. Aldershot: Ashgate.

Gordon, J. (1603) *A panegyrique of congratulation for the concord of the realmes of Great Britaine in vnitie of religion, and vnder one king*. London: R. Read.

——. (1604a) *Enotikon or A sermon of the vnion of Great Brittannie, in antiquitie of language, name, religion, and kingdome*. London: Eliot's Court Press.

——. (1604b) *England and Scotlands happinesse in being reduced to vnitie of religion, vnder our invincible monarke King Iames*. London: V. Simmes.

Gower, K. (2002) 'Pursuing the Chemin and the Coquilles St. Jacques in Paris.' *Peregrinations*, 1.3: 1–8.

Gray, A. (1939) *Shakespeare's son-in-law John Hall*. Cambridge: W. Heffer.

Hakluyt, R. (1599) *The principal nauigations, voyages, traffiques and discoueries of the English nation*. London: George Bishop, Ralph Newberie and Robert Barker.

Harbus, A. (2002) *Helena of Britain in Medieval Legend*. Cambridge: D.S. Brewer.

Harvey, R. (1593) *Philadelphus, or A defence of Brutes, and the Brutans history*. London: John Wolfe.

Hastings, F. (1598) *A watch-word to all religious, and true hearted English-men.* London: Felix Kingston.

Hingley, R. (2008) *The Recovery of Roman Britain 1586–1906: A Colony so Fertile.* Oxford: Oxford University Press.

Hopkins, L. (2003) 'Paris is Worth a Mass: *All's Well That Ends Well* and the Wars of Religion.' *Shakespeare and the Culture of Christianity in Early Modern England.* Ed. D. Taylor. New York: Fordham University Press. 369–81.

Horstmann, C. (1887) *The Early South English Legendary* I. EETS, OS 87. London: Trübner.

Jansen, K. (1999) *The Making of the Magdalen: Preaching and Popular Devotion in the Later Middle Ages.* Princeton: Princeton University Press.

Jones, G.R. (2001) *The Cult of St Helen.* Available at: www.le.ac.uk/users/grj1/helen.html (Accessed: 1 September 2010).

Koebner, R. (1953) 'The Imperial Crown of this Realm: Henry VIII, Constantine the Great, and Polydore Vergil.' *Bulletin of the Institute of Historical Research*, 25: 29–52.

Lane, J. (1996) *John Hall and his Patients: The Medical Practice of Shakespeare's Son-in-law.* Stroud: Alan Sutton.

Lloyd, L. (1590) *The consent of time.* London: George Bishop and Ralph Newberie.

Maguire, L. (2007) *Shakespeare's Names.* Oxford: Oxford University Press.

Mancall, P.C. (2000) *Hakluyt's Promise: An Elizabethan's Obsession for an English America.* New Haven, CT: Yale University Press.

Maxwell, J.C. (1969) 'Helena's Pilgrimage.' *Review of English Studies*, 20: 189–92.

Mulligan, W.J. (1978) 'The British Constantine: An English historical myth.' *Journal of Medieval and Renaissance Drama*, 8: 257–79.

Parsons, R. (1602) *A manifestation of the great folly and bad spirit of certayne in England calling themselues secular priestes.* Antwerp: A. Conincx.

Roberts, J.A. (1991) *The Shakespearean Wild: Geography, Genus, and Gender.* Lincoln, NE: University of Nebraska Press.

Schoenbaum, S. (1977) *William Shakespeare: A Compact Documentary Life.* Oxford: Oxford University Press.

Shakespeare, W. (2007) *All's Well That Ends Well.* Ed. G.K. Hunter. London: Cengage Learning.

Shell, A. (2006) 'Why Didn't Shakespeare Write Religious Verse?' *Shakespeare, Marlowe, Jonson: New Directions in Biography.* Ed. T. Kozuka and J.R. Mulryne. Aldershot: Ashgate. 85–112.

Southwell, R. (1591) *Marie Magdalens funeral teares.* London: John Wolfe.

Spenser, E. (1596) *The faerie queene.* London: Richard Field.

St Helena Foundation (2010) *Historical Chronology.* Available at: www.sthelena.se/history/cron.txt (Accessed: 1 September 2010).

Tiffany, G. (2000) 'Shakespeare and Santiago de Compostela.' *Renascence*, 54.2: 86–107.

Voragine, J. de (1969) *The Golden Legend.* Trans. G. Ryan and H. Ripperger. New York: Arno Press.

Wager, L. (1567) *A new Enterlude, neuer before this tyme imprinted, entreating of the Life and Repentaunce of Marie Magdalene.* London: John Charlewood.

Waller, G. (2007) 'From "the Unfortunate Comedy" to "this Infinitely Fascinating Play": The Critical and Theatrical Emergence of *All's Well, That Ends Well*.' *All's Well, That Ends Well: New Critical Essays.* Ed. G. Waller. London: Routledge. 1–56.

Warner, W. (1597) *Albions England*. London: Orwin.

Weever, J. (1631) *Ancient funerall monuments*. London: Thomas Harper.

Wilcox, H. (2007) 'Shakespeare's Miracle Play: Religion in *All's Well That Ends Well*.' *All's Well, That Ends Well: New Critical Essays*. Ed. G. Waller. London: Routledge. 140–54.

Williamson, E. (2009) *The Materiality of Religion in Early Modern English Drama*. Aldershot: Ashgate.

Wilson, R. (2004) 'To great St Jaques bound: *All's Well That Ends Well* in Shakespeare's Europe.' *Shakespeare et l'Europe de la Renaissance*. Ed. Y. Peyré and P. Kapitaniak. Paris: Actes du Congrès de la Société Française Shakespeare.

Wood, M. (2003) *In Search of Shakespeare*. London: BBC Worldwide.

13

Imagining the enemy: Protestant readings of the Whore of Babylon in early modern England, c.1580–1625

Victoria Brownlee

I sawe a woman sit vpon a skarlat coloured beast, full of names of blasphemie, which had seuen heads, & ten hornes. And the woman was araied in purple & skarlat, & guilded with golde, & precious stones, and pearles, and had a cup of golde in her hand, ful of abominations, and filthines of her fornication. And in her forehead was a name written, A mysterie, great Babylon, the mother of whoredomes, and abominations of the earth. (Rev. 17:3–5)[1]

The last book of Scripture, the Revelation of John the Divine, is home to the Bible's most infamous woman, the Whore of Babylon. Dramatically entering John's apocalyptic narrative on a seven-headed beast, she emerges as an outlandishly costumed seductress who elicits sex, intoxication and horror. John's visually emotive description of the Whore's person and threat in Revelation 17 positions her at the forefront of the Antichrist's ranks. But for many reformed commentators, the chapter's painstaking detail also revealed the identity and workings of their greatest enemy, the Roman Catholic Church.[2] Martin Luther declared the Whore's Roman Catholic identity by including a woodcut depicting her in the papal tiara in his 1522 New Testament and, as this interpretation gained credibility among reformers on the continent, it accrued similar respect and popularity in England through the work of John Bale, John Foxe and Heinrich Bullinger.[3] Read by some as the Pope, and by others as the Roman Catholic Church, Revelation's 'great Whore' (Rev. 17:1) became a recognisable symbol of Catholicism among Protestants across post-Reformation Europe. Indeed, so pervasive was the Whore's visual and ideological presence in this period that Alison Shell deems it 'almost impossible to overestimate her ubiquity' (1999: 31).

Early modern scholarship has readily accepted the Whore of Babylon's popularity and synonymy with Catholicism, and her evocation within discourses of anti-popery has been acknowledged in studies of Catholicism and discussions of dramas set in southern Europe.[4] Yet, in spite of widespread recognition of the Whore's symbolic importance to Protestants in England, there exists no sustained investigation into the exegetical framework that underpinned her identification with Rome. This essay seeks to address this need by tracing how the Whore's biblical narrative, as told in Revelation 17, was read, understood and applied by Protestants in early modern England. It is interested in the way in which reformed commentators worked to square complex and imaginative exegesis of Revelation's Whore with their commitment to reading Scripture literally. Reformed exegesis imbues the Whore's body, as well as her seductive and deceiving nature, with a host of attendant ideologies about Catholicism and, as this essay demonstrates, a series of reoccurring, and related, tropes centring on her glittering apparel, dissembling seduction and corrosive female body can be found across sermons, commentaries and literary re-imaginings of Revelation 17. Within this tradition, the essay considers Book One of Edmund Spenser's *The Faerie Queene* (1590) as a nexus point where the Whore's most popular tropes imaginatively converge in the figure of Duessa, and concludes with a brief discussion of how these stock characteristics shift in line with changing national and international circumstances in Thomas Dekker's 1607 play *The Whore of Babylon*.[5]

The prominence afforded to the Whore of Babylon in reformed thought emerged as part of a broader commitment to apocalyptic theology which advocated viewing present circumstances through an eschatological lens.[6] The Reformation, and its subsequent religious and political fallout, could be understood in light of the Bible's prophecies about the upheaval and hardship of the last days, as outlined throughout the Book of Revelation, as well as portions of Daniel, the Gospels and Paul's letters.[7] While interpretation of these biblical prophecies may have differed, it was generally accepted that in the final days of history, Satan would persecute the faithful through earthly representatives, such as the Antichrist and Whore of Babylon, until Christ returned and inaugurated the eternal reign of truth. Detailing this struggle at length, and culminating in the eternal victory of truth over the forces of evil corruption, the Book of Revelation was popularly mapped onto the on-going struggle between Protestantism and Catholicism.[8] Among the most heavily interpreted biblical texts of the early modern period, this book, it was claimed, supported Protestantism's identification as the true church and offered proof that the English Church would, eventually, triumph.[9]

For reformed commentators on Revelation, exposition of John's mysterious vision was possible because society stood on the cusp of an apocalyptic ending. The Reformation and its legacy were understood as clear indicators that John's prophecies were presently coming to pass and that his text could now be properly understood. In the first of many sermons on the Book of Revelation, George Gifford explains that the text's 'darke riddles' were a mystery to previous generations because 'they liued before the times in which they should be fulfilled, which now vnto vs that have seene them come to passe, haue a cleere and an vndoubted exposition' (1599: 3). The exegetical significance of the historical juncture is clearly established at the outset of William Perkins' 1606 commentary which positions readers in the midst of an apocalyptic disclosure:

'the Prophecie being fulfilled, wee can now tell what was foretold in it' (A1v). By the turn of the century, then, a tradition of reading the Book of Revelation historically was well established in England. Earlier exegetical works, such as those by John Bale (1545) and John Foxe (1583), had popularised a methodological approach that sought to ascertain the connectedness of biblical and secular history, and prove how, from the early church, history had been progressively building towards the break with Rome. Within this tradition, the Book of Revelation did not only prove that the entirety of sacred and secular history was part of a unified narrative, it also verified the existence of a definitive ending that gave meaning to past, present and future. The Second Coming of Christ, detailed in Revelation 19, signalled, in the words of Bale, the 'complet summe' and 'whole knitting vp' of history (1570: 1.A3v). As the end point in a typological chain of meaning that stretched from Old Testament to New, and from New Testament to the present age, Christ's arrival promised eternal victory to the true church of believers.[10]

Although the Second Coming was clearly the final antitype, or fulfilment, in Christian history, John's text detailed how it would be preceded by multiple apocalyptic disclosures which, if understood, would help believers to withstand the threats of the last days. Ascertaining the arrival and nature of these precursory revelations became a major task for reformed exegetes but it was one that had to be reconciled with their commitment to Scripture's 'one sence which is the literall sence' (Tyndale, 1528: R2v). English interpreters regularly noted that as a prophetic work, admittedly written in a symbolic manner (Rev. 1:1, 3), Revelation's meaning was not explicit. For example, the Somerset clergyman Richard Bernard described John's vision as 'but shadowes and resemblances' and his words as 'figuratiue ... and almost altogether Allegoricall'. The text's metaphorical style prompted him to call readers of his commentary to 'looke further' than the text's rich symbolism to discern 'the letter and naked relation of things' (1617: 130). Bernard's instructions demonstrate that the reformers did not abandon their commitment to the literal but instead accepted a form of literalism that was, paradoxically, figural. As John Donne explained in a sermon on Revelation given at St Paul's Cathedral in 1624: 'in this later book ... a figurative sense is the literall sense' (1962: 62). Donne's statement illuminates the tensions inherent in the reformers' commitment to literalism and is suggestive of the complexities of an exegetical method that enabled Revelation's contents to be applied to the early modern present. Importantly, however, commentary on the Book of Revelation and, more specifically, discussion of the Whore, tends to sidestep the convolution of its readings, instead suggesting that, to 'those that haue their eyes opened', the text's meaning is easily discernible (Gifford, 1599: 340).

In a sermon dedicated to Revelation 17, Gifford identified the Whore of Babylon as the hermeneutic centrepiece of John's text explaining that 'the exposition of the mysterie of this woman, and of the beast that beareth her, is a cleere opening of the greatest part, and euen of all the chiefest matters in this prophecie. This chapter is euen as the key to open the closet of the mysteries of this booke' (1599: 323). As he goes on to explain, it is because John makes it 'most euident … that Rome is this filthie whore of Babylon' that the book may be confidently understood to speak of the secular struggle between Catholicism and Protestantism (340). The hermeneutic buoyancy of Gifford's commentary is detectable across reformed writings on the Whore of Babylon. According to Foxe in *Actes and Monuments* (1583), John reveals in 'playne woordes' that the Whore signifies 'the City of Rome' (1778) and, for Patrick Forbes, her Catholic identity is 'largely and cleerely exponed' in Revelation 17 (1613: A4r). Writing some time later, and extolling the virtues of a rather Foxean comparison of biblical text with secular history, David Pareus declares that 'if we rightly consider the experience of the present times, two nuts are not more alike, then is the *Beast and Purpled Whore* to the Papacy' (1644: 10).[11] These assessments are suggestive of the confidence with which the Whore of Babylon was interpreted in the period and demonstrate that her association with Rome was by no means considered to be an interpretative leap. Rather, the insistence that the Whore's identity was plainly revealed in the text demonstrates how the reformers semantically strived to reconcile highly figurative readings of Revelation with their commitment to literalism.

For most commentators, the confident identification of the Whore with the Pope or Roman Catholic Church rested, at least initially, on the geo-political details provided in Revelation 17. For Bale, because the Whore is associated with 'the greate cyte which rei[gn]eth ouer the kinges of the earth', 'must thys whore b[e] Rome' (1545: Q3r). In the tellingly named *A plaine discouery of the whole Reuelation of Saint Iohn set downe in two treatises* (1593), John Napier states 'for assured certe[n]ty, this whorish & mystical *Babylon*. is verilie Rome' because John describes her sitting upon 'seuen mountaines' (35–6). The geographical detail of Revelation 17 also made the Whore's identification unmistakable for the Essex minister Arthur Dent who notes that 'onely Rome of all Cities in the world is situated vppon seuen hilles … *the whoore of Babylon*, or Antichrist *sitteth vpon seuen mountaines: ergo* shee sitteth at Rome' (1603: 210–11). Yet, it was not only the Whore's location in a city with seven mountains that was found to definitively reveal her Roman Catholic identity; her distinctive physical appearance was understood to be a similarly obvious marker of Catholicism.

It is perhaps no surprise that John's detailed description of the Whore's apparel excited biblical commentators. Arrayed in 'purple & skarlat, & guilded with golde, & precious stones, and pearles' (Rev. 17:4), the Whore is Scripture's quintessential ornamented woman. Unsurprisingly, her bejewelled appearance was invoked to dissuade women from the vanity of adornment, but this was not its most popular function.[12] Rather, among reformed readers, the Whore's ostentatious appearance became emblematic of Roman Catholic clergy and wealth. Thomas Mason reminds readers that 'the ordinary attire of the Pope and Cardinalls is scarlet' and suggests that the Whore's 'guilded' appearance matches that of 'Popes, Cardinalls, Bishops, Prelates' (1619: 80–1); while Thomas Cartwright's posthumously published personal commentary, *A plaine explanation of the vvhole Revelation* (1622), finds her regal appearance a more general marker of 'the exceeding great riches of that Church of Rome' (105). Yet, the significance of John's description of the Whore's apparel in Revelation 17:4 was understood to run deeper than the physical hallmarks of the Roman Catholic Church. Ideologically, the Whore of Babylon's appearance revealed the nature and threat of Catholicism; as Bale explains: this portion of text embodies 'a wanton folyshe and fantastycall relygyon / a vayne gloryouse pompe / and a shynynge pretence of holynesse in superstycyo[n]' (1545: Q6r). Claiming that the Whore of Babylon and Catholicism ultimately possess a shared nature, that is, 'shynynge pretence', Bale's scathing commentary is suggestive of the popular association drawn in reformed exegesis between the Whore's external appearance and Catholicism's emphasis on visual beauty.

The Whore's highly ornamented body was widely understood in reformed readings to be a symbol of Catholicism's propensity towards idolatry. Her apparel, contrived to seduce the gaze of those who see her, was considered reminiscent of the gaze invited by Catholicism's sacred objects and visual rituals such as the mass. Gifford elucidates this connection explaining that because the Whore is 'decked and trimmed aboue all other' she is emblematic of 'their whole religion, and you shall see nothing but pompe, glorie, & beautie in outward things: and by these they have dazzled the eyes of high and lowe, and haue drawn them into superstition and idolatrie' (1599: 325). Both visually emotive, the Whore and Catholicism are understood to induce similar effect and, to that end, the choice of the word 'dazzled' is telling. Gifford's use of 'dazzle' suggests that the visual components of Catholicism not simply are attractive but also command an attention that, in line with early modern definitions of the term, had the ability 'to overpower, confuse, or dim' (*OED*, 2013). 'Dazzle' is deployed with similar suggestiveness in the opening lines of Dekker's *The Whore of Babylon* when the play's titular Whore celebrates her court as 'we, in pompe, in peace, in god-like splendour, / With adoration of all dazeled eies' (1964: 1.1.1–2). Encapsulating both the allure and effect of idols, the term 'dazzle', and its derivatives, reoccurs in anti-Catholic writings but, in reformed exegesis of Revelation, it is regularly turned to describe the idolatrous potential of the Whore's specifically female body.[13] For Forbes, viewing the Whore's enticing female form has spiritual, rather than moral, consequences: 'The woman is glorious in all worldly pompe, and royall magnificence, whereby shee dazeleth the eyes of men; shee is a most abhominable Harlot, prouoking to detestable Idolatry and superstition' (1613: 174). Here, the Whore's ability to dazzle is elided with

charges levelled at the Roman Catholic Church to make clear that the fornication she tempts men into is not sexual, but spiritual. It was this threat of spiritual
whoredom that prompted Bale to warn his readers that, although the 'whore at
the fyrst ... semeth onlye a woman', she was in fact a 'stynkynge strompett' who
induced the 'most shamefull whoredome in the sprete' (1545: Q6v, Q4v–r). The
association drawn between the Whore's female body and spiritual whoredom
was well established in the Old Testament, particularly in portions of Isaiah
and Hosea, a point not lost on reformed commentators.[14] Thomas Brightman
explains that the Whore's sexual promiscuity is a 'most usual Metaphore in the
Scriptures, because the Spirituall Adultery is equall yea surpassing in filthines,
and wickedness with the bodily, as whereby a man reuolteth from the true God'
(1616: 714). Powerfully embodying the ideological alliance in Scripture between
physical and spiritual whoredom, the Whore of Babylon was understood to
entice men into illicit sex, the outcome of which was emotional disarmament
and spiritual sickness.

While the threat posed by the Whore's body is explored at length in the
period's sermons and biblical commentaries, a number of literary writings are
similarly preoccupied with the seductive potential of this biblical woman. The
Whore's position as a sexual temptress who provokes spiritual adultery is imaginatively explored at length in Book One of Spenser's *The Faerie Queene*, 'The
Legende ... of Holinesse'. Adultery provides the book's central narrative as the
knight, Redcrosse, whose quest Book One traces, must choose between Una,
allegorically styled as truth, and Duessa, the embodiment of duplicity or false
truth.[15] Una and Redcrosse enter the narrative together, his loyalty to her signified through his commitment to avenge the imprisonment of her parents (1987:
1.1.5).[16] Yet, after being duped by Archimago in Canto Two, Redcrosse abandons
Una and is seduced by the gloriously clad Duessa who appears to the wandering
knight as

> A goodly Lady clad in scarlet red,
> Purfled with gold and pearle of rich assay,
> And like a *Persian* mitre on her hed
> She wore, with crownes and owches garnished. (1.2.13)

While Redcrosse reads her apparel as the markings of a 'goodly lady', for a
biblically literate audience, the details of Duessa's embroidered attire clearly
align her with the Whore of Babylon who is similarly arrayed in a 'skarlat' robe
embellished with 'golde, & precious stones, and pearles' (Rev. 17:4).[17] From the
outset, the 'tinsell trappings' (1.2.13) of Spenser's Whore dazzle Redcrosse and
the narrative reveals that her appearance has a blunting effect on his senses when
it describes how 'He in great passion all this while did dwell, / More busying
his quicke eyes, her face to view, / Then his dull eares, to heare what she did
tell' (1.2.26). This initial encounter makes clear, then, that it is a sensual lust for
Duessa's body, what he sees, that drives Redcrosse into infidelity. The knight's

adulterous intentions are evocatively suggested when he responds to Duessa by constructing 'a girlond for her dainty forehead' (1.2.30), a symbolic declaration of his shifted allegiance that marks Spenser's Whore as his new queen.

Subsequent stanzas reiterate that Redcrosse's adultery is the result of being visually overwhelmed by Duessa's appearance, a consequence that clearly chimes with the conflation of the Whore's bejewelled body and idolatry in reformed thought. Duessa's idolatrous potential is suggested in the narrative's repeated insistence on her shiny visage. She is described as 'sunny bright' with 'gold and jewels shining' (1.5.21) and, elsewhere, her twinkling visage is implied by the 'tinsell' and 'golden bels' she wears which produce a 'glorious show' (1.2.13, 21). Importantly, her glistening female form induces the dazed state that reformers typically warned against in exegesis of Revelation 17 as she is termed one who 'bewitched all mens sight' (1.2.39) and causes those who view her to 'gr[o]w amazed at the sight' (1.5.21). The text draws a significant distinction, however, between Duessa's idol-like dazzle and the radiance of Una. Una's beauty issues 'blazing brightnesse' and 'glorious light' (1.12.23) but such descriptions of her appearance always associate her with whiteness or clearness rather than the coloured lustre of Duessa's body. Una exudes a pure light 'as doth the morning starre' (1.12.21) and appears 'whiter' than her 'snow white' ass (1.1.4) in a garment 'All lilly white' (1.12.22). As a vision of whiteness, Una contrasts pointedly with the coloured gaudiness of Spenser's Whore and the celestial imagery used to describe her appearance, such as her 'sunshyny face' (1.12.23), clearly align her with the women of Revelation 12 who is 'clothed with the sunne' and wears 'a crowne of twelue starres' (Rev. 12:1).[18] Like Spenser, reformed commentators regularly distinguished between the glorious raiment worn by the woman of Revelation 12 and the superficial shine of the Whore. William Fulke explains that the purity of the Woman Clothed with the Sun is symbolised by the fact that she is arrayed in 'heauenlye matter' rather than 'earthly preciouse stones' and further understands the Whore's colourful apparel as an indicator of her depraved nature noting that John 'with sundrie colours paint[s] oute Antichrist' (1573: 75, 110v).[19] Engaging with this tradition of analysing the apparel detailed in Revelation 17, Spenser's painted Whore and her colourless counterpart attest to the important distinction the reformers drew between that which was clearly shining and shining clearly.

It is, Book One suggests, because Redcrosse fails to catch the subtleties of this distinction, and is unable to decipher the Whore's shining beauty as gaudy pretence, that he ultimately finds himself 'defilde' (1.9.46). Duessa's stupefying seduction and Redcrosse's adulterous lust reach their zenith in Canto Seven. Here, after a brief parting, the pair 'bathe in pleasaunce of the ioyous shade' and the suggestive descriptions of the stream, with its 'bubbling waiue', 'fleshly well' and 'fountaine like a girlond', imply that their reunion is sealed sexually (1.7.4). Yet, the bubbling waters used to denote the pair's sexual union in the

Canto's early stanzas shift to suggest a liaison that exceeds physical infidelity as the narrative progresses. The grove's eroticised waterways include a mystical stream that causes those who drink from it to grow 'faint and feeble' (1.7.6) and it is Redcrosse's ingestion of this enchanted water that first reveals the consequences of his liaison:

> Hereof this gentle knight vnweeting was,
> And lying downe vpon the sandie graile.
> Drunke of the streame, as cleare as cristall glas,
> Eftsoones his manly forces gan to faile,
> And mightie strong was turned to feeble fraile. (1.7.6)

If the water is suggestive of Redcrosse's sexual union with the Whore, here the potent effect of consuming this body is reminiscent of the intoxicating properties of the Whore's 'wine of ... fornication' that flows from her 'cup of golde' (Rev. 17:2, 4). The Whore's cup was regularly elided with the mass chalice in reformed exegesis of Revelation 17, and the magical properties of Spenser's watery grove recall the popular reformed suspicion of the enchanting properties of the Catholic mass.[20] The grove's bewitched waters are further aligned with the Whore's intoxicating wine as they spread through the knight's body like a 'feuer fit' (1.7.6) and, in doing so, recall the later, more blatant, revelation of Duessa's possession of a 'golden cup, / ... replete with magick artes' that spreads a 'secret poison through [the] inner parts' (1.8.14). The fever induced by Duessa's elixir evokes the popular belief, expressed by John Mayo, that the 'Romish Babilon' would 'infect you with her poisoned cuppes' (1591: 34) and more broadly engages with what Jonathan Gill Harris terms the 'unmistakable pathological connotations, specifically of venereal disease' that the Whore had acquired by this period (Harris, 1998: 64). Emblematic of Catholicism's corrupting, foreign influence, the Whore's infecting body, as Canto Seven explores, threatens the spiritual health of believers.

'The Legende ... of Holinesse' explores the consequences of contact with the Whore's corrupting form as the decisions of the fever-stricken Redcrosse leave him 'both carelesse of his health, and of his fame' (1.7.7). Because the encounter has necessitated the removal of his armour, the knight's body has become vulnerable to external attack as well as internal infection. According to the poem's allegory, the loss of Redcrosse's armour at this moment becomes emblematic of his spiritual, as well as physical, unpreparedness for battle, a point made clear when the giant Orgoglio enters the grove and Redcrosse finds himself 'vnready' (1.7.7).[21] Here, Redcrosse is ill-equipped not simply because of his lack of weaponry but because of his altered spiritual condition. The fever he suffers from has produced a spiritual dis-ease and he faces battle 'disarmed, disgrast, and inwardly dismayde' (1.7.11). Unable to defeat the giant, Redcrosse finds himself imprisoned in a 'Dongeon deepe' (1.7.15), a physical and spiritual captivity that prevents him from fulfilling his divine service to both Una and

Gloriana. In Spenser's narrative, then, Revelation's hyper-sexualised Whore is imaginatively used to embody both the threat and far-reaching consequences of spiritual adultery.

Duped by the semblance of a 'goodly Lady' (1.2.13), Redcrosse's lust for what he sees has led him into the deadliest form of whoredom, idolatry. The enticing shimmer of the idolatrous Whore that dazzles believers into defilement was a common trope within anti-Catholic exegesis of Revelation 17, one that was constantly associated with fakery. Bale describes the Whore's ornamentation as a 'case' that seeks to 'counterfeite godlinesse' and likens it to the 'painted chu[r]ch' of Rome 'which is but a glittering colour' (1570: 2.S3r–4v). These allusions to the existence of false surfaces are characteristic of reformed readings of Revelation's Whore and, as Alison Shell has shown, 'metaphors of concealment have a long history in anti-Catholic polemic' more generally (1999: 26). Certainly, descriptions of Spenser's Whore persistently alert the reader to the presence of a truer surface that resides beyond her striking visage.[22] Shortly after Redcrosse meets Duessa, he is warned by the ruined knight, Fradubio, of a woman of 'forged beauty' who, despite being 'like a faire Lady', was in reality 'fowle *Duessa* hyde' (1.2.36, 35). During the parade of the House of Pride, Duessa's fairness is again positioned as a mask when she is oxymoronically termed 'that false Lady faire, the fowle *Duessa*' (1.4.37), and later her speech is similarly rendered deceptive, described as 'fowle words tempting faire, soure gall with hony sweet' (1.7.3).[23] The opening speech of Dekker's Whore of Babylon similarly evokes this trope of fabrication noting that her 'Image' is widely believed to 'blanch'd copper, or but guilded brasse' (1.1.36–9). The ornamentation of the Whore of Babylon, then, like the statues, vestments, paintings and visual rituals it was understood to represent, was always a shroud that concealed inner corruption. Gifford elucidates the contemporary connection between Catholicism's emphasis on visual beauty and the Whore's bedecked appearance. He explains that the 'Church of Rome', like this Whore, 'trimmeth vp her selfe' with 'outward glorie, and in goodly shewes' but, he warns, if 'you take away all … there will remyne nothing that is worth the looking on' just as when

> notorious harlots which … put into mean apparel, and the painting of their faces gone, are as homely and as hard fauoured women, as man shall lightly see. And this is the very case of the great whore of Babylon, the Romish Church … shee is the most euill fauoured and beggarly whore that may be. (1599: 326–7)

Here, the Whore's ornamentation necessitates a moment of disclosure in order that her true nature might be known, an uncovering that has its basis in Revelation 17:16 when John foresees how those 'that hate the whore … shal make her desolate and naked, & shal eat her flesh, & burne her with fyre'. Conflating the Whore and 'the Romish Church', Gifford's narrative strips both of their beautifying apparel to reveal to his parishioners 'the most euill fauoured and beggarly' female body.[24]

It was not uncommon for the disclosure of the Whore's identity to take the form of a voyeuristic and scornful attack on the female body. In Spenser, Duessa's nature is revealed to Redcrosse through a literal disrobing. Duessa, who has been taken captive after Arthur defeated Orgoglio, is placed before the knight as Una vows to reveal 'that wicked woman in [his] sight' (1.8.45). The language used to describe the ensuing revelation is intensely violent. Una gives a command to 'spoile [Duessa] of her scarlot robe' and the narrative recounts the various stages of her uncovering in detail:

> So as she bad, that witch they disaraid,
> And robd of royall robes, and purple pall,
> And ornaments that richly were displaid;
> Ne spared they to strip her naked all.
> Then when they had despoild her tire and call,
> Such as she was, their eyes might her behold. (1.8.46)

The language used here communicates a ruthlessly physical plundering of the Whore's body and reiterates the devastating completeness of the disclosure. In doing so, this moment exemplifies, as Jane Grogan explains, how stripping a body is 'the most brutally physical form of discovering it, of enabling viewers to see through appearances to the truth-speaking interior in an act that, in Spenser's hands, need not be construed erotically' (2009: 93). Certainly, the attack on Duessa is charged with misogyny rather than eroticism, particularly because her freshly stripped body prompts disgust and repugnance among those who view it. Deprived of garments, the group view her 'Such as she was' and find 'her misshaped parts did them appall' (1.8.46). The following two stanzas chart these malformed features working from her bald head to her 'most monstrous' feet, but especial venom is reserved for the monstrosity of her specifically female body:

> Her dried dugs, like bladders lacking wind,
> Hong downe, and filthy matter from them weld;
> Her wrizled skin as rough, as maple rind
> So scabby was, that would haue loathd all womankind. (1.8.47)

Importantly, the Whore's breasts are found to operate unnaturally, emitting 'filthy matter', rather than life-sustaining nourishment, and become objects of shame and loathing for all women. In a manner reminiscent of Canto One's lactating monster Errour, who similarly possesses 'poisonous dugs' (1.1.15), this moment of apocalyptic disclosure firmly reveals the female body to be the locus of the narrative's physical and spiritual threat.[25]

Readings of the Whore of Babylon as a mother whose female body produces and sustains corruption have their biblical basis in Revelation 17:5 where she is termed 'the mother of whoredomes, and abominations of the earth'. Reformed commentators had much to say about the maternal role afforded to Revelation's Whore. In language that aligns her with Eve, that Old Testament mother of sin, Bale elaborates on the significance of John's description: 'for she ys the oryginall mother / the cause / the begynninge / the rote / the sprynge / and the fountayne of all spirituall fornyca[t]yons / and in a maner of all fleshlye abhominacyons also done vpon the earth' (1545: Q7r). In line with the repercussions of the Genesis Fall, Bale positions the female body as the cause, as well as the distributer, of sin. It is not difficult to see how the Whore's position as a corrupting spiritual mother was taken as further evidence of her Catholic identity. Commentators on Revelation 17:5 made much of the Roman Catholic Church's claim to be 'the holy mother Church' (Perkins, 1604: 356), reiterating, as Thomas Wilson does in his dictionary on the Book of Revelation, that this Church has been heard 'proudly boasting herselfe to bee the Mother-Church, the head of Christianity' (1612: 121). Inverting the Roman Catholic Church's claim to be the foundation of all other Christian churches since Christ commissioned Peter, this spiritual mother is, like the Whore, found to induce corruption; as Wilson explains she is 'the Mother and the Nursse of wickednesse of all sorts & kindes' (1612: 100). David Pareus uses nursing imagery to connect the spiritual maternity of the Whore of Babylon with '*Popish Rome* ... the Mother of Churches' explaining that 'in very deed the whole East [s]ucked their abominations and idolatries from her as from the paps of a mother' (1644: 345).

Such readings of the Whore as a lactating mother who transmits her corruption to her progeny, the Church, are central to Thomas Dekker's conception of the formidable Empresse of Babylon. The *Dramatis Personae* of his play states that she 'figure[s] Rome' (1964: 469) and the play itself reveals her more precisely to be the embodiment of the maternal Roman Catholic Church by declaring her 'the mother of Nations' (4.3.31). From the outset, Dekker's Whore is associated with reproduction urging her Court, comprised of cardinals, friars and the kings, to 'Be fruitfull as the Vine, in sonnes and daughters' (1.1.4). It quickly becomes clear, however, that the Empresse's desire to extend her spiritual family is impeded by current temporal conditions, particularly those within the Fairie kingdom that 'weares a girdle wrought of waues' (1.1.97) and is protected by the valiant 'Fairie Queene' (1.1.46), Titania, who represents Queen Elizabeth.[26] The extension of the Empresse's spiritual kingdom must, then, include the temporal takeover of 'Fairie land' (1.1.195) but, rather than a militaristic invasion, she urges her political allies to engage in a more covert attack on the body of the Queen. The Kings of France, Spain and the Holy Roman Empire are to 'wooe (like louers)' and secure the kingdom by marrying Titania; to this end, she advises them in the arts of deception: 'Draw all your faces sweetly / ... giue out smiles / ... Dissemble, flatter ... / And beg shee would but with us ioyne' (1.1.100–12). While the dissembling manners and seductive ploys devised by Dekker's Empresse are reminiscent of the tactics used by Spenser's Whore, Duessa, the apocalypticism expounded in *The Whore of Babylon* is, as the inclusion of temporal kings suggests, much more politically pronounced.

In the seventeen years that divided Dekker's play from the first instalment of
The Faerie Queene, England's religious-political landscape had shifted considerably.[27] The country had a new monarch with, as he explained to Parliament on
22 March 1603, a vision for 'a general Christian Union in religion' (House of
Commons, 1802: 144) and a firm commitment to peace in Europe.[28] Particularly disturbing for England's more militantly minded Protestants was the fact
that King James began his reign by brokering a peace settlement with Spain,
signing the Treaty of London in 1604, and was undeterred from his policies of
religious and political conciliation by the attempt to blow him and Parliament
up in 1605. Emerging within two years of the Gunpowder Plot, Dekker's play
joined a growing number of militant Protestant voices who wished to make
clear that England, and the religious truth it protected, faced continuing threat
from anti-Christian aggressors.[29] Vividly representing the alliance between Rome
and the political powers of southern Europe, the play refracts the views of those
Protestants who believed that Catholic gains made in England were for 'the
Bishop of Rome, or the king of Spaine' (Abbot, 1604: 145) and chimes with the
more extreme opinion, expressed by some later readers of Revelation, such as
Brightman, that Revelation itself spoke of a conjoined Spanish-Roman threat:
the Whore's '*Purple, Scarlet, Gold, precious Stones*, and *Pearles* are among those
wares of *Merchandize*, by which *Spaine* is signified ... [and] shew that *Rome*
should bragge and relie most of and vppon the Spaniards aid' (1616: 724).[30]

While the play visualises the Whore's scheming with temporal kings, the
threatening alliance between Rome and southern-European powers is most
powerfully symbolised through the use of maternal imagery. The attempt by
the King of the Holy Roman Empire to woo Titania is enmeshed with a tribute
to the Empresse, who is pointedly termed 'Our aged mother' (1.2.137). The King
attempts to persuade Titania by celebrating, and offering, 'those sacred breasts /
From whence we draw our nourishment, would runne / *Nectar* to you (sweete
as the food of life)' (1.2.134–6). These lines elide the Whore's role as a spiritual
mother with the spiritual maternity claimed by the Roman Catholic Church in
a manner similar to writings discussed earlier; but, as the lactating metaphors
are developed within the play, the threat posed by this conjoined maternal body
is amplified and extended.[31] After Titania publicly rejects the seductions of the
three kings, they determine to 'Flie to our Empres bosome, there sucke treason,
/ Sedition, Herezies, confederacies ... / And when ye' are swolne with theis,
return againe, / And let their poison raine downe here in showres' (1.2.254–5,
259–60).[32] While the maternal bond between mother and child is once again
turned here to embody the powerful connection between Rome and England's
political enemies, these lines also enlarge the Whore's maternal threat as her
body leaks political treachery as well as spiritual corruption. Her body, that is
the feminised body of the Roman Catholic Church, is found to support and
sustain the temporal threat to the English state. In line with changing religious

and political circumstances, Dekker's play reveals a Whore of Babylon who is the mother of both political and spiritual abominations.

The politicised maternity of Dekker's Whore is further established in the closing representation of the 1588 Armada attack. These concluding scenes are, as Regina Buccola has noted, laden with images of pregnancy and childbirth (2007: 152–3). The Empresse's bountiful fleet is described as a pregnant body whose 'rib and belly are so great' (4.4.72) and later, when seen at sea, Fideli recalls how 'the windes haue got the sailes with childe, / With such big bellies' (5.2.17–18). The Empresse herself describes the attack on England in terms of birthing and operates in the role of mother and guiding midwife when she instructs: 'let our Galeons feele euen child-birth panges, / Till their great bellies be deliuered / On the soft Faiery shoares' (4.4.15–17). These descriptions of the Whore as a mother whose labour induces a political attack adhere to Catholicism's association with what Frances E. Dolan terms 'monstrous conceptions' and the tendency in anti-Catholic writings to describe 'Catholic plots … as monstrous births' (1999: 39). While the Empresse's threatening maternity is certainly a marker of the perceived dangers posed by the spiritual body of the Roman Catholic Church, it has been considered by some as a sticking point in the play's ideological framework, particularly because maternal imagery is attached to her counterpart, Titania. Commenting on the opposition of the play's female figureheads, Buccola notes that 'one of their vexing similarities is Dekker's persistent association of both characters with a mystic maternity' (2007: 145).[33] While there are certainly ideological rifts in the fabric of *The Whore of Babylon*, it is possible to reconcile the play's maternal imagery within its oppositional framework if these metaphors are read in light of the two contrasting mothers within the Book of Revelation.

In Revelation 12, John notes that the Woman Clothed with the Sun is 'with childe and cryed trauailing in birth, and was pained readie to be deliuered' as she is pursued by the dragon (Rev. 12:2). Among Protestant readers, this woman was most commonly understood as a 'figure' of the 'Church militant vpon earth' who, although persecuted, labours 'with paine to bring [Christ] forth' across the earth (Gifford, 1599: 217, 219).[34] Like the Whore, she is a spiritual mother, but one who travails to bring spiritual rebirth, rather than death, to the soul. Dekker's Titania, whose name, derived from Titan, and description as 'like the Sun' (2.1.262) align her with this apocalyptic figure, is a similarly fruitful mother.[35] Florimell likens Titania's ships to fertile bodies that 'beare the most royall freight / That the world owes (true hearts:) their wombs are ful / Of noble spirits' (5.2.168–70) and, importantly, ties his vision of her fleet to the birthing of the spirit at 'Pentecost' (5.2.174). Indeed, the atmosphere of merriment among the 'iollie youngsters' and 'gay mutitudes' who see the ships depart is understood to precipitate both the literal birth of Titania's army and the spiritual rebirth of the nation, as Florimell declares 'So many Faieries neuer dwelt at once / Neuer so many men were borne so soone' (5.2.179–80). Titania's association with fruitful, or natural maternity is further suggested when, after the Empresse's retreat, Plain Dealing reveals the birth of 'a man childe i'th Camp: a boy that looks as if he would shoote off already' (5.6.36–7). Directly echoing the words of Revelation 12:5, which detail that the Woman Clothed with the Sun 'broght forthe a man childe which shulde rule all the nations wit a rod of yron',[36] this moment suggests that the maternal representations of Titania and the Empresse draw on Revelation's opposing visions of motherhood.

Aligned with an apocalyptic mother who protects the 'man childe' Christ, Titania participates in a birth that is ideologically distinct from the Empresse's maternity. While Titania's labour inaugurates life and spiritual rebirth, descriptions of the Empresse's maternity clearly mark her labour as a harbinger of death. Florimell ominously observes how the Empresse's fleet 'beates the waues, / Boasting to make their wombs our cities graues' (5.2.7–8). The association of her maternal body with destruction is reiterated again later when she gives birth to ships that are likened to 'roaring Whales' that come 'with deuouring wombs / To swallow vp' the kingdom of Fairyland (5.6.59–60). In these climatic scenes, the Whore continues to operate as an unnatural wet nurse when she urges her armies to snatch babies from their mother's breasts and instructs when they 'crie for milke, let them sucke bloud' (4.4.123–4). Here, the Empresse's bloody breast solidifies her association with death but it also reiterates her identification as the Roman mother Church by evoking the way in which the Catholic faithful, according to the doctrine of transubstantiation, are spiritually nourished with blood during the mass. The Whore's body is found to harbour both physical and spiritual death and, once again, the denunciation of the Roman Catholic Church's threatening spiritual body hinges on the denigration of Whore's specifically female body. In Dekker's play, the Whore's corrupting materiality operates not as emblem for the threat faced by the individual believer, as is the case in Book One of *The Faerie Queene*, but as a symbol of the danger faced by the collective body of the state. Expanding the Whore's target in this way, and demonstrating her allegiance with southern-European powers, *The Whore of Babylon* amplifies and extends the tropes of Spenser's Duessa within a more politically determined apocalyptic framework. While the Whore's stock characteristics, such as her dissembling nature and corrosive presence, remain here amid fears that religious reform would be eroded by King James' conciliatory policies, the Whore of Babylon modulates from a dangerous seductress into a cunning political schemer.

Alongside the theological writings considered above, 'The Legende … of Holinesse' and *The Whore of Babylon* illuminate how the Whore of Babylon evoked a constellation of attendant meanings about Catholicism and the threat it posed to the individual believer, reformed faith and the English state. The Whore's bejewelled body warned of the dazzling potential of Catholicism's visual beauty and elicited a form of whoredom that promised spiritual dis-ease and death. Ornamented with the gaudy trappings of the world, her glistening appearance was understood to mark, and conceal, corruption, and the exegetical process of revealing this inner nature regularly involved the revelation of a repellent female body or maternal process. Such readings of the Whore, as with Eve, position the maternal body as a site that creates and sustains sin and, while this conceptualisation of corruption undoubtedly had consequences for early modern women, the Whore of Babylon was not typically deployed, as is the case with so many of the Bible's women, as a standard against which appropriate female behaviour could be measured. Instead, reformed readings of the Whore of Babylon illuminate how her body became a transnational symbol of Protestantism's enemy, Roman Catholicism, her nature the embodiment of the spiritual and political threat against which both individual and state must prepare.

For Protestants, reading the Whore of Babylon was central to a broader attempt to create and maintain a strict opposition between the opposing factions of Christianity. As an avatar of the false Church of Rome, the Whore, glistening, seducing and corrupting, always operated in contradiction to what she was not, the innocent, plain and pure reformed church. The widespread use of the Whore of Babylon to delineate Protestantism's distinction from Catholicism crystallises the means by which reformed Christianity, despite its insistence on literalism, was in fact deeply committed to an allegorical means of definition. Indeed, the reformers' complex use of the contents of Revelation to establish a legitimate identity within Christ's true church in the aftermath of the Reformation illuminates how an allegorical ontology perforated this supposed literalist faith at every medium. Certainly, as Dekker and Spenser's intricate allegories suggest, the process of decoding the significance of the Whore of Babylon in a post-Reformation context ironically gave rise to a set of complex and highly imaginative allegories befitting the historical moment. Always glistening, always corrupt, always Roman Catholic, there is perhaps no other figure in Scripture that so clearly reveals the figurative inclinations of the newly reformed faith as the Whore of Babylon.

Notes

1 Biblical references have been taken from the Geneva edition (1560, rpt. 2007).
2 Throughout the essay the terms 'reformed', 'reformers', 'Protestant' and 'Protestantism' are used as a means of describing a religious outlook that, however fragmented by understandings of the Eucharist or the limits of free will, was theologically distinct from Catholicism. Key points of agreement that have a bearing on this chapter include the doctrine of *sola scriptura*, a vocal commitment to Scripture's 'literal' sense and a broadly conceived anti-Catholicism.
3 For more on how apocalyptic theology was supported by the adoption of Lutheran-

ism as the state religion in many countries across Europe see Hill (1971: 9–13). Both Bale (1545: R2r–5r) and Foxe (1583: 1775–9) interpreted the Whore in relation to the Roman Catholic Church and Bullinger's lengthy sermon series on Revelation, which espoused a similar reading, was disseminated with royal approval (see 1561: 507, title-page). See O'Hear (2011: 135–98) for a discussion of the woodcuts used in Luther's New Testament.

4 Shell (1999: 25–31, 41–8) and Dolan (1999: 6–9) acknowledge the Whore's importance to conceptions of Catholicism within broader discussions of the tropes of anti-Catholic writing. Her reimagining within early modern drama has been suggested in the following works: Gasper (1990: 62–75); Parker (1995: 251–69); Davidson (2002: 64–94); and Streete (2009: 230–54).

5 For discussion of Spenser's apocalypticism and consideration of his engagement with Revelation more generally see: Parker (1979: 74–6); Hume (1984: 73–106); Sadler (1984: 148–74); and Gless (1994: 118–24).

6 Apocalypticism was not a new phenomenon and a number of studies have demonstrated the importance of these ideas in the medieval period. See Reeves (1969); Cohn (1970); and Emmerson and McGinn (1992).

7 See in particular: Daniel 7–12; Mark 13; Matthew 24; Luke 17:22–37, 21; 1 Corinthians 15:20–8; 2 Corinthians 5:1–31; 1 Thessalonians 4:15–18; and 2 Thessalonians 2:1–12.

8 For a discussion of the popularity and importance of apocalyptic theology in the sixteenth and seventeenth centuries see: Ball (1975); Bauckham (1978); Christianson (1978); Firth (1979); and Backus (2000).

9 Although, by comparison, Catholic eschatology of the same period is less insistent, the charge of antichristianism was turned against Protestants by some Catholic commentators. See Firth (1979: 111–13, 161); as well as Clark (1997: 340–5, 356–7).

10 For the connection between typological and apocalyptic thought see Brownlee (2012).

11 Unless otherwise stated, the italics that appear in quotations from early modern texts are preserved from the original.

12 Thomas Bentley, for instance, cites the example of the Whore to dissuade women from 'abhominable pride, paynting their faces, and decking their bodies with superfluous attyre' (1582: 96).

13 In her discussion of the connection between Catholicism and female beauty in anti-Catholic writings, Shell acknowledges the Whore's presence within reformed charges of idolatry (1999: 30–32). See also Streete's (2009) discussion of Bianca's idolatrous beauty, as well as her association with the Whore, in Thomas Middleton's *Women Beware Women*. It should also be said that the connection drawn between the Whore's body and idolatry was part of a more general understanding of women and Catholicism as both 'intrinsically idolatrous, superstitious and carnal' (Marotti, 1999: 4).

14 See for example Isaiah 57; Hosea 1–3 as well as Jeremiah 3, Micah 1; 1 Corinthians 6.15–16.

15 A number of scholars have considered how Spenser explores religious truth and falsehood through these opposing women and noted that Book One is peppered with the tropes of religious error and expresses an interest in learning to read truth correctly. In particular see King (1990: 49–93) and Wood (1997: 30–79).

16 All further references to *The Faerie Queen* have been taken from this edition and are formatted according to book, canto and line number.

17 Duessa's 'Persian' mitre also marks her as a stranger and ties her to the East, and, more specifically, to Babylon. It is also important because, as Dolan (1999) has shown, Catholicism was associated with foreignness.

18 Unlike medieval and Catholic readings that commonly understood the woman of Revelation 12 as Mary, in the reformed tradition, this woman is typically understood to be the persecuted Church (see for example Gifford, 1599: 219).

19 The significance afforded to colour in exegesis of Revelation 17 operates within the more general opposition of reformed truth, styled as 'perfect glasse' or 'christall', and the 'coloured abuses' of Catholicism (Batman, 1569: A2r). For more see Shell (1999: 29).

20 Bale (1570) likens the mass chalice to the Whore's cup because it 'dayly ministereth ... false religion' (2.S4v). For more on the association drawn between the mass and Catholicism generally and magic and witchcraft see Clark (1997: 360–1) and Parish (2005).

21 In his explanatory letter to Walter Raleigh, Spenser likens the knight's armour to the spiritual 'armour of a Christian man' described by Paul in Ephesians 6:10–16 (1987: 17).

22 For Catholicism's association with false surfaces see Shell (1999: 26–31) and Rhatigan (2012: 176–94).

23 The multiple references to Duessa's bejewelled and shining appearance, noted earlier, similarly imply the presence of a false surface because, within anti-Catholic polemic, jewellery promised 'either a dazzling revelation of corruption or a revelation of dazzling corruption' (Shell, 1999: 29).

24 The conflation of the Whore with the Roman Church in reformed readings meant that her stripped body was often considered to be emblematic of Catholicism's loss of power and riches across Europe. See for example Pareus (1644: 439).

25 For a sustained consideration of Errour see Hume (1984: 77–9).

26 For discussion of how the play operates as a tribute to Elizabeth and her victory over the Armada see Perry (1997: 153–87) and Watkins (2000: 161–3).

27 Dekker's obligations to Spenser are obvious in his use of fairy imagery as well as names such as Florimell and Paridell. For discussions of Spenser's influence on Dekker see Hoy and Bowers (1980: 300–3); Sadler (1984: 148–74); and Watkins (2000: 156–68).

28 For a discussion of how James styled himself as *rex pacificus* see Smuts (2002: 371–87).

29 Gasper (1990) defines militant Protestants as those who 'regarded the Reformed Church as the only True Church, and conceived of it as a single, international body. They ... thought that a unified, active defence was necessary in order to survive in the struggle against their great adversary, Rome. In practical terms, this meant seeking alliances with Protestant powers abroad ... Alliances with Roman Catholic powers, however advantageous they might appear, were to be distrusted and shunned' (2–3). In light of this definition, Gasper terms *The Whore of Babylon* as 'the definitive militant Protestant play' (9). It should be said that the play's obvious political motivation was probably a decisive factor in its failure, noted by Dekker in the *Lectori* (1964: 497). Howard (1994: 53) notes that Jacobean audiences no longer had the appetite for the overtly didactic drama that had been popular in the Elizabethan period.

30 The play reiterates the dangers posed by a Spanish-Roman alliance by drawing on historical attacks, such as the Armada, as well as the supposed poisoning attempt by the Rodrigo López. For a discussion of these episodes, as well as the play's other political allusions, see Gasper (1990: 81–8) and Krantz (1995: 271–91).

31 This speech also reveals that the Empresse operates as a female Pope as she wears the distinctive 'trible crowne imperiall' (1.2.121), a description that recalls Duessa who similarly appears with a 'triple crowne set on her head' (1.7.16). In representing female Popes, both texts engage with the views of Protestant writers who 'described what was wrong with the Roman church by suggesting that its hierarchy was actually dominated by women' (Dolan, 1999: 53). It is also worth noting that this representation is part of a broader interest in the Whore's androgyny (see the descriptions of Duessa's 'nether' parts at 1.8.48 and 1.2.41 and the Empresse at 5.2.4) that chimes with accusations of Papal androgyny found within some reformed writings (see for example Mayo, 1591: 33–4; as well as Dolan, 1999: 53).

32 Scott (2004: 67–95) has considered the images of contagion in Dekker's play and reads the Empresse specifically as a syphilitic wet nurse.

33 Critics who have questioned the security of the play's oppositional structure include: Howard (1994: 524–60) who argues that the play's theatricality undermines its ideological project; Dolan (1999: 55) who suggests that Titania and the Empresse coalesce in their challenge of gender conventions; and Harris (1998: 64–73) who traces how the play's imagery of poison and medicine entangle.

34 Sadler (1984: 164) notes that the reformers shifted the emphasis of Revelation 12 from Mary to Queen Elizabeth particularly during the 1580s and then again after the Queen's death.

35 Gasper (1990: 71–3) has shown how Titania's association with the woman of Revelation 12 and Queen Elizabeth emerges from an earlier Tudor tradition established by Foxe's allegorical drama *Christus Triumphans* (c.1556) and Spenser's *The Faerie Queene* (1596). For more on the relationship between Titania and Spenser's Una see Sadler (1984: 148–74).

36 In line with her exploration of the Marian imagery attached to Titania, Buccola (2007: 157) also reads this climactic birth as that of the Christ child and connects it to Gospel accounts of the nativity. Alternatively Gasper (1990: 96–9) suggests that this moment represents the reign of King James I.

References

Abbot, G. (1604) *The reasons vvhich Doctour Hill hath brought, for the vpholding of papistry.* Oxford: Joseph Barnes.

Backus, I.D. (2000) *Reformation Readings of the Apocalypse: Geneva, Zurich, and Wittenberg.* Oxford: Oxford University Press.

Bale, J. (1545) *The image of bothe churches after reulacion of saynt Iohan the euangelyst.* Antwerp: S. Mierdman.

——. (1570) *The image of both Churches after the most wonderfull and heauenly Reuelation of sainct Iohn the Euangelist.* London: Thomas East.

Ball, B.W. (1975) *A Great Expectation: Eschatological Thought in English Protestantism to 1660.* Leiden: Brill.

Batman, S. (1569) *A christall glasse of christian reformation wherein the godly maye beholde the coloured abuses vsed in this our present tyme.* London: John Day.

Bauckham, R. (1978) *Tudor Apocalypse: Sixteenth Century Apocalypticism, Millenarianism,* and the English Reformation: from John Bale to John Foxe and Thomas Brightman. Oxford: Sutton Courtenay Press.

Bentley, T. (1582) *The sixt lampe of virginitie conteining a mirrour for maidens and matrons.* London: Thomas Dawson and Henry Denham.

Bernard, R. (1617) *A key of knowledge for the opening of the secret mysteries of St Iohns mysti-call Reuelation.* London: Felix Kyngston.

Brightman, T. (1616) *The Reuelation of S. Iohn illustrated with an analysis.* Leyden: John Class.

Brownlee, V. (2012) 'Reforming Figures: Biblical Interpretation and Literature in Early Modern England.' PhD thesis, Queen's University Belfast.

Buccola, R. (2007) 'Virgin Fairies and Imperial Whores: The Unstable Ground of Religious Iconography in Thomas Dekker's *The Whore of Babylon*.' *Marian Moments in Early Modern British Drama.* Ed. R. Buccola and L. Hopkins. Aldershot: Ashgate. 141–60.

Bullinger, H. (1561) *A hundred sermons vpo[n] the Apocalips of Iesu Christe.* London: John Day.

Cartwright, T. (1622) *A plaine explanation of the vvhole Revelation of Saint John.* London: T.S.

Christianson, P. (1978) *Reformers and Babylon: English Apocalyptic Visions from the Reformation to the Eve of the Civil War.* Toronto: University of Toronto Press.

Clark, S. (1997) *Thinking with Demons: The Idea of Witchcraft in Early Modern Europe.* Oxford: Clarendon Press.

Cohn, N. (1970) *The Pursuit of the Millennium: Revolutionary Millenarians and Mystical Anarchists of the Middle Ages.* Oxford: Oxford University Press.

Davidson, C. (2002) *History, Religion, and Violence: Cultural Contexts for Medieval and Renaissance English Drama.* Aldershot: Ashgate.

Dekker, T. (1964) *The Whore of Babylon. The Dramatic Works of Thomas Dekker.* Vol. 2. Ed. F. Bowers. Cambridge: Cambridge University Press.

Dent, A. (1603) *The ruine of Rome: or An exposition vpon the whole Reuelation.* London: T. Creede.

Dolan, F.E. (1999) *Whores of Babylon: Catholicism, Gender, and Seventeenth-Century Print Culture.* Ithaca, NY: Cornell University Press.

Donne, J. (1962) *Sermons: Volume 6.* Ed. G.K. Potter and E. Simpson. Berkeley: University of California Press.

Emmerson, R.K. and McGinn, B. (1992) *The Apocalypse in the Middle Ages.* Ithaca, NY: Cornell University Press.

Firth, K.R. (1979) *The Apocalyptic Tradition in Reformation Britain, 1530–1645.* Oxford: Oxford University Press.

Forbes, P. (1613) *An exquisite commentarie vpon the Revelation of Saint Iohn.* London: W. Hall.

Foxe, J. (1583) *Actes and monuments.* London: John Daye.

Fulke, W. (1573) *Praelections vpon the sacred and holy Reuelation of S. Iohn.* London: Thomas Purfoote.

Gasper, J. (1990) *The Dragon and the Dove: The Plays of Thomas Dekker.* Oxford: Clarendon Press.

Gifford, G. (1599) *Sermons vpon the whole booke of the Revelation.* London: Thomas Man.

Gless, D.J. (1994) *Interpretation and Theology in Spenser.* Cambridge: Cambridge University Press.

Grogan, J. (2009) *Exemplary Spenser: Visual and Poetic Pedagogy in The Faerie Queene.* Farnham: Ashgate.

Harris, J.G. (1998) *Foreign Bodies and the Body Politic: Discourses of Social Pathology in Early Modern England.* Cambridge: Cambridge University Press.

Hill, C. (1971) *Antichrist in Seventeenth-Century England.* London: Verso.

House of Commons (1802) *Journal of the House of Commons,* Vol. 1: 1547–1629. London: HMSO.

Howard, J.E. (1994) *The Stage and Social Struggle in Early Modern England.* London: Routledge.

Hoy, C. and Bowers, F. (1980) *Introductions, Notes, and Commentaries to Texts in 'The Dramatic Works of Thomas Dekker'.* Vol. 2. Cambridge: Cambridge University Press.

Hume, A. (1984) *Edmund Spenser: Protestant Poet.* Cambridge: Cambridge University Press.

King, J.N. (1990) *Spenser's Poetry and the Reformation Tradition.* Princeton: Princeton University Press.

Krantz, S.E. (1995) 'Thomas Dekker's Political Commentary in *The Whore of Babylon.*' *Studies in English Literature, 1500–1900,* 35.2: 271–91.

Marotti, A.F. (1999) 'Alienating Catholics in Early Modern England: Recusant Women, Jesuits and Ideological Fantasies.' *Catholicism and Anti-Catholicism in Early Modern English Texts.* Ed. A.F. Marotti. Basingstoke: Macmillan. 1–34.

Mason, T. (1619) *A revelation of the Revelation wherein is contayned, a most true, plaine, and briefe manifestation of the meaning and scope of all the Reuelation.* London: G. Eld.

Mayo, J. (1591) *The pope's parliament, containing a pleasant and delightful historie.* London: Richard Field.

Napier, J. (1593) *A plaine discouery of the whole Reuelation of Saint Iohn set downe in two treatises.* Edinburgh: Robert Walde-graue.

O'Hear, N. (2011) *Contrasting Images of The Book of Revelation in Late Medieval And Early Modern Art: A Case Study in Visual Exegesis.* Oxford: Oxford University Press.

Oxford English Dictionary (OED) (2013) Oxford Dictionaries Online. Oxford: Oxford University Press.

Pareus, D. (1644) *A commentary upon the divine Revelation of the apostle and evangelist,* Iohn. Amsterdam: C.P.

Parish, H.L. (2005) *Monks, Miracles and Magic: Reformation Representations of the Medieval Church.* London: Routledge.

Parker, B.L. (1995) 'The Whore of Babylon and Shakespeare's *Julius Caesar.*' *Studies in English Literature, 1500–1900,* 35.2: 251–69.

Parker, P.A. (1979) *Inescapable Romance: Studies in the Poetics of a Mode.* Princeton: Princeton University Press.

Perkins, W. (1604) *Lectures vpon the three first chapters of the Reuelation.* London: Richard Field.

——. (1606) *A godly and learned exposition or commentarie vpon the three first chapters of the Reuelation.* London: Adam Islip.

Perry, C. (1997) *The Making of Jacobean Culture: James I and the Renegotiation of Elizabethan Literary Practice.* Cambridge: Cambridge University Press.

Reeves, M. (1969) *The Influence of Prophecy in the Later Middle Ages: A Study in Joachimism.* Oxford: Clarendon Press.

Rhatigan, E. (2012) 'Reading the White Devil in Thomas Adams and John Webster.' *Early Modern Drama and the Politics of Biblical Reading.* Ed. A. Streete. Basingstoke: Palgrave Macmillan. 176–94.

Sadler, F. (1984). 'The Faerie Queene, An Elizabethan Apocalypse.' *The Apocalypse in English Renaissance Thought and Literature: Patterns, Antecedents, and Repercussions.* Ed. C.A. Patrides and J.A. Wittreich. Ithaca, NY: Cornell University Press. 148–74.

Scott, S. (2004) '"The Empress of Babylon's 'carbuncles and rich stones'": The Metaphorizing of the Pox in Thomas Dekker's *The Whore of Babylon*.' *Early Theatre*, 7.1: 67–95.

Shell, A. (1999) *Catholicism, Controversy, and the English Literary Imagination, 1558–1660.* Cambridge: Cambridge University Press.

Smuts, M. (2002) 'The Making of Rex Pacificus: James VI and I and the Problem of Peace in an Age of Religious War.' *Royal Subjects: Essays on the Writings of James VI and I.* Ed. D. Fischlin and M. Fortier. Detroit, MI: Wayne State University Press. 371–87.

Spenser, E. (1987) *The Faerie Queene.* Ed. T.P. Roche and C.P. O'Donnell. Harmondsworth: Penguin.

Streete, A. (2009) '"An old quarrel between us that will never be at an end": Middleton's *Women Beware Women* and Late Jacobean Religious Politics.' *Review of English Studies*, 60.244: 230–54.

The Geneva Bible: A facsimile of the 1560 edition (2007) Ed. L.E. Berry and W. Whittingham. Peabody, MA: Henderson Publishers.

Tyndale, W. (1528) *The obedie[n]ce of a Christen man and how Christe[n] rulers ought to governe.* Antwerp: J. Hoochstraten.

Watkins, J. (2000) '"And yet the End was not": Apocalyptic Deferral and Spenser's Literary Afterlife.' *Worldmaking Spenser: Explorations in the Early Modern Age.* Ed. P. Cheney. Lexington, KY: University Press of Kentucky. 156–74.

Wilson, T. (1612) *A Christian dictionarie.* London: W. Iaggard.

Wood, R. (1997) *Metaphor and belief in The Faerie Queene.* New York: St. Martin's Press.

14

Afterword

Dympna Callaghan

Sir John Harington's 1590s manuscript sonnet, *Of a certayn man*, is a jest on the problem of over-zealous and wrong-headed exegesis especially as it pertains to women in the Bible.

> There was not certaine when, a certaine Preacher
> that never learnt and yet became a teacher
> And having thus in Latten red a text,
> Of *Erat quidam homo*, much perplext.
> Hee seemd the words with diligence to skan,
> In english thus, There was a certaine man.
> But now (quoth he) good people note you this
> He saith there was, he doth not say there is,
> For in this age of ours it is most certayn
> Of promise, oath, worde deed no man is certayn,
> Yet by my teshe (quoth he) this comes to pass,
> That surely once a certaine man there was,
> But yet I thinke in all the Byble no-man
> Can find this text: *There was a certaine Woman.*

(Harington, Folger MS. v.a. 249)

The poem's paronomastic jocularity centres on the word 'certain', which in its biblical context typically refers to a particular individual whose name is unknown or whose role is clearly confined to a specific biblical incident. The biblical text that Harington has his preacher focus on, however, is not the kind of substantive pronouncement that might make it amenable to exegesis. Instead, it is the oft-repeated phrase that prefaces biblical narratives, *Erat quidam homo*, 'There was a certaine man'. Harington thus puns on the misogynistic suggestion that there are no women of entirely unimpeachable virtue in the Bible. The poem also edges towards an even more outrageous claim: that there are no women – or at least, no clearly discernible ('certaine') women – in the Bible at all, that is, none who are singled out as the protagonists of significant biblical events. That Harington's preacher is completely wrong about the absence of the phrase, 'There was a certaine woman', is amply demonstrated by the answer poem composed by Lady Mary Cheke (1532/3–1616), which locates the precise phrase *Erat quaedem mulier* in both the Old and the New Testaments:

That no man yet could in the Bible find
A certaine Woman, argues men are blind
Blind as the preacher, having little learning
The certaine cause of this is ill discerning.
A certaine Woman of the multitude
Said blest be the paps that gave our savior food
A certaine Woman too, a millstone threw
And from the wall, Abimilech she slew.
(There likewise was, as holy writ doth say
A Certaine woman named Lydia
Nay more though we by men be overswaide)
The text records there was a certaine maid.
Which proves directly, certaine women then.
And certaine maids, more certain sure than men.
Nor marvail then, Your preacher stood perplext
To see how grossly he belied his text
And blush his Sermon was no Better suited
Than by a Woman thus to be confuted.
Yet for this Comfort, one true note he had
When there is now no certain man he said. (Cheke, 1605)

'Men are blind' to women's role in the Bible because, claims Lady Cheke, they are gender blind. To such ignorant men virtuous women are simply textually inconspicuous or even invisible: women do not signify and if they do, it is for nothing good. Her response is a poem with a kick – a couplet tail that indicts male pretentions to superior moral standing. Cheke casts her textual evidence at Harington beginning with the woman who praises Christ, and especially his mother's body, as the origin and sustenance of divine wisdom: 'a certain woman of the company lifted up her voice, and said unto him, Blessed is the womb that bare thee, and the paps which thou hast sucked' (Luke 11:27).[1] Abimelech's spirited adversary at his assault on the tower of Thebez is Cheke's next, and particularly apt, piece of evidence: 'But a certain woman cast a piece of a millstone upon Abimelech's head, and brake his brainpan' (Judges 9:53–4). Abimelech was remembered for having, in his dying moments, begged to be run through with a sword so as not to be known as a man who was killed by a woman. Her penultimate piece of evidence is of a named woman: 'And a certain woman named Lydia, a seller of purple, of the city of the Thyatirians, which worshipped God, heard us: whose heart the Lord opened, that she attended unto the things, which Paul spake' (Acts 16:14). The annotation in the Geneva Bible offers further ballast to Cheke's case: 'God beginneth his kingdom in Macedonia by the conversion of a woman, and so showeth that there is no [exception] of persons in the Gospel.' Lydia is of unassailable ('certain') virtue and the woman who threw the millstone is a decisive agent ('certain') in biblical history. As for Cheke's concluding evidence, there are, in fact two 'certaine' maids in the New

Testament, both of whom have acute powers of discernment. One is in Acts ('And it came to pass that as we went to prayer, *a certain maid* having a spirit of divination, met us ...' Acts 16:16, emphasis added) and another in Luke's Gospel where she is the woman who recognises Peter after Jesus' arrest: 'And *a certain maid* beheld him as he sat by the fire, and having well looked on him, said, This man was also with him' (Luke 22:56, emphasis added). This 'certain maid' is certain of Peter's identity and thus helps fulfil Christ's prophecy that the rock of the Church will deny him three times. More than either of these, the 'certain maid' connotes Mary upon whose incontrovertible virginity Christ's divinity necessarily depended for all parties of the Reformation schism. It is Mary more than any other woman who refutes the preacher's contention that there are no definitively, sexually continent women, whether in the Bible or anywhere else.

When she was only fifteen in 1547, Lady Mary Cheke married Sir John Cheke (1514–57). Sir John was personal tutor to Edward VI and a significant force in shaping the young king's unequivocally Protestant identity. He was also Regius Professor of Greek at Cambridge, and had worked on Anglicising biblical words of Greek and Latin origin for monolingual English readers (Tadmor, 2010: 18). Having a decade of such a marriage behind her meant that Cheke was rather well positioned to offer a riposte to Harington's cheery misogyny. However, the perfect pitch of her retort may have also been the product of another aspect of her experience with her learned first husband who had described her as a woman of 'a strong affection and a weak reason', and as 'feeble headed and strong hearted' (Bryson, 2004). She was, then, in every way poised and prepared to take on Harington as well as the scriptures and the tired cultural common-places about women's inferiority.

I begin with these poems because they reflect in miniature many of this volume's key themes, especially the inextricable connection between misogyny and exegesis in early modern England and between the various confessional certainties about women's virtues and vices and women's own attempts to inter-pret biblical women. *Biblical Women in Early Modern Literary Culture, 1550–1700* explores the multiple, sometimes contradictory and often explicitly antithetical, interpretations of women in Scripture. The stakes of biblical polemic were high in early modern England because, as Victoria Brownlee and Laura Gallagher explain in their introduction, the Bible, functioning as an 'omnipresent history', determined the liberties and restrictions that were imposed on the entire population, but especially upon women. As in Harington's poem, even the most anodyne of expressions might be torqued or wilfully misread for ideological ends, and, as in the case of the literalist preacher, reformist *sola scriptura* did nothing to diminish such reading practices. What is new in the early modern period is that women become readers of the Bible as never before, and despite Henrician legislation that had sought to limit their direct access to the scrip-ture (Molekamp, 2013: 2), many women rifled the Bible to defend themselves from misogynist onslaught and to reinterpret Scripture to their own advantage. Women's interventions now helped to shape the debate about the spiritual, social and political status of women, from Lanyer's *Salve Deus Rex Judaeorum* in 1611 (examined by Brownlee and Gallagher, Elizabeth Hodgson, and Alison Thorne) to the women petitioners of the Interregnum (also discussed by Thorne). While the aristocratic Lady Cheke's access to rebuttal in the 1590s was based on privilege, crucially, in the course of the seventeenth century, women from a much wider range of class positions succeeded in securing for themselves the right of reply.

The essays included here demonstrate the degree to which early modern culture was saturated with knowledge of biblical women, far beyond the Blessed Virgin and Mary Magdalene, although as Laura Gallagher and Thomas Rist demonstrate, Catholic cults of these saints survived well into the seventeenth century. Alongside the host of nameless women like Cheke's 'certaine' maids, early moderns were fully cognizant of the women of Jerusalem whose role in Lamentations and Josephus is discussed by Beatrice Groves. They knew also women such as Lot's Wife or Jesus' sisters, known only via their relationship to men. Further, early moderns were much more familiar than we are today with the named women in the Bible from Abigail, Anna and Athalia to Zeresh, Zillah, and Zipporah. Harington's ignorant preacher notwithstanding, the Bible, albeit the key text of early modern patriarchal thinking, could hardly be said to fail to represent women in all their infinite variety. Although the current volume does not aim at encyclopaedic or even alphabetic inclusivity, it does show that, in a culture which overall sought to erase or at least diminish women's agency in the historical record, the interpretation of their irrefutable biblical presence became, perhaps surprisingly, increasingly problematic and increasingly complex with the demise of medieval, allegorical interpretation. Predictably in a society that condemned celibacy and tirelessly reiterated St Paul's doctrine of wifely submission, early modern interpreters focused overwhelmingly on negative biblical images of women while the virtues of heroic women, whose behaviour was to serve as a paradigm of godly femininity, became increasingly 'uncertain' and contested in the process of Protestant exegesis. As Michele Osherow demonstrates, early modern exegetes had a hard time distinguishing between a heroic woman and one who was simply 'froward', mendacious and insubordinate.

The 'problem' of women in the Bible begins, of course, with Eve. It was a woman's weakness that led to the exile from paradise when, persuaded by the wily serpent, and directly against the order of the creator, she took the fruit of the tree of knowledge. This was a bad rap, and early modern women couldn't shake it, though as Brownlee and Gallagher argue, Lanyer tried very hard to do so by making Adam the source of Eve's frailty since her physical substance was an extract of his body. Eve, however, *was* an agent in Genesis. It is she, not the cloddish Adam (literally and onomastically 'made from earth'), who makes the critical decision to bite the forbidden fruit. While this means she bore the blame for the postlapsarian condition, this also made her, as Elizabeth Hodgson shows in 'A "Paraditian Creature": Eve and her unsuspecting garden in seventeenth-century literature', a more interesting character for early modern writers of both sexes, a figure in whom they seem much more invested than her allegedly less sinning husband. Hodgson demonstrates the complexity of the Genesis story and its astonishing discursive reach from Lanyer to the Royal Society in the course of the seventeenth century. Eve's guilt attenuated as her garden became the emblem of a new form of specifically horticultural salvation. Thus reframed and, in several instances, rehabilitated among some of the male poets of the later seventeenth century, Eve develops a more positive literary afterlife than was accorded to her in Protestant theology.

That there are shifts and reconfigurations both dramatic and subtle around narratives of biblical women is one of the central tenets of this volume. This is particularly visible in the dexterous ideological footwork required in relation to questions of female government in treatises by Protestant Scottish writers of the 1550s as they broached the issue of political liberty. Adrian Streete's 'Christian liberty and female rule: exegesis and political controversy in the 1550s' unpicks the knotty contradictions in the writings of those who disapproved of the authority of women but sometimes had to recuperate biblical women in the service of arguments for Christian liberty – that is, the requirement to place obedience to God before that to any temporal sovereign or magistrate. Thus, John Ponet condemns Jezebel as the tyrant precursor of Mary Tudor. But Jael, who drove a peg into the head of Sisera, received his unqualified approbation. Thus, it is through female figures that the contradictions around obedience to the state are drawn out and though which the idea of spiritual freedom is advanced. The radicalism of this idea cannot be overestimated. It is, after all, what at a subsequent historical moment would be called a duty to conscience above all other, and yet it finds its expression in gender hierarchies of the Old Testament.

Whatever the ambivalence about female government, female domestic supremacy, as Michele Osherow demonstrates in 'Wives, fears and foreskins: early modern reproach of Zipporah and Michal', became in the early modern period subject to criticism in a manner that marked a significant departure from medieval Jewish commentary. The quick-thinking Zipporah who saved her husband's life by smartly producing the foreskin of the child he had neglected to circumcise and throwing it at his feet, was now seen as a troublesome bundle of strife. Commentators argued that Zipporah erred by usurping the male prerogative to perform a religious rite. Similarly, Michal, wife of David whose bride price was a hundred Philistine foreskins (which he doubled), became the focus of early modern opprobrium. Ostensibly, this was because after she helped him escape certain death, she lied about his absence and used an effigy (an idol) to hide it. However, what these narratives have in common is that they both rely upon a connection with the proto-castration that is circumcision, and therefore both women pose a threat, albeit an unacknowledged one, to the male member. And early moderns, much more than their predecessors, found this unsettling.

In contrast to such definitively masculine anxiety, Alison Thorne's essay, 'The politics of female supplication in the Book of Esther' investigates the dynamics of supplication. She asks what Esther, who was both a supplicant and one to whom supplication was made, meant for women, from Aemilia Lanyer to the women petitioners who were caught between the necessity of pressing their cause to Parliament and the restrictions on female speech imposed by conduct literature. That the same biblical narrative could be used to silence or to empower women is clear from the treatment of Esther and other biblical women in early modern commentaries. Danielle Clarke's 'Gender and the inculcation of virtue: the Book of Proverbs in action' also explores these contradictions around female speech. Since speech is understood to be the prerogative of men, women's self-representation becomes almost impossible, at least without simultaneously sacrificing the certainty of women's virtue and reputation. The exception to the injunction upon female speech is the Book of Proverbs where godly utterances are permitted. Robert Cleaver's laudatory account of the good woman from Proverbs summons up the alarming vision of an early modern Stepford wife whose humourless and leaden speech acts are confined to faith, repentance and fear of the Lord. She would acquire this winning disposition, as Juan Luis Vives suggested, from reading the Bible under male supervision. Then, women themselves, purged of all that was trifling, 'liyght', rash or indiscreet, might police their own conduct by applying to it the model of Proverbs' exemplary wife. Arguably, this programme offered women a certain ideological wiggle room since their active participation in this patriarchal project was encouraged or, perhaps, required. On the other hand, making women themselves agents of patriarchal restraint may have served only to tighten the web around female self-expression. Funeral sermons of the period that eulogize deceased women use Proverbs 31 and suggest that, at least once they were dead, women were understood to have dutifully acquiesced to patriarchal dictates about female reading, writing and speech. Clarke's essay reveals what is at times the surprisingly uneven ideological weight of endlessly reiterated, exemplary biblical femininity, and argues that we should pay more attention to the ideological work of sheer repetition.

For all that, early moderns were much more invested in biblical images of female transgression and evil than they were in depictions of virtue and submission. One of the most disturbing accounts of women in the Bible is of the mother who devours her offspring. Maternal cannibalism is recorded in Lamentations during the first destruction of Jerusalem and prefigures Josephus's account of the second destruction of the city, where again femininity is so depraved in the despoiled city that mothers eat their young. Beatrice Groves 'Christ's tears and maternal cannibalism in early modern London' examines how early moderns linked the fate of the insistently feminised Jerusalem to that of plague-ridden London, known by the start of the seventeenth century as a metropolis, the mother city. This image is taken up in its most lurid form in Nashe's *Christ's tears over Jerusalem*, which is, Groves contends, a parody of tub-thumping homilists, 'a sustained polemic against bad preachers' who twist Scripture to their own ends, and do so with particular force in relation to powerfully negative images of biblical and quasi-biblical women.

In contrast, the image of the divine mother remained a potent reminder of the world before the Reformation, and the Blessed Virgin came to signify the grief for all that had been lost. The virginity of Christ's mother, as we have noted, was one element of Christian orthodoxy not contested during the English Reformation. However, for Protestants, she was downgraded from supreme intercessor to merely the holiest woman in the Bible, she whose virtue was indubitable and therefore might be emulated by godly women. Yet, her cult could not be eradicated overnight and veneration of the Virgin continued despite the destruction of shrines and statues, and the prohibition of what had been, along with the Lord's Prayer, the most ubiquitous orison in Christendom, the 'Ave Maria.' Thomas Rist's 'Mary of recusants and reform: literary memory and defloration' examines how this proscribed prayer persisted, especially among male lyricists Jonson, Constable and Verstegen. In the latter, Mary is also represented as the specifically and insistently somatic figure whose womb bore Christ and whose breasts nourished him and finally, in a figure for the condition of the English Church, whose body was belatedly penetrated when her heart was pierced with sorrow at the crucifixion. Around this vignette in biblical history, a powerful devotion arose in the thirteenth century, and the sorrowful mother who stands at the foot of the cross became one of the most widely promulgated images of the medieval Church. Laura Gallagher's '*Stabat Mater Dolorosa*: imagining Mary's grief at the cross' asks what was to be done with Catholic tropes that had infused the culture but were now officially proscribed. For Catholics, Mary's tribulations were to be shared by the faithful so as to more fully understand Christ's sacrifice. Gallagher shows, however, that this residual image, still being disseminated for an English recusant audience, survived in part by metamorphosing into a model for the performance of mourning, which shaped and intersected with early modern ideas about the expression of grief in the culture as a whole. Thus, Catholic ideas are not retained and transmitted without alteration but rather with inescapably dynamic engagement with the dominant culture that has proscribed them.

During the Reformation, images of unequivocally virtuous women did indeed vanish from the horizon of visual culture with the wholesale destruction of statues of saints. However, female saints persisted in discursive form, and especially in imaginative literature, as part of a common cultural heritage.

Furthermore, as Lisa Hopkins' essay on 'St Helena of Britain in the land of the Magdalene: *All's Well That Ends Well*' shows, they could still do cultural work. Hopkins indeed demonstrates the degree to which literary texts are steeped in early modern religious and biblical associations, ones readily apparent to early modern readers and playgoers but ones that now require the exertions of scholarly archaeology to recover. Such apparently medieval allusions are endowed with further contemporary relevance since these travelling saints became, in early modernity, associated with exploration and travel to the New World, so that geography became a way of mapping a now proscribed hagiography. In this instance, the allusions to St Helena of Britain and Mary Magdalene also offered commentary on political and social issues, especially the role of non-aristocratic women in the designs of dynasty and nationhood.

While Shakespeare's allusions to saints in *All's Well* seem relatively inconspicuous and well woven within his overall thematic design, the most conspicuous and most sumptuously dressed woman in all England, next to Elizabeth I, was arguably the Whore of Babylon from the Book of Revelation. Bedecked in scarlet and jewels and sitting aloft the many-headed beast, she cut an indelibly impressive figure across the early modern imagination. Victoria Brownlee's essay, 'Imagining the enemy: Protestant readings of the Whore of Babylon in early modern England, c.1580–1625' argues for the degree to which the Whore had captivated Protestant exegetes, for whom she was the magnetically obsessive focus of their virulent anti-Catholicism. Perhaps this is not surprising since the Whore of Babylon was from her inception entirely an invention of the male imagination. Her significance, however, intensified when, in the wake of the Reformation, she became the conspicuous (dis)figuration of papal power.

As the essays in this volume amply attest, there were many early modern commentators who might have concurred with Harington's preacher, with whom I began: that there were no virtuous women in the Bible, or at least none who excited their exegetical interests, while there were indeed some spectacularly wicked ones who did. The shared joke of his verse exchange with Lady Cheke was not only about the danger of biblical exegesis in the hands of the ignorant (about which both poets seem to agree). For these poems also reveal something about what it means for women to be discovered 'in' the Bible, and whether they were to be found represented or misrepresented there. In analysing these figurations across an array of genres, discourses and political moments, *Biblical Women* argues for a much more complex, although not necessarily less misogynist, account of scriptural femininity in early modern Britain. This volume also shows that early moderns of both sexes and of different political and confessional persuasions found that in negotiating the ur-text of Western patriarchy, they necessarily had to deal with its women.

Note

1 All biblical references have been taken from *The Geneva Bible* (1599)

References

Bryson, A. (2004) 'Sir John Cheke.' *Oxford Dictionary of National Biography*. Oxford: Oxford University Press.

Cheke, M. (1605) *Erat quaedam mulier*. British Library, Additional MS 15227, f 16.

Harington, J. (1605) *Epigrams*. MS. v.a. 249; Folger MS. v.a. 345.

Kilroy, G. (ed.) (2009) *The Epigrams of Sir John Harington*. Aldershot: Ashgate.

Molekamp, F. (2013) *Women and the Bible in Early Modern England: Religious Reading and Writing*. Oxford: Oxford University Press.

Tadmor, N. (2010) *The Social Universe of the English Bible: Scripture, Society and Culture in Early Modern England*. Cambridge: Cambridge University Press.

The Geneva Bible (1599) London: Deputies of Christopher Barker.

Index